Teaching English in High School

BY **ABRAHAM BERNSTEIN,** *Brooklyn College*

TEACHING
ENGLISH
IN
HIGH SCHOOL

RANDOM

HOUSE

NEW

YORK

ACKNOWLEDGMENTS

The Author and Publisher wish to thank the following for permission to quote material reprinted in this book:

Acuff-Rose Publications: the five lines quoted from "Wake Up, Little Susie," by Bryant and Bryant. Copyright 1957 by Acuff-Rose Publications.

Advertising Age: the material quoted from two articles: "Cultivate 'Jingly' Susceptible Teens, Fitz-Gibbon Says," and "Dailies Have Own Payola, Overplay Radio's: Sweeney," reprinted with permission from the June 8, 1959 issue and the December 7, 1959 issue of Advertising Age. Copyright 1959, Advertising Publications, Inc.

American Association for the Advancement of Science: the brief quotations from several articles in Science.

DeSylva, Brown & Henderson, Inc.: the line from "Where the Blue of the Night Meets the Gold of the Day," by Turk, Crosby, and Ahlert. Copyright © 1931 by DeSylva, Brown & Henderson, Inc., New York, N.Y.

Norma Millay Ellis: three lines from "Euclid Alone Has Looked on Beauty Bare," from Collected Poems, Harper and Brothers. Copyright 1923-1951 by Edna St. Vincent Millay and Norma Millay Ellis.

Harcourt, Brace & World, Inc.: the lines from "Four Preludes on Playthings of the Wind," in Smoke and Steel by Carl Sandburg. Copyright 1920 by Harcourt, Brace & World, Inc.; renewed, 1948, by Carl Sandburg.

Harvard University Press: the poem beginning "Farther in summer than the birds," by Emily Dickinson, from Thomas H. Johnson, editor, The Poems of Emily Dickinson, Cambridge, Mass., The Belknap Press of Harvard University Press. Copyright, 1955, by The President and Fellows of Harvard College.

Holt, Rinehart and Winston, Inc.: "Tree at My Window" and four lines from "A Hundred Collars," from Complete Poems of Robert Frost. Copyright 1930; copyright renewed 1949 by Holt, Rinehart and Winston, Inc. Also for the line from "Chicago" contained in Chicago Poems by Carl Sandburg. Copyright 1916 by Holt, Rinehart and Winston, Inc. Copyright renewed 1944 by Carl Sandburg.

The Macmillan Company: the first stanza of "Cargoes" from Collected Poems by John Masefield. Copyright 1912 by The Macmillan Company; renewed 1940 by John Masefield. Also for "Down by the Salley Gardens," from Collected Poems of W. B. Yeats. Copyright 1906 by The Macmillan Company, renewed 1934 by W. B. Yeats. Used with permission of The Macmillan Company, The Macmillan Company of Canada, and Mrs. W. B. Yeats.

New Directions: the stanza from "The Ballad of the Long-Legged Bait," from The Collected Poems of Dylan Thomas. Copyright © 1957 by New Directions.

Elvis Presley Music, Inc., and Lion Publishing Company, Inc.: two lines from Hound Dog, by Jerry Leiber and Mike Stoller. Copyright © 1956 by Elvis Presley Music, Inc. and Lion Publishing Company, Inc.

Remick Music Corporation: the four lines quoted from "Week End of a Private Secretary," by Mercer and Hanighen. Copyright 1938 by Remick Music Corporation.

CONTENTS

14. LESSON PLANNING

Curtain Raiser

To the Student

Possibly this book can improve your teaching; possibly not. Possibly you are improvable; possibly not. The guess here is that books on methods have something to say and that you can profit by them. You are familiar with the materials here discussed—English grammar, Shakespeare, the mass media, poetry, novels, and other matters—but your experience as a teacher is assumed to be limited, unfortunate, or nonexistent. Despite your knowledge of Shakespeare, have a copy of the plays at your side when you read Chapter 6. Similarly, have handy a copy of *Silas Marner* or *Giants in the Earth* for Chapter 5. Have a file of back issues of *English Journal* and *Scholastic* conveniently by because these periodicals are your most valuable single resource.

The book is designed not to be read once and then put aside, but to be a desk companion to which you return term after term, throughout your apprenticeship and for some time thereafter. Discussion and question materials are for use in actual classroom situations. Experiment with them, but above all investigate the feeling that English teaching is a major occupation of the times, as important as the work of the atomic scientist or the missile engineer. If your feelings and values are puerile, you will contribute to destruction. If your teaching and the feelings and values in it have power, you will contribute to survival. The book attempts to augment your power and your energy, in school and away from it, in your professional and private life.

The book is as practical as experience as a high school teacher, later work in educational research, and teaching hundreds of student teachers can make it, but practicality should begin with modesty. One methods

1

book will never make a teacher of you. You must seek out further materials and steep yourself in them. Supplementary materials exist in great abundance and are indicated here. Direct your attention to these, critically, because suggestions to the teacher do not always make sense; there is madness to some methods.

Methods courses are in occasional disrepute among some people who feel that for competent teaching knowledge of the material suffices. Hardly, even if your students were always willing to learn. Methods in your madness is not madness in your methods; the first will make you an interesting, even a good, teacher; not so the second; not all methods have merit, including, perhaps, some you may encounter in this book. If so, the fault lies with the author, not with the principle. Content is a necessary but not a sufficient condition for good teaching.

For that reason, your training combines the training of the artist and scientist, which is almost pure content, with the training of the salesman and the actor, which is partly content and chiefly manner, or method. You will deal simultaneously with content and presentation, if you respect your students. It cannot be otherwise when students too often balk at what you teach. Content alone will never carry the day for you; method must emerge from content; this book is devoted to showing how it can so emerge.

Use materials flexibly. Some questions dealing with Wang Lung in *The Good Earth* (p. 186) are applicable to Per Hansa in *Giants in the Earth* (p. 180). Discussion on "Richard Cory" (p. 233) and why men seek death can be applicable to Carton's death in *Tale of Two Cities* (p. 166) and *Romeo and Juliet* (p. 197). *Kubla Khan* (p. 250), as an example of organized, patterned fantasy, has points of contact with the fantasy in "Dream Children" (p. 257). This integration of materials makes you responsible for teaching imaginatively and provocatively. You will find throughout the book such attempts to integrate materials, but the space of a book is limited, so you must compensate by encouraging interpretation in yourself and in your classes. Add your insights and theirs to those offered here.

Go forward to your experiences and you will find yourself rewarded as few people are privileged to be. The thrill that the creative artist and scientist know—and few other people do—can be yours several days a week when lessons go well. How many people can be so fortunate? When teaching proceeds effectively, it is accompanied by an elation that keeps you young and your vital juices flowing. Seek this elation because it contributes to a better world and because it can be seized almost as often as you want it, by proper planning and by *method*-ically seeking it. In the classroom, your fate is what you choose to make it and you can arrange outcomes as you can nowhere else, provided that you know your material and how to plan your content and your manner of teaching it.

To the Instructor

Most English majors preparing to teach are brighter than they believe themselves to be. The better college campus, these days, is peopled by young scientists, mathematicians, and pre-meds who deprecate offerings in Education. Unfortunately, this rubs off on your students, who have misgivings about their life work. One of your more important jobs is infusing a stiff dose of morale into your classes. This book wants to help.

Paradoxically, although your students are less removed chronologically from their high school days than you are, they are more mistaken about them. Intervening experiences with college teaching make them believe that high school teaching is like college teaching and that the lecture method will serve them adequately. You know they are wrong, but they don't. They don't know that good questions are not only hard to come by, but are more productive of effective teaching than the most brilliant statements. For this reason, much of this book discusses question techniques, how to generate good questions, how to get a discussion off the ground, and how to keep it going. The good question is a jewel. In the student teaching you will observe, some questions in the book will work well on certain occasions and poorly on others. Assess the circumstances of success and failure with the student teacher for deeper analysis of the conditions of effective teaching.

The good question strengthens teacher morale. My colleagues have frequently twitted, "What do you teach in English methods?" and I have responded that much of my time is devoted to teaching students how to ask questions. The twitting stops and colleagues are respectful because they know that everything in science, philosophy, art, and the humanities depends on asking the right questions. Socrates' strength in discussion lay in this. This strength led to Socrates' morale.

Considerable attention is given to classroom climate and how it can profitably interact with teaching. The high school student can be vicious, unkind, or stupid. The teacher must not flee these but turn them to profit, and he can do so only by a sense of competence and assurance in any classroom climax, large or small; one can depend on the emergence of these a half-dozen times in most periods. Most often, they barely flicker into awareness; sometimes they are cataclysmic and terrorizing. The case studies in the book illustrate how the teacher can move forward into control of the classroom climate and how content leads to control, not spontaneously, but by the application of suitable method in conjunction with content. They show the teacher in the active, not passive, mood. Whether the teacher knows it or not, and likes it or not, he is perceived as managing the classroom and thereby, sometimes, becomes a target. The attempt to drag the teacher down to student level is understandable, though not acceptable; the attempt offers opportunities for method to show how content illuminates the attempt. The teacher, inevitably a model, sometimes one to emulate and too often, sadly, one to avoid, must know how content illuminates classroom climate; this is method, involving knowledge of the English syllabus as a beginning, but going on to inner attitude, confidence, techniques, and resources. A book on method, therefore, cannot be written without reference to content, but a book on content, even were it a thousand Cambridge Histories of English Literature, will not help settle class unrest at the end of the period preceding lunch or tell what to do about a board eraser flying across the room. It was the latter incident, indeed, that provided the idea for including case studies in this book on methods. Adapted from the paper of one of my graduate students, the incident goes:

> I was writing at the blackboard when I heard the soft *pow* of an eraser and an exclamation from the rear of the room, and I turned to see a student rising angrily from his seat, eraser in hand. He didn't know who had fired it but he was taking aim at the general source. I reclaimed the eraser despite his mutterings, and promised that justice would be done, if he'd give me a couple of minutes. However, I made him admit that justice would not consist in a free throw at the culprit, whoever he might turn out to be, but would be satisfied if I made the culprit admit his identity and clean the chalk marks from the victim's jacket. How could we determine the culprit?
>
> First I asked if the culprit had thrown a straight pitch, or had looped it, and I invited discussion. The class agreed that he could have looped it and remained in his seat or could have thrown a straight pitch, but would have had to get to his feet for that, because he otherwise might have hit one of the students in between. To have thrown a straight pitch and to have arisen meant that he had been seen and that there were witnesses. To have

looped it meant we were stuck for witnesses. On the board I wrote "Looped versus Straight Pitch." I then asked the class to consider if the culprit was right or left handed. If he were right handed, he could have looped it without being witnessed, but if he were left handed—since the pitch went from right to left—there might have been witnesses. The class got really interested, and somebody pointed out that a backhand throw would complicate my analysis, but then somebody else answered that a backhand throw was unlikely, and I added to the board "Right hander versus Southpaw." I asked the victim to show us how he had been sitting at the moment of impact; he had been copying the board work in his notebook, bent forward slightly, and the eraser had struck him back of the shoulder muscle. Had the source of the throw been forward or back of him? I wrote on the board "Rear half of the room versus front half of the room," and now the class began to turn its attention to the left rear quadrant of the room and the boys seated there fidgeted, most of them laughing and joshing with their accusers, but a couple frowning. I announced that I would form a jury of the entire class. The first vote was looped versus straight pitch. The majority voted for a straight pitch. The second vote was right hander versus southpaw, and the majority voted for a right hander. In the third vote, the majority voted that the pitch had come from the rear half of the room. Therefore the consensus was that a right hander had thrown a straight pitch from the rear half of the room. If so, the front half of the room was innocent and we had to look for the culprit in the rear of the room. Could we allow the rear of the room to continue as jurors? The front half of the room didn't think so and the rear half of the room objected to branding the innocent with the guilty. Just then one of the frowners in the left rear quadrant started to grin at me, arose silently, walked around the rear of the room to the victim, and with exaggerated obsequiousness started to brush his sleeve, pick lint from his jacket collar, and tidy him up generally. The class broke into laughter.

Coincidentally, I was teaching "The Devil and Daniel Webster," but it never occurred to me that I could have related the class as jury with the jury in the story. I missed a bet there, but when the class asked how I had located the culprit I said that detective work had nothing to do with it but that you catch more flies with honey than with vinegar. What was the honey? Just that, from the beginning of the incident on, I wasn't being punitive. Somebody else said it was like the carrot and the stick, which had to be explained to others in the class, and another student said it was like the sun coming out after the rain, drawing up all the mist from the fields. However, they got the point that it wasn't detective work that had solved the crime, but attitude. I'm still kicking myself for not having led into "The Devil and Daniel Webster."

This account is reminiscent of the physics teacher who was occupied with clerical work during a long home room period. He finished his work, noticed paper airplanes being thrown, and called out peremptorily, "Identify that plane!" He had students take out rulers, measure wing spread and length, and then, under official auspices, had them throw the planes and observe how the vagaries of flight were associated with dimension of length, width, and weight of paper.

The relationship of method to content is not always so palpable. On returning to my high school classes at the end of summer vacation, I never became accustomed to how in a few weeks my students had put on two, three, or four inches, and fifteen or twenty pounds. This sense of growth is no longer present even in the young adults you teach in college, but method must take account of it, must recognize that the teacher can resent it or take joy in it and that the identical content in the resenting teacher will not come out as it will in the teacher who takes joy in the growth all around. Method, like air, has weight, tangibility, quality, and a chemistry. Some people don't see it unless you present the classroom analogues to Von Guericke's Magdeburg hemispheres. Content alone will not give the answer to flying erasers or to paper airplanes, and, unless the answer is found through method, content will never have the proper opportunity to come forward.

I would like to thank Eleanor Justman for having read the primitive versions of this text, Harry Bernstein for having originally suggested the idea, Joseph Justman, Director of Teacher Education at Brooklyn College, for being a willing sounding board, Louis Rosenzweig, Deputy Chairman, Department of Education, Brooklyn College, for administrative succor. I also thank my daughter, Felice Bernstein, for her numerous illustrations of contemporary teen-age values; my wife, Belle Bernstein, for her inexhaustible faith and patience; and my students, undergraduate and graduate, for their assistance, interest, and co-operation.

Introductory: English and the Adolescent

The Adolescent Group

The first decade of life is affected chiefly by parental relationships, biology, and socioeconomic forces, but in adolescence a new circumstance is added by the gang or peer group. Group loyalties, ambitions, and perceptions set the major pattern within which the adolescent develops. Even sex, that most personal of all experiences, is suffused by group values.[1]

American and Western European urban culture testify to this. One hundred years ago, when American culture was predominantly rural and distance was a difficulty, the adolescent found his individual pattern of chores and family responsibility. Whenever possible, however, he went in gangs to and from school, in play, and in discharging his family and social duties, as the evidence in *Tom Sawyer, Huckleberry Finn, Hoosier Schoolmaster,* and elsewhere indicates. Group-mindedness seems built into the adolescent. Given opportunity, the adolescent will seek out other adolescents. We can quote yesteryear's cultural patterns and those of other societies, but our present concern is the teaching of English in American urban and suburban circumstances; here, clearly, the adolescent places greater store on group-approved behavior than on values originating with teacher or parent. It doesn't last forever—it just seems that way. By the time teen-agers reach

7

seventeen or eighteen, the mad rush to line up at the Paramount for Benny Goodman (1937) or Alan Freed (1957) has slowed down to a walk. But, although the discouraging spectacle doesn't last forever, it recurs forever.

The intensity of group feeling, the utter devotion to the gang—almost as if to a loved one—the noblest virtues of loyalty and self-sacrifice can operate in a gang of juvenile delinquents with concurrent brutality against out-group individuals and groups.[2] Inner organization is renounced for membership in a plural-person organization. Individual control, because it is onerous, is abdicated and a portion of control turned over to the peer group. The adolescent must find this abdication desirable, as his elders do; group policing makes behavior possible that would be otherwise unthinkable. In this subordination of self to the group, entire industries find profit.[3] This group sense is positive, an overriding push; let parents or teachers get in the way and resentments emerge, an observation easily documented by the elders involved.

American adult society must want its adolescents that way, despite complaints about teen-agers. The American adolescent has been planned. One can ask: "What of juvenile delinquency, teen-age crime, youthful drug addiction? Are these planned?"

These and general adolescent waywardness are the price we pay—and seem willing to continue to pay—for an adolescent society that is team conscious, loyal to the in-group, strongly partisan, and savage against the nonconformist. This behavior is sanctioned by a society that gets exactly what it thinks it requires for its preservation. Unfortunately, societies do not always know what is best for their survival. If they did, we would not have the roster of civilizations dead and gone. "Culture is an adaptation; but it is sometimes adaptive not to outer realities but to inner tensions." [4]

The chief danger of adolescent group-mindedness is not juvenile delinquency but inhospitality to the unusual and the off-beat, the group disparagement and encircling of the square, just as adult society is inhospitable to its unusual thinkers, its pioneering artists, scientists, scholars, thinkers, and revolutionaries. Adolescent group value systems are reflections of adult group value systems.[5] Adolescent group-mindedness—that reflection of adult practices that gives short shrift to the unusual man or woman—is nothing we can do anything about until the adult world takes itself in hand; meanwhile we remember that social feeling is on the whole a good thing. The adolescent wants his place within the group, either as leader or follower, as bully or butt, but he simply has to be in, there where his heart lies, so much power does group sense wield in him.

He who knows this gains tremendous leverage in affecting the adolescent. Peculiarly, those who should manipulate this leverage, parents and teachers, for example, often overlook or resent it. What are the fulcra of group life that you, as an English teacher, can turn to classroom profit?

Fulcrum 1: Groups stand in opposition to one another, in rivalry, competition, and enmity, as one team against another, or one neighborhood or block against another, sometimes to a homicidal extreme, more often in the various dilutions short of that.

Fulcrum 2: Rivalry requires group members to achieve competence, as athletes, as warriors, as Lotharios, as sharp dressers, as "cool," and even as artists and students. The group, to be worth anything, must be distinguished by such attainments in its members. The group has stature among other groups if its members have accomplishments.

Fulcrum 3: Therefore the adolescent is perpetually on the prowl for accomplishments in himself. If he can itemize these, he is satisfied. If he cannot, uncertainties, apprehensions, and anxieties develop. He pits himself against others, totals his assets and liabilities in bookkeeping procedures that are endless, involving his muscles, his complexion, his success with the opposite sex, his dancing ability, his athletic ability, his father's income, his mother's good taste, his family's standing, his popularity, in a neverending inventory. Give him only a few things to be certain of and he will be cocksure and assertive. Show him the instability of the world around him and he will throw himself at your feet, pleading for help. Point a way to true power and competence and you will be worshipped, because he can take it right over to his gang.

Look at these three fulcra. Ask yourself:

How does Fulcrum 1 express itself in school rivalry and intramural rivalry? How would you use it in debating? In organizing a discussion on current events? In comparing reviews of books, movies, or television programs? In a discussion of "Lady or the Tiger"?

How can Fulcrum 2 motivate good diction? A meaningful analysis of Hamlet or Lady Macbeth? The understanding of character in fiction? An effective recitation of Mark Antony's funeral oration?

How can Fulcrum 3 lead to effective theme writing? To self-understanding? To improved knowledge of parts of speech, grammar, and usage? To a sense for the topic sentence?

You are teaching English to make your group-minded student more competent as an individual. Here you are allies, because he wants the same. His very questions show the need to be competent as an individual, and his anxiety when competence is absent:[6]

> How can I be sure he (she) likes me and will date with me?
> Why don't people (my parents, teachers, friends) understand me?
> How can I tell when people are telling me the truth, or when they are lying to me?
> Is there a life after death?
> Where do I come from? How was I born?
> What makes classical music better than rock-and-roll? Where's the proof?
> Why do I have to obey?
> What makes my race, or religion, inferior?
> Why can't my father earn more money?
> Am I a dope because I can't read Shakespeare?
> Will there be a war? Will I survive? Why do men and nations fight?
> Why is necking wrong?

Note that each question can be restated as a topic for a composition assignment, and even in debatable form, so that points of view are defended and opposed, as recommended by the fulcra. As an example, the second question: "My friends understand me better than my teachers do" or "My parents understand me better than my friends do."

These questions reflect problems and anxieties, the answers the adolescent seeks, and what he would like to learn. Unfortunately, what is taught is not always what is learned, and external teaching not always equivalent to internalized learning. For example, what you consider a reward—or punishment—may not be so construed by your student, so that a reward in your eyes may be internalized by the student as a punishment;[7] teacher and student are not communicating. You may praise a student, causing him to be ridiculed by the class; you may ridicule a student and see the class make a hero of him.

Perhaps the chief contributor to this breakdown in communication between teacher and student is the group orientation of the adolescent. Rewards and punishments are not the same things to all men, but must be considered in a context of group values, and especially so in the adolescent, because his group's definitions of rewards and punishments are his guides.

For further discussion and teaching materials in this area, see:

1. Chapter 2, section on *The Fragment*, p. 62, for group work in composition correction;
2. Chapter 2, section on *Usage Versus Grammar*, p. 63 ff., for the teaching of usage;
3. Chapter 4, p. 134, on socializing reading experiences;
4. Chapter 5, section on *Two Old-Fashioned Novels*, pp. 162-176, on taking sides in discussions on literature.
5. Chapter 5, p. 184.

Research, Resources, and Techniques

"The attitudes of an individual have their anchorage in the groups to which he belongs. . . . Many attitudes can be changed more easily by making changes in certain properties of the group than by directly teaching the individuals, as individuals. . . . The conduct and beliefs of pupils is regulated in large measure by the small groups within a classroom, such as friendship cliques, and the cohesive groups of students within a school . . ." (William Clark Trow, Alvin C. Zander, William C. Maru, and David H. Jenkins, *Journal of Educational Psychology*, XLI [1950], 322.)

1. Show how the above statement can lead to class discussion and debate of the last line in George Meredith's sonnet "Lucifer in Starlight." (Hint: Does this sonnet, though written generations ago, tell us more about dealing with Russians or about dealing with ourselves?)

2. In Robert Frost's "A Prayer in Spring," have students debate: Does God fulfill or sanctify? Does man fulfill or sanctify? Why does the poet distinguish fulfillment from sanctification? Should he?

3. With material you are now teaching, adapt this procedure of having groups state beliefs and then having groups debate groups (rather than having individuals debate individuals).

Why Teach English?

Some years ago a student put a question to me, a question not easily answered. The student was of normal intelligence, hard-bitten, tough-minded, and not easily bluffed. He asked, "Teach', why do I hafta learn

English? I know a guy who can't sign his name, and he makes more than you do."

I have never had a class discussion more stimulating than the one that followed. The student was not taunting, but earnest. The others in class nodded their agreement. They too had evidence that illiteracy was no impediment to earning power far transcending a teacher's. True, one can give the statistical probabilities that people with an education are likely to earn more than people without—but the illiterate junk dealer of *Born Yesterday* who can bribe legislatures and mock at the laws is not unknown to high school students, and the exception that proves the rule can also demolish it.

After days of discussion the class concluded that English does not help the student make more dollars but more sense—of himself and his motives, of the people around him and far away, of the world, and of life. English will help him do a better job of analysis and appreciation, of synthesis and understanding, of figuring out what makes things tick (or tic!), of responses to beauty, of his emotions, his loyalties, his hates, and his loves. These reasons are general. We will later refine them because the reasons for studying spelling, *Tale of Two Cities,* journalism, and paragraph construction are different.

In part, this means that we teach English for adjustment. Arthur Bestor[8] and Jacques Barzun[9] have made "adjustment" a dirty word, but adjustment is the reason above all others that we teach, so that our students can live well armed and well nourished in mind and body, with data to hand that help them live compatibly within themselves and compatibly with others. Adjustment can be for anything you please, adjustment to the fullest self-realization, or adjustment to some society. You should expedite the adjustment process. English should teach us how to accept and transmit communication, how to enrich the blueprint of our lives, how to understand the order and design in ourselves and the world around us and the kinds of causativeness there are, and how to share in the lives of different places and people.

Unhappily, *Ivanhoe, Silas Marner,* grammar, spelling, and theme writing —English content in short—sometimes make not for adjustment, or dollars, or sense, or even scholarship, but for a threat to the student's status. Content may become a bugaboo, something he cannot handle, and he forever after hates the subject and calls himself a dope—and what do you want to make of it?—in this, the winter of our content. Depending on its handling, English can be an aid to adjustment or an impediment to it.

But, in addition, English these days has a social as well as individual importance. It stands between us and that mushroom-shaped column of smoke. Society requires an approach to English content that holds off an atomized world, that promises control of ourselves, of the world around us, and of insight into others and the world's past, present, and future. Society insists that its leaders certainly and its citizens preferably gain this English content.

Solid English content is therefore irreplaceable in the curriculum. Nobody in his right mind will deny it. The debate is how the adolescent can be confronted with content, not only in English but in the other curriculum areas—and here disputes in educational philosophy arise. Arthur Bestor opposes education for adjustment.[10] Harold Rugg wants to confront the individual most effectively with himself, before confronting him with content.[11] Now self-confrontation is the thing that human beings dread above all other things, yet Rugg assumes that self-confrontation is easily come by —as if Freud and Socrates had never lived or taught. Education for life adjustment constitutes the toughest and most challenging curriculum on the books and is not for the underendowed in the mental or spiritual realms.

On the other hand, to confront the student with content, with poetry, values, judgments, and beauty that moves to tears, wins you a cultivated gentleman, like the British civil servant dwelling in past values, culture, and Latin quotations and devastated by two victories as he has never been by defeats, or the sciolist of some *ancien régime,* or a pedantic chronicler occupying an academic seat. Cultivated men can be hamstrung by culture and content because they have not been enlarged by it—swollen, yes, but not enlarged. Bestor forgets that content must be internalized, must be involved with judgments, and must lead to wisdom, else it is empty pageantry, preciosity, or worse. Rugg forgets that without content attitudes degenerate to attitudinizing.

You, as an English teacher, must ask: How is my student to be confronted with himself, with content, with himself through content, and with content through his inner needs as an adolescent? The answer lies in the four-letter word "work."

For further discussion and teaching materials in this area, see:

1. Chapter 2, section on *In the Beginning Was the Name,* pp. 41 ff.
2. Chapter 2, section on *Grammar, Ego, and Self,* pp. 54 ff.

3. Chapter 2, section on *The Sentence Diagram and Inner Microscopy,* pp. 56 ff.
4. Case Study 9, p. 137.
5. Chapter 5, section on *Preliminary Consideration 1—Mute Inglorious Miltons,* p. 156.

Research, Resources, and Techniques

Compare the two quotations:

1. "I am aware of the special problems that exist in American public schools—that in localities where most of the pupils are the children of foreign parents, themselves illiterate in their native tongues, the instructor must be satisfied to teach them any English at all, that to exact from them a standard of correctitude becomes quite out of the question. I know that in some of our schools it is even as much as the teacher can do to avoid being murdered by his more aggressive students" (Edmund Wilson, *A Piece of My Mind* [London: W. H. Allen, 1957] p. 122).

2. " 'There are some classes,' you will say, 'who cannot be liked. There are some teachers who have really loathsome pupils. There are some schools where the girls think of nothing but sex, and the boys think of nothing but sex and fighting, and all of them hate the teachers, and the school, and education. . . . The boys and girls at these places do not want to learn' " (Gilbert Highet, *The Art of Teaching* [Vintage Books, 1954], pp. 27, 28).

Assume that you have been assigned to a school described in these quotations. Draw up a series of lesson plans for the teaching of *Macbeth* or *The Tempest,* to best insure motivation.

English and the New Leisure

Only through work will the student gain both competence and the answer to his questions. Work also reconciles divergent educational philosophies, come Bestor, come Rugg. But you, the English teacher, must work too, because student assiduity will be lacking without teacher assiduity. Your work is *precedent* to work in the student. If you work, the student will. To demand work without working yourself is hypocritical.

But work for what purpose? To what end? For what values? Unless you can answer, you will work for work's sake, and that is dull drill and rote chasing its own tail. Let's remember that status in the adolescent group is one goal attainable by work. Again, status for what purpose? To what end?

For what values? For the student's sweet solipsistic self? Only in part. If work leads to competence, if competence leads to status, if status leads to leadership, these must be for his peers, his neighborhood, his family, and his nation. Therefore, work has group outcomes as well as personal ones.

Groups, however, vary in privilege. If we want Negro, Italian, and Puerto Rican adolescents in New York's Harlem to work at their education, are we to promise them social mobility and social status enough to move out of their neighborhoods as a possible outcome? Then we are asking them to desert their origins. Most students scorn this disloyalty—and therefore do not work at their education, not when work leads to treason. Some teachers, agreeing that treason should not be a consequence of education, have used materials with ethnic overtones; thus *Ramona* has been taught to Spanish-speaking girls to fortify them in their cultural inheritance.

Let underprivileged youth work at their education and then return to their neighborhoods, their ghettos, and their slums, to stay there, live there, and improve them so that their dwelling places are no longer slums. Such work makes sense to the adolescent; it has outcomes in the world about him, in the world to which he owes his first loyalties: his friends, his neighborhood, and his family.

Similarly, more privileged youth must work for the appreciation of meaning, beauty, understanding, and expression. Without these things, status in society is boorishness and an evasion of responsibilities. When values and principles do not accompany privilege, tyranny is a consequence.

Thus with the deprived and with the privileged, work has a social, group-oriented reference; education is as imperative among the deprived as among the privileged, among the dull as among the talented.

But should we demand work of youth? What of the slow, contemplative, pleasant flowering of the spirit, as the unhurried adolescent[12] explores the possibilities and directions open to him? Good—unless exploration becomes diffuseness. The educated mind does a better job of exploration and daydreaming than the uneducated one, and exploration is neither daydreaming nor diffuseness, but work, or some aspect of it.

Work is not separated from play, according to the theorists of the New Leisure.[13] The work done by American businessmen and leaders would be physically and neurologically impossible but for the play interpretation put on work. Work is seen as the portal to play and play as the portal to work —to the three hour lunch (at which business is discussed), to golf (where deals are closed), to the elegant home or Florida hotel (where one meets useful people of the right kind), to expensive clothing and cuisine, so that a chilling amount of work-play can be undertaken if play-work is a promised outcome.

Your teaching, therefore, can be in a context of play or in a context of work—and the content will not have changed a whit. Nor does it make too much difference in learning outcomes, unless you feel that suffering must accompany learning, when actually suffering is an impediment to it. The appropriate interaction of work and play constitutes reinforcement of learning, leading in turn to competence.

How do work and play appropriately interact? By pace.

You must first slow down the student so that he has no sense of rush and grants educational problems—say homework assignments or English compositions—time enough to unfold themselves and himself time enough to think the problems over, whether he is a good or a weak student. Indeed you must comfort the poor student in his slowness. He cannot gain competence—in English, in the other disciplines, and in adjustment—except at his own internal pace. To sense the illogic of a sentence fragment or to improve reading takes time. The slow student needs this time.[14] The sense of *time enough* leads to the proper relationship between work and play.[15]

Second, you must believe in the improvability of your students. You cannot make the dull bright, but you can make them less dull, and you can put a higher polish on the others. You must have greater faith in students than they have in themselves, as any good athletic coach will tell you. You must show the possibilities of victory.

Finally, in this interaction of work and play, plan for one good laugh a period. Just one. No more is necessary. You want interaction of work and play, not dominance of one by the other.

For further discussion and teaching materials in this area, see:

1. Case Study 4, p. 55.
2. Case Study 7, p. 104.
3. Chapter 2, section on *Sentence Structure*, pp. 59 ff.

Research, Resources, and Techniques

1. "The usual way is to keep bawling into the pupil's ears as one pours water into a funnel, the pupil's business being merely to repeat what he has been told. I would have the tutor amend this method, and at the

outset, in order to test the capacity of the mind he has charge of, he should put it on trial. . . . I would not have him always to start the subject and monopolize the speaking, but to listen while the pupil speaks in his turn. Socrates, and after him Arcesilaus, first made their disciples speak, and then spoke to them" (Montaigne, *Essays* [Modern Library], pp. 127, 128).

2. "One of the most astonishing sights to be seen all too often in our schools is a teacher of civics or political science conducting a class in 'democratic government' with the pupils sitting in neat rows dutifully giving answers prescribed by the teacher and the book. A dictator can't teach democracy. It just can't be taught with a hickory stick any more than it can be taught with a bayonet. It can only be taught by a good listener" (Wendell Johnson, *People in Quandaries* [Harper and Brothers, 1946], pp. 480, 481).

How does the type of listening recommended in the above quotations help in integrating work and play? How does such listening relieve classroom tensions that lead to the one good laugh per period? What is the relationship between effective listening and effective questioning?

English as a Technological Necessity

Never in history has the work of the English teacher been of greater importance. Scientists cannot keep up with the abstracts of articles, much less with articles. Accumulating knowledge taxes storage capacity; our cataloguing schemes grow antiquated; man's mind can no longer keep in sight simultaneously all that man knows. The compartments of knowledge swell with additional information, burst, and proliferate new compartments. Chemistry becomes subdivided into organic, inorganic, biological, steroid, physical, isotopic, isomeric, or tracer; similar subdivisions appear in each of the disciplines, and boundaries between subdivisions become dim. A subdivision leaks over into its neighbor's area in complete disregard for hereditary privacy or leaps across several compartments, as when doctoral candidates in English become involved in content analysis (an aspect of sociology), in communications theory (an aspect of physics and engineering), frequency counts (an aspect of statistics), the language of fantasy (psychology, pharmacology, and chemistry).[16] As we grow in knowledge, the boundaries of the disciplines become increasingly permeable and knowledge grows thereby.

This affects you. The mass media have shouldered into the traditional English curriculum, and you are being urged to a redefinition of the communication arts, which may lead to an adulteration of the English program, with television substituting for reading, committee reports for individually undertaken compositions, and usage for grammar. Television viewing, committee work, and usage study are legitimate aspects of the English curriculum, but they must not be made adulterants, especially when teaching schedules are crowded, when there is no time to teach all we have come to know, no time to waste on diffuseness that masquerades as breadth.

Core reflects this crisis as one attempt to handle the burdensome accretion of knowledge, as does the survey course in college. The very breadth of core makes impossible any specialized competence—but the absence of specialized competence also makes impossible any breadth of knowledge. True, we cannot avoid the cross-disciplinary approach. We have no alternative. But when shall we teach it? At what point in the student's development? At first, before he has any knowledge of the field? Or terminally, when he can begin to synthesize? Core is desirable and inevitable in the world today—but it should be terminal, not introductory. Core should not be the springboard for subsequent specialized experiences in the traditional areas; instead it should be the outcome of prior specialized experiences, especially in English. In short, the English curriculum is too crowded for *premature* dilution with core concepts.

Your contribution as an English teacher is suffering for lack of time and the imposition of burdensome nonteaching responsibilities. The understanding of self and others, the sense of personal, artistic, and social values, the insight into economic, political, and literary motivations, the logic and causativeness in science and cosmos are all your proper domain as an English teacher. Technology and science make us the swiftest, strongest, and shrewdest of the animals, superior to all other animals in assessing, analyzing, and arranging our environment, but still incapable of making us human. We become human when we symbolize and conceptualize. Here you are the instructor of all your colleagues because symbol and concept are your merchandise, as is the degradation of these, the stereotype. Because language simultaneously helps us symbolize, conceptualize, as well as stereotype, a strange marriage has arisen between language and mathematics, called symbolic logic, at which Lewis Carroll was best man and which has borne fruit not only in important mathematical discoveries and in computing machines, but also in linguistics and grammar. The English teacher is at the heart—or perhaps the bottleneck—of technological and scientific matters these days and the pity is that so few know it.[17]

For further discussion and teaching materials in this area, see:

1. Chapter 4, section on *Words Our Apelike Ancestors Taught Us,* pp. 145 ff.
2. Chapter 5, section on *Homer Is the Hunted,* pp. 176 ff.
3. Chapter 3, section on *Native Woodnotes Are Usually Wild,* p. 82.

Research, Resources, and Techniques

Dr. Joshua Lederberg's Nobel Prize speech, dealing with his important contributions to genetics and biochemistry, discussed biogenetic mechanisms almost as if sentence structure were involved. Note these quotations from *Science* (Jan. 29, 1960, p. 271):

". . . Taking account of the code-duplication in complementary structures and the need to indicate spacing of the words in the code sequence, from three to four nucleins may be needed to spell one amino acid. . . . The coding relationship would then be analogous to, say, Morse-English (binary linear) to Chinese (pictographic). . . ."

Do the problems in "translating machines" require solution by the physicist or by the linguist? What do the physics teacher and the English teacher have in common that these machines can use? [18]

English and Family Living

But if your work intimately intermingles with science and technology, so does it with the personal world of the adolescent. While the adolescent's group life contributes heavily to the adolescent's personal world, so do home and family, which continue paramount, although in the background, unobtrusively, in this period.

Learning is an emotive matter. Therefore learning is a family matter, because emotive patterns are familial in origin. Successful learning is more a function of the home than of the school, as is poor learning. Evidence that the adolescent delinquent is a product of a delinquent home is overwhelming.[19] What's wrong in American education is attributable more to the American home than to "educationists," whether in spelling or in engineering education; bright and capable adolescents fail to continue beyond high school, or fall short of their possibilities in high school, chiefly because of misplaced loyalty to group and family aspirations.[20] Bestor's restoration of learning[21] must be preceded by a face-lifting job on American family life and such ideals as fathers give their sons and mothers their daughters. If children are television watchers, it's because their parents are; if children can't write well, it's because their parents don't read; if students are vocationally rather than culturally oriented, it's because these values are their parents' too.

Parents too often preach the value of education for their children but not for themselves, leading their poor lambs to the shearing they never accepted for themselves nor do now.[22] "I grew up and I know better now," the parent will alibi, but there is still time to read the significant books of the day rather than the popular magazines, to be interested in world affairs rather than sports or neighborhood gossip, to enrich the home with music and art and conversation. Where these are done, the course of learning in the school is easy and you, the teacher, far more effective. Where not done, we see the continuum of human waste from adolescent delinquency to boredom with education.

The influence of the home is prepotent; the school exerts the merest fraction of the home's influence in matters of emotive development. This, though virtually axiomatic, is not to say that you exert no emotional influence; you do, but in a direction already formulated in the home, where emotive tonalities and values will determine the child's emotive mechanisms in the school. Savage, sadistic, or even misunderstanding teachers were always fewer than parents; teachers have been less responsible for adolescent delinquency than parents. The level of understanding among teachers is higher than among parents and the school less decisive than the home, for which the school is but a sounding board, and especially so in those privileged communities which Riesman describes,[23] where the educational level of parents exceeds that of the teachers they hire. The angle of educational inclination is virtually always set by the parent and the home. The best teacher cannot reshape the adolescent's emotive world. All he can offer, in the worst instances, is an oasis. In the best, he can merely supplement and enrich the emotive climate in the home.

Furthermore, the law wants it so. The parent has means of enforcing the home's moral and emotive code that are denied you. Physical chastisement can become physical brutality in the home, with the voice of the law scarcely raised in objection, but physical chastisement is always physical brutality when administered by the teacher so that even the teacher's competence is questioned when such instances come to light. We are beyond the days of Wickham Squeers and Dotheboys Hall in our schools, but many homes are still there.

Any attempt by you to replace the home's moral and emotional code would invite the wrath of home, church, and community, which feel a special sacredness attaching to the family; intervention in family life is countenanced only under extreme circumstances. Therefore, accept the priority of the home in moral, ethical, and emotive matters. Where does this leave you and your domain? Since the family is so prepotent, what can you do when emotive problems and situations—familial in origin—walk into your classroom?

Be able to recognize them but do not properly feel morally responsible for their etiology, their course, or their alleviation, except as any enlightened citizen might. If, as an enlightened citizen, you know that the child draws its chief emotive sustenance from the home, you will further know that sometimes the sustenance is desirable and sometimes not. When desirable, rejoice. When undesirable, first quarantine the infection; second, offer wise understanding, patience, and fairness; third, do not become degraded or tarred with whatever brush smeared the child; fourth, avoid any semblance of therapy of the home situation.

To repeat: you have no right to change the emotive pattern laid down in the home, but, if the emotive pattern is nonetheless dragged into your classroom, you are not to mold the child, nor reshape the child's emotional states, nor reform the child. Your responsibility is to make the emotive pattern more discernible to the child, nothing more. Using the materials in the English course of study, you should inform—not reform.

How? Using what techniques? It is easy to say, "Make the emotive pattern more discernible to the child," but what means does the teacher use to do so?

For further discussion and teaching materials in this area, see:

1. Chapter 2, Case Study 4, p. 55.
2. Chapter 4, Case Study 8, p. 134.
3. Chapter 4, Case Study 9, p. 137.

Research, Resources, and Techniques

1. One hundred years ago, Herbert Spencer, in *Education*, wrote: "The great error made by those who discuss questions of juvenile discipline, is in ascribing all the faults and difficulties to the children, and none to the parents. The current assumption respecting family govern-

ment, as respecting national government is, that the virtues are with rulers and the vices with the ruled. . . . When we canvass the misbehavior of juveniles, we habitually take for granted that these culpable men and women [parents] are free from moral delinquency in the treatment of their offspring! So far is this from the truth, that we do not hesitate to say that to parental misconduct is traceable a great part of the domestic disorder commonly ascribed to the perversity of children. . . ."

2. "Many boys and girls who are chronic offenders come from homes broken by divorce, desertion, or death, or cracked by parental disharmony. Many are subject to one or several of the following conditions: a parent who is chronically ill, mentally ill, a drunkard, a prostitute, or criminal; spoiling or discipline that is overstrict or inconsistent; faulty care due to lack of interest, lack of time, or outright rejection . . ." (Norma E. Cutts and Nicholas Moseley, *Teaching the Disorderly Pupil* [Longmans, Green, 1957], p. 4).

3. ". . . These teachers frequently harbor a most grandiose and self-defeating expectation of omnicompetence in the classroom. They expect themselves to respond sympathetically to individual problem-children, even psychotic ones that would baffle an experienced psychologist. . . . They may resist the expectation that there is no child they cannot handle, no child to whose needs they cannot minister" (David Riesman, "Thoughts on Teachers and Schools," *Anchor Review,* No. 1, p. 49).

In your class you encounter children of the kind described in the above quotations. You may be teaching character analysis of the great villains in literature—Macbeth, Cassius, Claudius, or, on a lower level, Ichabod Crane. How do you teach the self-defeating quality of evil? Or you are planning a unit in self-expression and your students find it difficult to express themselves. What questions can you *properly* ask that will help them analyze the impediments in themselves to self-expression?

English and the War between the Generations

Fair verdicts on adolescent behavior are hard to arrive at because adults are hostile, parents are hostile, teachers are hostile, and English teachers not less so than any other adult group. On the other hand, it is especially important for you to be aware of this pervasive adult antipathy because the English course of study is particularly effective in dealing with, as well as being blind to, it. Contradictory? Consider:

Infants are far more trouble than adolescents. The elementary school child is more demanding and requires more concentrated attention than does the adolescent. Even the years beyond adolescence are more congenial to adults—the sex decisions made by people in their twenties and thirties are acceptable to us even though such decisions affect other people, children, neighbors, and, in general, a wider orbit of human beings than do the sex decisions of adolescents. Adolescent sex affairs are rarely as disruptive of social relationships as are adult sex affairs, yet so deeply ingrained are our aggressions and hostilities toward the adolescent that we find these sex patterns sometimes disturbing, sometimes offensive, and sometimes comical, in a reaction disproportionate to the stimulus conditions.

Bad manners, defiance, loudness, vulgarity are what we expect from adolescents. When we see adolescents in public conveyances, we automatically brace against the possible impact of young bodies violently tossed about. In movie houses we expect noisiness from raucous young throats. How often have our expectations come true? Are adolescents obstreperous in public places—or hearty? Are they violent in public vehicles—or active in horseplay? Are they rambunctious in a movie—or responding to a poor show?

On occasion the adolescent group becomes destructive. But we expect destructiveness all the time, we expect violence all the time, we expect irresponsibility all the time. We have these expectations because we are soured on adolescents and this dislike warps our perceptions. If we reserve special venom for any particular age group, it will be for adolescence. Why do we dislike—even hate—them so? Perhaps because: (1) They are all we once were and never shall be again. (2) In them sheer animality is as unobstructed as it ever is after early childhood and before senility. (3) They are more athletic, tireless, and sexually potent. Adolescent girls don't need Slenderella. (4) Their presence tells us to prepare to get out of the way, for they are coming to succeed us. They will survive us; they will live to see us lowered into our graves. (5) We can't win. They can't help but win.

These reasons are not definitive. You can furnish your own. The adult's disapproving eye—a jaundiced one—may be the arena of events without counterpart in actuality. The opinion of such an adult is not lost on the adolescent, who may react to it with bitterness, sarcasm, or other forms of assault. Thus, the shortest way to an East Harlem girl's heart is a glancing roundhouse blow on the deltoid muscle of her shoulder. This states: "I like you. You're my girl." To this nonverbal communication an East Harlem girl responds with squeals of displeasure, or frowns of haughtiness, or self-removal, or a counterpunch—whichever invites further pursuit.

How interpret a blow on a girl's shoulder? An ungentlemanly, badly brought-up brute? And the girl not better than she deserves to be? But I have seen the same gesture-language in settlement houses, swank summer camps, urban school systems in Pennsylvania, New York, Delaware, and New Jersey, and in privileged schools in Montclair, Manhasset, Great Neck, Westchester County, and Fairfield County, among delicately reared adolescents in upper-class suburbs. This is adolescent courtship in East Harlem and in wealthy Summit, New Jersey. The girl understands because many a true word is spoken in gesture. The patterns of communication are different in adolescence and in maturity.

The adult disapproves. He always has. Elvis Presley follows an earlier Valentino, a Rudy Vallee, or a younger Sinatra, formerly greeted by responses equally excessive even if not libidinous; if your grandma feels prim and self-righteous, remind her of Chauncey Olcott. Indeed, millennia tell the same story. Cicero defended the memory of an earlier matinee idol, the actor Roscius, "Quis nostrum tam animo agresti ac duro fuit, ut Roscii morte super non commoveretur? . . . propter excellentum artem ac venustatem, videbatur omnino mori non debuisse. Ergo ille corporis motu tantem amorem sibi conciliarat a nobis omnibus." (Who here so poor-spirited and hard-shelled as not to be moved by Roscius' recent death? . . . if only for the high level and true beauty of his art, he ought never have died. Especially his winning body gestures won great esteem from us.)

Eulogizing Presley so is premature, but *plus ça change, plus c'est la même chose.* Adolescence recurs; it had better, if we want the race to survive. The boogie-woogie and rock-and-roll of our days are the same mass tic and socialized pulse beat of the tarantism of the Middle Ages, or circus-tent evangelism, and Dionysus-worship. Because the adolescent is highly suggestible to forces and values *not* of the adult world's making, he is not readily controlled by the adult world. The adolescent seeks rapture, transport, enthusiasm, on the evidence of thousands of years.[24] Consider how the adolescent adopts off-beat coiffures, the d.a.[25] (more primly, the d.t.), the crew-cut, and how hair states loyalty to affiliation not only in Amish (Pennsylvania) and Chassidic (Williamsburg, Brooklyn) religious societies but also in adolescent societies.[26]

Throughout, the adult finds fault and calls names. You may find the adolescent and his ways in poor taste. Perhaps they are, but you would think so simply because adolescence is somewhere about. You, the English teacher, the guardian of taste and discrimination, know how taste and discrimination can become priggish, sanctimonious, and sterile. Intrinsically, a d.t. is not in worse taste than a crew-cut, nor the bell-bottoms of a couple of generations ago in worse taste than Ivy League dress today. The objection to these is their insularity, and your job is to break down this insularity of taste, not by preaching or admonishing, but by an Observant Eye, and an Accessible Ear.

The most successful teacher (and successful parent, and successful psychotherapist, and successful human being) has the ability to listen—just plain listen. Listening is the highest form of communication you can establish with your class of adolescents. The Observant Eye and the Accessible Ear say more than verbalization, no matter how persuasive and eloquent—that you are interested, that you have no antipathy, and that you are sympathetic. They say far more than a big mouth, an unflagging tongue, and a yammering from the sidelines.

"Hold on!" you say. "Am I never supposed to say anything? When I see the impermissible or the inadvisable taking place, do I shut up? If so, I'm abdicating my responsibilities rather than assuming them!" But the impermissible and the inadvisable will be less likely if you have first done a stint of listening. Youngsters can do foolish and heedless things. You can best prevent these by first learning why such things are undertaken and then forbidding them as a second stage. But listening and observation come first. You are paid to tell of many things: of spelling and punctuation, of agreement in number, of Brutus and Lady Macbeth, of "The Monkey's Paw," Antigone, and the death of Mary White. But telling is not teaching. Telling is only part of it. It must be supplemented by listening and observation, if teaching is to be at highest effectiveness. Learning to listen is not easy. It requires drill and exercise. Observation does not spontaneously come to us. We offer training, drill, and exercise in these later on.

For further discussion and teaching materials in this area, see:

1. Chapter 5, section on *Two Old-Fashioned Novels,* pp. 162 ff.
2. Chapter 5, Case Study 10, pp. 174.
3. Chapter 3, section on *Some Painful Truths,* pp. 96 ff.
4. Chapter 5, Case Study 11, p. 184.
5. Chapter 3, section *Below-the-Skin Diving,* pp. 102 ff.

Research, Resources, and Techniques

1. From the W. H. D. Rouse translation of Plato's *Republic* (Mentor, p. 222), notice the applicability of what Socrates says to the modern adolescent's predilection for rock-and-roll:

"For the methods of music cannot be stirred up without great upheavals of social custom and law; so says Damon, and I believe it. . . . The fort of safeguards . . . must be built . . . in music. . . ."

If, as Socrates says, poor music has abrasive effects on the minds of the young and even on society, would you outlaw rock-and-roll from discussion in your class?

2. Socrates says (p. 152) that it is impossible for anybody living in society to be altogether and completely evil: "Now when we say that the just are shown to be wiser and better and more able to act effectively, and the unjust to be incapable of accomplishing anything together, and when on the other hand we add that in fact those who do accomplish something with strong united action are yet sometimes unjust people— then we are not saying what is wholly true; for they could not have kept their hands off each other if they were absolutely unjust; it is clear that some justice was in them, which kept them from wronging each other as well as those they attacked, and by this justice they accomplished as much as they did. They set out on their unjust way only demidevils in wickedness, since whole villains, and men perfectly unjust, are perfectly unable to act effectively."

In what circumstances does the presence of others in the same classroom lead to accord? In what circumstances to discord? In what circumstances does the presence of others cause misbehavior? In what circumstances good behavior? How is the presence of classmates constricting? How is it expanding?

English and Self-Knowledge

The very nature of the English class invites excessive verbalization, and the temptation may be especially great if you have traveled, read, and moved through the world. The English teacher who knows all the answers should be particularly careful not to give them until the class is worked up to a proper pitch of interest and involvement. This means questioning, rather than telling. It means provoking a series of problem situations, or what Hollywood writers call "cliff-hangers"; the anguish formerly known by movie audiences when the heroine was left dangling on a precipice is the kind of anguish you should provoke in setting the stage for discussion and teaching. Like the script writer, you know how the predicament ends, but you aren't telling—not quite yet.

This technique requires silence. Do not rush in with answers. Be satisfied if no hands wave eagerly; if instead you observe fidgeting, lip-biting, and a fighting for ideas and words that elude expression. In learning how to keep your mouth shut you will learn improved observation of others and self. Don't use words as though you were a Russian fleeing wolves across the snowy steppes, throwing wife, infants, and a dear babushka to the slavering pursuers, to keep the oncoming vulpine horde off your neck. Excessive teacher verbalization similarly attempts to satiate the classroom wolves, but with words, unnecessary yammering, and the protective word-curtain between teacher and class. Better silence based on a simmering problem—a cliff-hanger—that leads to analysis, thought, and response. The chances are that the wolves are running to keep warm, nothing else.

We are only saying silence is golden and leads to improved observation. Improved observation, in turn, leads to understanding and sympathy—things the adolescent too often has been denied by the adult. Let adolescents come to your class knowing that you offer insight, that the absence of yammering in your class sets the stage for thought, that this restriction on excessive communication encourages self-communication, self-understanding, and the solution of inner problems.

Yet self-understanding comes hard. Socrates said, "Know thyself," but psychology shows that self-knowledge is the most difficult thing in the world to attain, far harder than the knowledge of nuclear physics. But this is your job. Why is self-knowledge for most of us, and despite our interest in it, *terra incognita*? If a man cannot, by taking thought, add a cubit to his stature, he cannot any more easily get at the roots of himself. Literature, poetry, and grammar help, and we shall later on discuss the contribution that these make to the adolescent's self-understanding. The self-expression that composition writing encourages leads to self-understanding. These, however, are interpersonal communications; intrapersonal communication is equally important. Here the adolescent communicates with nobody but himself.

CASE STUDY 1   The teacher of a third-year class in a senior high school said to the students, "This is a lesson in talking to yourself. The lesson has two sections. In the first section you will talk to yourself as you first remember yourself, from your earliest memory. In the second section you'll talk to yourself in the various stages you've grown through. In neither section do you recite to the class, but you do recite to yourself. Let's see how well you can recite to yourself. Here's section one:

"What is the earliest memory you have? The very first thing you remember? Recall it as fully as you can, and in as much detail as you can. Now ask yourself—

"1. How old am I at the time of this memory?

"2. What is the scene? Where does it occur?

"3. Who are the people involved? Who is there?

"4. What is the event? What is taking place?

"5. What is my emotional reaction to the event?

"6. Do I feel the same way, at my present age, about the people in the memory? Do I feel differently? If the event were to take place today, would I feel the same or differently?

"7. Can I say that I am any different today from me then, in my emotions and in what makes me happy and sad?"

In discussing section one, most students felt they would still react—not act—the same way today. They admitted they were emotively the same as they were at the age of three or so—the period most often remembered. *If the events in the memory were to take place today they would react—not act—in a similar manner.* They had, in emotive areas, changed little. Emotions had come and gone, states of mind had succeeded one another, pleasure had been supplanted by pain, pain by joy, joy by sorrow, and then back again to pleasure, but amid these emotional shifts and swings they had remained emotively the same, even though their very chemistry had changed. A residual emotive *me* had always remained. What was this residual self? Whatever their emotional development, the emotive residue had not altered, almost as if, in this area, they had no internal history, for the emotive residue seemed unaffected by any history they had lived through—or almost, as we shall soon see—but there still remained this persisting, hard, inner emotive core, or emotive style of life, affected so little.

The second section, on the contrary, showed that there had been changes and that aspects of life were in constant flux:

The teacher said to the class: "Multiply your present age by twelve." After the class had done so, the teacher said, "That number is your approximate age in months. Let's call it X. At half that number, or X/2, or half your present age, now recall:

"1. Where were you living at that time, when you were X/2 months?

"2. Who was your favorite movie star? Your favorite sports star?

"3. Who were your friends? What favorite game did you play with them?

"4. What did you prefer doing with spending money?

"5. Who was your teacher? What was your favorite subject?

"6. What was most fun? What was most punishment? What was your greatest ambition?

"7. Now do the same (from 1 to 6 above) for X/3, for 3X/4, and for 5X/8."

Here comparisons showed how the adolescent had changed—the values, friends, and interests he had abandoned. Students began to see that alongside the residue within them that had no history, unchanged since earliest memory, other areas had seen considerable change and development.

Student response to these two assignments is varied. Some see no sense in them, calling them a waste of time. Others are challenged, piqued, and excited either by the lack of change or by the excess of it. Many are embarrassed at being outcomes of circumstance rather than molders of it, passive rather than active in living their lives.

Your job does not include therapy, but you should understand the mechanisms unremittingly at work below the surface. Your job does not go beyond the surface aspects of behavior, but you deal more effectively with surfaces when you are aware of the subterranean forces. The surface is job enough and important enough, and it matters enough, especially in adolescence. Increased inner understanding is the heart and soul of the curriculum, of life, and of civilization today; without it, doom and catastrophe will overtake the human race and that particular class you are teaching and for which you are responsible. You are neither idiotic nor fanatic when you remember that language is related to science, religion, myth, and human happiness.

You need this toughness of conviction and sense of mission. This toughness is best achieved by understanding adolescents and teaching them how to understand themselves.

For further discussion and teaching materials in this area, see:

1. Case Study 3, p. 47.
2. Chapter 2, section on *Spelling, Symbolism, and the Sense Modalities,* pp. 77 ff.
3. Chapter 4, p. 121.
4. Chapter 3, p. 85.
5. Case Study 12, p. 246.

Research, Resources, and Techniques

1. John Dewey has said: "That a man may grow in efficiency as a burglar, as a gangster, or as a corrupt politician, cannot be doubted. But from the standpoint of growth as education and education as growth the question is whether growth in this direction promotes or retards growth in general. Does this form of growth create conditions for further growth, or does it set up conditions that shut off the person who has grown in this particular direction from the occasions, stimuli, and opportunities for continuing growth in new directions? What is the effect of growth in a special direction upon the attitudes and habits which alone open up avenues for development in other lines? I shall leave you to answer these questions, saying simply that when and *only* when development in a particular line conduces to continuing growth does it answer to the criterion of education as growing. For the conception is one that must find universal and not specialized application" (*Experience and Education* [Macmillan, 1956], p. 2).

Can intrapersonal communication, as described in this chapter, lead to introversion and withdrawal, and hence impede growth? How can inner understanding help in the growth process? What are the dangers in teaching for inner understanding?

Escaping the Imprisonment of Time and Space

Toughness, further, is incompatible with self-commiseration, particularly with the self-pity that deals with time and space and their ever-present weight.

Anyone in a teacher's room, or in a faculty dining room at the moment the bell strikes, will not hear, " 'Tis the knell that summons thee to heaven or to hell," but its equivalent, the repetition *ad nauseam* of the ritualized, choral sigh, "Back to the salt mines." The necessity of having to appear at a classroom promptly, when the bell tells you, and terminate a lesson because the bell says so, makes a sensitive teacher feel like an automaton. How give amplitude to a life marked off by a bell schedule, and liberation from clanging regularity?

But you are enslaved to space as well as time.

The classroom is an arena, partly in the Marquess of Queensberry sense, partly in the hospital delivery room or operating room sense, and even partly in the sense of a house of worship, where the business of education is transacted. Infrequently you can plan for an excursion or trip, and occasionally an assembly period or a library period will remove the class from the classroom, but most of your contact with the students will be under the same, unalterable conditions of lighting, room design, furniture, view, and general setting. Not only do you meet your class at the same time, but at the same place. You are enslaved to time and space, and your psychology becomes too often that of the prisoner.[27]

Yet there are forces and groups trying to break into this prison. Business, labor, the National Association of Manufacturers, the A.F.L.-C.I.O., the broadcasters, newspaper publishers, anybody with anything to sell, an idea, a product, a point of view, will furnish truckloads of free teaching materials in the form of films, comic books, brochures on guidance. Why should anybody want to break into a prison? A firm like General Electric will not consider it *infra dig* to supply educational comic books free to any high school class. Literally thousands of free teaching aids are available from all kinds of sources, trying to crash this prison.[28] Perhaps those on the outside do not construe the schoolroom as a prison, despite what students and teachers think?

Beyond all other teachers, you are able to liberate yourself and your classes from this oppression of time and space, specifically in your attitude toward the homework assignment. The homework assignment, believe it or not, is the greatest single means of overcoming the confinements of time and space, of giving breadth to the classroom. What is the homework assignment generally? What ought it be? Why has the homework assignment become an additional manacle fastening teacher and student to the deadening regularity of a bell schedule and the routinized recurrence of place?

The typical orientation to the assignment is that it is work assigned in school to be completed away from school. The orientation recommended here is in sharp contrast: *the assignment ought to be work originating out of school to be completed in school.* The differences are not verbal. They are basically dissimilar. Only the term *work* is common.

Next, homework assignments are inevitable if children are to get an education. A high school student cannot learn mathematics, languages, social studies, English, and science on school time alone. There is not time enough in the school day.[29] Hence there is no way out of homework. If, then, assignments ought to have their origin *outside* the classroom walls and be completed *within* the school walls, what can such assignments be? How are they best described?

We talked before about the Observant Eye and the Accessible Ear. Let's aim these ears and eyes at the adolescent, to learn what movies he sees, what songs he sings, what television or radio programs he watches, what obtains his attention and interest. With this information we develop our assignments, on nonschool experiences. These may be Elvis Presley hysteria, pigeon-raising, clothing fads, the height of the building in which the student lives, the most recent altercation in which he took part or which he witnessed, the variation in costs between related products in rival supermarket chains, plans for a forthcoming party, overcrowded playgrounds, a Sunday drive with the family, important factories nearby, or what happens when he salts his soup. The ear-to-the-ground or eye-on-target is amply codified in state syllabi, in *English Journal,* in the better methods textbooks,[30] and in curriculum sources like the Citizenship Education Project of Teachers College.[31] These cannot be used unthinkingly, because they lead to a new variant of rote learning unless modified. They can also be inordinately time consuming, unless you have a clear sense of direction.

Consider this execration:

> You ain't nothin' but a hound dog
> Cryin' all the time. . . .

Is this Elvis Presley aria what the ear-to-the-ground picks up? Yes, out of the throats of students singing it by the millions. Grammatically, it is equivalent to something you might encounter in a work book, "Mr. Jones is not the bank teller being promoted," and could be used as effectively to teach the noun, the copulative verb, and the predicate nominative if you want Presley aficionados who do not know a verb from a preposition to do some thinking about what goes on within them when they shout, scream, sing, or just plain ordinary talk.

Millions of high school adolescents do not know what a noun is. Take some popular song, like the instance above, and ask students to encircle the *names*—not nouns, because they wouldn't know what you're talking about. What is a name? Is *you* a name? *nothin'?* *hound dog?* *all?* *time?* What is the naming process? What is the nature of identity and what do we mean by the word *identity?* What are the ways of identification that we use when we name? Though we here talk about proper, common, and abstract nouns, we still call them *names.*

This is *not* too abstract for students. The author has tried it in dozens of classes, with high I. Q. groups and with vocational school groups. It not only works equally well with either, but is virtually self-motivating.

Go further and ask what are the names (not *nouns!* not yet!) doing (or being)? What is *you* doing (or being)? What is *hound dog* doing? What, therefore, is an action (or, after a judicious while, a verb)?

Grammar is thought-analysis as much as language-analysis. Let students bring in their flimsy lyrics from the outside. In class, teach them *themselves,* how they name, what an action is, and—most important of all—how they cannot even think without having names perform actions, or, in grammatical lingo, without relating subject and predicate. They think all the time, whether on the lazy levels of fantasy or the highest levels of creativity. Molière's Jourdain had been speaking prose without knowing it, and your students are thinking every second of the time. If they were to stop, they would become psychopaths. Thinking uses certain intellectual antibodies to fight off psychopathology, called nouns, verbs, prepositions, adjectives, and adverbs. We can teach formal grammar via the juke-box and we ought not be ashamed of it. We can improve the Kallikaks by the jukes.

In greater depth, you can discuss rock-and-roll lyrics, and the heavy hand there of sex, suffering, unrequited longing, and the way the rhythmic twitching, which may not knock their brains out of shape, can in overdose, put them on a clackety-clacking railroad track that means something inside them is screaming, and what can that be? You must never be patronizing about rock-and-roll; that would be dreadful. A bit of it isn't bad, isn't harmful, and can even be fun—hasn't it torn a rent in the Iron Curtain?

Vocational school excitement about gang warfare and street fights have motivated an intense reading of Santayana's essay on war. Low I. Q. girls worried about dates and how to snag a boy have converted these in-securities into an avid reading of a great expert in this area, Jane Austen in *Pride and Prejudice*. Was not the death of James Dean, the late actor, still mourned by adolescents, an appropriate introduction to *Lycidas* or *Thanatopsis*? Cicero's "Defense of Archias" on the anguish of the women of Rome at the actor Roscius' death reminds us of mass behavior at Dean's death and Valentino's. Let's not be snobs. Arthur Koestler, in a brilliant essay, says that snobbery is a clash of two value systems, one unrelated to the other; in conjunction, they breed snobbery. "Our appraisal of any work of literature or art is never a unitary act, but the result of two independent and simultaneous processes which tend to distort each other. . . . The social hostess with the musicality of a cow, who raves about Yehudi [Menuhin] and longs to have him for a cocktail party, is a snob, because she pretends to measure value by one quality whereas in fact she measures it by another." [32] Read Koestler's essay. Compare con-temporary rock-and-rollatry with the seizures of medieval teen-agers in historic tarantism, Aldous Huxley's discussion of spasm in *The Virgins of Loudon,* and Arthur Miller's *Crucible*—and then allow the adolescent to follow through on the comparison. The author has seen them shocked into maturity.

Students will learn effectively and you can teach with powerful impact, although surrounded by bell schedules and fixed room programs, when the assignment begins *outside the classroom.*

But students will fake and copy homework one from the other, will they not? Will there not be a loss in character development and in indi-vidual responsibility? "A student should do his own work," some teachers insist, but how much "his own" is it if the homework assignment is identical with the assignment everyone around him is getting? "His own" means that it is compounded out of *his own* experiences, otherwise it is a mass-production job. He feels no sense of personal involvement, no moral obliquity, and so fakes and copies. *His own* experiences lie outside the classroom and outside the bell schedule. The homework assignment must be integrated with his life beyond the school walls. This done, cheating is impossible. You'll have, instead, the superior backing up the inferior, the quick helping the slow, the educationally desirable goal of the brighter helping the duller. Group sharing in the responsibility for assignment completion in the school is a simple reflection of group and team life outside the school.

For further discussion and teaching materials in this area, see:

1. Chapter 2, p. 41.
2. Chapter 6, section on *The Tempest*, pp. 206 ff.

Research, Resources, and Techniques

1. In the Book of Job (2:13), we read the dynamic power of silence to get discussion going: "So they sat down with him upon the ground seven days and seven nights, and none spake a word unto him: for they saw that his grief was very great. After this opened Job his mouth. . . ."

2. Glenn E. Smith says, "It is axiomatic that the counselor be a good listener in the counseling situation. Likewise, he must be skilled in the use of the silence technique, knowing when listening is likely to be effective with the counselee. . . . Use of the listening technique is much more difficult than the uninitiated might imagine . . ." (*Counseling in the Secondary School* [Macmillan], p. 119).

3. Dr. Ralph R. Greenson says: "The silence of the analyst is another element which permits transference reactions to develop . . ." (*The American Handbook of Psychiatry* [Basic Books], II, 1409).

4. What is the relation of the above quotations to what has been said about the Observing Eye and the Accessible Ear? Does the following quotation from Edward Sapir make adolescent language patterns more acceptable to you? "The outstanding fact about any language is its formal completeness. This is as true of a primitive language, like Eskimo or Hottentot, as of the carefully recorded and standardized languages of our great cultures. . . . All of its expressions, from the most habitual to the merely potential, are fitted into a deft tracery of prepared forms from which there is no escape. These forms establish a definite relational feeling or attitude towards all possible contents of expression and, through them, towards all possible contents of experience, in so far, of course, as experience is capable of expression in linguistic terms. . . . A language is so constructed that no matter what any speaker of it may desire to communicate, no matter how original or bizarre his idea or his fancy, the language is prepared to do his work" ("The Nature of Language," in *Selected Writings of Edward Sapir* [University of California Press, 1949], p. 153). Would you interpret this as saying that the language of your students is as ordered and as orderly as your language? Is it possible to have order in language and still have disorderly language habits?

Homework and Individuality

Be mindful of the recent warnings against excesses in group- and team-mindedness[33] and the abandonment of individuality for conformity. The homework assignment can reinforce individual qualities and individual resources, as we here describe the desirable homework assignment.

We have thus far stressed the group- and team-mindedness of the adolescent. But every one of us, and every adolescent too, has frequent need to flee the world and the people around us and be with ourselves, retreat into ourselves, and taste some privacy. Most adolescents require this occasional privacy even if they do not realize it. The pleasures of privacy must be discussed with them, the privacy that in no way indicates disloyalty to the group or team. Privacy is valued but hard to come by or even unobtainable in a crowded home. Students can recall, without divulging personal particulars either to you or the class, when they needed to be alone, how it helped at the time, and what good things come out of occasional solitude.

Can your student gain this privacy? Yes, by using the magic words, "I have homework to do." People leave him alone when he utters these mysterious syllables. People hush other people, they try to leave a silence around him, they tiptoe away, and, even if he lives in a crowded home with a large, noisy family, something happens: he gets at least some degree of privacy, when he declares, "I have homework to do." Importunate friends who ask, "Can't you do it later?" don't object too much if he repeats the magic incantation. Parents who want an errand run will get another child to run it or will undertake it themselves. This temporary self-banishment into solitude furnishes strength and vigor for the next sally into the world. It offers a chance to rehearse without embarrassment, so that he is spared unnecessary mistakes and the humiliations the adolescent dreads, and he can try out the sensible, advisable things, whether it's a new dress or tie, a new dance step, a new laugh, that gesture of the arm to accompany the speech the dopey English teacher expects, or the sneer for the mathematics teacher when the student does a perfect job of proving the theorem.

There is danger here. Such rehearsal, to avoid becoming fantasy, requires techniques of judgment, forethought, predicting possible alternatives, and discrimination between the relevant and irrelevant. Doing homework will gain privacy, but the homework must have realism, applicability, and discussable outcomes. This is your responsibility, so to frame the assignment as to avoid busy-work and drill without goal. The assignment requires not less thought of you than of the student.

Finally, the assignment should have feedback qualities. You should react and interact with the student's output, assessing, approving, disapproving, and evaluating, giving reasons why every step of the way. The teacher who does so is in a powerful position in the hearts and minds of his class. When assignments are handled so, assignments are done. The student who fails to do an assignment is the exception who feels himself an isolate because everybody else has done his homework, including you.

Feedback takes time. If you cannot find time, do not object when classes don't do homework. If you find time, assignments will be done amid high excitement about what you will have to say. Nevertheless, time for feedback is scanty. Where is it to come from?

From other things, naturally. Just as you expect the student to take time from family, friends, fun, and the neighborhood ice-cream parlor to get his homework assignment done, levy the same expectation against yourself. Your job—insufficiently paid for—is to react conscientiously to the jobs the students turn in. If you have not the time to do so, do not issue assignments. If you ignore the homework you assign, or casually check off its being or not being done, the worst type of man's indifference to man emerges—the kind that takes place in a classroom, at the expense of the young and helpless.

Conversely, the assignment, if properly thought through by you and accompanied by proper feedback, can usher in the richest and most thrilling of all teaching experiences—the successful communication between man and man of feeling, thought, idea, and emotion.

For further discussion and teaching materials in this area, see:

1. Chapter 3, section on *Discipline, Task Therapy, and Classroom Writing,* pp. 115 ff.
2. Chapter 14, *Lesson Planning.*

Research, Resources, and Techniques

1. Read the quotation from Robert L. Heilbroner for a parallel to your energy investment in the homework assignment and the return on your energy investment in your personal life after school: "Hence in the final analysis, the economy hung on the amount of investment which business carried out. When investment was low, the economy shrank in size; when investment was high, it pulled the nation up with it; if invest-

ment failed to *remain* high, it permitted the cycle of contraction to begin. Riches and poverty, boom and slump, all depended on the willingness of business to invest" (*The Worldly Philosophers* [Simon and Schuster, 1953], p. 262). Will an investment in your classroom duties, in energy and enthusiasm, diminish your energy and enthusiasm in after-school activities, or increase them?

2. From a review by Charles Calitri: "Frustration comes when a child mutters, 'Teach me to read, will ya?' and there is no time for him because there are thirty others. . . . Anger comes too when certain fellow teachers, having let themselves become too involved with their work, and having been beaten by the surrounding walls they have tried desperately to confront and challenge, have become soured and cynical because that is the only protection they have against the acceptance of defeat" (*Saturday Review,* Feb. 13, 1960, p. 51). Does this, in contrast to the first quotation, mean that you ought to refrain from making an investment of energy and enthusiasm?

3. Compare two issues of *The New York Times,* nineteen years apart, describing two similar scenes of teen-age enthusiasm. The first, the issue of January 27, 1938, describes the behavior of high school adolescents at a Benny Goodman swing concert at the Paramount Theatre. Almost a generation later, the issues for February 23, 1957, and February 24, 1957, describe an Alan Freed rock-and-roll performance at the same theater.

Read these news stories to your class. Elicit comment on: (a) the reasons for recurrence of adolescent behavior patterns; (b) the needs in adolescents for such behavior patterns; (c) the needs in adulthood that cause the disappearance of these patterns. Compare with Case Study on p. 55.

4. Bernice Fitz-Gibbon, an advertising consultant, in an address, urged executives to advertise in *Seventeen* for these reasons: "You know you can't sell anybody anything unless he has the yen and the sen, the desire and the dollars, the longing and the lure, the compulsion and the cabbage. Because what profiteth you if people have the scratch but don't have the itch to own?

". . . Almost 9,000,000 teen-agers want things hard. And that can't-do-without urge, along with the $4 billion they have to splurge on the urge, makes them a store's gold mine.

"Sure, momma's got shekels, poppa's got shekels, all God's chilluns got shekels—but the chilluns, they got shekels to spend. Mommy-and-daddy money is no good to you. It's tight money. It's not all lovely and loose and jingly like teen-age money.

"It's tied up. It's all spent before poppa's paycheck comes home—on the mortgage and taxes and insurance premiums. . . .

"While father gets poorer, his teen-age daughter is living high on the hog; . . . her allowance has a sacred place on the ledger; . . . she is a big money earner. . . .

"Think of all that tender, young, rosy-leafed cabbage circulating around. . . . The teen age is the green age—green meaning young, budding, flowering, healthy, strong, alive. Green meaning money. . . .

"A girl in her teens is a woman. . . . There's nothing like that wonderful, heart-rending, world-shaking day when flat-chested Susie comes tearing into the home waving her first bra and shrieking, 'Look, Mom! No concavities.'

"Teen-agers are reachable. They are open minded, impressionable, easy to sell. . . . They are not sated. . . . They have not learned how to tune out, to edit out selling messages and sounds and impressions. . . . From 21 on, it's downhill all the way. . . .

"Follow the camp which has the desire as well as the dough, the oomph as well as the oof—cater to the teen-ager with the warm, glowing dream in her eye as well as the cold, hard cash in her hand" (quoted in *Advertising Age*, June 8, 1959, p. 3).

(a) How applicable to a classroom is Miss Fitz-Gibbon's advice? (b) Is this advice related to the chapter's discussion on teaching Santayana and Jane Austen and the integration of James Dean's death to the teaching of "Lycidas"? (c) Would the approach recommended to business executives tend to destroy the teacher's status or increase it? (d) What lessons can you prepare to protect teen-agers from becoming financial dupes of advertising campaigns?

5. As a beginning teacher, you will want to read—*critically!*—Grace Daly Maertens' article "Organizing the Class to Care for Individual Needs" (*English Journal,** Oct. 1958, p. 414). Decide for yourself: (a) How practicable and manageable are these ideas for the beginning teacher? (b) Do you have the experience to handle these suggestions? Or do the suggestions presuppose too much maturity and contact with classroom realities? (c) Which suggestions are in accord with statements in this chapter? Which are antithetic?

5. Read Arthur Koestler's "The Anatomy of Snobbery" (*Anchor Review*, No. 1, p. 1), for some soul laundering. After reading it, check yourself on whether your values in teaching are genuine or snobbish. Are your reasons for teaching grammar and poetry, for example, derivative from the opinions you have heard and read? They should be, in great part, but do they remain superficial or have you chewed these over to make them your own?

6. Before reading the list of texts, read David Riesman's "Thoughts on Teachers and Schools," available in the same paperback with Koestler, above, for the ideas of a well-known contemporary thinker on methods in teaching (*Anchor Review*, No. 1, p. 27).

* *English Journal* is referred to hereafter as *E. J.*

7. Here are some texts on principles in secondary education, history of secondary education, and curriculum in secondary education:

a. Nelson L. Bossing's *Principles of Secondary Education* (Prentice-Hall, 1955) is thorough and scholarly. It offers an excellent treatment of the history of secondary education and of secondary education abroad. A fine book.

b. Ralph K. Watkins' *Techniques of Secondary School Teaching* (Ronald Press, 1958) is especially good in its Chapter 9, "Appreciation Building." The book has some interesting ideas on classroom teaching.

c. Jean D. Grambs, William J. Iverson, Franklin K. Patterson, *Modern Methods in Secondary Education* (Dryden Press, 1956) has a practical, classroom-oriented approach to the questions and problems of the beginning teacher. Deals clearly with administrative and supervisory matters.

d. Somewhat less useful than the above citations are Herbert J. Klausmeier's *Teaching in the Secondary School* (Harper and Brothers, 1958) and Philip W. Perdew's *The American Secondary School in Action* (Allyn and Bacon, 1959), both of which are nonspecific.

8. Norma E. Cutts and Nicholas Moseley, *Teaching the Disorderly Pupil in Elementary and Secondary School* (Longmans, Green and Company, 1957), should be read in conjunction with Hymes. The title is indicative of the contents.

9. Jerome M. Seidman (ed.), *The Adolescent: A Book of Readings* (Dryden Press, 1953), like other books in this area, has chapters on adolescent psychology and sociology, in relation to reading (p. 167), television (p. 230), and school (p. 570).

CHAPTER 2

The Mechanics of English

In the Beginning Was the Name

Why teach grammar? The answer is easy: to show how we think. We have mentioned how even Elvis Presley can illustrate the language, grammar, and thought of the naming process.

The naming process differentiates men from beasts. Cassirer says: "The Babylonian-Assyrian myth of creation describes Chaos as the condition of the world when the heavens above were 'unnamed' and on earth no name was known for any thing. In Egypt, too, the time before creation is called the time when no god existed and no name for any object was known." [1] Creation was accompanied by naming. Science these days rejects the literal Biblical version of geological or cosmic creation, but, as a description of the creation of individual consciousness, how perfect, apt, and accurate! In Genesis, order emerges from Chaos as in psychologists like Piaget[2] consciousness grows in the newborn child, who, as he looks about with his original vision, has no conception of light and dark, of wetness and dryness, of chairness, cribness, wallness, windowness, floorness. There are no boundaries between things because he does not know where *wall* ends and *floor* or *ceiling* begins. Things are without form and void. Soon enough forms and entities emerge, identification is established,

41

and the groundwork is laid for the naming process. McCarthy says that the first words are names, used as sentences.[3] If language begins with the name, the study of grammar should begin there too. We cannot talk without names. We cannot talk without grammar. Even illiterates speak grammatically, because we cannot think without using sentences—a name doing something. Language in the illiterate is as ordered as in the linguistic purist, even if not socially accepted. All else is the language of schizophrenia.

What constitutes a name? Put the following sentences on the blackboard, or distribute mimeographed copies to your class, and have students underline the names:

1. John is walking.
2. John enjoys walking.
3. Walking is fine exercise.
4. John is exercising.
5. Exercising is good for you.
6. You are an honest boy.
7. Honesty is the best policy.
8. The best is what she deserves.
9. The group will meet tomorrow.
10. We will group the class according to size.
11. John will size up the situation when he arrives.

Ask the class: Why is *walking* a name in sentences 2 and 3 but not in sentence 1? *Exercising* a name in sentence 5 but not in 4? *Best* in 8 but not in 7? *Group* in 9 but not in 10? *Size* in 10 but not in 11? How have our thoughts been formulated so that the same word is now a name and now not? What has gone on in our minds? How have we grouped ideas, traits, and characteristics to identify them?

I have walked around a classroom, gestured to a student, and asked, "What's your name?"

A look of puzzlement, a shrug, and then the watchful answer: "Danny Brown." I have then pointed to another student and asked the same question. This time a look of apprehension, a frown, and then the answer: "Steve Ritter." I have asked a third student, a fourth student, a fifth student, and then, when they have been ready to explode with objections because I knew their names, I have pointed to the object before which I sit. "What's the name of this?" "A desk." Then to the transparent object at the side of the room. "A window." Then to the opaque object at the front of the room. "The blackboard." And the white cylinder in my hand. "Chalk." I have written with the white object on the opaque one:

> "Sweet Adeline! My Adeline!
> At night, dear heart, for you I pine.
> In all my dreams, your fair face beams.
> You are the darling of my heart, Sweet Adeline!"

and have then asked students to identify the names.

Or I have written:

> "O little town of Bethlehem, how still we see thee lie
> Above thy deep and dreamless sleep, the silent stars go by.
> Yet in thy dark streets shineth
> The everlasting light.
> The hopes and fears of all the years
> Are met in thee tonight."

And:

> "I come from Alabama, with my banjo on my knee. I'm going to Louisiana, my Susanna for to see. Oh, Susanna! Oh, don't you cry for me! For I come from Alabama with my banjo on my knee."

And, from the Ten Top Tunes:

> "The movie wasn't so hot.
> It didn't have much of a plot.
> We fell asleep.
> Our goose is cooked.
> Our reputation is shot."

Or suitable selections from that day's newspapers and sports sections, cut on a stencil, mimeographed, and distributed, with your instructions:

> 1. In the passages below, circle all the names. Are they the names of people? Of places? Of things?
> 2. Why are some names in capitals? How are they different from the other names?
> 3. In *Bethlehem,* is "thee" a name? Is "thy" a name? Why is one a name and the other not? What of "hopes" and "fears"?

Try it on your classes, but be sure *you* know grammar.

The student cannot sing, think, talk, listen, or live, except as he knows what a name is. The differentiation comes later: into names that are proper, common, and abstract; male, female, and neuter; pronoun, pronominal adjective, and the rest. From all kinds and varieties of examples, from the sacred and the profane, give your students drill in raising the naming process from the automatic to the conceptual. Difficulties in identifying names will not occur with people or places, but with the abstract, as in:

The *hopes* and *fears* of *all* the *years, or*
Our *reputation* is shot, *or*
Exercising is good for *you, or*
Walking is fine *exercise, or*
To err is *human.*

Remediation of grammatical ignorance begins with fundamentals and the naming process is the elemental fundament, where your student sees that things weightless, unfelt, unseen, and unheard can be grouped and identified into entities, hence named. Why does he have a name, whether *Danny Brown* or *Steve Ritter?* Because he has characteristics, because he is describable, because he constitutes an assemblage of traits, attitudes, and dimensions. This is true of *Susanna* and *banjo* in the song, of *reputation,* of *hopes* and *fears,* of *walking, exercising, honesty,* and *to err.*

How have we come to have various names for *automobile?* We have *Ford, Buick, Chevrolet, Cadillac, Chrysler,* and so on. Eskimos have as many names for *snow.* If we have a need to discriminate among brands of automobiles, so have Eskimos the need to differentiate among the kinds of snow and ice; life and survival depend on it. What of our culture is revealed by the numerous subnames for *automobile?* What of Eskimo culture by the numerous subnames for *snow?*

Your examples of the naming process draw on areas of discourse important to the adolescent, like the songs he knows and things he thinks about privately, but can also draw on newspapers, formal literature, poetry, essays, and fiction. But there is no hurry about calling a name a noun. The usual nomenclature can be introduced afterward, after the notion of action, to which we now turn.

Research, Resources, and Techniques

1. Perhaps you need the support that these articles give to jazz in the classroom:

a. Frederick S. Kiley's "Served on a Black Platter" (*E. J.,* Nov. 1956, p. 483) tells how the author used popular songs to teach poetry. Indeed, relating popular song to poetry is not particularly new.

b. In *E. J.* for Nov. 1958, p. 467, Hugh L. Smith, Jr., in "Jazz in the American Novel," shows how writers have dealt respectfully and sympathetically with the jazz phenomenon—and why teachers should too.

c. In *The New York Times Magazine*, Jan. 12, 1958, p. 16, Gertrude Samuels in "Why They Rock 'n' Roll" offers reasons for the popularity of this most recent jazz manifestation among adolescents.

d. Also in *The New York Times Magazine*, Dec. 8, 1957, p. 24, John S. Wilson's "What Makes 'Pop' Music Popular" shows why the teen-ager is not altogether idiotic in his liking for hit tunes.

2. René A. Spitz's *No and Yes* (International Universities Press, 1957) presents an interesting discussion, from the psychoanalytic viewpoint, on the genesis of human communication and the reasons why negatives come more easily to us than positive, constructive attitudes. "No" precedes "Yes" in human development, and the author tells us the consequences.

3. For a good discussion of how psychological investigation approaches verbal behavior, speech, symbolism, meaning, and syntactic organization, see Charles E. Osgood's *Method and Theory in Experimental Psychology* (Oxford University Press, 1953). A specific discussion on these areas will be found in Chapter 16, "Language Behavior," pp. 680-727.

4. Similar material is covered by George A. Miller in his article "Information and Memory," *Scientific American* (Aug. 1956, p. 42). This article should persuade you that *everybody's* language is highly organized —even the illiterate's. The article deals with memory and thinking and the way language, grammar, and sentence structure aid them.

5. Here are three classics on which much of the discussion so far is based:

a. A pioneer work is *The Meaning of Meaning*, by C. K. Ogden and I. A. Richards (Harcourt, Brace, 1953). See especially Appendix A, "On Grammar," p. 251.

b. From Otto Jespersen's *Growth and Structure of the English Language* (Doubleday Anchor, 1955) you will learn that function should precede glib nomenclature and easy definitions of what a noun, verb, or sentence is.

c. Benjamin Lee Whorf's *Language, Thought, and Reality* is published jointly by the Technology Press of Massachusetts Institute of Technology and by John Wiley (1956). Read especially the chapter "Languages and Logic" in which this important sentence appears (p. 242): "With a suitable grammar we may have intelligent sentences that cannot be broken into subjects and predicates. Any attempted breakup is a breakup of some English translation or paraphrase of the sentence." Do you agree?

6. To adapt the semantic approach to language study to your classroom, read Cleveland A. Thomas' *Semantic Concepts for Secondary School English* (*E. J.*, March 1960, p. 186).

What Is an Action?

CASE STUDY 2   *Scene:* a classroom. The teacher stares congenially at a student; the student fidgets uncomfortably; the class wonders what is going on between the two of them, or what the teacher has caught the student doing. But the teacher looks pleasant enough and even asks pleasantly enough, "John, what are you doing?"

"Nothing. I wasn't doing anything," Johnny expostulates.

"You sit there and say you do nothing?" the teacher demands.

Righteous outrage rises in Johnny. For once he knows he is innocent; thrice armed because his cause is just, and with the strength of ten because his heart is pure (at the moment), he glares at the teacher and says bitingly, "That's all I was doing."

Teacher's mobile eyebrows shoot triumphantly ceilingwards as he pounces. " 'That's all,' he says! You sit there and claim you are doing nothing! Were you doing nothing or weren't you? Come clean!"

A grin breaks over Johnny's face at the way he was caught and trapped, even if it was corny. "Sorry. I mean I *was* doing something. I was sitting. Is that what you mean?"

The teacher nods quickly. He is off on a new chase, tracking a new quarry. He asks the class, "When a man sits still, is he doing anything? Of course he is. His heart beats, his lungs breathe, his blood pulsates, his nerves are alert. He is hearing, seeing, and touching. He is sitting, but is he acting and doing and being? Yes. In thousands of different ways. Is sitting an action? Yes. Is thinking an action? Yes. Is running? Yes. Is sleeping? Yes. Is running the same as sleeping? No, but they're both actions. What, then, is an action?"

Action is inevitable. Action is inescapable. If we sit, or sleep, or think, or run, we are immersed in rhematic action. We cannot even conceive of an actionless state. Invite—nay, defy—your class to think of one; just as we cannot think of a name—and what that is has just been discussed— except in terms of its acting or receiving an action, a thought requires that a name be acting, doing, or being.

For example, ask your class to think of infinite space. The word "infinite" may be difficult. Let them close their eyes and imagine the outermost ends of space. How large is the universe? Very, very, very large. Think of its limits. Now think of its going beyond those limits. There's always a further extent to which you can reach in your mind. Is this additional bound occupied by matter? No, it is empty. But is it? Is it not occupied by your mind? Hence, though the universe may be truly limited—and mathematicians say it is—it is expansible by our minds. Our minds rush in to fill the vacuum that nature abhors. We can neither conceive of nor tolerate airy nothings but must endow them with a local habitation and a name. In this exercise the student thinks of space beyond space beyond space, presumably empty, but it is not. Why? Because his mind and thoughts are there. How empty can it be when you are there? Just by being there you have enlarged the universe. Hence, being is a kind of action too.

We can now say that an action, in the grammatical sense, is what a name does, or what is done to a name, or what a name does to another name, or what a name is, or what a name is being. But something additional is needed for proper conceptualization: the relationships of names and actions.

CASE STUDY 3   The teacher asked a student, "What is your name?"

Knowing by this time that the teacher had something in mind, the student responded, "Andy Miller."

The teacher paused, stumped, but dissimulating. He expected a complete sentence, "My name is Andy Miller," from which he could have proceeded to the point he intended making, but the student, characteristically, didn't come through the way the teacher planned. But this teacher, experienced and flexible, continued, "And how old are you?"

"Sixteen," the student answered. Again a partial answer, still not a complete sentence, but the teacher persevered. "What color are your eyes?"

"Brown."

The teacher sighed and tried another tack. He said, as he went to the blackboard, "This is what I understood you to say." He wrote:

(My name is) Andy Miller.
(I am) sixteen.
(My eyes are) brown.

He looked inquiringly at the student. The student nodded. "This is what you were actually saying," the teacher pointed out as he erased the parentheses, leaving:

> My name is Andy Miller.
> I am sixteen.
> My eyes are brown.

Now the teacher was at the point he wished originally to be. He proceeded, writing on the board:

> My name is sixteen.
> My eyes are Andy Miller.

and turned to the class, asking, "What's wrong?" of one of the other students.

The student laughed. "It doesn't sound right."

"Why not?"

"They don't go together."

Now the teacher struck. "In other words, names must go with actions. They must match!"

The match of action with name (of subject and verb) has greater force if impromptu, if the teacher from that day's newspaper selects sentences, designates the subject, and has the class find the matching verb, or uses a current magazine, or some material the class is reading. Agreement in person and number is concurrently illustrated as is the inescapable and infinite complexity with which actions accompany names. Examples of mood, tense, verbals, verbids, infinitives can be selected from newspapers, magazines, current juke-box favorites, and partially from work books and grammar texts to show the plasticity of verb and subject and verb and object combinations.

Thus, present a series of sentences to your class, like the one below, with instructions: "Underline all the names. If the name is doing or being something, lead an arrow from the name to the word it is doing or being. If the name is not doing or being anything, encircle it."

Notice that the examples contrast active and passive voice, transitive and intransitive forms, tense, and mood with the same verbs, showing their versatility and the patterns of action. Notice also that these examples require that *you* recognize the issues involved in these contrasting sentences, why, for example, in 1 a and 1 b, and 2 a and 2 b below, the subjects are not the same. Will you be able to explain to your class? How can they put the nominative in the objective without a prepositional phrase? How can they put the object of a prepositional phrase into the nominative? How do active-passive comparisons tell us the same thing now from John's point of view (1 a), now from the horse's (1 b), now from the coach's (2 a), now from the sprinters' (2 b)?

1 a. John hobbled the horse.
 b. The horse was hobbled by John.
 c. The halfback hobbled to the bench.
2 a. The coach will time the sprinters.
 b. The sprinters will be timed by the coach.
 c. Officer, time that speeder!
3 a. He ran for the train.
 b. He was run down by the train.
 c. He has been running for office.
4 a. Joan flew to her defense.
 b. The airplane was flown in safely by the copilot.
 c. The pilot flew the jet skillfully.
5 a. I prepare to leave.
 b. I am preparing to leave.
 c. I am being prepared to leave.
 d. I prepare myself to leave.
6 a. I feel ill.
 b. I feel the merchandise.
 c. I am ill.
 d. I am Joe Jones.

Research, Resources, and Techniques

1. Here are four articles dealing with language and usage. Do you know that scientists are interested in these matters? Note that they all appeared in *Scientific American*.

a. Hans Kurath's "The American Languages" appeared in *Scientific American* on Jan. 1950, p. 48. A perspective-broadening piece.

b. Perhaps the relationship between verbs and mathematics is not so remote. To prove that being is a kind of action and that copulative verbs are in part actions, read Hans Hahn's "Is There an Infinity?" in *Scientific American* for Nov. 1952, p. 76.

c. An article on the English your students will be speaking after *you* are dead and gone, and one which should make you more humbly respectful of neologisms and slang, is Jotham Johnson's "The Chang-

ing American Language," in *Scientific American*, Aug. 1955, p. 78.
d. An amusing satire on Basic English, and on some parochial concepts of usage too, is H. B. G. Casimir's "Broken English," in *Scientific American* for March 1956, p. 96.
2. These materials are further explored in two inexpensive paperbacks:
a. Charlton Laird's *The Miracle of Language* (Premier Books, 1957) is an excellent background on grammar. Chatty, informative, and well presented, it covers an amazing variety of ground that you can use in the classroom.
b. More remote from classroom considerations, but very scholarly and giving an excellent integration of how mathematics has answered some problems in language is Joshua Whatmough's *Language: A Modern Synthesis* (Mentor, 1957).

The Preposition

In my early days as a teacher, I had trouble teaching the prepositional phrase, but luckily a popular song of those days, which reached the blessed estate of the Ten Top Tunes and hence was known by my classes, began:

> I went *to Havana*
> *On one of those cruises*
> *For forty-nine-fifty*
> To spend a few days.

Thereafter, whenever appropriate, I used the Hits of the Week as a teaching resource in grammar. Though popular songs are short-lived, adolescent interest in them is continuous. I am not ashamed of this. If the function of a prepositional phrase is to attach a name to some part of a sentence, and if a popular song can illuminate this in a context additional to

> Quinquereme *of Ninevah from distant Ophir*
> Rowing home *to haven in sunny Palestine*
> *With a cargo of ivory,*
> And apes and peacocks

then the very amplitude of illustration serves the teacher's purpose.

(Somewhere hereabouts nomenclature is justifiably introduced, so that students see that language knowledge is codified. Nomenclature is evidence of data on the patterns of language and thought. At this time, also, work books and grammar texts are proper, despite current disparagement of them, because they regularize the *ad lib,* impromptu tone and offer the ordered analysis that should characterize language study.)

In responding to

> The patients are trained *in skills in use at the hospital, from typing and carpentry to electrical maintenance,*

students will sometimes designate the prepositions (*in, at, from, to*) as action words. Such confusion arises from:

> To arms!　　On guard!　　At ease!
> On your toes!　　To the lifeboats!

What causes confusion? In the above errors—as in most errors—the student's feeling that the prepositions are action words and hence verbs is partially true, for we are saying:

> (Run) to arms!
> (Be) at ease!
> (Go) to the lifeboats!
> (Be, Stand) on guard!
> (Be) on your toes!

Prepositions especially invite this confusion. Fifty years ago, Krapp[4] illuminated this confusion with *I will look into it* and *He ran up a bill,* in which *it* and *bill* are direct objects, not prepositional objects, and we can say further:

> I *am going with* (accompanying) you.

in which *you* is the direct object of the compound verb *am going with,* in the sense of *accompanying,* rather than of the preposition *with.* We see this absorption by verb of preposition when we say:

> Don't stand on ceremony.

Are we here using *on ceremony* as a prepositional phrase, or *don't stand on* as the verb with *ceremony* as the direct object (or even as an adverb!), or do we intend a single predication in the imperative mood? The teacher will find that intentions vary in a given class and that more than one answer can be defended. If, in

> The general puts on his uniform

puts on (dons) is the verb and *his uniform* the direct object, then in

> The general puts on his uniform a campaign ribbon from the Korean campaign

puts alone is the verb and the student will see how action must be differentiated from connectedness. If we wish to add to confusion, consider, from Gilbert and Sullivan's *Patience,*

> When I first put this uniform on

in which *on* becomes an adverb and is no longer a preposition, or else it is possibly still a preposition but introduces the phrase *on* (*me*), or the two alternatives already discussed.

In brief, the teacher should understand how the student sees the construction; then get him to see that it is one of several possible alternatives and when these alternatives are or are not defensible.

In

> Keep off!
> Keep off the grass!

there is no single right answer. *Off* may be an adverb, a preposition, or part of the verb, depending on how we see it. But we must know what we see and how others see it.

Prepositions disguised as adverbs are the motif for fun and confusion in Noel Perrin's *New Yorker* piece "Wake Me Up for the Hoedown" (Nov. 28, 1959, p. 46). Thus:

1. a. He ran down the path.
   b. He ran down her reputation.
   c. He ran down the guest list.
   d. He ran the guest list down.
   e. He put down the rebellion.
   f. He put the rebellion down.
   g. I must go down to the seas again.
2. a. The Babe swung at a fast ball.
   b. The Babe swung like a rusty gate.
3. a. While there, I ran across Jones.
   b. He ran across the road.

Studying the preposition is not merely a memorization of *on, around, above, below,* and so on; it also requires analysis of a word that sometimes works closely with a verb, sometimes with a noun, and sometimes independently goes into business for itself.

To test yourself, how would you teach:

1. He came to.
2. He came to the drawbridge.
3. The bridge was drawn to.
4. He finally got across.

5. He finally got across the point.
6. He finally got the point across.

With this further evidence of the subjective, inner aspects of grammar, we now turn to descriptive processes.

The Modifiers

If an adolescent says, "I don't feel good," using an adjective for an adverb, we call the doctor despite the grammar. We modify names one way and actions in another, but communication does not break down if we fail to do so. In some groups of our pluralistic society, it hurts to use adjective and adverbial modifiers interchangeably, while in others you are suspected if you don't. *To do good* is not the same as *to do well,* and *spinach is healthful* not the equivalent of *spinach is healthy.* Fineness in discrimination is only one reason for not confusing adjective and adverb. We can say *the boy struck powerfully at the ball* or *with a powerful swing the boy struck at the ball* and we are not talking about the same thing in *the powerful boy swung at the ball.* Similarly *the girl walks beautifully* and *the girl has a beautiful walk* are not quite interchangeable. We can wreck a reputation by *Jane is fast* but not by *Jane is quick.* We can say *make the transition gradual,* modifying the noun, or *make the transition gradually,* modifying the verb, and be right in either case, depending on what was intended.

Grammar has complexities and nuances not easily seen by students unless you furnish comparisons and contrasts. Using *John likes her* as a springboard, have your class match

    John likes her family
    John likes her appearance
    John likes her dancing
    John likes her convertible

where *family, appearance, dancing,* and *convertible* are direct objects, with

    John likes her very much

where *very much* is an adverbial, and

    John likes her friendly

where *friendly* is adjectival (despite the *-ly* ending!), with

    John likes her friendliness

where we again have a direct object.

Not all students will see what is going on; then you must back away, offer more comparisons, and let instances incubate. But if students shake their heads in incomprehension, you cannot merely urge them to think patiently about the differences between names and actions until illumination comes; you must offer the opportunities for understanding that drill provides.

Here is a drill suggestion:

Turn your newspaper over to a boy who will copy on the blackboard a sentence from the sports page previously selected by you; have a girl copy a sentence from the women's page, or the fashion section. Analyze and diagram the sentences with the class. Put your paper away and go on with the lesson you have planned. Make it seem spontaneous, but include this diversion every day for a few minutes at the outset of each period, and, sooner than you surmise, students will come into their grammatical birthright.

The ability to differentiate between an action and a name is part of the student's bloodstream. In communication the student does differentiate, else his speech would be gibberish. If so, he must—on one level at least—understand the difference. What in him resists further understanding and analysis of the difference, and what makes him uncomfortable about pushing the inquiry too far?

Research, Resources, and Techniques

1. Nothing will better illustrate how prepositions and adverbs are often interchangeable than the Noel Perrin piece in *New Yorker*, cited above, for Nov. 28, 1959, p. 46, called "Wake Me Up for the Hoedown." It's fun to read.

2. Read *Psychology in English*, by Margaret M. Bryant and Janet Rankin Aiken (Columbia University Press, 1940), pp. 72-75, for a discussion on the preposition. Compare the illustrations (p. 76):

> Happily he did not die.
> He did not die happily.

What is being modified in each sentence?

Grammar, Ego, and Self

The student is not sliding away from grammatical information, but rather from information about himself. For a long time now, psychologists and psychiatrists have experimented with free-association techniques.[5] In describing its Freudian form, Ernest Jones says, "Freud was deeply imbued with the principles of causality and determinism, so pronounced in the Helmholtz school that had dominated his earlier scientific discipline. Instead of dismissing the wandering associations as accidental, unconnected, and meaningless, as others might have done, he felt intuitively that there must be some definite agency, even if not evident, guiding and determining the course of these thoughts." [6]

Galton, an even earlier pioneer with free association, describes his own discomfort: "It would be very instructive to print the actual records at length, made by many experimenters . . . but it would be too absurd to print one's own singly. They lay bare the foundations of a man's thought with a curious distinctness, and exhibit his mental anatomy with more vividness and truth than he would probably care to publish to the world." [7]

Afterward, Kent and Rosanoff, Jung, Cofer and Foley, Balken and Masserman, and Boder[8] accumulated evidence from free association and related techniques that words are dynamite. Osgood, Suci, and Tannenbaum,[9] in more controlled word-association techniques, took a deep, deep plunge into subconscious processes.

CASE STUDY 4   A teacher, after reading how word-association techniques reveal personality, wrote on the board

Good work improves reputation

and told students to draw four columns in their notebooks with *good, work, improves,* and *reputation* at the head of the four columns. Optimistically, he then asked students to look at the four words and write immediately and spontaneously all that occurred to them.

One student, reflecting the attitudes of several others, asked, "What's the idea?"

"Try it," the teacher urged.

They did try, but one after another laid down pencils, looked about with boredom, and after five minutes the teacher saw that even those who were trying were having difficulty. The class wasn't balking. It just wasn't finding the task easy.

In discussion, the teacher asked, "What went wrong?"

"Couldn't think of anything," the answer came.

The teacher accepted the disclaimer and then said, "Look at the last word you have written. Look at it hard. What does it remind you of? Is there a connection with something very personal? Or is there no connection whatever? Is that why you found it hard to go on?"

There were some nods, some grins, and hands went up. The teacher shook his head. "Keep it to yourself. It's your secret." Since associations become increasingly personal, the teacher did not collect the papers. The teacher instead placed this problem before the class and, like Pontius Pilate, neither waited for nor fished for answers: "Why did you stop at that particular word? Why couldn't you go beyond it? Why couldn't you think of anything else at that point?"

The following day the teacher was implored, "Let's play that game again!"

The teacher did not probe. The point of the above exercise was that words apparently flat and abstract led to subterranean levels where emotion is rampant. The teacher wished to show how the reluctance to understand the grammar of names, actions, and their modifiers is also an avoidance of self-understanding.

Hence, when you face a student of average intelligence who in actual speech differentiates names and actions but cannot tell a noun from a verb, put the responsibility where it truly belongs—not on an inability to differentiate but on a reluctance to push toward inner understanding. You should not intrude or probe or go further than the surmise that grammar can teach the student something about himself. If students avoid such self-understanding by an indifference to grammar, respect this reluctance. However, know that discomfort about too much self-understanding, rather than grammar, is involved.

You are being paid to teach grammar. If you teach grammar—not grammatical classifications—successfully, you will inevitably teach students the beginning ways of self-understanding.

The Sentence Diagram and Inner Microscopy

Which comes first, diagraming or sentence sense? You cannot diagram without prior sentence sense; all the diagraming in the world will not give sentence sense. However, nothing visualizes sentence sense like diagraming.

The diagram structures the orthodox. Where unorthodoxy sneaks in, diagraming breaks down. In

> Go to your teacher for advice you can trust
> Go to your teacher, somebody you can trust, for advice
>
> Your electrical appliances get all the current they need
> Your electrical appliances need all the current they get
>
> I get all the money I need
> I need all the money I get

placement and sequence alter significance. The diagram helps visualize relationships already recognized and is to that extent useful, but it is an outcome of understanding, not a precursor to it. Nonetheless it is a useful tool. In

> A wonderful vacation has been planned for you if you want to take advantage of it

the adverbial *if you want to take advantage of it* includes the verbal *to take* with its object *advantage,* followed by the adjective modifier, the prepositional phrase *of it*—unless you interpret *to take advantage* as an infinitive, in which case *of it* becomes adverbial. Diagram it both ways for your class to help them visualize the complexities of interrelationships and the involvements of action and name.

By all means, diagram—it visualizes, it clarifies, but it works best with the student who has already seen grammatical light.

Research, Resources, and Techniques

1. Dora V. Smith, in "Teaching Language as Communication" (*E. J.,* March 1960, p. 167), feels that "research" proves that diagraming is futile in the improvement of writing—contrary to the viewpoint expressed here.

2. G. H. Vallins, in *The Pattern of English* (Pelican, 1957), considers developments in the construction of the English prose sentence. The appendix has an especially interesting discussion on "People who live in glass houses shouldn't throw stones" versus "People, who live in glass houses, shouldn't throw stones." Are they diagramed the same way? Hence, what is the logic of sentence sense that must precede diagraming? How, thereafter, can diagraming be used to greatest advantage?

Grammar and Primitive Man

Ask a class why we say *John is swift* and *John runs swiftly* and students will demand, "What's the difference?"

Their inability to differentiate between name-modifier and action-modifier develops from a primitively seen universe in which names alone are the vehicles of prehuman, or humanoid, thought. Anthropology testifies amply to this primitivism in which a name reifies actions, behavior, and mysterious forces.[10] Hence, *John is swift,* where a quality is given to a name, is on a more primitive level than *John runs swiftly,* where an action is described. Adverbial modifiers are generally more subtle and complicated than adjective modifiers.[11] A more challenging and difficult formulation is called for in

> No matter how I try to forget her, I still love the girl with the three blue eyes

than in

> I still love the girl with the three blue eyes, whom I have tried to forget[12]

and in

> When I am old enough, I shall shave

than in

> Anybody shaves who is old enough.

For further consideration and comparison, here are alternative adverbial and adjective modifiers:

1. The girls *eagerly* offered to bake the cake.
   The *eager* girls offered to bake the cake.
2. The lady with the large hat stood *in front*.
   Will the lady *in front* remove her hat?
3. John is reluctant *to wash* his neck.
   The time *to wash* your neck is now.
4. He walks *five miles* every day.
   He enjoys his *five mile* walk.
5. I did it *as I was told to do*.
   I did the job *that I was told to do*.

In presenting these and similar pairs to the student, peel away layer after layer of opacity in the student until the cry "What's the difference?" is not heard in the land. The student must recognize what word or idea is being modified, described, or qualified and abandon the primitivism that equates naming, action, and description. In the five paired specimens above, he will generally find it easier to identify the name-adjective than the action-adverb or modifier-adverb combination. Originally his first breakthrough came when as a child he learned the names for things and what thingness was. The second breakthrough comes with the sense of relationships. A verb is one such statement of relationship. Description, modification, and qualification are others. (Form-equivalence, in nuclear physics, is another kind.) An adverbial relationship is more difficult to grasp because it depends on more intermediate contingencies than does an adjective relationship; it depends on a prior presence of a verb or modifier, which depends in turn on the prior presence of a name, whereas an adjective modifier depends only on the prior presence of a name.

Space limitations here forbid further examination of this topic. Work books, if properly used in conjunction with other aspects of student language, like newspapers, magazines, and popular songs, are not to be disparaged. They are a helpful supplementary resource.

Research, Resources, and Techniques

1. A whetstone of an article that should sharpen up your eye for certain errors in the use of nouns and their modifiers is Norman C. Stageberg's "Some Structural Ambiguities" (*E. J.*, Nov. 1958, p. 479). Use the excellent examples to differentiate names, actions, and the ways we describe each. Excellent.

2. Here are two articles that deal with the same area.

a. Robert D. Williams' "Linguistics and Grammar" (*E. J.*, Oct. 1959, p. 388) presents a general discussion, with a few illustrative sentences for you to borrow—they'll be helpful in the classroom as examples.

b. Also use Sumner Ives' "Linguistics in the Classroom" (*College English*, Dec. 1955, p. 170).

Sentence Structure

We turn now to the sentence, the sentence fragment, and the clause. We have already said that a sentence is a name plus an action. We have said that being is a kind of action, so that a sentence is also a name plus a verb of being.

Write on the blackboard:

> Where the blue of the night meets the gold of the day, someone waits for me.

The class, instructed to underline the names in the sentence, does so with *blue, night, gold, day, someone,* and *me*. It agrees that the verbs are *meets* and *waits,* giving six names and two verbs. What names go with the verbs? After discussion, it is seen that *the blue meets* is one sentence and *someone waits* is the other. But now comes the question of subordination, dependence, and independence. Many students will say that the introductory adverbial clause is the important sentence, giving a variety of reasons: it is longer; it has more names; it comes first; it sounds more important. All true, except for that single word *where,* which is like the hook at the end of a fireman's ladder. It needs a wall, a ledge, a window sill, something to support and maintain it.

We can set other puzzlers for them. Which are the grappling hooks here, and which the supporting walls? In other words, which are the dependent clauses here and which the independent ones?

> While the richly dressed ambassadors, the handsomely decorated officers, and the beautifully gowned women chatted, a mouse ran across the floor.
>
> As he gasped his last breath, and as the nurses rushed about, the doctors worked feverishly, and the crowd outside waited in tense anticipation, a leaf fell from a tree in the courtyard.
>
> If he did, he'd lose.

What happens when we remove the hook from the end of the ladder? Grappling hooks are moved and removed in

> While John breathlessly rushed aboard, the whistle sounded.
> John breathlessly rushed aboard. The whistle sounded.
> While the whistle sounded, John breathlessly rushed aboard.

Subordination can be altered where we have simultaneity of occurrence, but not readily otherwise. In

> As ye sow, so shall ye reap

we cannot alter subordination without altering logical meaning because

> As ye reap, so shall ye sow

is not the same.

Clausal independence and subordination can be illustrated by substitution. *Where the blue of the night meets the gold of the day, someone waits for me* can be rewritten:

> Someone waits for me there

and *While the richly dressed ambassadors, the handsomely decorated officers, and the beautifully gowned women chatted, a mouse ran across the floor* can be rewritten

> Meanwhile a mouse ran across the floor

in which single words are substituted for the dependent clauses to reveal what is subordinate and what superordinate despite the deceptive greater length in the dependent clause, or seemingly greater importance. Though single words cannot always be substituted, show that the clause behaves like a single word, whether adverb, adjective, or noun.

Research, Resources, and Techniques

1. A defense of the new structural grammar and an attack on conservatism in grammar teaching—indeed, a veritable blast!—can be found in James Sledd's "Grammar or Gramarye?" (*E. J.*, May 1960, p. 293). A strongly held viewpoint, which will illuminate your own, no matter on which side of the fence you sit.

2. A similar defense of the structural linguistics approach will be found in J. J. Lamberts' "Basic Concepts for Teaching from Structural Linguistics" (*E. J.*, March 1960, p. 172).

3. More temperate in tone is that outstanding book by Robert C. Pooley, *Teaching English Grammar* (Appleton-Century-Crofts, 1957). The discussions are fine. Furthermore, you'll find appropriate materials for classroom use. Strong on theory, but equally strong for practical classroom application.

4. Dona Worrall Brown, Wallace C. Brown, and Dudley Bailey's *Form in Modern English* (Oxford University Press, 1958) will yield many useful illustrations of the discussions here. With some modifications, you'll find examples that can be readily used in class. Very helpful.

The Fragment

The sense for subordination is missing in the sentence fragment. The fragment should be related to the neighboring idea, or else it should be set up on its own as a going entity. Again we return to the basic consideration of a name and an action, for in

Going down town. I met my friend.

the student must see that *going down town* can be: (a) an action divorced from a name, or (b) a name divorced from an action, to be corrected in various ways:

1. I was going down town when I met my friend.
2. As I was going down town, I met my friend.
3. I was going down town. I met my friend.
4. Going down town was fun because I met my friend.

In the first three sentences the fragment is seen as an action, with the auxiliary and the name added, while in the fourth sentence the fragment is seen as a name and the action added for completion.

The fragment is unacceptable in all compositions except the superlatively outstanding. When the student amply indicates his ability to write, the fragment is a permissible change of pace, or a means to a dramatic, staccato style, or an attempt to burst through stylistic rigidities. Do not stand in the way of such experimentation, if ability to handle English is demonstrated in the remainder of the paper, thus furnishing evidence that the student knows what he is doing. More often the fragment proves the student does *not* know what he is doing. He does *not* know that he has failed to put down what he was thinking. The chief objection to the fragment is its inadequate reflection of what is in our minds. As we have said earlier, we cannot think except in terms of names undertaking actions. The fragment is a distortion of what we are thinking. Its chief offense is that it misrepresents the writer, not grammar.

Correction of the fragment and instruction in sentence sense originate in the student's own verbal output. The appropriateness of newspapers, magazines, the popular song, and work books in grammar instruction has been indicated, but avoidance of the fragment is best taught from student compositions. Unfortunately, your schedule leaves little time for composition correction; to expect you to react intensively to more than five or six full-dress student compositions a term is illusory. Intensive analysis requires a

500-word composition, where you go at spelling, punctuation, paragraph organization, transitions, and idea content, as well as sentence structure. The shorter composition, of paragraph length, will give you adequate opportunity for improving sentence sense. Average class size being what it is, you have restricted opportunities for the analysis and correction required, a frustrating matter because the sentence fragment and its accomplices, the comma splice and the run-on sentence, account for much language disability. (These are linked to punctuation errors. Indeed, punctuation is a major hint to the teacher of the presence or absence of sentence sense. A student who effectively uses the comma simultaneously indicates that he can manipulate his ideas and organize a logical sentence. We shall discuss punctuation soon.)

All this, as we say, is time consuming. The following technique may help the troubled teacher who lacks time. To avoid student self-consciousness and shyness, I have, at the beginning of the term, assigned a number to each student and have had students copy composition correction symbols (p. 98) into their notebooks. Occasionally, when short compositions of paragraph length are returned, I have students put their numbers (not their names) on the top of a fresh sheet and have them list the errors according to category. Thus, under *frag.,* the student has entered all the sentence fragment errors indicated, under *p.* all punctuation errors, under *sp.* all spelling errors, and so on. This sheet, identified only by number, is turned over to a committee which in turn mimeographs sample errors by classification and, after each error, sets in parentheses the number of the paper from which it came. The mimeographed sheets are distributed, the errors are analyzed, and the class learns what the errors have been, though not the perpetrators; furthermore the class knows that these are actual home-grown errors, not synthesized by some work-book author. Short of individual conferences, this is a worth-while experience that saves considerable time, spares personal feelings, respects privacy, and gains high involvement. The procedure requires at least two students who can cut a stencil with fair accuracy.

Usage versus Grammar

Usage is not grammar.

Usage is to grammar as etiquette is to behavior. Behavior simply notes what people do; etiquette sets a stamp of approval or disapproval upon actions, or sets up standards to guide actions. The specific business of usage, therefore, is to determine what choices and discriminations are made in the use of English, and then to analyze the forces, social and psychological, which determine the choices. In practical terms, usage is the study which notes the variety of choices made in the use of English, observes the standards set up by such choices or created to influence such choices, and attempts to evaluate the validity of such standards.[13]

This side of schizophrenic discourse, all language is inescapably grammatical and hence no more to be approved or rejected than any other physiological manifestation. Usage is another matter. It is accompanied with value judgments, acceptance, and rejection. If a student says, "Him and me is goin' to the movies," his language is completely grammatical and grammatically acceptable. What is objectionable is the usage, in that employing the accusative rather than the nominative, and a singular verb form rather than a plural, the student has simultaneously stated an adherence to a particular group in society, has identified himself as coming from a certain background, has limited his communication possibilities, *even though in his mind the accusative is a nominative and the singular is a plural*. Teach usage for seemliness, not seaminess, in social behavior, for greater adaptability to a variety of social circumstances, to break through the chains of regionalism, provincialism, class, and caste. In a pluralistic democracy, the teaching of the standards of usage should imply no denigration and no pejoratives. *Him and me is goin' to the movies* is not wrong; it is merely limiting. We do not wish to remove it from the student's repertoire of response, but to supplement it with alternative forms more appropriate in alternative circumstances. Usage should therefore be taught in social terms, inductively, and by examples, rather than deductively, as grammar is. This requires rote learning, drill, memorization, and contrasting instances. Almost always, when I have written

> Him and me is goin' to the movies
> He and I are going to the movies

students have selected the second as the proper option. Their reason has been, "It sounds better." But does it? In exploring this reason with them, they have arrived at a better explanation, that the second option doesn't brand you as readily as the first, that both options are available to you depending on the good judgment you use about the people you are addressing and the social context. We cannot say that *He don't like me* is less preferable than *He doesn't like me* unless we determine whom we are talking to. This determination must be made in assessing usage.

Having determined the varieties of social context, a friend, a parent, a teacher, an employer, a stranger, we must learn when *I coulda came on time* is less appropriate than *I could have come on time* and we must memorize the difference. *Lie* and *lay, sit* and *set, most* and *almost* offer forms and alternatives that correspond to no logic and must similarly be memorized. Rote learning, in other words, is inseparable from the teaching of usage— but rote teaching is another matter. Rote learning is respectable. How else can you learn spelling and the multiplication table? But rote teaching, especially in the teaching of usage, is snobbish and leads to what the British, in one of their lighter moments, have come to classify as U and non-U speech.[14] Recognize the difference, else your teaching of usage can become hide-bound, class-bound, caste-bound, and resented.

To avoid rote teaching, associate the rote learning of usage with group differences in democratic society. Do not curb language parochialisms but supplement them. Agree with the student that there is nothing wrong with the way he speaks right now, provided that he does not confuse other social groupings with his and doesn't indiscriminately use the same verbal behavior under all conditions. He will not thereby become disloyal to his present social contexts, but he will be able to function effectively in others. The classroom, or a social context additional to the bosom of the family, or the ice-cream parlor, or the pizza palace is suitable for rehearsing usage, to feel at home and comfortable in other segments of society.

A paradox thereby follows. If a student comes from a home and social group in which language and usage are "acceptable," are you to make him aware of language and usage which are not? If a student habitually uses "proper" English, are you to drill him, by rote methods, in usage employed across the tracks? Do you not, in that case, degrade his quality of language?

Groups and classes are ranked, and some usage is ranked as superior to other. Thus, *Him and me is goin' to the movies* ranks low in acceptance by most groups because identified with one particular group low in the social hierarchy. *He and I are going to the movies* carries no corresponding stigma. Students who habitually use good English should be taught the existence of alternative usages and the social backgrounds that give rise to them, whether Pennsylvania Dutch, or Negro, or Down Easter, or New York, or Southern. This does not become a usage slumming party. Just as we want students who speak effectively to employers, so ultimately we will want employers who understand their employes. We want students who realize that there is nothing wrong with the way the other person is talking or expressing himself simply because it is different. This is not new. Mark Twain said it in the preface to *Huckleberry Finn* and so did Shaw in *Pygmalion*. Furthermore, in the larger view, this hospitality to the other fellow's mode of expression leads to a richer, subtler, far more flexible language —and society too.

CASE STUDY 5   The example *Him and me is goin' to the movies* is associated with one English teacher's dramatic experiences, a high-water mark that remains in the memory for years. The teacher was discussing the nominative and the objective pronouns and their case endings. He had put on the board:

> John kicks him.
> John kicks he.
> John likes him and me.
> He and I are going to the movies.
> Him and me are going to the movies.
> I am going to the movies with he.
> I am going to the movies with him.

Discussion followed on the pronominal case endings and how the nominative in the examples undertakes the action and how the objective receives the action. A Negro boy in class who had been leaning back in his seat suddenly bent forward over his desk and blurted out: "I ain't never gonna say that again!"

The teacher was puzzled at this unexpected outburst, and asked, "What are you talking about?"

"That!"

"What?"

" 'Me and him is goin' to the movies,' " the student answered.

"Why?"

The student explained, almost venomously, "Why should I put myself on the receiving end? I'm on the receiving end enough! When I talk like that, it's like dishing it out to myself even if nobody else is. Why should I? It's like pointing the finger at yourself and accusing yourself. I ain't ever gonna say *me* when I should say *I*."

How true!

"It's a habit," the teacher answered. "How will you stop it?"

The boy shook his head stubbornly. "I'll figure it out."

The class arrived at a point in the discussion where students saw that they were prisoners of lifelong habits of usage, with choice and volition playing minor parts in their patterns of utterance. In addition, this lifelong imprisonment to usage reflected imprisonment in social circumstance. They would have to make up their minds. Either they would consent to remain prisoners of social circumstance as long as they lived, on the accusative or receiving end, or they would make up their minds that they, in their words, would beat the rap by taking steps, beginning with their speech and usage patterns, to make themselves available to far wider social circumstances. And, finally, they would make up their minds in accordance with their levels of morale. If they felt licked, they would continue as they were. If not, they would move forward, beginning with the way they talked. It was as simple as that—or is that simple?

Work on usage begins with an acceptance of student usage habits and goes on to student acceptance of the usage habits of others and thereafter to drill, memorization, use of work books in conjunction with written work, and a pervading classroom atmosphere that language parochialisms will not be accepted unless the user acquaints himself with other patterns of language. Students are ready to buy this *quid pro status quo*. If these conditions are laid down, they will read a humorous *New Yorker* editorial on suggestions to baseball writers on the use of verbs,[15] the reports of John Crosby in the *New York Herald Tribune* on the neologisms created by the advertising world of Madison Avenue (see p. 290), the Welshman, the Irishman, and the Scotsman in *Henry V*, Ring Lardner's stories, and the high-gloss finish in Sir Walter Scott, with the feeling that these are all equally English—and are legitimate supplements to their own daily language.

The danger of preciosity and snobbishness is great. Teachers of English, who are not authorities, are more likely to fall into these traps than the experts, who have ever been far more hospitable to language variants and verbal heterodoxy.

Thus, the student may see the double negative as an intensification of a negative statement, rather than as a canceling of two negatives to yield a positive, as in algebraic multiplication. The student is not wrong in seeing this possibility in the double negative, but English is not algebraic multiplication. It is, through its manifold forms, itself; the double negative will not destroy communication but will certainly cause unseen, unfelt, and unconscious—and you can sometimes remove *un*—barriers to arise between speaker and listener. In learning usage, the student should project himself beyond his present circumstances, whether upper upper or lower lower on the social scale, and undertake a stint of role-playing because ultimately role-playing is what the teaching of usage comes down to.

Actually, history is on the student's side when he says *He don't want it,* because if he ignores agreement between subject and verb, so do we ignore the original inflection of *it* in the Old English accusative. Why should we ignore one kind of accidence but hold the student responsible for another? *It* is not inflected for the accusative, and *He don't want it* is heard in Congress as well as on street corners. The student has evidence from radio and television that many of our leaders have less than an adequate grasp of English.

Furthermore, he fears ostracism from his group, in any attempt to widen usage, lest his own people make fun of him. The author recommends a class exercise where students in their normal, daily course of contacts see how often parents and friends find out when the student surreptitiously amplifies his repertoire of usage. Almost always, people do *not* find out, removing the primary impediment to the motivation of usage study. What relief accompanies student reports, in this version of television's *I've Got a Secret,* that nobody caught on, that they have been listened to more attentively, that they have gained—not lost—status, when they adduce instances of increments in power and in self-esteem, gingerly, apprehensive attempts to use a new addition to their vocabulary, uncertainty about how it would be received, and then, minutes or days later they have heard it used by someone else in the group and felt the reward: It Worked. Here you and your students enter jointly into a conspiracy, with nobody else having to know. Once in a while a student reports that a friend cocked an eye at him, and even said, "Look at him! Getting fancy! Five dollar word!" but defenses can be planned. A student, having used *rigorous* in describing preseason football practice, reported this reaction from a questioning friend. The student scratched his head, stared a while, and answered the friend, "I saw it on the sports page. How else could you say it?"

"What's the matter with *hard?*" his friend demanded.

The student agreed. "I guess so. They mean the same." No fights. No disputes.

"So whyn't you say *hard?*" his friend continued.

The student shrugged. "That's what I read on the sports page. You want to pick an argument? Pick an argument with the reporter." A few days later the friend was heard using the word in describing a pro football game seen on television.

Research, Resources, and Techniques

1. Not only is usage culturally determined, but so unexpected a thing as posture. The way we sit, kneel, stand, or crouch is governed in part by anatomy, but also in great measure by social patterns. For a discussion on this read Gordon W. Hewes' "The Anthropology of Posture" (*Scientific American,* Feb. 1957, p. 122). Our social origins accent our speech and stance.

2. Here are three contributions to our discussion on usage, all from *English Journal:*

a. For an overview of the contentions in this area, read Charles V. Hartung's "Doctrines of English Usage" (*E. J.,* Dec. 1956, p. 517).

b. In his usual statesmanlike way, Robert C. Pooley specifies the usage that schools should prescribe in "Dare Schools Set a Standard in English Usage?" (*E. J.,* March 1960, p. 176). Pooley argues that standards exist and should be taught.

c. "Approaching Usage in the Classroom," by V. Louise Higgins (*E. J.,* March 1960, p. 181), discusses how the teacher is in the hot seat, hot potato in hand, in determining for students what's "right" and "wrong" in usage and how he can duck out of the way gracefully. Not as forthright as Pooley's article.

Punctuation

We turn to the apostrophe and to haplology.

Consider the concept of possession and how the apostrophe expresses possession. Cattlemen in the old West expressed ownership by a brand. We express ownership at summer camp by a name tape. The cattle brand, the name tape, and the apostrophe express possession, but not in parallel ways; the cattle brand and the name tape label the thing possessed; in language we label the possessor. Therefore we write the *cow's horns* and not the *cows horns'*. We ask *Am I my brother's keeper?* and not *Am I my keeper's brother?* The physicist speaks of *the spin of the nucleus* and *the nucleus of the spin;* whether it is *the spin's nucleus* or *the nucleus' spin* is one of the unsolved problems of modern physics. If we ask *Which came first, the chicken or the egg?* we want to know if it is *the chicken's egg* or *the egg's chicken,* like a geneticist speaking of the phenotypical versus the genotypical.

In teaching the apostrophe for possession we use a combination of concept and rote. The exceptions, *yours, hers, theirs, ours,* are learned by rote, but *Jones's hat, Smith's book, Burns's poetry* require some sense of logic for differentiation from *the caucus' vote* and *the principals' opinions. Who's* and *it's* have nothing to do with possession because we use *whose* and *its* —requiring rote again. Do not push logic beyond its proper domain. Know that the apostrophe is a matter of social acceptance, of what is congenial to custom, of printing conventions, and thereafter of conceptualization.[16]

I have often used a series of silly little jokes to facilitate rote. Students seem to find them amusing:

> 1. A little duck was heedlessly waddling across the railroad track. Just then the train came along. Most of the duck had crossed, but the train caught the duck's tail, sending the duck skittering in one direction, while the feathers flew off in the other. A passenger, seeing the shower of feathers, asked the conductor, "What's that?" The conductor pointed to the tail, then to the duck, and answered, "It's its!"
>
> 2. Make up your own story, using the combinations *he's hers, who's whose, there's theirs,* and *she's hers.*

Or we can deal with the apostrophe in contraction and offer reasons of informality, change of pace, change of appearance, and closer conformity with spoken language. *I'm, he'll, we've, they're, they've* are contractions, meaning that something has been squeezed out: *I (a)m, he (wi)ll, we (a)re, we (ha)ve, they (a)re,* and *they (ha)ve.* The apostrophe signals the act of contraction. Signals are important in baseball, football, transportation, life, and punctuation. A student indifferent to language signals is indifferent to the other man, or contemptuous of the whole business, or unable to understand the signal system.

Thus the comma signals the nonrestrictive and restrictive, the apposite, the parenthetic, and the series. Teaching comma use involves teaching these concepts. The process of learning comma use is automatic, once these concepts are absorbed into thinking. Hence, your first concern is with the conceptualizations involved in comma use. If conceptualization is effectively taught, the usual work book will offer adequate exercises and drills. Even if, thereafter, comma faults occur in student compositions, communication toward correction has been established. Refer the student back to the work book for examples of what is meant and refer him to his concepts of the appositive, the parenthetic, and the series.

CASE STUDY 6 | A teacher made a wager with a colleague that comma use in restrictive and nonrestrictive clauses could be successfully taught to a slow tenth-year group. The colleague thought the concept too complex. They agreed that the colleague would be the sole judge of the success of the endeavor and that the unit would be taught in two sessions. The bet was paid after the first session, when the colleague admitted that the outcome was predictable. The first lesson went as follows:

The teacher began, as in a lesson described earlier, by asking a student, "Who are you?" The student gave his name. The teacher shook his head. "I didn't ask your name. I asked, 'Who are you?' " The student looked puzzled. So did the class. The teacher addressed a second student, who also offered his name, a little vaguely, and again the teacher rejected the answer. Similar blanks were drawn from a third and a fourth student. The teacher returned to the first student, asking, "Who are you?" A spark caught, for the student answered, "I'm five-seven, I weigh 128, I've got two sisters and three brothers, I live on Claremont Avenue," and drew breath to continue, when he was interrupted by the teacher's nod of acceptance.

A student's hand shot up. "You shouldn'ta asked 'Who are you?' but 'What are you?' Then we'd know what you meant."

The teacher agreed. "Good point. Suppose I ask 'Who *aren't* you?' "

The student who objected said, "That's easy. I'm not anybody else. I'm not him, not you, not anybody."

Again the teacher agreed. "Now I'll ask, 'What *aren't* you?' "

This, the class agreed, was difficult. Nevertheless things were either you or non-you, it or non-it. Thus, in "Boys who are stupid always fail," and "Boys, who are stupid, always fail," we had two contrasting philosophies, and the class agreed that we weren't saying the same thing. In one, specified, defined boys fail. In the second, all boys fail without restriction. Both sentences made sense—depending. But what kind of sense did we intend to make? Did we want to say that some boys will fail or that all will fail? The comma depended on what we believed about boys.

The teacher wrote on the board:

> Here are the students who come from this school.
> The students who come from this school are here.
> The students, who come from this school, are here.

The teacher asked, "Does the comma give additional information, or does it repeat the same information in different words? Does it add or repeat?" The class chewed that over. If the clause identified, restricted, defined the antecedent more closely, as Sir Ernest Gowers said, then we used *no* comma. But if it repeated the same information in different words, we used a comma.

A hand went up and a voice asked incredulously, "You mean they're all correct?"

The teacher nodded, "Depending. They're not saying the same thing. Did you ever squeeze a pit from a grape? The pit's the comma. If you narrow the grape, out comes the comma—oops! sorry!—I mean the pit. If you narrow the sentence, and restrict it, so that you're sharpening up the information and not just adding the same information in different words, you squeeze out the pit—oops! sorry!—I mean the comma." He wrote on the board:

> The pits that come from grapes are seeds.
> The pits, that come from grapes, are seeds.

"Both," he assured the class, "are correct, depending." He leaned forward, challengingly. "Depending on what?"

There were some preliminary frowns, and then the answers came. The colleague smiled, nodded, and the teacher grinned back. He told the class, "Open your work books, and we'll do some drilling on when we get additional information and when we repeat the same information, and how the comma comes into the picture."

The bet was paid gracefully.

The concept of identification is a necessary precursor to the teaching of the comma and the sense of restrictedness and nonrestrictedness in the adjective clause. The comma sends out a signal, "No identification needed here!" The absence of a comma signals, "I am identifying." We cannot do both simultaneously. (This is reminiscent of the psychologist's explanation of figure-ground relationships where, if we see the figure, we do not see the ground,[17] and conversely if we see the ground, we do not see the figure. The physics of Heisenberg analogously states that we cannot simultaneously know the position of a particle and its velocity. Similarly, an adjective clause cannot simultaneously be in apposition and further identify, qualify, or describe its antecedent.) We must determine what we are saying before we can determine whether punctuation is called for. Thus, the correct options in the following pairs depend on what we plan to say:

> The man who was ill yesterday feels better today. (Identification.)
> The man, who was ill yesterday, feels better today. (Apposition.)
> Turn in your SO money to the teacher who will be there. (Identification.)
> Turn in your SO money to the teacher, who will be there. (Apposition.)

Each sentence is correct, depending on what we intend. Are the adjective clauses used to identify or used in apposition? In restriction or in nonrestriction? We can call our shots either way, in the above pairs, depending on what we want to say.

How will students react to grammar taught this way? How effectively does this approach motivate? Is it too fancy, too prolix, too metaphysical for the average high school group?

Not a bit. Leading to sound sentence-analysis and self-analysis, challenging, thought-provoking, and not relying on artificial definitions, this approach depends hardly at all on rote and almost completely on the problem-solving ways of teaching language and grammar.

Observe that contrasting examples are offered, that instances come paired and compared. If you offer one sentence at a time, indicate how it can be transformed by commas into an alternative possibility. As you cull examples from whatever work book your school uses, you will notice how readily the comma lends itself to such matched illustrations, beginning with that old standby, "John said Jim was an idiot," versus "John, said Jim, was an idiot," and its numerous derivatives.

Such comparisons, unfortunately, are not too available with introductory adverbial clauses. Furthermore, to teach comma use with the introductory adverbial clause requires that you simultaneously teach recognition of the adverbial clause. This task is more formidable than teaching the adjective clause in restrictive and nonrestrictive use precisely because illuminating comparisons are so hard to come by. Hence recognition of the adjective clause is no obstacle in teaching the comma in restrictive and nonrestrictive use, but ability to recognize the introductory adverbial clause is the chief roadblock in teaching that the comma separates the remainder of the sentence. What should you do? Don't push for the impossible. If students recognize an adverbial clause when they see it leading off a sentence, you can teach them that a comma should set it off from the independent clause. If they can't recognize an introductory adverbial clause, they'll never learn this use of the comma.

As an example, you can ask even a slow class, "In which sentence are you sure that the store has more than one salesman?"

> The salesman who took the order made a mistake.
> The salesman, who took the order, made a mistake.

But you can list sentences like the following and understanding will come hard because the comma is not involved with meaning but merely with custom:

> If I can come, I'll telephone.
> Whenever you come, you're welcome.
> As soon as he saw her, he fainted.

Meaning is not drastically affected by removal of the comma after these adverbial clauses. Because it isn't, illuminating comparisons are hard to find, and the topic hard to teach. Don't stress it.

With comma use in series, show how reading the sentence aloud and listening for pauses offers hints on comma placement. (More on this in the Rosenson and Hatfield articles mentioned below.) Unfortunately, this device may lead some students to the comma-splice, in which a comma substitutes for a period. More than one student has said: "I did what you told me. I read it out loud. My voice dropped, so I put a comma there." Be prepared. The comma separates many things, but not sentences; a stop can be abrupt, gradual, or tentative; unwise stops cause traffic jams. A new driver learns how to apply and release the brakes, and so in writing. Do they want to make themselves understood? They must then learn how to stop and go, how to end ideas, begin them, and separate them.

Research, Resources, and Techniques

1. Two articles that deal with the difficulties in teaching punctuation and how these can be met by having students speak their sentences aloud:
a. Julius S. Rosenson's "The Oral Approach to Sentence Sense" (*E. J.*, Oct. 1958, p. 425) relates punctuation to intonation. What are the

advantages to this approach? The limitations? How does it supplement or contradict the recommendations you have just read?

b. Similarly, W. Wilbur Hatfield's "Will Structural Grammar Help?" (*E. J.*, Dec. 1958, p. 570) discusses how inner speech (intonation) helps in teaching punctuation. Compare both articles.

2. That breezy paperback by Harry Shefter, *Short Cuts to Effective English* (Pocket Books, 1956), has a particularly good chapter on the comma and its proper use.

Grammar and Research

For almost two generations the teaching of formal grammar has been under attack. The controversy has been carried on in *The English Journal* and elsewhere. The attack is summarized in DeBoer,[18] and a more balanced account given in Pooley.[19] The attackers quote research studies[20] to the effect that the teaching of grammar does not improve written English and that, to improve writing, practice in writing is preferable to practice in grammar. An interesting straw man, because no one can possibly disagree. Improvement in writing comes with opportunity to write. However, the "research" confuses practice in grammar with practice in *usage,* another matter entirely. Furthermore, these "studies" fail to equate control and experimental groups, fail to control for I. Q., or else test for transfer effects without teaching for transfer effects. The "research studies" that have intimidated English teachers into abandoning grammar are untrustworthy guides.

Not all research is good. A substantial amount is poor. The English teacher, respectful of "research," should not credulously accept results. Grammar study *does* transfer, with the better student. With the inferior student, less transfer, and here we are reduced to rote memorization of correct forms. "Rote" is a dirty word these days and goes disguised under the euphemism of "enriched drill." Tear off the disguise and reveal that four-letter word to which the author has no objection, because rote and the conceptualization of grammar study are not mutually exclusive. Both are legitimate parts of the English curriculum. Too much "research" recommends drumming grammar out of the curriculum to admit the rote study of usage, but your student should have both experiences, the rote of usage study and the conceptualization so inevitable to grammar study.

Should diagraming be taught? Yes. Should grammar be taught? Yes.

But doesn't "research" indicate that grammar has no relationship to improved writing and expression?

Such "research" is of a piece with recommendations that algebra, geometry, and nuclear physics not be taught because most students in adult life will have little occasion to use these subjects and that the curriculum in high school therefore be turned over to driving instruction and citizenship education. Why the doctrinaire mutual exclusivity? Medieval youth was taught equestrianship; modern youth should be taught the workings and manipulation of an automobile. Periclean youth was taught civic responsibility; so should modern youth be taught citizenship. That most of us in mature life do not use the binomial theorem or Euclid is irrelevant. What is relevant is that our minds be opened as wide as our capacities permit. Diagraming a sentence widens our perceptions of language; therefore diagraming should be taught. Does diagraming improve expression? Not always, but why should it be expected to? However, evidence exists that it does—chiefly with brighter students. Every experience is grist to the brighter person, and the brighter person can transfer from one experience to another, especially if he is taught to transfer. That's why he's bright.

To say that all diagraming does is improve the ability to diagram is to say that breathing merely improves the ability to breathe. "Research" on behalf of this argument, when the experiments are poorly designed and methodologically weak, is doctrinaire. The author has yet to encounter a single well-designed experiment that proves that diagraming and grammar study—not usage study—fail to contribute to sentence sense and expressional improvement.

Research, Resources, and Techniques

1. Richard Corbin's "Grammar and Usage" (*E. J.*, Nov. 1960, p. 548) is another overview of the battles raging in this area.

2. The point of view in John J. DeBoer, Walter V. Kaulfers, and Helen Rand Miller's *Teaching Secondary English* (McGraw-Hill, 1951) disagrees with the opinions expressed here. By all means form your own opinion.

3. Read Ingrid M. Strom's two contributions here:

a. Her doctoral dissertation is called *A Study of the Relationship between the Ability to Read Materials of an Informative or Literary Nature and the Ability to Analyze the Grammar and Syntax of the Materials Read* (unpublished; Univ. of Minnesota, 1955).

b. More readily available and easier to read is her article "Does Knowledge of Grammar Improve Reading?" (*E. J.*, March 1956, p. 129), in which she indicates that knowledge of grammar *is* associated with higher reading ability.

4. In Ray Charles Muize's "Two Methods of Teaching English to College Freshmen" (*Journal of Educational Psychology,* Jan. 1954, p. 22), forty compositions in the experimental group were contrasted with fourteen in the control group. Apparently the forty were not read by the experimenter, who claims that improvement occurred anyhow. Does this mean that feedback, correction, and discussion were not necessary? Compare this research with Eric Johnson's article in *English Journal* (Feb. 1958, p. 76), discussed below.

Spelling, Symbolism, and the Sense Modalities

Somewhere in the Australian bush, an aborigine's eye is caught by an animal hair in the bark of a tree or by a track in the sand or by a ripple in the grass. His senses are on the alert, picking up hints, clues, and messages to assure his survival, his food, his life. His awareness of signs and signals marks his ability to endure to the next day or week.

Somewhere in America, a man's eye is caught by a message in his pay envelope, by a newspaper, a letter of application, a menu, a television commercial. Instead of signs and signals around him, leading to survival or death, he is surrounded by symbols, words, statements, directions leading to more successful survival or less successful survival. The aborigine must discriminate among signs and signals, and the American must discriminate among symbols. Responses in either case can be adequate or inadequate.

The chief symbol is the word. When slight differences in words are lost on us, when our senses lapse in differentiating between the appearance and sound of words, when the barely perceptible becomes the imperceptible, our competence in surviving successfully becomes endangered. We will live if we cannot spell well, but we will not live with as much awareness of that world in which we chiefly live, the world of the symbol.

Spelling requires perhaps the last vestige of eye and ear alertness that remains to us, not with sounds and sights and sniffings, but with the symbols by which our lives are so closely governed, the words and language that we see and hear. Not less than with the aborigine, the auditory and visual modalities must be on the alert. We no longer have much opportunity to exercise eye and ear, except in terms of the word. Spelling offers such exercise. Even more, it offers exercise in the subtlety of our understanding with symbol use, the symbols by which, in modern life, we live effectively or less than effectively.

Too often spelling is taught for the wrong reasons, so that we may be proper secretaries or write a letter of application for a job; these are reasons for being toadies or lackeys, not for being properly implemented or armed as symbol-using citizens. Spelling should not be a means to training subordinates. The vocational purposes of learning spelling are legitimate, but they are subordinate to the *personal* purposes.

Spelling is observation or it is nothing. To motivate spelling we must motivate the willingness to be observant. Some students take pride in being observant. These students can learn to spell. Others see nothing wonderful or important about the observational qualities that enter into spelling. These will never learn. They are not necessarily the duller students. Some extraordinarily bright students are indifferent because spelling offers little intellectual challenge. A fine mathematics or science student can become interested in the analytic process in grammar and syntax and be bored by the factitious norms of acceptable spelling.

The businessman who blasts the high school for sending him secretaries who can't spell is one source of pressure on the high school to turn out good spellers, but most students do not plan to be secretaries. By and large, they do not envisage many occasions in their lives for letter-writing or spelling, and when they do, the conditions are unhappy: they are suppliants for a job, or writing a letter, or ordering something, or stating a complaint. Spelling in these circumstances is a cheerless chore.

Yet spelling is an important way of acknowledging the power of the word. Correct spelling is virtually a ritual in which we manifest our respect for the written word or else indicate that it means nothing to us. We can share in the ritual or ignore it. The responsibility is ours. Most students have this respect; the possibilities of the dignity and esteem that accompany words are not lost on them. Think of the mail-order courses on encyclopedias, five-foot-shelves, synopticons, and word-power courses to see how impressed people are by the forceful command of the language and the word.

But are high school students equally impressed? Of course. An effective assembly speaker, whether adult or adolescent, can hold a school auditorium enthralled. Difficult classes, taught by mediocre teachers, will become interested and involved—almost, indeed, to excess—at the possibility of a spelling bee. The spelling bee offers most to the better spellers and least to the poor ones, but all students get carried away by the excitement of the competition.

Competition alone won't raise the spelling competence of a class. We come back to the desirability of observation and the few ways left to the modern urban or suburban or heavily mechanized rural American to use his senses. This is where spelling comes in.

In the movie version of *Guys and Dolls,* Marlon Brando puts his hand over Frank Sinatra's shirt front, obscuring Sinatra's tie, and offers to bet him that he doesn't remember its color. Sinatra loses the bet. I have employed a similar device when teaching. After addressing a class for fifteen or twenty minutes I would turn my back, raise my coat collar, keeping it tightly closed, face the class, and ask how many could describe the tie I had on. It was the rare student who could. On one occasion, in fact, a girl had admired my necktie at the beginning of the period and yet was no more successful than the others when the time came to describe it.

This is one device that brings home to students their failure to use their senses, even when these are directly assaulted. In another class exercise, the author has asked students to remember how many steps on the stairway leading from their homes to the street or from the school's main entrance to the street. The degree of error is tremendous.

In self-defense, students ask, "What's so important about that? Why do I have to remember how many steps?" One should hope for this demurrer, because the teacher can then move in with the haymaker.

"In the first place," I have said after successfully teasing this answer forth, "you do it every day, day after day. But in the second place, you may be right. Perhaps it has little to do with you. But let me show you something that is part of you. Put your hands on the desk, flat, palms down, and tell me which finger is longer, the index finger or the ring finger."

The answers are sex-linked. Boys answer that the ring, or fourth, finger is longer. Girls answer that the index, or second, finger is longer. Puzzlement and consternation. Nobody has noticed this anatomical fact before. The evidence is in and conclusive that they do not use their senses, whether with things remote or as immediate as their own hands. Are they missing anything? Far more than they even suspect.

Such are the ways in which I have motivated the use of eyes and ears and thereafter set these to work on spelling. However, eyes and ears do not play equally important roles. Is it *ei* or *ie, er* or *ar, ent* or *ant?* Your ear won't tell you. Your eye, if trained, always will. The painter is more likely to be a good speller than the musician.[21] The good speller is both eye- and ear-minded, but he will place greater weight on how a word looks than on how it sounds, because the pay-off in correct spelling is not the kind of noise it makes but the appearance it presents.[22]

Since the number of spelling demons is finite, students are generally amenable to spelling tasks and hence frustrations chiefly inhere in spelling errors on compositions with words that have been gone over in class, tested, and thereafter misspelled. Why does this happen?

The error *looks* satisfactory. In the rush to get other things down on paper spelling becomes secondary. Indeed, it should be, because ideas have priority. But once ideas are down, editing should have priority, and an observant eye should be cocked for spelling errors. The editing habit should be meticulously called into action because good writing and good spelling are an aspect of editing, rewriting, and second and third drafts. The teacher should insist on such editing before compositions are turned in. Editing becomes synonymous with the sharpened use of eye and ear.

Also important is the determination of the specific trap in the spelling demon. Why is the tendency to spell *seperate* or *comeing* or *completly* or *dissapointed* or *definately* so recurrent? Is the student being led down the primrose path by *operate* when misspelling *separate?* by *familiar* when misspelling *similar?* In *coming* we drop the *e* and in *completely* we retain it; should students therefore memorize the governing rule? What makes it possible for the experienced teacher to predict with pinpoint exactness what the specific error will be? *Definitely* can be misspelled in a variety of ways but in actual practice the misspellings take a limited number of forms. *Definately* seems to be the chief offender. *Definitly* and *definatly* are less frequent. Similarly it is *seperate* we encounter most often, and the author suspects that *operate* is the villain lurking behind the scene and responsible for the error.

Therefore we can set specific targets in the teaching of spelling. We not only know the spelling demons but we also know the specific errors that occur within each of the demons. The traps to be avoided can be identified and partioularized. In presenting the list of demons the teacher should hammer away at the particular hideout that the error in a specific word frequents and wherever possible contrast the demon with the source of its downfall. For example:

in*sistent*	irresis*tible*	irritate	acknowle*dg*ment
con*sistent*	exci*table*	irrigate	knowle*dg*eably
per*sistent*			
as*sistant*	frag*ment*	congratul*ate*	favor*able*
re*sistant*	frag*rant*	defin*ite*	leg*ible*
	flag*rant*		
		occa*si*on	defi*ance*
*dis*pell	sep*arate*	om*ission*	differ*ence*
*miss*pell	op*erate*		
		di*s*tance	in*noc*uous
*dis*appoint	benef*ited*	exi*st*ence	inoculate
*dissim*ulate	sub*mitted*		
		*im*migrate	
acciden*tally*	examin*er*	*e*migrate	
intent*ly*	dicta*tor*		

Resource materials are available in great quantity, even in paperbacks. Radke[23] has an excellent chapter on spelling. Shefter's paperbacks[24] are inexpensive and very useful. Bolenius,[25] over two generations old, has an excellent assortment of homonyms.

At the end, however, it will be necessary for the student to develop his senses so that the eidetic[26] is exercised and a photographic talent developed for seeing the word as well as sounding it.

Research, Resources, and Techniques

1. Falk S. Johnson's "New Rules for 'IE-EI' Spelling" (*E. J.*, May 1960, p. 347) should be mimeographed and distributed to your classes.

2. You may be interested in the kind of research that has gone into the analysis of spelling difficulties. If so, read:

a. Joseph F. Comerford's *Perceptual Abilities in Spelling* (unpublished doctoral dissertation, Boston University, 1955);

b. David H. Russell's "A Second Study of Characteristics of Good and Poor Spellers" (*Journal of Educational Psychology*, March 1955, p. 129).

3. The general concern about poor spelling, extending beyond the English teacher, is reflected in:

a. Samuel Wehr's article on spelling in the *Bulletin of the National Association of Secondary School Principals*, May 1958;

b. Edna L. Furness' contribution to *Clearing House* for March 1958.

4. Harry Shefter's highly recommended paperback *Six Minutes a Day to Perfect Spelling* (Pocket Books, 1954) should be in the hands of every student with weaknesses here. Though it is a self-help book, you should not hesitate to give assignments from it.

Composition and Expression

CHAPTER 3

Native Woodnotes Are Usually Wild

Many years ago Paul Klapper wrote, with apparent plausibility:

> The child must be led to recognize that he has "composition ability" of no mean degree. Teachers, too, must realize that most children are not deficient in the art of composition. As we listen to a narrative of a ten-year-old lad who is giving a friend a verbal picture of the athletic game he saw, or to a description by his sister, half his age, of the particular doll that has caught her fancy, we become convinced that the art of composition is not foreign to the child. In the formal classroom lesson the life of the informal narrative and the charm of the child's description are ruthlessly crushed by the formidable technical laws of grammar and rhetoric which are imposed upon children. How to transfer this native ability to compose, so manifest in informal intercourse, to the formal language lessons, is the problem. . . .[1]

We disagree. Spontaneous utterance has not the charm that Klapper supposed, unless training and experience accompany it. If spelling and poetry are the easiest areas for the competent teacher to teach, then the hardest are composition and theme writing. Despite Klapper's opinion, spontaneous discourse is not effective, not picturesque, not well-ordered, and not efficient communication. Candid microphone recording proves that spontaneous discourse is sloppy, thoughtless, and maundering. Composition requires that we *compose,* that we arrange, that we put our thoughts and words in order. Only after experience in composing and arranging will our spontaneous utterances have effectiveness. A trained artist can with a half-dozen economical strokes of a pencil convey the sense of a figure; those half-dozen strokes distill years of experience. No beginner's spontaneity can substitute for it. Similarly, only a thoroughly trained musician can improvise. In short, spontaneity is an outcome of practice.

Effective writing is the result of such practice plus analysis and correction, and this is where you come in. The more practice the better, but have you the time to correct and analyze more than a few compositions each term?

Let's begin with the typical beginning. In September, when classes reassemble, you assign a topic for a composition. What qualities should the composition have? You remember that the best writing is personal, something experienced at first hand and familiar to the writer. What more natural, then, to assign that fresh and recent topic "How I Spent My Summer Vacation"? And how puerile an assignment it turns out to be!

Though one reason is unoriginality, another is the reluctance of students to talk about themselves. Talking about yourself is not easy. The personal does not come trippingly to the tongue. We must be taught ourselves and how to talk about ourselves, describe ourselves, and assess ourselves. Our experiences are difficult to disentangle. Our motives are closed books to us. A course in biology is required to understand that there are millions of unicellular structures within us, enzymes, hormones, chemical reactions, amino acids, and an infinity of activities about which we are never conscious. Similarly, we must be taught how to understand and thereafter express ourselves so that the ideas within us can be brought to the tongue or to paper. Aside from banality, what is wrong with "How I Spent My Summer Vacation" is spurious subjectivity. True subjectivity, on the other hand, is the heart of composition writing and requires that the student probe himself, his ideas, and his use of language. We can transform the banality and spurious subjectivity of "How I Spent My Summer Vacation" by seeking the topic's components:

1. Why I looked forward to this summer vacation
   a. experiences last term
   b. what school meant to me
2. What I planned to do
   a. why I arrived at these plans
   b. why my plans did (didn't) work out

3. People I met
   a. and liked
   b. and disliked
4. Things I did
5. Things I saw
6. How my plans for next summer are affected
7. How the summer affects my attitude toward school this year
   a. favorably
   b. unfavorably
8. Things about which my former opinion was
   a. changed
   b. confirmed
   c. confused
   d. modified

We want depth. "Where did you go? Out. What did you do? Nothing." symbolizes not the absence of inner resources but the absence of digging techniques by which the student gets a good bite on what he has experienced.

Just as students do not know what goes on in their bodies, so they do not know what goes on in their minds. They will grant their ignorance of what goes on in their bodies, but be less willing to concede ignorance of what goes on in their minds.

Try this. First, differentiate between awareness and knowledge and show that we can be aware of bodily states without any knowledge of what these states are. What happens when we are hungry, thirsty, sleepy, or when we bleed? Is the same thing true of our minds? When we hate, love, despise, need, repulse, agree, laugh, cry, we again have awareness of mental states, but is this the same as knowledge?

Good writing begins with observation, whether of the inner or outer worlds. Even before we teach the use of the appropriate word, we must teach how to observe appropriately. Appropriate observation is in turn dependent upon logic. In the sentences below, determine whether the appropriate area of observation is the written page on which these sentences appear, or your own thoughts:

1 a. This way he can see the problem.
  b. The way he can see the problem.
2 a. What made him do it?
  b. What made him do it.
3 a. Who is there?
  b. Who is there.

The first sentence in each pair is complete, but the second is a fragment. The difference in each pair are minuscule, but these slight differences reflect different internal states. In the first pair, how does the first word—the source of inflection—lead to logical and syntactical difference? For an answer, let the student stare within himself, at the way he thinks, rather than at the words on the page. In the second and third pairs, the difference caused by punctuation and inflection also reflects different internal expectations. What the student must observe in these three instances is something within, the workings of his own mind as he uses language. A whole inner system of language and symbol is involved so that in one case we get the sense of completeness and in the other not, although each sentence is almost indistinguishable from the other.

A similar kind of inner observation is called for when you assign a deceptively simple composition like "How to Tie Shoelaces" or "Description of a Spiral Staircase" or a description of the view from the classroom window. The last topic can be extraordinarily challenging if you first read your class Walt Whitman's "Miracles" and then ask them to look around the classroom and through the window to ascertain the "miracles" that they can see, or that Whitman could have, if they can't. The subsequent discussion can serve as introduction to your assignment on inner observation:

Why, who makes much of a miracle?
As to me I know of nothing else but miracles,
Whether I walk the streets of Manhattan,
Or dart my sight over the roofs of houses toward the sky,
Or wade with naked feet along the beach just in the edge of the water,
Or stand under trees in the woods,
Or talk by day with any one I love,
Or sit at table at dinner with the rest,
Or look at strangers opposite me riding in the car,
Or watch honey-bees busy around the hive of a summer forenoon,
Or animals feeding in the fields,
Or birds, or the wonderfulness of insects in the air,
Or the wonderfulness of the sundown, or of stars shining so quiet and bright,
Or the exquisite delicate thin curve of the new moon in spring;
These with the rest, one and all, are to me miracles,
The whole referring, yet each distinct and in its place.
To me every hour of the light and dark is a miracle,
Every cubic inch of space is a miracle,
Every square yard of the surface of the earth is spread with the same,

Every foot of the interior swarms with the same.
To me the sea is a continual miracle,
The fishes that swim—the rocks—the motion of the waves—the ships with
    men in them,
What stranger miracles are there?

You will find it easier to select complex topics than simple ones. Fight that temptation! This is especially true with a brighter group whose facility with language may make them use words to disguise reality rather than penetrate it.

Give this assignment:

> When you entered school this morning, you:
>   a. walked
> *or* b. strolled
> *or* c. ambled
> *or* d. rushed
> *or* e. sauntered
> *or* f. skipped
>
> Decide which you did and discuss the reason why; also discuss why, this morning, you did not do the others. [*Note to teachers:* In some classes you must explain these words!]

In this exercise, recollection and analysis precede the choice of a word. The student must first remember a physical action and thereafter must match action and precedent condition with an appropriate word. After selection, the student must analyze and furnish reasons.

We have here all the elements of paragraph development. Paragraphing represents the pursuit of ideas. If we *sauntered,* and did not *rush,* to school this morning, we must look within ourselves for inner occurrences and reactions that make one word rather than the other the preferred choice. Did we saunter because our homework was done, our consciences clear, and the morning pleasant? Or did we saunter because we hadn't done our work and hated to get to school any sooner than necessary?

We have thereby introduced further matters. *Sauntering* versus *rushing* emerges as a consequence of precedent conditions: work done, state of conscience, the weather. These conditions, in turn, like door beyond door, open upon further matters. We may have rushed because we arose late; we arose late because we went to bed late; we went to bed late because we were socializing, or working at an after-school job, or preparing homework.

Students resist this continuing substitution of knowledge for awareness.

Feeling states are as important as cerebration; because cerebration threatens the feeling state, any endeavor to organize and compose the feeling state, as in paragraphing, is frequently fought. This is as true of adults as adolescents, as true of teachers as of their students, and re-grettably, of this author and of you too. Paragraphing requires thinking and thinking comes hard.

Thinking—paragraphing—requires that we ask questions of ourselves. Have some fun in your class by inquiring, "Have you ever asked yourself a question? We generally ask questions of others, but when was the last time you asked yourself a question?" Do not expect immediate response. This probing requires time for thought. After a while answers will come forth. List them on the board. When you have a dozen or more samples of the kinds of questions your students have asked themselves, you should then inquire, "When you asked the question, were you completely ignorant of the answer or did you have some partial idea, some information, that would help getting the answer?" Students will see that it is impossible to frame a question in the absence of information. Some information must be already at hand, else the question cannot be formulated at all. Hence, questions do not emerge from total ignorance but from partial information.

Teach your students to ask questions of themselves. The question, re-phrased as a declarative sentence, becomes the topic sentence of the paragraph. The answers to the self-addressed questions constitute the development of the paragraph. (See the examples below.)

Sometimes answers do not lie within us. We must undertake research to locate answers, particularly in writing the expository paragraph. Even so, the research cannot be undertaken until we have first enunciated the question. If we put the questions well, the research will be all the more fruitful.

Though self-expression and paragraph construction require digging as much as building, and the digging is inward, you must designate the real estate where digging is to take place and where pay dirt is likely to be encountered. You should know, for example, that most boys are interested in sports and most girls in popular music and relations among people. What are the broad themes in sports? in popular music? in other areas of adolescent interest—loyalty to friends, relationships with parents, sex, and the effects on our thinking of the mass media?

Next, set up regions of debate so that the class is dichotomized, with some students defending one point of view, some another, with opinions, ideologies, and loyalties polarized in opposite and conflicting directions, thus:

> *Sports:* Playing to win, rather than for the fun of the game, leads to dirty play, crookedness, and professionalism. On the other hand, playing for fun is sissyish. [*Note to the teacher:* Do you know William James on sports and the moral equivalents for war? It's appropriate here.] Do you tighten up, get tense, and play more poorly when you compete, or do you play more effectively? An example from tennis is playing a match versus volleying practice; from baseball, hitting in a pinch versus practicing fungoes and batting flies; from golf, playing a driving range versus playing a course; and so on.
>
> *Popular Music:* Is it more fun to listen to slow music by yourself, or with your friends? To music with a strong beat? Your favorite singing star is appearing next Saturday. Choose one song you want him to sing and give reasons why you'd prefer that song rather than any other.
>
> *Loyalty and Friendship:* In order to get money a boy gets a job delivering orders at a neighborhood store. His best friend secretly talks to his employer, offering to work for less, and gets the job which the boy loses. Would this happen to you and your friends? Tell why. Have you ever heard about a similar incident? Tell what happened.
>
> *Family Relations:* Three students were having a discussion. One said the worst punishment was being scolded. Another said the worst punishment was silence. The third said the worst was being spanked. What do you believe?

Observe that each suggestion contains a question. The student must decide how to answer. This answer becomes part of his topic sentence or it may be the topic sentence entire. Note also that different points of view may be taken, thus opening debate possibilities.

Composition requires the mobilization of ideas, if any. If none, no great damage, because we can mobilize feelings. These must be caused to emerge and clothed in words, not a simple matter; it comes easily to the bright student and with more difficulty to the slower one. The bright student has techniques by which he can pursue an idea. He sets up relationships, connections, generalizations—in other words, he establishes transitions.

Transitions show how ideas are connected. Direct student attention to the way conversations wander. Do they really wander? Are there not hidden connections? Two students eavesdropped on the way a lunch-room conversation went: from homework the next day, to dates, to the World Series, to neckties, to neighbors who had complained about playground noise. They were asked to bridge the gap by their own surmises as to how the students involved in the conversation had set up transitions. Such eavesdropping is not only excellent observational practice but is also an introduction to the handling of transitions. In ordinary conversation, the freewheeling leap from topic to topic is apparently haphazardly anarchic. Is it? Can the student figure out why conversation hopped from one point to another seemingly unrelated? What were the invisible, the unspoken connections?

You can freely, with your students, consider the nature of thought. They'll be fascinated. First ask: "What are the beginnings of our thoughts, the middles, the ends?" Unless we know this, we can neither tell a story, nor develop a paragraph, nor fully understand what others are saying. Because we are allowed no reprieve from the necessity of doing our thinking, and organizing our thinking in public, composition digging can also be public.

Next, discuss this: students share in the universal experience, in a dispute, of being at a loss for a rejoinder, only to have, hours afterward, too late, the perfect retort come to mind. Everybody in your class has some such rueful reminiscence. Ask why the retort doesn't appear when needed but later, with the second-best comfort of, "If I'd have said *that,* I'd have ruined him!"

The class will tell you: "I was rattled." "I couldn't pull myself together." "I couldn't think straight."

Can they learn to keep calm and organize their ideas under stress? Yes. It needs practice. Determining boundaries, outsets, conclusions, where nature recognizes none, requires decisiveness. We must make up our minds and say, "Here is where I'll begin and here is where I'll end." In keeping out the extraneous we find, as Hegel says, that everything in the universe is related to everything else, which is no help at all because when everything else crowds in we cannot organize our ideas, or a paragraph, or an apt retort. In paragraph construction, in sentence structure, in the handling of ideas, we must maintain more an internal consistency than an external relatedness, achieving a uniformity that omits the jarring and unexpected and is determined not in nature but by man. Hence, the student is the ultimate arbiter of order and disorder, of sense and nonsense, coherence and incoherence. The job is the student's because he must dredge these out of himself and nobody else in the world can do it for him. This is an act of determination, and this is where the teaching of paragraph structure is motivated.

We teach this determination by insisting that the student clarify, for himself first, what he has in mind or whatever he opts to talk or write about. Let him look out of the window and look and look. What does he see? Does he see any of Whitman's "miracles" worth writing about? If so, let him say so, succinctly. If not, let him look around at his classmates. And so on. What does he think is worth writing about? He can come up with an idea or say, succinctly, "Nothing!" Then he is indeed in a bad way for he is saying that he cannot clarify, or else he refuses to take the time to clarify, a single idea. He cannot mark it off from its fellows and, having done so, proceed to develop it.

Ask them, "What is an idea?"

A usual answer is, "Something in your head."

Only in your head? Can it be in your heart, your fingertips, your insides? Yes, but only if your head knows it's there. An idea is in your head.

"Your head knows, but how do you?" the teacher asks.

The student retorts, "Who knows better than I do?"

"Can you prove it?" the teacher demands. The proof lies only in words, nowhere else—or so the lesson should proceed. No idea, no words. If you can't put it into words, you have no ideas. (For the brighter and more disputatious class, show how the mathematician has a special set of words, known as mathematical symbols and relations. The musician has notation, phrases, intervals, themes, and harmonies. The painter has color, space, and design. These are special languages where ideas become "words" in a special idea-word transformation.)

Invite the class to put ideas into words. List these on the board, twenty-five, fifty, one hundred, and have them copied into notebooks. Thus, by concretizing words from ideas, we have begun by enumerating topics.

Now we must go backward. What made us phrase these ideas as we did? What was the *prior* state within us that made us give these ideas their *final* verbalization? This list on the board is an outcome, an end-result, a final wrap-up of precedent states, conditions, moods, feelings, and experiences, rather than an augury of the future pathways paragraph development can take. Indeed, this analysis of prior conditions *is* paragraph development; in paragraph development we go back rather than forward, down in depth, rather than upward into the insubstantial.

We have attempted to lead the student within himself. We have tried to get him to recall when a suitable rejoinder did not come trippingly to the tongue, a rather general experience which we would like to relate to other experiences that are immediate, deeply personal, and still universal. What can these be? All around us, underfoot and under our very noses, or in something called the syllabus, are such experiences. We can integrate them with paragraph development. To illustrate:

1. Has anybody ever high-hatted you? Did you ever have the experience of being snubbed and humiliated? ("Richard Cory")

2. Is there anybody you dislike, or hate? In feeling this way, are you destroying yourself or strengthening yourself? Is there anybody you love? In feeling this way, are you destroying yourself or strengthening yourself? Do you live more fully, enjoyably—and longer—if you love or hate? Who lived longer in the hearts and minds of people, Sidney Carton or Madame Defarge? (*Tale of Two Cities*)

3. What does ambition require of the ambitious man? What does hopelessness have to do with ambition? Can you be ambitious and still feel hopeless? Which requires greater strength, ambition or hopelessness? Is the unambitious man strong or weak? (*Julius Caesar*)

4. Here is practice in what psychologists call free association. Close your eyes. Take a specific idea, say the desk in front of the room. Using that as a beginning, what other ideas come into your head? After five minutes, come to attention and be prepared to tell what idea is in your head at that time, how one idea led to another, how you finally arrived at the last idea, and what the connection between ideas was. (Paragraph construction and transitions)

5. What do we do when we name things? What makes *John Smith, Mary Jones, desk, hat, fingers, table, blackboard, jumping, hating, skating, thinking* names? What do we group and identify in the naming process? What is an action? Can you have an action without a name? What is being? Can anything have being without having a name? (Sentence structure)

6. Can you be described? Can people be described? Can things be described? Are people and things described as we describe actions, or not? If we didn't describe, would it be possible to speak? Would it be necessary to speak? Why the difference? (Parts of speech)

7. Is the better commander the man who can take orders or the man who resents taking orders? If you destroy everybody in your way, do you build yourself up or destroy yourself too? How can we tell when our leaders can also control themselves? Should they? (*Macbeth*)

8. You are on the *Seawolf* on the first submarine voyage under the North Pole. Write a monologue on your experiences, as you tell them over the telephone to a friend on your return or to a newspaper reporter. (Other options are being on a jet from which you are forced to bail out, or on the first voyage to the moon, or caught in a sudden squawl while out on the water, or in an unexpected blizzard. Adventures reported in

the daily papers are a never-ending source of ideas like the above. Here you, the teacher, capitalize on the semisensational.)

9. You are on a rescue mission and you can take out only one person. (Occasion: a blizzard, a tornado, a flood, people stranded on an ice floe.) Do you take out a mother or her infant? A boy or a girl? A father or a mother? (See discussion below on *Hours on Freedom,* p. 111)

10. Why do men leave home and go to sea? ("Sea Fever," *Moby Dick, Odyssey*)

11. Go through the "Letters to the Editor" section in a newspaper or in *Time* to see what issues people take opposite sides on. Which side are you on? (Journalism, speech) What is your reaction to letters complaining about teen-agers?

12. Have you ever seen anything, or heard of anything, that would make a good television play? (Narrative, creative writing) (You will find this, in most classes, a successful question. Students preen themselves on the extent they have been around, and the interesting things they have encountered. They also have ideas on the kind of television show they would like to produce, or see produced. Compositions on topics #11 and #12 evoke amazing effectiveness and you will find that students surpass their usual standards for reasons not altogether clear.)

Paragraph structure requires that students peel down to one idea and strip away excrescent verbiage and concepts so that one idea and its ancillary subideas, and nothing else, are treated in the paragraph. Almost always, this stripping away will leave the student with a unified, compact, hard-hitting paragraph.

How can you illustrate this? Allow the student to write his paragraph any way he can. Do not interfere with the process of birth. Your sideline coaching at this point should be confined to the theoretical and to examples of good paragraph structure. (You will find in Strunk and White's *The Elements of Style* examples of sentence stripping down, and in Harry Shefter's excellent paperback *Guide to Better Compositions* comparisons of good and poor paragraph structure and how the second can be edited into the first.) But the theorizing and the examples may not work. Don't expect too much. Nevertheless, your student must know that the paragraph deals with a single main idea, that the single idea is strengthened by relevantly supporting ideas, and that the paragraph's main idea is clear-cut and unmistakable.

You have told him, you have illustrated what you mean, and the paragraph he turns in is a horror. You haven't communicated anything beyond the principle. Now let his blood flow, via your red pencil or red ballpoint.

Start excising every unnecessary word and phrase. In doing so, you will be leaving great, yawning gaps. Link the surviving words with transitional words and phrases, and show him the technique of transitions. (Shefter is very good here.) He will begin to see, as no theorizing or didactic examples can illustrate, that, in J. N. Hook's words, the paragraph has unity, coherence, and emphasis—or, in the words of your students, that the paragraph has singleness, direction, and punch.

The outcomes are startling when you correct this way, rather than by the usual correction symbols. The difference is like a textbook discussion of anatomy versus the dissection of a cadaver. The student witnesses the dissection of his own verbal cadaver. It hurts. It's violent. But it works far better than all the composition symbols in the world. You have drawn blood, always upsetting. And it takes more time than you have. That's more upsetting than anything else.

From Strunk and White: "Planning must be a deliberate prelude to writing. The first principle of composition, therefore, is to foresee or determine the shape of what is to come and pursue that shape." [2]

From Hook: "Teaching straight thinking is, in large measure, the teaching of organized, methodical thinking. Random thoughts lead only to other random thoughts." [3]

From Shefter: "The most natural thing in the world is proper planning, whether something is being built up or being torn down, whether it is alive or inanimate, whether it is a tree, a building—or a composition! And since careful preparation is so essential, it is always puzzling to your teachers why you are often reluctant to spend the necessary time to organize your ideas before you write." [4]

All true, as we said above (p. 82) in stressing the *composing* that goes into composition and into paragraph structure, and the outlining that must precede the composing. But what precedes outlining? Experience in editing and practice in revising—surgery, in brief, on the words that the student loves so dearly. Teach him how to hack his composition to pieces, how to shorten it, how to throw out all unnecessary words, phrases, and sentences. Do it for him, using his compositions for the surgery, or take specimen paragraphs from the daily newspaper, thus:

> (A) Obviously what our gifted young artists need is more musical discernment on the part of American audiences. If such discernment existed in greater measure, young artists could make more headway without having to be swept to fame by well-publicized contests. But

contests will probably remain with us until American audiences have more interest in artistry for artistry's sake and more power of sizing up artists, regardless of verdicts by juries (Ross Parmenter, *The New York Times,* Oct. 30, 1960).

(B) Obviously, gifted young artists need more musical discernment in American audiences. If more discernment existed, young artists could succeed without contests. But contests will probably stay until American audiences seek artistry for its own sake and can size up artists without juries.

Continued editing and revision lead to skill in outlining, as knowledge of anatomy helps the painter with the human figure and the sculptor with his armature. Outlining is learned when the student learns how to slash his work.

Composition is taught through decomposition.

Research, Resources, and Techniques

1. Here are three references which bear on Klapper's point of view that opened this section:

a. John Dewey, in *Democracy and Education* (Macmillan, 1939; p. 6): "Nor is the one who communicates left unaffected. Try the experiment of communicating, with fullness and accuracy, some experience to another, especially if it be somewhat complicated, and you will find your own attitude toward your experience changing; otherwise you resort to expletives and ejaculations. The experience has to be formulated in order to be communicated. To formulate requires getting outside of it, seeing it as another would see it, considering what points of contact it has with the life of another so that it may be got into such form that he can appreciate its meaning." Here, of course, Klapper's point of view is attacked.

b. On the other hand, John C. Adler's "The Metatextbook Factor in Writing" (*E. J.,* Dec. 1959, p. 511) defends the Klapper approach and shows how the accepting teacher can develop expressional ability in students. This is an excellent piece that realistically demonstrates how it can be done and how personalized writing can awaken effective writing.

c. In Lionel Trilling's *The Liberal Imagination* (Doubleday Anchor, 1953), read the discussion "The Kinsey Report" (p. 228) on naturalness in response and then see how this is related to control and planning —therefore outlining—in responses of all kinds.

2. Lou LaBrant's "Inducing Students to Write" (*E. J.,* Feb. 1955, p. 70), says that to get students to write, the following must obtain:

a. The teacher must write.

b. The teacher must be accepting and respecting of student effort.

c. Topics must be interesting. Suggestions: "the difficulty of waking in the morning; the dread of losing consciousness at night; the competition of the family for the morning paper, the radio program, the use of the car or bathroom."

d. There must be time enough for writing.

e. There must be response to student effort—or what is here called "feedback."

f. Revision, rewriting, and editing must be included in the writing program.

3. In Mabel M. Staats' "Continued Next Week" (*E. J.*, Feb. 1960, p. 112), the "cliffhanger," or suspense, approach to paragraph writing is described. The article also has some relevant comments on why the personalized composition doesn't work, though on the surface it should.

4. You may want to compare two articles for certain differences and similarities:

a. Carl G. Wannberger's "Writing—A Way of Life" (*E. J.*, Feb. 1959, p. 66) stresses some of the things said in this chapter. Though this article will be more useful to the experienced teacher, it may offer you a few of the values to be kept in mind when you teach composition.

b. For another viewpoint, read Bertrand Evans' "Writing and Composing" (*E. J.*, Jan. 1959, p. 12), which deals with the techniques of inner digging. The article asserts that ideas are more important than amount of writing done, and more important than accumulation of data. You may question Evans' estimate of the amount of writing done by high school students, but he seems correct in his feeling for the primacy of thought over writing and outlining. First think; then outline; then write.

5. Robert P. Saalback's "Teaching Students to Organize" (*E. J.*, Nov. 1958, p. 505) declares that organizing material on somebody close to you and presumably well known to you—a brother—can present difficulties. The article illustrates that outlining is not merely the arrangement of the simple, but rather the analysis of the complex. Compare the article with the outlining approach above of My Summer Vacation, in this section.

6. Marion Marshall's "Helping Seventh Graders to Spot Plots" (*E. J.*, Nov. 1958, p. 507) is mistitled. *Spot* should be *Spin*. However, two points are made which bear upon material in this chapter. First, theme topics require much pinpointing. Second, you yourself should write and not merely assign writing for others to do.

7. Don M. Wolfe's "Fruitful Long Paper: The Autobiography" (*E. J.*, Jan. 1956, p. 7) offers some approaches to narrowing down composition topics, to making them more manipulable, and to helping students define topics more analytically, for easier handling.

Some Painful Truths

Let us now be realistic. The best way for students to write effectively is for them to write regularly and often. But every paper written requires that you react. This, however, takes time. Behold the bottleneck! You do not assign the composition work that students should be doing because reading, correcting, reacting to, and grading compositions take time. Students should have dozens of writing experiences a term, but have you the time or strength to handle this flood?

If your lack of time is the bottleneck, what can be done? Of what good are our fine words about composition, decomposition, editing, revision, and outlining, when you cannot grade more than five or six papers per student per term? What's that buzzing in your ear about teacher aides hired to correct papers?

An English teacher, Eric Johnson, reported in *English Journal:*

> Any teacher of English understands that to teach writing and remain sane and healthy, he must constantly compromise; he cannot do everything he knows should be done, and what he does often has to be done only half as well as he could do it if he had unlimited time or a student load of twenty instead of 125. Nothing could be worse than for us to lead a joyless, paper-filled life, conscientiously dealing with every comma on every paper and resenting the casual way the pupils ignore the results of our slaving. We must have time to read, relax, and recreate, and therefore, we must boldly cut corners where we can. Here are some time-savers. . . . I take in the papers at the end of the class and later quietly throw them away. I think this is perfectly moral if not done too often or with papers on which the students have spent much effort.[5]

A sad, sad statement and an honest one.

Some teachers and teacher organizations oppose the use of teacher aides, or teacher assistants, now being tried in some schools. Favorable reports are beginning to come in from administrators and teachers.[6] These assistants are selected for competence in clerical work and in composition correction. But these supplements to your energies may not be available to you. What then?

You must get others to supplement your job requirements, or you must make use of technology. You are strongly urged to turn to student assistants at the very opening of the term. Supplement the diagnostic tests in grammar and spelling that you use to get the term's work going by a diagnostic composition. Having by class discussion intensified interest in an international, national, local, sports, or human-interest topic, assign a composition of 200 words. You will, naturally, save time by correction symbols (see p. 98), but you will also personalize the correction process by writing a few words of opinion on each paper, a matter of tremendous importance. Last, you will select the three or four best papers, meet with their writers separately, and designate them as your assistants. Once a week you will assign a composition topic. You will collect the papers and turn a half dozen or so over to each assistant for correction in spelling, grammar, punctuation, and sentence structure. Papers corrected by the student assistants will not be graded unless you go over the paper.

Technological devices offer another way of by-passing the bottleneck. The balopticon, opaque projector, and Vue-Graph make it possible to correct compositions on class time and with the class as witness to the surgery. The effect is impressive, somewhat like seeing an X-ray of yourself. If your school does not have this equipment at present, get the sales material from a nearby sales agent and put it on the desk of your department head or principal or person from whom all budgetary blessings flow. With these technological devices, you get an image of the student's composition on a screen or blackboard, visible simultaneously to the entire class, and thereafter you proceed to dissect the composition, with the class as witness. You will find it possible to correct ten or twelve compositions during a class period, if you move smartly along. This is not too big a dent in the volume, but your able student assistants will get an idea of what you want, and the saving in time thus becomes considerable. Naturally, in using these devices you will take precautions about the anonymity of the student whose paper is being publicly corrected. Use a scissors, or black out the name.

This public display takes precedence over the practice of having students read their compositions to the class. The correlative practice of having other students criticize the compositions has its dangers. The frequent degeneration into destructive critical cannibalism, captiousness, carping, and petty sniping at the unimportant is bad. Students must be taught how to criticize, and they are best taught by operating along one dimension at a time. When the student has offered his sacrifice, you may say, "Now let's state the same thing, but in fewer words. Will you read the first sentence again?" Thereafter call on students to shorten the sentence, nothing more. The possibilities for doing so are presented and considered, and the class goes on to the next sentence, thus criticizing one aspect of the

Correction Symbols *

Symbol	Meaning
agr	agreement
amb	ambiguous
ant	antecedent
awk	awkward
cap(s)	capital letter(s)
cl	lacks clarity
coord	faulty coordination
cs	comma splice
d	faulty diction
del	omit
dmod	dangling modifier
frag	fragmentary element
g,gd	good
illog	illogical
lc	lower case (not capital) letters
n	wrong number
nc	no capital
np	no punctuation
npar	no paragraph
o	omit
p	faulty punctuation
red	redundant
ref	faulty reference
ros	run-on sentence
s	faulty sentence construction
sp	spelling error
stet	restore deleted words
ww	wrong word
¶	new paragraph needed
no ¶	no paragraph needed
?	unclear

* There are many other correction symbols, but these are the ones most commonly used and most convenient.

composition at a time, using marksmanship rather than a shotgun. You also by-pass the jaundiced, the wise-guy, or the apple-polisher who contributes, "He said 'wuz' and shoulda said 'was,'" and thus compounds the felony by adding his own errors in the act of correction. Student criticism is desirable, but it should be serious and responsible.

In schools where there are students for whom English is a second language, like the New York high schools, a buddy system is set up, in which a Puerto Rican newcomer is paired with a classmate who has achieved mastery in composition and language skills. The classmate helps his buddy in assignments, and compositions are sometimes done jointly until the newcomer is able to take off on his own. This buddy system can be adapted for pairing good and poor writers.

The perceptive reader—you, it is hoped—will have noticed some contradictions in the advice and suggestions offered here. If students are reluctant to talk about themselves, as you were told earlier, does not the approach recommended in this chapter tend to probe unduly into interests, attitudes, needs, and aims—areas of very great privacy? Agreed. It does so for greater student competence within and with himself. Involved are the publicly personal, the privately personal, and timing, because what is intrusive at the beginning of the term is permissible at the end.

Thus, a well-known and widely used educational film on classroom methods shows a young, comely teacher meeting her class for the first day. She smiles at the class—a dubious procedure because one doesn't smile at strangers—and requests that the students arise and introduce themselves to the class, telling their names, their interests, and their backgrounds. Methods films are not distinguished for realism. One does not ask strangers to reveal so much of themselves. In many classes such conduct at the initial meeting of the class will lay an egg as often as not, because this recommendation to the beginning teacher is strictly for the birds, who are oviparous, but is not for you.

The new teacher, on first meeting a class, should be courteous but not friendly, and certainly not ingratiating. These students are strangers to you and you are one to them. Be aloof, but not remote; interested, but not involved; flexible, but not flaccid. You do not gush with strangers and you should not expect them to confide in you. Your students are assessing you, the first few days, and you ought to be coolly assessing them too. Confidences can come later, after you know one another. Do not

cheapen the regard in which you are held by prematurely thrusting yourself forward. You do not offer friendship to everybody you meet. Perhaps
friendliness or, better yet, interest—but not friendship. This is precious,
takes time to achieve, and must be earned. At first contact students are
reluctant to talk about themselves—and they are right. Personal background, at this point in your relationship, is none of the teacher's business,
and you should be particularly careful about requesting students to
divulge anything of a personal nature—even hobbies—before the class.

On the other hand, you may be an experienced teacher who has been
in the school four, five, or more years. The student underground has trans-
mitted all the scuttlebutt on you, so that students know of you before they
first set foot in your room. The rumors and gossip about you have gotten
around. You can afford to be warmer, more intrusive in your assignments,
and you can relax more readily. You're known.

Even with the new teacher, however, after formality has been established
and some weeks have passed, there comes a time when it is perfectly appropriate to assign topics like:

> If you had your life to live over again, you would . . .
> Your parents, as compared with your friends, are . . .
> (I) (My friends) need (my friends) (me) more than (they) (I) need
> (me) (them), because . . .

More important than topics assigned is the esteem you have gained.
Topics will be successful to the extent that you establish yourself in the
eyes of your students. A teacher who is foolish will not do well with the
best of topics. But if you, as the weeks pass, confirm in your students the
feeling that you make sense, that you are mature, that you are a sound
person, then you will get outpourings that ring with sincerity and effort,
despite the misspellings, sentence fragments, and punctuation errors. For
correction of such mechanical errors see the time-saving suggestions on
page 98. Composition and expression, however, transcend the attainment
of minimum essentials in the mechanics. They involve the pursuit of ideas,
the joy in words, the sense of form. These can be taught only if you are
the kind of teacher who can kindle students.

This brings us to you.

Research, Resources, and Techniques

1. In reading the discussion on use of teacher aides below, remember that some people are opposed lest the aide encroach on the teaching function. Do you agree? Do you think that the presence of a nurse augments or lowers the status of the physician?

a. Paul B. Diederich's "The Rutgers Plan for Cutting Class Size in Two" (*E. J.*, April 1960, p. 229) is a tremendously important article on what is basically involved in readjustment of class size and in the use of teacher assistants—human and mechanical. A truly professional and practical article.

b. A piece in *The New York Times* for August 28, 1960, describes Diederich's "Rutgers Plan": (1) College-trained housewives are hired to correct compositions, enabling the teacher to assign weekly compositions without sacrificing his eyesight and sanity. The teacher continues to correct every fourth paper. (2) Each English teacher divides each class in half. Half the class spends two periods a week in a reading room, doing independent reading, and two hours in discussion sessions with the teacher. The fifth day in the teacher's week is devoted to individual conferences with students. On that day, all the students also take tests and work with "programed exercises" (sometimes called "teaching machines") on rules of grammar.

c. Sally van Schaick's "The Composition-Reading Machine" (*E. J.*, April 1960, p. 237) discusses the technical problems of setting up a teacher-aide program for composition reading, its benefits, hazards, and headaches. Note that those underprivileged communities that most need such a program will be least likely to find adequate aides! First, because of financial stringency and, second, because such communities will not have the trained, educated people required.

d. The November 1959 issue of *Atlantic Monthly* was devoted in part to the situation of the English teacher. One of the articles was Henry Chauncey's "The Plight of the English Teacher" (p. 122), which was a recommendation that teacher aides and lay readers be widely used in high school writing and composition programs.

2. Another way of reducing your work load in composition correction is by the use of students:

a. Loren V. Grissom's "Student Leadership in Evaluating Compositions" (*E. J.*, Sept. 1959, p. 338) shows how students correct the compositions of classmates before they are turned over to the teacher. Hence your students are your assistants.

b. Janet Emig's "We Are Trying Conferences" (*E. J.*, April 1960, p. 223) blueprints an individualized writing program for the college bound and tells how it was made possible by reducing class size and teaching load; in other words, give the teacher time to teach writing and writing will be taught.

c. Jane Z. Carroll's "A Plan for Meeting Individual Differences in Composition and Reading" (*E. J.,* Nov. 1959, p. 466) discloses some techniques in drilling students in correcting composition errors. Required is a stock of remedial materials, which the author calls her "drug store."

3. See Howard E. Blake's *Class Size* (unpublished doctoral dissertation; Columbia University, 1955) for research here.

Below-the-Skin Diving

Some students have ideas, others not, but all students experience emotive states and feelings. Ideas require time for emergence and statement. Again, the difference between the able student and the poorer one is the time required for feeling states to emerge as ideas. Furthermore, this emergence is not comfortable and, with the slower student, can be painful and psychologically difficult, as it can for the bright, emotionally tied-up youngster.

The student must be taught to dive within his skin—another kind of skin-diving—to fetch among feeling states and emerge with ideas. The chief requirement here is imposed upon the teacher, not upon the student. Students, if without mental defect, can do this fetching if you have faith in their resources and determination enough to drive them to do the underwater exploration among these resources. The pursuit of ideas and the sifting of feeling states must be done under your direction. You must know in what directions to send them. With the burden of proof on you for this development of ideas, what kind of person must you be?

We have said little so far about teacher quality, but this consideration is imperative in the teaching of composition and expression. The mental hygiene of the teacher is not a primary consideration in most areas of English teaching, at least not more so than with your colleagues in mathematics, science, foreign language, or social studies. Nor is it particularly crucial in teaching usage or spelling, though even here it is an asset. Your mental health emerges with greater importance in the teaching of literature and is absolutely indispensable in the effective, as contrasted with the routine, teaching of composition and expression.

You must yourself have experience with yourself before you can justifiably expect such inner experiences in your students. You too must be sensitive to the forces that have made you what you are, and if you assign a composition on some autobiographical matter, you must guard against presumptuous intrusions by having had recent experiences of your own with some autobiographical skin-diving into yourself. Have you done so? If not, do not compel your students. With perhaps little recent occasion to write to a friend, what have you written of late to yourself? Unless you have had reason to write, why should you compel your students to? Every day, every period, experiences accumulate and slip by, forever lost to memory or to fruitful use, unless reduced to paper. What anecdotal records have you kept, what diary, what autobiographical data have you organized that you require your students to? Have you recapitulated "How I Enjoyed My Summer Vacation" that you should ask your students to? Have you a hobby and have you described it to yourself? If not, you are a fraud to force on the young and helpless what you do not demand of yourself. Only the teacher with writing experience can instruct in writing. All others are traveling under false passports.

Have you considered if *you* rushed or sauntered to school this morning and why? You'd better, else the suggestions in this and any other book on methods and every volume in *English Journal* and *Scholastic* ever printed will be no good. You will remain as stilted and as artificial as before. You too must write and on topics similar to those you assign, you must organize paragraphs of your own, and you must sit and think about what is going on in your soul. You must try on yourself what pages 84, 91, and 95 suggest you try on students. You must practice composing ideas and expressing them.

Many things happen thereby. You are brought closer to creativity and to students, and they are brought into more understandable range. Somehow, also, you simultaneously find yourself less grudging of the time spent and energy expended in correction of their compositions. Do you want them to write often and well? Do you likewise.

You are, provided you are a person of breadth and understanding, in a strong position to have students come to you and reveal themselves, their hopes, curiosities, doubts, and convictions. To repeat, this does not mean that students are ready to talk, even about matters close to them. Indeed, here they may be most reluctant; shyness may get in the way, stubbornness, or a staunch refusal to allow you to invade their privacy. Nor should you invite yourself into these areas without permission. Such prying can become dangerous. Generally, the English teacher does not have the training, background, or experience to handle the seething volcanoes lying around and should avoid unloosing them.

On the other hand, the student has a wealth of experiences that have a valuable place in the classroom. How can the student become involved enough to adduce these experiences in no trivial way, but meaningfully, without prying, while you elicit significant participation? This way:

The matters that affect us are less private than they seem. If we are in love, we seem uniquely so, in a way nobody has been before. If we know joy or hate, are moved to tears or laughter, the experiences are not sensed as a state all humanity knows but an enclosed universe in which we alone dwell. Do we feel these experiences more richly and intensely because they are so individuated? Or does the individuation warp and diminish emotive sensitivity? (Hysteria and aberration are not defined as emotion here, but as the ways of error in which emotion sometimes goes.) Emotion is enriched when seen as a common experience, even though intimately and personally felt. Perhaps, indeed, emotion becomes deeper and truer if, as one teacher said to her class, "What makes you think you are an exception?"

CASE STUDY 7 Because of illness the regular teacher had been absent for almost a month and the class covered by a substitute, a pretty, giggling, and inexperienced young woman. When the regular teacher returned, the class had lost all discipline. The teacher soon restored order. The substitute secured another assignment in the school, and the regular teacher conferred with her about the work covered. During the conference the substitute said, in a compound of silly giggles and vanity, "One of the boys telephoned me for a date. It was after you returned. I should have punished him otherwise."

The teacher said pleasantly, "I can't blame him for trying."

"The surprising thing was he was one of the quieter ones. He never gave me any trouble." The regular teacher was curious about the student's identity, but he wondered why the substitute hadn't hung up at once before engaging in this kind of flirtation or else put the telephone call on another level. "First he didn't want to give me his name, but then I teased it out of him, before I turned him down." Then she mentioned the boy's name. The teacher was troubled. The boy was a sensitive, conscientious, and shy student.

The next day, in class, the teacher said: "I've got something to say to a few of you." The class looked up, wondering. "I'm not mentioning names." A quick buzz began, to be as quickly stopped by interested class members. "Some of you know whom I'm talking about. The others can listen and guess if they want to. When students walk into a class, they don't walk in alone. They bring their parents, their brothers and sisters, the things they did they shouldn't, what they admire about their parents and what they hate, a father who spends his salary Saturday nights at a bar, a mother who scolds without stopping, or a family that is happy and getting along the way families should. When a student walks into a class, there are really two students, one that you see and one that's hidden. What do I mean by that? Can you explain?"

Hands went up. Discussion grew more eager, almost incandescent. The teacher resumed:

"I'm not talking about one student," he lied, forgivably, "but about a half dozen who've been on the telephone, when they shouldn't. These students behaved foolishly. They thought they were three or four years older than they were. Instead, they were that much younger. Why is it, when we try to be older and more grown up than we truly are, when we jump the gun on our years, we only grow in the infantile direction?"

Again hands went up. Discussion was more good humored, less incandescent, though students were burningly curious about what had happened and who was concerned. The one culprit involved did not participate in the talk, which ranged over good judgment, the need to be older, and the point the teacher was chiefly interested in, the typicalness of such behavior among adolescents. He continued:

"People don't always know what's bothering them. Sometimes they don't know how to know. Those half-dozen students who shouldn't have telephoned didn't know either and didn't know others had telephoned too! Each thought he was the only one. We feel we're the only ones who get certain ideas, or have certain emotions, and that nobody else does. Why?"

Students disagreed with the teacher. They felt they shared ideas, feelings, preferences, and aversions, with their contemporaries. By now the class was consumed with curiosity, and resentments were arising that the teacher had told so much without saying more, but the teacher had an audience of one particularly in mind.

"I can't mention names. They're not important anyhow. What's important is the poem I'm going to read. It tells you everything I could say. It's Yeats' 'Down by the Salley Gardens' and it's why you shouldn't telephone until you're old enough," and he read:

> Down by the salley gardens my love and I did meet;
> She passed the salley gardens with little snow-white feet.
> She bid me take love easy, as the leaves grow on the tree;
> But I, being young and foolish, with her would not agree.
>
> In a field by the river my love and I did stand,
> And on my leaning shoulder she laid her snow-white hand.
> She bid me take life easy, as the grass grows on the weirs;
> But I was young and foolish, and now am full of tears.

The teacher looked up from his reading. "How would you explain 'take love easy' and 'take life easy'?" There was some preliminary fidgeting and the hands went up, the culprit's among them. The teacher looked around, shook his head, and said (quitting when he was ahead!), "No time for full discussion. Put your ideas down on paper, in a composition, and we'll have the compositions read to the class."

The papers were interesting. The culprit's was excellent, in accordance with his usual performance. He made no reference to his telephone call, but thereafter, for the remainder of the term, he was no longer shy and the painful sensitivity in him disappeared. Indeed, he became more companionable with the more aggressive boys in the class, as if he wanted to find out who his companions in crime had been!

Research, Resources, and Techniques

1. For an ingenious, original, and easily done idea, see how John Sanders combines free association with a class newspaper in his "Begin a Theme with Proust" (*E. J.*, Nov. 1956, p. 488).

2. How the analysis of inner experience makes external expression less stilted, more interesting, less forced, and more stimulating to read and write is discussed by Robert Lambert and Dorothy Mack in "Anecdotal Autobiographies" (*E. J.*, Dec. 1959, p. 528).

3. Carl G. Wannberger's "They All Can Learn to Write" (*E. J.*, Nov. 1956, p. 455) points out the primary importance of the accepting teacher: ". . . I had really done nothing at all. I hadn't even suggested that anyone write poetry and I certainly gave no marks or credits. I had merely kept the kind of class in which it was possible for a football captain to

write poetry without being laughed at." Read also in this article what is said about teachers who never write themselves: "It is obvious that such persons cannot teach composition." An excellent, outstanding, realistic, honest contribution.

The Committee Report

Until now we have been talking about the individual composition and individual expression. Now consider group work in composition and expression.

Research in social psychology and group dynamics reveals that people will work with improved effectiveness if they feel their efforts backed up by those around them. Improved output is an outcome of such group morale. For this reason group reports sometimes succeed in pulling the reluctant writer into activity that would terrify him if he were solely responsible for the assignment. Collaborative writing efforts are familiar to your students. They see them in newspaper coverage of a World Series, where different reporters write on different aspects of the event, or in an opera opening, or in coverage of a national election. Much can be learned from collaborative composition work, not least of which is that every group has at least one free-loader who will depend on others to get his work done for him. Aside from this major peril to group cohesiveness, groups learn how to take a general assignment, break it down to its constituents, assign specific responsibility for research and writing, and combine the parts with whatever logic the assignment requires. Some rather impressive writing can be done this way, so impressive that the technique has important public relations aspects. That classic French movie, *Passion for Life,* shows how a class in a collaborative writing effort turned a sleepy French town upside down. Although later, in the chapter on the teaching of narrative, we shall deplore the dilution of English by social studies considerations in core, we say here that, in the collaborative composition, units with social studies are truly enriching and immeasurably broaden the opportunities for themes, compositions, and essays.

The mechanics of the collaborative effort are not too complex. Class committees are set up. Chairmen for each committee have responsibility for final synthesis of individual efforts, for a unified group contribution, and committees are set in competition. One elementary precaution. The make-up of each group must be representative of low, middle, and high achievement students. The chairmen should be the best people in the class. Within each committee collaboration and co-operation should rule. Between committees competition rules.

Resources are numerous. Thus, you can administer the following questionnaire to the class and have different committees support different points of view. Note that this is an adaptation of the Kuder Interest Inventory, not originally intended for group composition work, but well suited for such use:

Select *one and one only* of the choices in each group. Put a circle around the letter of your choice, and discuss with your group how each of the options selected should be answered. Then proceed to organize your answers.

I WOULD PREFER TO:

1. (a) have a few good friends and acquaintances; (b) know a lot of interesting people; (c) take care of my family and not bother with other people.

2. (a) have many friends; (b) have a big family; (c) have an important job.

3. (a) be independent; (b) be clever; (c) be sympathetic.

4. (a) play cards; (b) go to a big party; (c) go to the movies.

5. (a) be comfortable when I get dressed up; (b) be neat when I get dressed up; (c) have people make favorable comments when I get dressed up.

6. (a) associate with average people; (b) associate with unusual people; (c) associate with carefree people who have fun.

7. (a) go to an interesting party with strangers; (b) go to a familiar party with friends.

8. (a) have people treat me as a comrade; (b) have people look up to me; (c) have people pay no attention to me.

9. (a) have work I like with low pay; (b) have work I don't like with high pay; (c) have an easy job with good pay.

10. (a) show up an enemy; (b) show up a show-off; (c) pacify an argument.

11. (a) be friendly; (b) be important; (c) be famous.

12. (a) carry an argument through to the finish; (b) tell a person why I disagree but not argue about it; (c) change the argument when people don't agree with me.

13. (a) say what I think even if it's unpleasant; (b) say something nice to a person even if I don't like what he has done; (c) not tell a person what I think if it is unpleasant.

14. (a) avoid a person who has hurt my feelings; (b) have it out when a person has hurt my feelings; (c) act as though nothing has happened with a person who has hurt my feelings.

15. (a) have my picture in the paper with a friend; (b) have my

picture in the paper with a famous person; (c) have my picture in the paper alone.

16. (a) be a modest person; (b) be a person who stands up for his rights; (c) advise people on what to do.

Set up committees to defend one of the points of view against those of contending committees. Here is another simple example of collaborative composition work:

Check one of the following and give reasons for your choice:

1. It is right for men to spend more money on clothes than women do. Yes . . . No . . . Why? . . .

2. When meeting people, it is better for a man to feel well-dressed than to feel comfortable. Yes . . . No . . . Why? . . .

3. When I get dressed up, I feel more comfortable . . . conspicuous . . . Why? . . .

4. The man who takes care of himself likes to dress well . . . comfortably. . . .

More complicated endeavors in collaborative composition writing can be adapted from sources like Celia B. Stendler's *Field Projects and Problems:*[7]

1. To which of these experiences would you expose a six-year-old child? A twelve-year-old?

Seeing a dead person . . .

Attending a funeral . . .

Watching a mother nurse a baby . . .

Seeing a baby born . . .

Seeing a movie of a birth . . .

Watching baby animals being born . . .

2. Interview three of the people listed below. Ask each person what he considers the chief job and responsibility of people your age. Analyze the replies for agreements and possible conflicts.

Professional man

Businessman

White-collar worker

Skilled worker

Unskilled worker

Areas of agreement . . .

Areas of conflict . . .

3 a. Mary's father had been out of work for some time and there had been no money to buy lunches at school. One day she helped herself to a quarter on a neighbor's desk at school. She remembered how much she needed money and thought it would be all right.

3 b. John's father was very poor and John had no money for school supplies. One day when he was in the Western Union Telegraph Company, where he worked after school, he saw the cash box out on the desk and helped himself to fifty cents. He figured he needed it so much it was all right.

Who did the worse thing, Mary or John? Why do you think so?

4 a. Harry was the last one getting dressed after gym one day and noticed a pair of tennis shoes hanging out of one of the lockers. There was no one around and so he helped himself to them. He knew most tennis shoes looked alike and that he could get away with them.

4 b. Donald worked after school for a large corporation where rubber shoes were made. One night when it was quitting time he slipped a pair of rubber shoes into his jacket. He knew he would be safe in doing this for no one had seen him.

Who did the worse thing, Harry or Donald? Why do you think so?

[*Note to the teacher:* if, for rubber shoes, you substitute carpet slippers, do you think you would get a different set of responses?]

5. In her first teaching job, Miss O'Rourke finds herself in an elementary school in a slum district of one of our large cities. There her middle-class values receive quite a blow. The children's language on the playground is racy and blasphemous; she overhears two first-graders talking together over toy telephones, using a vocabulary liberally sprinkled with vulgar and profane words. In the toilet rooms, the children help themselves to paper towels with abandon, showing no regard for the sign which admonishes them to use only one to dry their hands. They write on the school building and show disregard for public property in other ways.

Miss O'Rourke, however, does not take measures to correct these behaviors. "I don't believe in inflicting middle-class mores on these children," she says. "And besides, I don't want to appear to be criticizing their parents by telling my class that nice people don't behave that way. Most of these are only surface behaviors. I want to build more fundamental values."

Do you agree with Miss O'Rourke's decision? Why or why not? If you do not, outline a plan for changing children's behavior. What methods would you use with third-graders? With ninth-graders? Write your answers:

I think Miss O'Rourke is (right) (wrong) for the following reasons . . .

To change the third-grader's behavior, I would use these methods . . .

To change the ninth-grader's behavior, I would use these methods . . .

6. The accusation is sometimes made that the schools contribute to delinquency. The schools are too easy, it is claimed; if they would "use the rod" more frequently, children would learn that they can't get away with wrongdoing. Write a paragraph defending or attacking this theory.

Might the statement ever be true that an individual teacher or a school contributes to delinquency?

Lack of discipline in the modern school contributes to delinquency by . . .

Do the schools contribute in any way to delinquency? . . .

7. Below are listed some traditional beliefs that you have undoubtedly heard expressed by many Americans. Discuss the conflicting beliefs:

The government should stay out of the business of making and supplying electric power, but . . .

The farmer should have his just share of the national income, but . . .

We should have lower import duties in order to foster better international relations, but . . .

Other resource materials for the collaborative composition can be found in Paul Mort and William Vincent's *Modern Educational Practice*[8] and by the Citizenship Education Project of Teachers College, Columbia University, especially in the Project's Practice Resource Box and its *Hours on Freedom* series.[9] Generally, such resources have debatable aspects that enable you to pit one student committee against another. Careful reading of newspapers or magazines will enable you to accumulate additional materials without too much trouble.

Research, Resources, and Techniques

1. William G. Fidone's "The Theme's the Thing" (*E. J.*, Dec. 1959, p. 518) offers a variety of reading lists based on the common theme approach, including fiction, biography, and nonfiction.

2. Virginia Alwin's "Developing a Unit" (*E. J.*, Sept. 1959, p. 315) elaborates practicably on the work done in a class on the theme "Disaster." So well presented is the material that it's ready to use by you with minimum adaptation. The author warns that you must make sure that relationships to the central theme, from various student contributions, must be checked and maintained. "Recognizing such relationships . . . must be planned for." And this takes time.

3. Emily Betts Gregory's prize-winning "Managing Student Writing" (*E. J.*, Jan. 1955, p. 18) requires that twenty per cent of class meeting time be turned over to writing. Do you think this excessive? Very important is her discussion on assignment to student committees of the task of correction and how this, in turn, spared the teacher time and energy, thus making it possible for students to write more.

The Letter

Though among the dullest things in the world, the block form of the business letter and the indented form of the friendly letter, when placed in the historical framework of the typewriter, become interesting matters for class discussion.

Why do you head a business letter in block form

> 3523 Third Avenue
> Cleveland 33, Ohio
> January 19, 1960

and a friendly letter in indented form

> 3523 Third Avenue
> Cleveland 33, Ohio
> January 19, 1960

and what is the connection of block and indented form with typewriting and handwriting?

Have your class discuss why, at one time, before the use of the typewriter, the indented form was correct both for business and friendly letters. (Some people still prefer it for handwritten letters.) Can the class see why the typewriter's tabulator key changed the form of the heading?

Those students who have had contact with a typewriter should be able to reason out the relationship of tabulator key to change in acceptable form for a letter heading. The tabulator key, which made it possible to begin the next line directly and precisely underneath, introduced a new esthetic into letter writing, the block form, which now prevails in all typed letters, business or friendly. The block form is sensible, efficient, and easy to use in typed letters, just as the indented form disguises imprecision in spacing in handwritten letters, which is why it is preferred by some people.

Similarly, ask students why printed letterheads, now available for personal letter use in many stationery stores, dictate that date should follow address and not precede it. The printed letterhead makes it possible to begin with the date.

Why is there no punctuation at the end of lines until we come to the end of the salutation? Because the end of each line is signal enough, is it not?

3523 Third Avenue
Cleveland 33, Ohio
January 19, 1960

Mr. Olin Jones
The Jones Hat Company
538 Smith Street
New York 17, New York

Dear Mr. Jones:

We avoid abbreviation. In the business letter, form follows function, but business firms have their own slight variants, to avoid empty, meaningless custom. Thus the letter of application for employment, so sedulously taught to your students, is replaced in many firms by the résumé, a compact statement that describes the applicant in bill-poster style:

> *Name:* Frank Young
> *Address:* 3523 Third Avenue, Cleveland 33, Ohio.
> *Birth:* Akron, Ohio. May 11, 1940
> *Marital Status:* Single. Living at home with parents.
> *Telephone Number:* WOrth 7-6670
> *Education:* Graduated Patrick Junior High School, June 1954. Awarded medal for proficiency in history. Graduated Fredericks High School, January 1958. Editor school newspaper; vice-president Arista; school honor roll. Currently attending Cleveland College at night, majoring in accounting.
> *Employment History:* Assistant to manager, Economart Stores, February 1958-date. Present salary $4500 yearly. Duties include correspondence, sales supervision, and merchandising.
> *Reasons for Seeking Change:* Interested in wider opportunities in marketing and advertising, where my writing ability and merchandising experience can be more effectively utilized.

Deplore it as you will, but picking up the telephone is easier than writing a letter. A student teacher, in trying to motivate the writing of the friendly letter, once asked a class: "If you were in the hospital, would you prefer to get a letter from your friends or would you prefer to get a telephone call?" The class unanimously voted for the telephone call, and that ended that. Many of the class declared that they would even prefer a printed, commercial get-well card.

Correct letter form, handwritten or typed, business or friendly, is easy; it's rote. What is hard is knowing what to say between the salutation and the complimentary close. Indeed, why write unless you have something to say? How frequently do *you* have occasion to write the friendly letter? Naturally, if the telephone had never been invented we'd all be writing more often than we do, and so would your students, and thereafter the letter-writing assignment would seem more realistic to them.

Yet the letter has something precious about it; thus people keep old letters. It perpetuates the moments that slip so quickly by. Letters that are years old recapture for us the feelings and emotions we once felt. Do your students have such experiences that they'd like to look back on, that they'd like to remember three, five, and ten years from now? Are they too self-conscious and embarrassed to tell their friends about this in a friendly letter? If so, why not write the friendly letter to a complete stranger? Who can the stranger be? What about the star in the film your student saw that moved him to tears, or caused him to laugh as he never had before?

The fan letter offers the opportunity for frankness in expression and spares the student the risks that his friends may pull his sentiments to pieces. With the knowledge that only the teacher and the person to whom the fan letter is written—or the person's secretary—will ever see the letter, your students will turn in some amazingly honest reactions and perceptions. After you correct the letters and return them, there is no reason why the student should not keep a corrected copy for himself and mail off the corrected original to the addressee. Allow the student to say whatever he wishes, as long as it is coherent and in good taste. Will there be replies? Certainly. This is how fan clubs flourish.

Furthermore, it's good practice for learning how to write the political letter to senators, congressmen, and other legislators. Here again you can anticipate replies from the mightiest in the land, because a citizen's letter is a highly important matter to sapient politicians.

Research, Resources, and Techniques

1. Harry Shefter's *Guide to Better Compositions* (Washington Square Press, paper, 1960) has an excellent section on the letter; matters of form and content are treated clearly and explicitly. Shefter prefers the block form for friendly and business letters. Other authorities prefer the indented form for the friendly letter and the block form for the business letter, because a plumb line cannot be drawn for the handwritten letter, but the tabulator key on the typewritten business letter does so. With this exception, the chapter on the letter in the Shefter book is heartily recommended.

2. Sir Ernest Gowers' *The Complete Plain Words* (London, Her Maj-

esty's Stationery Office, 1954) has excellent material on false standards in letter writing.

Discipline, Task Therapy, and Classroom Writing

This section is specifically aimed at the new teacher.

In addition to matters discussed earlier, the composition may be regarded as a disciplinary technique. Composition work is a constructive, positive means of maintaining classroom control and of helping students learn self-control. This use of composition should begin within the first days of the term, particularly with the new and inexperienced teacher.

New teachers take heed. What follows is of importance. Early in your contact with your classes assign a writing exercise done on *uniform* theme paper. The uniform theme paper sold by the National Council of Teachers of English may be worth the slight additional expense because, even if not formidable, it is more formal in appearance than the usual kind of theme paper. It looks as if it means business. Having the writing done in class may also, initially, furnish more formal, disciplined auspices than the composition assigned to be done at home.

Correct the papers within the next day or two. Comment objectively and constructively, almost as if you were chatting with the author, enter the grades, and return the papers. At once start a discussion that will set the stage for the next assignment, this one to be done at home and to be turned in as soon as the class schedule permits. After you collect this second set of papers, repeat the process of correcting objectively and constructively, commenting fully, and getting the papers back to the class within a day or two.

You will find this correction an arduous job, but, if you want to retain control, you have little choice. As an inexperienced person you are fair game. If you want to retain the control of the class, that means composure within yourself, and you must work for it, work that sets up feedbacks to the class. The class wants to know what you think. The correction process is the feedback that lets the class know. This knowledge is the basis for the inner discipline you aim for. If you feed back in this way, your class will not groan when you assign themes and compositions but will write in eager anticipation of what you will have to say. Students will write without complaint if you correct as immediately, as fully, as objectively, and as constructively as you can. You may, meanwhile, become half-blind and lose sleep, but you will have surmounted the chief terror of the new teacher; you will have your class under control. The blindness will be temporary and the fatigue bearable because the satisfaction of control will be more than adequate compensation.

Students, like all authors, get much satisfaction from the feeling of an audience reacting. Make yourself fully available as audience to them. In this sense, composition is indeed composing.

You will find students who will never learn how to write. Their writing may be sincere, heartfelt, and feeling, like the letters in Nathanael West's *Miss Lonelyhearts,* but stilted in expression, infantile in style, and awkward in manner. This fact does not diminish your responsibilities to feed back in the correction process we have described, because something more dominating than a finished composition is involved—the feeling that you are listening and that you are there. If competence in expression will never be gained by these limited students, self-assurance will. Therefore when you, in despair, return composition after composition in which the same errors, inelegancies, and gaucheries persist no matter how often you have corrected them, remember that more important business is being transacted. You are encouraging students to speak their piece and their minds, something far preferable to muteness or acquiescent silence.

Most students, however, can improve considerably if opportunity for writing is given, if you feed back in the correction process, and if you teach them sensitiveness to expression in poetry, on the sports page, on television, in newspaper headlines, and in fashion advertising copy. This is in addition to the models found in Shakespeare or in the narrative the class may be reading.

By this time, perhaps, your eyes have given out. You are spending weekends and evenings in correction. You are irritable. You have had it, and more, in spades. Your classes are writing, enjoying it, and draining your last strength. The growth of eagerness to communicate makes you grateful, but debilitated. How long, you want to know, must this hell continue?

Now comes the time for students to learn how to edit their work without you. As usual, you start discussion and assign the relevant topics. On the appointed day work is brought in and put on their desks, but—and here is the switch—you do not order the papers sent forward. Instead, you tell them to correct their papers themselves, according to the editing process they should by this time have learned from you. They are to view the papers with as critical an editing eye as they have learned to expect from you.

Give them five or ten minutes for this editing job. Then have students exchange papers, to see what neighbors can pick up that may have escaped. Have papers sent on to another neighbor, who will in turn scrutinize the paper for needed corrections. Then have the papers returned to the writers.

Do you collect them? No. Do you grade them? No. Then what is the point? Simply, to get yourself out of the student's way at last, just as you want him out of your sore and battered eyes. You both have by this time had enough of each other. You have sufficient grades on composition entered. He has learned all he can from you and your particular feedback. From now on he should be writing for himself and for others, but no longer for you. Give him every opportunity to write and have others feed back, but remove yourself from the communication network. Students may want to know why you continue giving writing assignments if you don't intend correcting and grading them and you must be persuasive that not you or your corrections or your grades constitute the *raison d'être* of their writing. What is most important is their getting into the habit of expressing themselves with words on paper so that they can become more competent with words and with themselves. Your grades and corrections are only way-stations to this outcome.

Have each student maintain a folder file of compositions. Continue to check these, as assigned, even though you are no longer actively correcting. You may even say that the compositions, though no longer corrected and graded, will be considered in case you have doubts about final grades.

Finally, at this stage, your class can move on to higher levels of student writing by issuing a class newspaper.

The class newspaper, as a terminal endeavor, spares your eyes but involves you in greater generalship. Your judgment will be needed more than ever, but the brute low-level work of correction and grading will be spared you. From their folders students will select the one composition that they deem most satisfactory. This composition will be turned over to the typewriting committee, those half-dozen or more students who can peck at a typewriter with fair accuracy, whether with ten fingers or two. Have available and ready mimeograph stencils, correction fluid, styluses, and templates, which these students will need. Assign an artist to each typist and then show the principles of interesting and attractive page layout.

A letter count of each composition, with the information on the stencil as to line length and type size, allows students to determine heads, captions, spacing, placing, and the area to be allotted to the accompanying art work. Use second-sheets to rough up layout. Make sure that each composition is given a by-line. Run off not less than five mimeographed copies per student. You will see why when the finished, stapled copies of the class newspaper (or you can call it a class magazine) are distributed. "Lookit! My name!" Be indulgent about the tremendous pleasure your students will get from seeing their names there for the world, or at least their families and friends, to see. Such a small thing and yet so contributory to student *élan!*

Research, Resources, and Techniques

1. Write the A. B. Dick Company (they are the manufacturers of mimeographing materials) for material on the publication of class newspapers.

2. Louis Zahner's article in *Atlantic Monthly* (Nov. 1959, p. 114), "Composition at the Barricades," deals with the difficulties—some insuperable—of preparing students adequately in expression and composition, and with the primacy of thoughts over words.

3. Elizabeth R. Barlow's unpublished doctoral dissertation, *Improving Sentence Patterns in Written Compositions in Grade Nine* (Boston University, 1955), may be of help to you.

4. In Inez Robb's article, "Price of Nonconformity," in the *New York World-Telegram* for June 20, 1960, some words of caution are offered, relevant to the topics you may assign. The article deals with a boy's rejection of graduation awards because he disapproved of the principles of the group making the awards, the American Legion, the recrimination to which he was subjected, and the way school authorities behaved under fire. Therefore use care in matching prize-seeking student compositions to prize-awarding sponsoring organizations. The article states in part: "What happens today when a youngster of 17, just about to grasp his high school diploma, stands on his own two feet and exercises the rugged individualism that youth is being urged to practice? He gets clobbered."

5. An indication that writing improvement is greatest when the teacher comments freely on student compositions and full feedback takes place is offered in Ellis Batten Page's "Teacher Comments and Student Performance" (*Journal of Educational Psychology,* Aug. 1958).

6. You will find some workable suggestions on how to stop yourself from going blind with composition correction and still have your students do a respectable amount of writing in William W. West's "How to Avoid Work" (*E. J.,* Dec. 1956, p. 537). Practical and useful ideas here.

7. More on the importance of feedback in composition correction is given in Katherine Keene's "Students Like Corrections" (*E. J.,* April 1956, p. 212). Students prefer having papers corrected to having them thrown in the wastebasket.

8. Even animal psychology proves that organisms, whether people or rats, prefer having notice taken of them to being ignored. The laboratory rat gives evidence that feedback in composition correction is important; if rats do better by being noticed than by being ignored, so do the human beings in your class. Seymour Levine's "Stimulation in Infancy" (*Scientific American,* May 1960, p. 81) states: "Both painful shocks and gentle handling enhance the development of normal stress responses in infant animals. The absence of such treatment leads to behavioral disorders when the animal matures. . . . We subjected a group of infant rats to mild electric shocks. . . . For control purposes we placed another group in the shock cage, but did not give them shocks. A third group of infant rats was left in the nest and not handled at all. We expected that the shocked rats would be affected and looked for emotional disorder when they reached adulthood. To our surprise it was the second control group—the group we had not handled at all—that behaved in a peculiar manner. The behavior of the shocked rats could not be distinguished from that of the control group which had experienced the same handling but no electric shock." Then would it not seem better to correct rigorously, even punishingly, than not to correct at all?

Stray Suggestions

1. Local and national organizations offer prizes for meritorious compositions on various subjects. When possible, integrate your composition program with such occasional opportunities. Your better students will like the feeling of competition. Poorer students will forget their inadequacies and will even think they have a fighting chance, especially if the rules of the contest permit a teacher to edit the student's original work. In the event of success, school authorities and the community will be pleased. In case of failure, no damaging consequences attend your effort.

2. You have seen "In twenty-five words or less, plus box-top . . ." contests. Do not be repelled by the crass commercialism. Where such box tops exist in the student's household, why not? But there is fun in adapting the technique to more direct classroom purposes. For example:

> In fifty words or more, write on:
> a. The television program for which I'd stay up late is . . .
> b. The last time I bought something advertised that I didn't need . . .
> c. I'd improve the car card bus advertising by . . .

d. I pay most attention to advertising on television . . . radio . . .
magazines . . . newspapers . . . when . . .
    e. I'm writing a fan letter to . . .

3. In a modification of Stevenson's "sedulous ape" technique, have students bring in a newspaper and read a national columnist's article in class. Have them put the papers aside and write a topic sentence that recapitulates the article. Then have them write a paragraph or two in which they restate the content, not in their own style but in the closest possible imitation of the original writer.

Research, Resources, and Techniques

1. Marc Raeff's "We Do Not Teach Them How to Think" (*The New York Times Magazine,* Jan. 26, 1958, p. 7) is a call for more rigorous instruction in the high school. Can composition and expression help in gaining this rigor? Does the essay examination offer a greater challenge than the objective type of examination? Which requires more organized thinking?

2. Here are two thoughtful contributions to the discussion in this chapter:
a. *The Elements of Style,* written by William Strunk, Jr., revised by E. B. White, and published by The Macmillan Company (1959), is terse and hard-hitting. It makes much of the virtues of brevity and how to achieve it.
b. Did you know that the educated have special kinds of usage errors? There is abusage on both sides of the intellectual tracks. Stuffiness in style is as troublesome as illiteracy. See Sir Ernest Gowers' *The Complete Plain Words* (London: Her Majesty's Stationery Office, 1954).

3. Arno Jewett's "Creative Activities for Observing the Lincoln Sesquicentennial" (*E. J.,* Jan. 1959, p. 26) shows how the past and present are combined to gain up-to-the-minute values; keep this article in mind when your students enter prize contests.

The Teaching of Reading

CHAPTER 4

Confessions of a Doctoral Candidate

Once a time came when circumstances caught up with me: I had guidance responsibilities, the loving care of the school newspaper, a full teaching program, and was further boxed in by examinations for my doctorate, ten days off. I told my departmental chairman that I would be out for the next few days, and why. The chairman regretfully pointed out that I could not get paid for the days out—Board of Education regulations—and suggested an alternative, that I come in, give my classes some busy work, and meanwhile sit at my desk preparing myself, and suffer no cut in pay.

The prospect was appalling. How keep classes going for a full week without giving them anything to do? Open revolution would greet the assignment of a week's worth of writing. A reading of textbooks? One period and they'd have had it. Give them free periods? There'd be whispering, mischief, scuffling, and the author would be unable to concentrate. "Nevertheless," the departmental chairman said gently, "they'll do better with you here than with a substitute." Settled.

What I needed was a week of quiet and peace, in which disciplinary problems would not emerge, students would be self-policing, and fidgeting young

121

people would not intrude on my preparations. How could matters be arranged? Seemingly, I hit upon some magic, a most unusual experience with one of the classes involved. This was a lower junior group, slower than my other classes, meeting the last period of the day and hence restless, when the sun shone in with a harsh, mid-afternoon glare, and the traffic noises seemed especially heavy. Shades could be drawn against the glare, but little could be done with the traffic.

The library had a good set of back issues of the *Saturday Evening Post, Reader's Digest, Popular Mechanics,* and other periodicals. I also had my own collection of paperbacks, short stories, and text editions of novels, essays, and plays in my class closet. The librarian had the periodicals carted in at the beginning of the week, and the stage was set with the periodicals and the contents of the class closet in full view.

To each class: "I've got some work to do this period and I'll be busy. Help yourself to one of the books in the closet, or one of the magazines, one row at a time. Read quietly at your seats and, when you are finished with one of the magazines or books, you may replace it for another." There was generally some fumbling and inability to come to a decision in some students, others indifferently took the first copy to come to hand, and rows were called up while one or two students from the previous row were still trying to make a selection, but by the time the last class of the day appeared the mechanics of distribution had been ironed out. Three or four piles of *Saturday Evening Post* were grouped, as were the other periodicals; there were twenty or more small piles of magazines on various surfaces of the room and students did not have to clump up by the half dozen in front of each pile, snatching and contending for a specific issue. The instructions to the last period class were the same, and they made their selections with no bickering, while I sat at my desk, my own task for the week in my hand, and watched until all selections had been made and all class members had returned to their seats with their choices.

I resumed my preparations. This was the class about which I had been most concerned. The reading level was low, and for the first few minutes students turned pages idly, yawned, and poked one another, while I doggedly read and took notes, determined that I would get my private headaches out of the way. Minutes passed and the sound of turning pages grew quieter. I was still determined that only a fire drill would cause me to abate my concentration. Now and then a student arose to exchange a periodical, but even this sound became progressively infrequent. When my teacher's instinct told me that the bell would sound in a minute, I looked up from my material and saw a class of adolescents reading in various postures, none of which would be recommended in any text on the teaching of reading, in light dimmed by shades drawn against the sun, and in a state of complete relaxation. I stared, quietly closing my own book, at the still-ness and the hush into which the bell shortly broke. Here and there a student slowly drew a deep breath, resumed normal posture, rubbed an eye or two, and looked around. Others kept on reading. Nobody bolted for the door. Some individuals arose, stretching, and ambled toward the pile of periodicals or the book closet. The others lethargically prepared to follow. A student asked if he could take his home; he wanted to finish it. Another had the same idea. Permission was granted provided that the material was returned before the first period next day. The class dribbled out of the room, unhurried.

They came in the day following to find the materials similarly distributed on various surfaces. I announced, "Help yourself the same as yesterday," and immediately turned to my own work. For several minutes there was bustling, to which I resolutely paid no attention, and again silence grad-ually descended. There was no squirming, no fidgeting. The class read, and read, and read. This class of slow readers, having no alternative outlet, was quiet and at peace with itself. The class had a greater than usual share of any reading disabilities you'd care to name—reversals, vision, intelligence level, emotional blocks—but there was ease and relaxation in looking at words that you did not understand, in fixating on a word not in your vocab-ulary, and in moving your lips even though it slowed down your reading. Nobody was asking you what the passage meant, or timing you, or asking you to look up the word in the dictionary, or testing you on comprehension. You weren't being bothered. You were in a haven, with nothing to do except sprawl comfortably, and there was no other way to keep busy except this.

The relaxation in them the fourth and fifth day was marvelous to behold, and a great help to the doctoral preparations. Some of them would come rushing along the corridor, excited and overstimulated, enter the room, see the materials racked up and ready, sigh a bit, and slow down perceptibly. No challenges here today, no threats, a period's worth of safety with something to read and nobody, no friends, no parents, no teacher, on your back. Incredible to report, the relaxation in them continued through the term. Did they become better readers? Not by any evidence I could gather.

My experience was similar in the other classes, though not as dramatic, for the other classes had always been brighter, more tractable, and more available to the written word. This class had a number of interpersonal and intergroup conflicts and there were ethnic difficulties, but these disappeared. Something seemed to have mesmerized them that week. They had been introduced to the possibilities of peace. And this is the description of an actual occurrence—when a class encountered words and found them good, because they were left alone with them.

I subsequently attempted to analyze the experience and concluded that I had accidentally stumbled on an important reason for reading, one that I had never come across in any of the texts, which say students should read to gain information, esthetic pleasure, understanding, insight, relaxation, and a sense of discrimination. All these reasons are valid but an important one is omitted. Reading helps us fall asleep. For many readers this purpose is paramount, accounting for the sale of bed lamps. Something in the students fell asleep, and had they fallen completely asleep I doubt that I would have recalled them to a waking state.

Ever since, I have been uneasy about the premise that the good reader not only reads rapidly but comprehends. Ease with the written word must first be engendered. If you can fall asleep in the face of a threat, you reduce the threat. If words are threatening, if anything helps you fall asleep in their presence, and if you are encouraged to fall asleep in their presence, ease develops when words stare back at you. Reading remediation texts are compulsive about the value of rapid reading and comprehension. They occasionally refer to the relaxation benefits of reading but never mention the ultimate in relaxation, how words can make your eyes grow heavy and send you off to dreamland.

However, administrators are not happy about having somnolence in a classroom interfere with scorable results and per cent point gains in reading rate and comprehension. Ultimately, we want our students to become better readers, but initially they must be made easy in their minds about themselves, by providing reading materials in great variety, allowing students no alternative outlets, and then oneself—always a symbol of threat —retiring to the sidelines. In the incident just recounted, I was no threat, having been rendered harmless and neutralized by an important task. I have no evidence as to reading improvement, but I am positive that the *attitude* toward reading improved. Why? Not only was reading material provided, but also the opportunity to fall asleep.

Most classes are not as uniformly poor as the one described. Harris points out, "A difference of five or more years in reading grade between the best and poorest readers in a classroom is normally to be expected. The overlapping of reading ability in different grades is also tremendous." [1] This means that you must be prepared to attack the reading problem on various fronts. The retarded reader who is reading up to the level of his low I. Q. does not present the same problem as the student with a gap between reading level and I. Q. The techniques for the improvement of reading are extensive and many materials are available for the bright student retarded in reading,[2] the slow student reading up to his level of intelligence, the student with physical defect, the student with emotional block, and other categories of reading disability. In any given class, not one but a variety of reading programs should operate. Some will deal with the far away, the long ago, and the imaginative; others with the here and now. The best reading program is orchestral, a term we shall now define.

The diversity of reading ability and reading impediment in any given class means that the reading program should also be diverse. Reading interests and disabilities are individuated. Hence reading programs should be. But do not such centrifugal programs tend to become uncontrollable and complex?

No reading program will work that breaks the teacher's back. Such programs will be quietly sabotaged and deserve to be. Reading programs are corrosive of morale if a simulacrum of them is put into action without funds and without honesty, as when an administrator latches on to the reading program bandwagon, neglecting to provide the money or staff the program requires. A reading program needs money for special reading teachers, for smaller class size, for special materials and resources, else it becomes a public relations opportunity for the administrator, with the teacher caught in a cross fire. Any reading program that puts an additional load on the classroom teacher is unrealistic. Administrators cannot stretch the school day enough and the most eager, compliant teacher will give somewhere at the seams in attempting to please the administrator or supervisor in a spuriously ambitious reading program. Unless the school can afford to detach a teacher or two from all duties except the responsibility of teaching reading—or, far better, reduce class size to the maximum of twenty so that you can truly individuate teaching—optimum or even meaningful results are remote. Any gains will come from simple maturation, rather than merit in the program.

The truly individuated reading program died with the WPA remedial reading program a generation ago. In those days it was possible, with Federal funds, to undertake individuated reading programs on a mass basis, paradoxical though that sounds. The WPA remedial reading teachers did a remarkable job,[3] and one that cannot be realistically duplicated or even approximated by the classroom teacher with so many other responsibilities. It would be suicidal to try.

Hence, you must defend yourself, as a first step, if you are sincerely interested in getting a *practicable* reading program under way. Secondly, you must know that effective reading programs are possible if the community makes up its mind that such a program is worth the money. Third, you should realize that such communities are scarce and the probabilities are that you are not working in that kind of community. Fourth, you can depend on nobody but yourself and your relationships with your students, because few communities put money into reading programs, into small class size, or into reading specialists. Where reading specialists exist without smaller class size or without a reading budget, one can justifiably wonder about administrative pretexts that remove a favored person from the classroom situation. Playing politics, favorites, and nepotism are not unknown in American schools. They have also been known to masquerade as reading programs. Only where a community pays for small class size has it put its money where its mouth is. Otherwise skepticism had better govern, and you should keep your reading program within manageable limits.

The pity is that we know so much about the teaching and improvement of reading. In no other area has educational psychology worked as intensively. Materials exist, diagnostic procedures are as refined and exact as in any other area of mental, psychological, and intelligence testing, and one thing only lacks—the willingness to implement the research findings. The utmost ingenuity has been expended in developing the spectrum of reading materials in diagnosis, correction, and remediation, but no substitute has been found for putting the eye to the printed page under the tutelage and encouragement of a teacher freed from other responsibilities. The simple reluctance of a student to invest time in reading that he would rather invest in other matters is one complication; another is that the diagnostic procedures in reading are not only beyond your time schedule; usually they are beyond your training.

Such diagnosis can be divided into: (a) physiological; (b) psychological; (c) intellective:

(a) Physiological diagnosis relates reading defect to physiological defect, as in vision, co-ordination, glandular imbalance, or malnutrition, because these and other areas of physiological impairment are known to contribute to reading defect. Students, vain of their appearance, may refuse to wear glasses, even when they have had eye examinations. The lack of physical tone caused by poor eating habits is reported to have contributed to reading defect. Medical remediation here is prior to reading remediation.[4]

(b) Psychological impediment is strongly suggested when no physiological or intellective impairment exists. Thus an intelligence test may reveal normal endowment or better, while reading lag is present. Here again you are not competent to remediate but can be aware of the situation and the resources that the school offers in the way of psychological services and act accordingly, aiming modestly.

(c) Intellective underendowment is the chief source of reading disability. However, a fourteen-year-old, with 80 I. Q., reading at the seventh grade level, is reading up to his intelligence level, if not up to grade level, and therefore is *not* a reading problem.

In these three areas, you are generally not competent to diagnose, but can be justifiably sensitive to situations where diagnostic procedures are indicated.

Withal, a modified reading program need not be a murderous addition to your already burdensome load. Indeed, such a program can organize and integrate your planning and work day. We shall now consider the characteristics of such a modified, practicable, realistic program, dealing with an inner need to read in all of us, your responsibility for materials and resources, and the perfectly obvious matter that one learns to read by engaging in reading.

We are driven, nay forced, to read. The waiting rooms in a dentist's or doctor's office, the barber's, the beautician's, indicate that we are so constituted neurologically that we cannot sit around, idle, as time accumulates. We cannot relax, doing nothing, while waiting our turn. For similar reasons, newspapers and magazines are available at bus stops and railway stations, because we cannot let time or the scenery go by without some focus of attention. The student who walks into the English class without having done his reading assignment will have a comic book rolled up in his back pocket because he too must read at some dead spots during the day when nothing seems to be happening, and one of those times might be your class.

Two psychological experiments, one done in 1885, in the pioneering days of experimental psychology, and the other recently, indicate that our minds cannot be idle, must find work to do, must feed on something, must forage for stimuli, and therefore we read. We are stimuli ingesting creatures as much as food ingesting creatures.

Let's go back to 1885 and the state in which psychology, as a budding science, found itself. In the other sciences, for example chemistry, entities had been isolated, identified, excluded from other entities, and their units, weights, smells, characteristics described. But not in psychological research. Ebbinghaus[5] tried to correct this defect by developing the "nonsense syllable," a unit of language which would serve to test rapidity and circumstances of learning and memory, hoping that one nonsense syllable would be as completely devoid of meaning as another, hence giving a pure and uncontaminated unit of measurement. In the examples given, note that a nonsense syllable has a vowel with initial and final consonants and has no meaning—presumably:

    zud   mek   zas
    kul   mas   laj

Unfortunately for methodological rigor in psychology, Glaze in 1928 found that some nonsense syllables were learned more rapidly or remembered better than others because they had more meaningfulness, sense, or associative values, but in every case the "non-sense" syllable had some attachment to sense and meaning. Inevitably some meaning rushed in to fill the vacuum. It always does, whether with the nonsense syllable of the psychological laboratory, or with the mysteries of the universe, therewith accounting for myth, religion, scientific hypothesis, art, error—and behavior at the doctor's, the dentist's, the barber's, and bus stops. Our minds must busy themselves. If nothing is around, we turn to daydreaming and fantasy. We put a rolled-up comic book in our back pocket in case the English class gets dull. In other circumstances, we will pick up a book and read it even if we don't understand it, provided there is nothing else to do.

Nonsense syllables[6] are still used extensively in psychological research, but they have been graded according to their associative values because we know that sense cannot be entirely divorced from the non-sense.

More recently, the isolation studies of Donald O. Hebb, of McGill University, similarly indicate that man must send forth meaning to structure the voids around him, and the student in a classroom must similarly occupy himself. If reading materials are available to the student and he cannot find other activity, he will read, whatever his level of reading ability. In Hebb's isolation studies, the subject of the experiment is, as you might suppose, placed in isolation in a darkened, soundproof room from which all outside stimuli are blocked out, so that the subject can neither hear nor see anything. He emerges only for meals and for elimination functions and remains in such isolation as long as reason holds out. But reason rapidly crumbles because this hyper-rest cure, or air-conditioned solitary confinement, where all external stimuli are excluded, requires that the neurological system furnish its own stimuli, which turn out to be bizarre fantasies, visions, and sounds that are almost actual to the subject.[7] Just as we must lend sense to the "non-sense" syllable, and Hebb's isolates must create sounds and sights where there are none, so students in the English class, to avoid doing nothing, will turn to comic books, movie romances, and Shakespeare. Armed with this knowledge, the practicable reading program leads from strength, not weakness. Students in the functioning range of intelligence, from 80 I. Q. up, must, if the circumstances are right, inevitably read. They cannot help themselves. The reading program can be less concerned with persuading, cajoling, teasing, or high-pressuring the student into reading. Instead, it will set up the circumstances in which reading will be inevitable—chiefly, there is nothing else to do and alternative forms of activity are absent. This, however, is a negative approach, the exclusion of competing stimuli.

More positively, there must be a focus of attention. This brings you into the scene. The exclusion of competing stimuli is a difficult task, requiring that you keep firmly under control the itches, twitches, whispering, nudging, musing, poking, and scuffling. Sounds fine, but how? We have just debarred you from any major role in diagnosis of reading disability, and we should now like to assign to you dominant responsibility in resources and materials available, where you are expected to be professionally competent. The area of reading resources, sources, and materials is vast but uniquely and specifically your domain; you should know what comic books, magazine articles, short stories, novels, sport stories, newspaper features, or experiential materials are available for the particular reading situations in your class. This is a full-time commitment, dealing with the up-to-date as well as with the warehouse of language and literature. How do you amass these resources?

Research, Resources, and Techniques

1. For a very informative collection of articles on the nature of the reading process, methods of teaching reading, phonics, vocabulary, emotive aspects, audio-visual aids, and other matters in this area, see Oscar S. Causey's *The Reading Teacher's Reader* (Ronald Press, 1958). Up to the minute.

2. Three discussions on the effects of isolation and the light they throw on motivation to read are:

a. Woodburn Heron's "The Pathology of Boredom" (*Scientific American,* Jan. 1957, p. 52), which deals with Hebb's isolation experiments at McGill University and with the need of the human organism to ingest stimulation and experiences as much as it must ingest food;

b. Daniel Lang's "Man in Space" (in the Reporter At Large section, *New Yorker,* Nov. 15, 1958, p. 111), which relates the isolation experiments to the difficulties that the astronauts in interstellar space will encounter. You can in turn relate this to your teaching of reading and the need to exclude competing stimuli.

c. But Jack Vernon, Theodore Marton, and Ernest Peterson, in "Sensory Deprivations and Hallucinations" (*Science,* June 9, 1961), claim that isolation has no such effects, and that the Hebb experiments require additional corroboration.

3. *Atlantic Monthly* for November 1959 contains two articles on the teaching of reading:

a. Robert L. Filbin's "Teaching Reading" (p. 125) is a plea for wider use of phonics in the reading program.

b. Helen R. Lowe's "Solomon or Salami" (p. 128) gives actual experiences with poor readers, the sources of their difficulties, and some suggestions for improvement. You might ask your classes why the "Words Used" list below was seen as the "Words Read" list. Their conjectures might be interesting. Here's the list, for your amusement:

Word Used	Word Read
delicacy	delinquency
bivouac	bifocals
timid	diminished
groceryman	clergyman
hurricane	hammer
bos'n	cow
neurosurgeon	trapeze
phosphate	phosphorus
hydride	hydroxide
God knows	good news

Word Used	Word Read
antiseptic	adhesive
Oxonian	example
inert	inherent
industrial	international
imbecility	implicitly
Solomon	salami

4. V. E. Leichty's "How Slowly Do They Read?" (*E. J.,* May 1956, p. 257) is an excellent defense of reading for understanding, for savor, and for taste, rather than for the sprinting records and for "comprehension" that have as much relationship to appreciation as a vaudeville fiddler has to Heifetz, who, poor fellow, can't stand on his head while playing.

5. James R. Squire's "Literacy and Literature" (*E. J.,* March 1960, p. 154) claims that more reading is going on in the country than ever before.

6. Here is a provocative statement from David H. Russell's "Some Research on the Impact of Reading" (*E. J.,* Oct. 1958, p. 398): "We at least know enough to take care in using reading to help pupils solve their personal problems for often they may fail to understand, they may misinterpret, or they may consciously or unconsciously block the desired responses. . . . Reading by itself has little effect on a person's deeper layers of feeling and behavior." Does this statement bring you more into the picture, if it is true, or does it exclude you?

7. A typical work book for reading improvement suitable for the junior high school level is Joseph C. Gainsburg and Samuel I. Spector's *Better Reading* (Globe Book Company, 1952). Such books offer drills and exercises in comprehension, word study, and speed.

8. What can psychologists tell us about reading? Mark R. Rosenzweig and Leo Postman, in "Frequency of Usage and the Perception of Words" (*Science,* Feb. 7, 1958, p. 263), describe experiments in word recognition and the techniques of measurement used. The readiness with which words are recognized is related to the frequency with which they have been encountered.

9. A distinguished psychologist, B. F. Skinner, in his *Verbal Behavior* (Appleton-Century-Crofts, 1957), says, "Macaulay claimed in his last illness that an interesting book acted as an analgesic" (p. 160). Hence, as was said in this chapter, one important reason for reading is the increased ability to fall asleep! Elsewhere in the book Professor Skinner makes a comment relevant to the reading and understanding of poetry: "In T. S. Eliot's 'Gerontion,' for example, expressions like 'dry month,' 'hot gates,' 'decayed house,' 'windy spaces,' 'dry brain,' 'dry season,' have an over-all effect which is independent of their order or of any syntactical arrangement in the poem. The adjectives 'modify' much more than the words which follow them." Which would seem to mean reading comprehension

transcends literal understanding. There must be poetry in the reader for him to understand the poetry to be read.

Improving the Teacher's Reading

Your reading cannot be idle, as the reading of the editor or of the reviewer is not idle. The literary pro does not read for fun, most of the time, nor should you. The professional musician does not go to a concert with the ear or values of the lay audience, nor the painter to an art gallery with an innocent eye. Similarly your reading must be methodical, purposeful, and filed for reference. You should read knowledgeably, shrewdly, and with a goal in mind. Reading for fun is for amateurs and is not as rewarding or as enriching as the aware approach of the reviewer or the editor, which leads to far greater harvests of insight, illumination, and satisfaction, as long as it is not jaded or jaundiced. You must never sit down to read an article in *Reader's Digest,* or the latest volume of Camus, or *English Journal,* or *Harper's,* or the newspaper without a file card handy and in your mind the questions: Where is the peg in the curriculum on which I can hang this? To which students can I refer this? What in the term's work does it illustrate? How much intelligence is necessary to grasp this? How does it fit in with the other subject matter areas? Does it appeal to adolescents?

The answers go down on the file card, which should contain the author, title, source, estimated reading difficulty, and some indication of the most relevant curriculum area, as well as a brief précis.

Resources accumulate, after a while, and become unwieldy. Periodically they must be stripped of the out of date because the wheels of the printing presses grind rapidly and in large quantity, unlike the mills of the gods, and the pity is that there is not time enough to read all the good things and that so much time is wasted on the shoddy. Luckily, there are filtering agents. *English Journal* does an excellent job of reporting on available materials. The local library will be glad to mark off against the master list of *English Journal* its recent acquisitions. *Publishers' Weekly* classifies new books according to age interest. *The New York Times Book Review* and *Saturday Review* are indispensable if you maintain your role as the resource specialist in the reading program.

Incidentally, décor is important. Book jackets, as many teachers know, are a fine way of dressing up the drab walls of a classroom. Your classroom bulletin board should vibrate with up-to-the-minute cartoons from *New*

Yorker, Saturday Evening Post, and *This Week.* Travel posters, excellent sources of color though they are, should be changed frequently. Montages of headlines, photographs, story titles, and art work from magazines should be taped on the blackboard. Masking tape in various colors lends additional chromatic value and can give a bold outline to the display. This visualization of material in exciting and colorful presentation makes the prospect of reading a more tempting one than in the classroom that is dull and has not been enlivened by any attempt at interior decoration. This classroom decoration of materials from magazines and newspapers proves there is excitement in opening a periodical or a book. Hence the importance of décor. It sets the stage for motivating reading.

Reading Keynotes

At this point the student enters the scene. He is within the normal range of intelligence, his vision is adequate, he has no emotive blocks of any consequence, and he cannot be prevented from behaving, reacting, or learning—the things he wants to learn, that is—without taking an axe to him. He encounters you who have fulfilled your professional responsibility by having at your fingertips germane materials culled from newspapers, magazines, books, and even advertisements, but, more important, you know that the student has all kinds of antenna out for experiences, sensations, excitements, laughs, and the most sober of considerations, like:

How our families make us what we are.
How do you understand other people?
Sports in my life.
The bravest act I ever saw.
How he figured it out.
The funniest thing that ever happened to me.
Abandoned towns and ghost towns.
Animals:
  Leopards are dynamite.
  Jungle life.
  Hunting with bow and arrow.
  Pets.
  Camping and woodcraft.
Actors and acting.
Religion

How to get your way.
Why I had my last fight.
How people get rich.
How to answer back.
Behaving on a date.
Making ads tell the truth.
Billboards on the highway.
Academic freedom.
Sleepwalkers.
Hobbies:
  Gardening.
  Stunt flying.
  Clothing and dress.
  The ballet.
Adolescence and teen-agers.
Cave man.

Geriatrics—can we live forever?   Heart stoppers in:
How to become: Baseball.
  Beautiful.   Basketball.
  Strong.   Hockey.
  Rich.   The new writers.
  Popular.   The space race.
The most unforgettable character I ever
  met.

This list is the merest fragment, taken and paraphrased from the *Reader's Guide to Periodical Literature* and *The New York Times Index*. You can easily amplify this list from these sources and thereby keep a set of reading keynotes. However, a preliminary step must be taken, or, rather, a leap.

Incidents arise in a classroom. There is a scuffle, a laugh, inattentiveness, eagerness, friendship, responding out of turn or failing to respond—the normal concomitants of a classroom.

CASE STUDY 8

In the lower senior class, one student laughed, poked, teased, sought attention, caused mischief, and was generally the center of some hullaballoo that he had instigated. He was a handsome boy, well dressed, gay, smiling, without an ounce of viciousness, but bubbling and frothy. The teacher had a hunch. He went down to the record room, had his hunch confirmed, and was set for the next transgression. The expected occurred. The student again experimented with his repertoire of mischief. He leaned over to a boy in the adjoining aisle, not one seat in front, but two seats in front, perhaps to gain a wider orbit of observers, and pulled the shirttails out of the boy's trousers. The victim turned, involuntarily cursing, and jabbed back at his tormenter. It was all good-natured. Even the victim laughed with the remainder of the class as he stuffed his shirt back into position. The teacher wordlessly observed the incident. The class, in a usual reaction when a teacher maintains silence, subsided, waiting for reproof.

Instead, the teacher asked, "Vinnie, can you tell me something?"

The boy grinned. He was the cynosure of all eyes, and he loved it. He was full of merriment. "Sure," he answered. "What?"

The teacher asked, speaking slowly. "Are . . . you . . . the . . . youngest . . . son . . . of . . . a . . . large . . . family . . . of . . .

brothers . . . and . . . sisters?" It must have taken half a minute to get the words out. The boy's jaw dropped. His eyes widened. The other students looked on with interest, but Vinnie was the first to speak.

"How did you know?"

The question verified the implicit in the teacher's inquiry, there was a moment's silence, and curiosity, mixed with guffaws at Vinnie, broke out in questions from all quarters: "How d'ja know? How can you tell?"

The teacher donned a face like an inscrutable Buddha and pressed his advantage. "Is it true?"

Vinnie collapsed. He nodded and his voice was barely audible. "Yeah."

The classroom rocked. The teacher, accused of being a mind reader and of having second sight, ignored the class demand for illumination and remorselessly continued aiming at Vinnie: "How many brothers?"

"Four."

"How many sisters?"

"Three."

"And you're the youngest, aren't you?"

He nodded, began grinning again, and joined the demand of his classmates. "It's a trick, isn't it?" he asked, and others agreed that it must be.

The teacher shook his head. "No trick. I guessed that you had to be, from the way you behave."

"Me?" he asked in all innocence. "What about the way I behave?"

The teacher turned to the class. "What about the way he behaves?" the teacher echoed. "How could I tell from the way he behaves that he's the youngest in his family?"

Hands went up all over the room, and some answers exploded from students who had not been given permission to answer, but the teacher was not allowing one student to be made the butt of students who had heretofore been his butt, and he let the question remain rhetorical. Vinnie was good-natured, indulged, even spoiled, without a care, well dressed, as only the youngest child of a large family, all employed, could be. The psychology in this case was purely Adlerian,[8] but the shot in the dark, which was not so dark because the record room's information had verified it, led to a reading program which had as its keynote *How Our Families Make Us What We Are*. In the weeks that followed, students reported on these topics:

1. *Grapes of Wrath*. Life in a large, poor family.

2. Philip Barry's play *Holiday*. Rivalry between members of a family, and how it affects family loyalty.

3. *Johnny Tremain.* Experiences of a boy without family.

4. *Alice Adams.* A girl ashamed of her family.

Other students brought in from the popular magazines short stories dealing with family relations, magazine articles, and what they had been reading in newspapers and listening to over the radio—this being before the days of television.

Opportunities for the motivation of reading abound around us. One such opportunity exists in the competition in American advertising in automobiles, cigarettes, toothpaste, cake mixes, cereals, household appliances, clothing, furniture, and so on. An always interesting topic is "Which Would You Buy?" in which, as an example, Chevrolet, Ford, and Plymouth advertising is compared for advertising persuasiveness, or General Electric and Westinghouse appliances, or Pepsodent and Ipana. The national magazines have arresting copy. Institutional advertising understates selling and stresses the company's role in industry and American life, thus offering instructional value. John Hancock life insurance and Parke Davis drug advertising, Ford Motor's "American Road," much of women's fashion copy, not only are suitable reading for consumers but are instances of literary merit in commercial advertising.

Reading stimulation for boys is to be found in sports and adventure and for girls in fashion, dress, and romance. The research studies of educational psychologists like Wattenberg, Crow and Crow, and Hurlock[9] describe these reading interests of teen-agers. This information helps little with the reluctant reader, however, because these interests can be amply filled by the movies, television, and radio, without any recourse to print. But these are not the chief competitor to the adolescent's reading; socialized activity with friends is. Of course, other competitors do not lack, but, if we can reconcile reading with the need to be with the group, we can integrate reading, the presence of competitors, and a fuller life.

After all, there is something unnatural, or unusual, about an adolescent who would rather read than go to a party with friends, or go fishing, or go shopping for a new wardrobe. Or, if *unnatural* is too strong a word because there are adolescents who are perfectly normal in these respects but who are intellectually driven and intellectually insatiable, the typical adolescent will not go to the written word if his kind of people—the adolescents he groups himself with—are around and available. In these circumstances the reading program takes second place.

But there are ebbs and flows in these relationships. There are groupings and regroupings, loyalties and desertions; living with fantastic intensity in the moment alternates with vague and troubling goals. The reading program can justifiably take advantage of these matters. The teacher can contribute to keeping the student off balance and in a state of disequilibrium that only reading can remedy and restore to balance. This suggestion is not cruel, because the adolescent needs solutions rather than placebos, especially the reluctant reader who does not adjust well to the classroom or to the reading program. The reading program, no matter how effective, must contribute constructively to the disequilibrium already existing in the student of this type.

A supremely important aspect of teacher attitude now enters. The teacher who imparts the feeling that he knows more about the student than the student knows about himself has gained the secret of classroom management. This, when communicated, makes almost every other problem in teaching—and in the reading program—fall into place. But the teacher who *says* that he knows more about the student than the student knows about himself has, by verbalizing, revealed that he knows nothing and perhaps less than that. To say so is foolish and presumptuous. But the teacher in whom students *sense* insights into themselves that transcend any that they have, the teacher who never needs to put these into words, has set the stage for successful learning and for a successful reading program, especially when the teacher indicates the ways in which reading yields these insights.

CASE STUDY 9 ⏐ A behavior problem, a troublemaker who was also the leader of a half-dozen other boys in the class, was generally under control, or the semblance that he permitted, until his opportunity finally arrived. The class had been going for a month or more, national elections were being contested, and the class was involved in a journalism unit on the coverage of the elections. In the midst of discussion, the troublemaker called out a profanity, interpretable as a plague on both their houses, Democratic and Republican, and who cared a ———— anyhow?

In such instances a kind of shock descends on a class, a great uneasiness, as it waits for what happens next; even the giggles are uneasy and uncertain. The teacher was experienced. He smiled to give himself a chance to think and to reassure the class, and he looked at the troublemaker.

"Now I remember," the teacher said. "There was something about you that was familiar. I was wondering what it was."

"Is that so?" the student sneered.

"I read a book about you a couple of days ago. It was a book all about you," the teacher said pleasantly.

"You're nuts," the troublemaker said cheerfully. "Nobody ever wrote a book about me."

"It was all about you," the teacher said gently. "It was a perfect description. Honestly. I wouldn't fool you." His manner carried a world of conviction. The student looked at him with suspicion. "Of course, they don't say nice things about you. They're not flattering, or maybe the authors don't know what they're talking about."

"I don't believe you," the student said. By now he was spinning along on a course from which he could not retreat and his defiance was getting ever more out of hand. The teacher was baiting him, the class knew it, and the student knew it.

"It's not important to me if you do or don't believe me," the teacher said, smiling in his face. "I'll be here after school and tell anybody who's interested the names of the books and the authors, even you."

"I'll be here. You'll have to prove it."

"Bring witnesses," the teacher invited. "And now, if we can leave this matter until after school, I'd like to discuss name-calling, as we just saw it here, and how it connects up with the ways the political parties carry on campaigns. Can you describe in your own words what went on here just now?"

The class did so, as deftly as surgeons, because their confidence in the teacher had been restored, and the teacher extrapolated to the current campaigns.

That afternoon the troublemaker appeared, alone, and was greeted coolly. The teacher could have been understanding, sympathetic, and warm, but, in his judgment, this was the time for aloofness rather than cordiality. "Where's the book about me?" the student asked sullenly.

"There are *two* books," the teacher said. "I'll give you the names, but you'll have to write two book reports, one for each." The student demurred but the teacher was insistent. The student would be given the names and the authors of the two books that were so descriptive of him if he agreed to write the book reports, including how they threw light upon that day's incident in class. The student finally agreed. The teacher then administered the last mouthful of crow. He would next day announce the agreement in class because the class had been a witness and had a right to know. The student was ready to back out of the agreement, but the teacher said that in that case he would make another announcement, that the student had appeared, had been willing to do the job, and then had chickened out. The student was beaten. He asked for the names of the books. The teacher gave them. They were *Studs Lonigan* and Paul Eldridge's *And Thou Shalt Teach Them.*

The two reports were turned in, corrected, returned to the student, who thereafter submitted them for publication in the school newspaper. They were accepted. Who won? Call it a draw. But the student thereafter never caused a smidgen of trouble in class.

Reading can answer the problems that the adolescent faces. It is your responsibility to recognize these problems and to know the reading resources that are relevant. The student thereafter does the work. This work must be recorded and the records differentiated into two types—reading reports and book reports—with the student responsible for the maintenance of a record of his reading. The keynotes listed above (p. 133; see also p. 154) should be the springboard for each student's reading experiences and his reading assignments may revolve around one or more of these keynotes, with the student showing how his outside reading corresponds to one or more of the listed keynotes, or to one of his own making. Class members will go their individual ways in doing their reading but will, in reporting on the reading done, show how this reading is related to one of the suggested keynotes or to a fresh one. Hence the orchestration of topics we referred to earlier.

But materials vary in difficulty and students in reading ability; you must in each instance match level of difficulty with level of ability, *with the record of successive matches kept by the student or by student committees.* Such record keeping is not for you; you set up these records, determine what goes into them, and turn the bookkeeping over to the student or to a student committee. The records of reading reports, in a form that allows for mimeographing in quantity, might resemble the one reproduced here. Note that this is a reading report, *not* a book report. The reading report is not as ambitious, does not require the extended writing effort or the close analysis that should characterize the book report. Furthermore, the

OUTSIDE READING REPORT

Name of
student _____ Report
                        Number ___

Class _____ Date _____

Keynote _____

Author _____

Title and source _____

Brief outline of material:

How the material deals with the keynote:

New words:

New ideas:

book report is more an individualized effort than the reading report; the latter is related to a central keynote to which the entire class is simultaneously contributing. The reading report is centripetal; the book report is centrifugal. In the reading report the entire class is going in the same, or in a parallel, direction; in the book report students may ride off on their own hobby horses in unrelated directions.

Therefore, your assignment in the reading report is less permissive than in the book report. You must know the materials related to the keynotes selected and the difficulty levels of these materials. Only out of such knowledge can you control assignments so that students at different ability levels will be suitably matched with the materials you have in mind—and have mined—for them, and only thus can you assess achievement objectively. For you to know your reading resources and reading materials is as important as knowing your students and where they are individually as readers. The wealth of instructional, diagnostic, developmental, and remedial materials in reading is staggering, and much of your time is required to keep up with the flood. To keep abreast of developments in reading you must depend on students and student committees to do the clerical work and the bookkeeping that a good reading program requires. You have not the time.

Such reading records are prime tools in the reading program. They constitute files that are counterparts to yours. Only you can develop a file of reading resources. Only you can use it successfully, no matter what the program, or the student's reading level, or the seriousness—or lack of it —with which a reading program is contemplated by the community. This is as far as the usual English teacher, with the usual harassments, can go; but here you should go all the way. Thereafter, as in a relay race, you turn the baton over to the student for him to develop his own file and record of the reading he has done. His reading records and book reports are returnable to him at the end of the term. They are his property. Unfortunately, reports, so returned, can become negotiable commodities that are exchanged among students and a means whereby reading is avoided rather than pursued. What can you do about transactions among students for the exchange of book reports for the improved shirking of reading? On the college level, term papers and themes are similarly exchanged. Students in college and in high school borrow book reports, term papers, and themes, passing them off as their own because the risks of detection are worth taking, so infrequently are they caught.

Is this because students find reading a chore? No; writing is more responsible than reading for these derelictions. That a friend sees a movie, and even tells you about it, is more often a reason for seeing the movie than avoiding it. This is true about a book that a friend has read. If recommended, you read it. Reading does not cause barter of book reports. Writing does.

To overcome this contradiction between willingness to read and unwillingness to write, many teachers resort to oral book and reading reports or else have book reports and reading reports written in class. These substitutes are ineffective because students can continue to report on borrowed material. Best begin the reading program with a writing program. Here you request students to select one or more keynotes and to write a composition on reactions, opinions, and questions related to the keynote topic. The composition is graded and returned to the student, or the student committee, as the first element in the student's reading folder. These reading folders are like those issued by the National Council of Teachers of English.

The returned composition carries your recommendations on reading appropriate to the keynote. Moreover, it tells you what the student's interests are. Here built-in controls prevent the reading program from getting unmanageable, allow you to police cheating, and still allow for book reports written away from class—and hence with some degree of scope and ambitiousness—as well as for oral class reports. Finally, though highly individuated, it places far fewer demands on your time. Once you have selected the keynotes and the reading materials to back up the keynotes, your task is virtually done. From then on the student carries the ball of the reading program and your task becomes one of motivating, needling, provoking, stimulating, or posing questions that only further reading can settle.

One last reassurance on your file. The contents of magazines and newspapers are repetitive. Articles and news stories are grouped under types and categories. Magazine and newspaper editors try to keep a balanced table of contents, so that the *Saturday Evening Post* will have so many Westerns, suspense stories, love stories, success articles, and travel pieces over the course of a year, and *The New York Times* will even institutionalize this practice by having sections, as in theatre, sports, home furnishings, foreign, and human-interest pieces. Not only does this make your task easier, but it would be otherwise impossible to publish *Reader's Guide to Periodical Literature* or *The New York Times Index*. Articles reappear on sports, interesting personalities, styles and fashions, scientific break-throughs, and medical discoveries. Once you have set up your hundred-odd keynotes into which to slot and assort materials as these appear, the twin task of keeping up-to-date and combing out the stale will no longer be formidable.

So, too, student interests constitute a spectrum that is not infinite. These reappear in types and categories that are, within rough limits, predictable and applicable. However, though we know the categories of student interests, this does not spare you the responsibility of seeking contemporary expressions of these for your resource file.

Next, the reading experience should have socialized characteristics. After reading, the student should share reactions. The usual book report falls down here, since it is a private communication between student and teacher, with most of the class never sharing in the student's activity. Nevertheless, the writing experience is a useful one. The pity is that the reading and correction of book reports are so time consuming. One of these days, let us hope, class size will permit you to assign six book reports a term and time to read these attentively. No single experience in English can substitute for the full-dress book report, properly done. In the absence of this circumstance, teachers have taken to the substitute of oral reports. These too are useful, but they can often become dull and dutiful.

Oral reports on the same material tend to be repetitive and dull, but oral reports on the same keynote, drawing on different or supplementary materials, can be most stimulating. Here the approach is co-operative, rather than competitive. Also, when students have selected the same key-note, joint reports are useful provided the material is not the same. Thus reading reports can be combined with oral English, or with so-called "Club Day," when a more informal classroom attitude prevails.

Students need direction in the preparation of reports. In reporting on fiction, they frequently wander, mention characters without characterization, flatten out climaxes, and distort development. To avoid these pitfalls and to aid the listener, they must determine what is most important in that particular narrative—plot? character? setting?—and present the remainder in light of the type of story told. Many students have a knack for recounting a yarn; classes are fascinated when one of their colleagues is that kind of story spinner. Such students are themselves interested in gaining interest. They love it when they succeed and their classmates are proud of them when they do.

Nonfiction oral reports also need organizing and students should be encouraged to accompany such reports with suitable expository materials, like graphs, designs, cartoons, maps, or other props. One of the most interesting reports the author remembers was on the keynote of hobbies. A student, interested in pigeon raising, brought in a pair of homing pigeons and, at the end of his report, went to the window and released them. The class gasped. The pigeons fluttered a while and then, first on a wavering course and thereafter on an ever-more direct one, set out for home. The class flocked to the windows and watched for minutes, till the pair was out of sight.

Sometimes, such "read and tell" sessions can be interestingly converted to "read and don't tell." Fiction allows this. Thus, in "Ransom of Red Chief," a student told all the story except the end, which he defied the class to guess. Regrettably, much popular fiction is only too obviously plotted and students can frequently predict the end, even though they cannot always see how the end is negotiated. This technique can be adapted to non-fiction if the student analyzes the reader-interest "peg" that originally persuaded the editor that he had a publishable piece. Whether a *New Yorker* profile, or a *Saturday Evening Post* political article, or a travel article from *Holiday* or *National Geographic,* the student must decide what he can leave unsupplied and unspecified in order to leave his audience asking for more.

Written classroom reports, whether reading reports or book reports, also require direction. A class period is too short for a book report of scope; you should be definite about requirements, else the student will have difficulty. Furthermore, when a student has truly enjoyed a book, he wants to parade his pleasure. To restrict him to a routinized written classroom report, when he would like to bubble a bit, is unfeeling. Of course, when reading is a chore, and the student's approach stereotyped, the student, you, and the class are spared pain. On the other hand, reading, if accompanied by too much stately formality in reporting, can have all the pleasure taken out of it. Minima should be set, but maxima should depend on what the student feels he has got out of the reading he has done.

If students in junior high school do more reading than do students in senior high school,[10] as research studies claim, and if the junior high school "reading craze" abates in senior high school because of greater demands on the student's time, caused by school assignments and augmented social activities, this competition to the reading program must be answered by integration of the reading program with adolescent interests.

Research, Resources, and Techniques

1. Eric W. Johnson's "Stimulating Reading in the Junior High School" (*E. J.*, Feb. 1959, p. 74) deals with the outside reading assignment and how you can both encourage and control it.

2. Three unpublished doctoral dissertations which throw light on various aspects of reading are:

a. Harrison Bullock's *Helping the "Non-Reading" Pupil in the Secondary School* (Columbia University, 1955);

b. Algard P. Whitney's *Improvement of Reading Through Supervision* (Columbia University, 1955);

c. William S. Anderson's *An Investigation of Reading Achievement as an Affective Determinant in the Perception of Verbal and Non-Verbal Symbols* (Cornell University, 1955).

Words Our Apelike Ancestors Taught Us

My interest in Tarzan of the Apes goes back to Elmo Lincoln (which brands me as paleolithic), but I was not alone in my adolescent interest in the primitive then or now, because Tarzan has persisted in a succession of muscular avatars, from Weissmuller down to some contemporary sleek-muscled actor. This interest in the primitive caused me one day to ask a class what the language of their primitive ancestors must have been, what their lives must have been and what they looked like. I mentioned archaeological evidence that men ten thousand years and more ago looked so much like modern man that if you gave them a shave, haircut, and suit, they could proceed down Fifth Avenue without anybody's knowing the difference.

Similarly, I guessed out loud, we were speaking much the same language that our primitive ancestors used. Of course, some slight differences had crept in, but, as far back as we went, we could notice clear similarities between the English of today and the languages of thousands of years ago, like Greek, Latin, and Minoan. Indeed, I continued, more than half the English we use comes from the Latin. We're still speaking Latin, whether we know it or not.

Once, while teaching the *Odyssey,* I conjectured whether the man who invented the wheel was one-eyed, or whether the wheel was originally named after some man who had one eye. We were involved with Polyphemus, the Cyclops, and the one eye in the center of his forehead, the cycle, or circle, with the hub in the center which we these days call the wheel. There's no way of knowing, we agreed, but the guessing was fun and we were off into the detective-work of etymology, roots, suffixes, prefixes, and vocabulary improvement.

Improvement in reading demands improvement in vocabulary. Vocabulary improvement requires a sequential attack. First, preferably, the word should be encountered in reading. Second, the meaning should be guessed from context. Third, the dictionary should legalize this meaning. Fourth, the student should be able to use the word in new contexts. Fifth, the genealogy of the word should be learned.

Let's begin with beginnings. What was the first syllable we ever uttered? [11] Was it *m-m-m-m*? And then *ma-ma-ma*? We can compare *mater, madre, mother, mama,* and *pater, padre, father, pop.* We can go further in comparing *maternal, matriarch, matrix, metropolis,* and *maternity,* with *paternal, patriarch, patriotism, repatriate.* Such complexity from such simple beginnings! Similarly, *I* relates to the German *ich,* the Latin *ego,* and to *egoism, egotism, egocentrism.* We go home and watch *tele*vision, and what has that to do with *tele*phone, *tele*gram, *tele*scope, and *tele*pathy? We can guess and corroborate our guess by the dictionary and find further that *vision* leads to:

provision	revision	visual	visit
advise	division	Providence	evident
invisible	visage	interview	review

and *phone* to:

phonograph	focus

and *gram* to:

grammar	graphic	glamour

and *scope* to:

periscope	sight

Or, better yet, we can give this assignment: "Come in with five hard words, words you have never seen before, the meaning of which you don't know, and we'll operate on them here in class." In this surgical process, the students furnish the cadavers and the class, together, sees what the ancestral constituents are and the word's contemporary uses.

The longer the word, the easier the surgery because such words are likely to derive from the Latin or Greek and thus come equipped fore-and-aft with prefix, root, and suffix; if so, the task of reducing them to their clearly determinable constituents is not difficult. Thus *super-cilious, ante-diluvian, bene-volent, phil-anthropist,* can be fractionated into their parts precisely because they are long, and these parts become springboards for further word study. The multitude of combinations originating from a comparatively small number of affixes and roots additionally illuminates the importance of such word study because the mastery of the small number of these leads to the attainment of a larger vocabulary and widened understanding.

Picture a class which has had distributed to it this list:

antedate	replete	childish	uninterested
antidote	deplete	childlike	disinterested
benevolent	entomology	distrust	affect
malevolent	etymology	antitrust	effect
censor	philanthropist	continuous	ingenuous
censure	misanthropist	continual	ingenious
discover	reduce	displace	climatic
uncover	conduce	misplace	climactic

Suppose, further, that the teacher says, "Someone in your family has just swallowed poison. What word will you need to know how to save his, or her, life?" Many will know, but how can they prove, by word-surgery, that the word is *antidote* and not *antedate*? Did Columbus discover America, or uncover it? When the family has had Thanksgiving dinner, and the larder is empty, what is replete and what depleted? If a woman were to reduce, to what would that conduce?

Or to use another available approach to the same material, is it possible to have an idea without having its opposite? Thus:

good and bad (*bene* and *mal*)	above and below (*supra* and *infra*)
before and after (*pre* and *post*)	to and from (*ad* and *ab*)
love and hate (*phil* and *mis*)	present and absent (*in* and *de*)
in and out (*in* and *ex*)	large and small (*macro* and *micro*)

mean that *benevolent* and *malevolent, prescription* and *postscript, philan-thropist* and *misanthropist* arise from the opposites that we must have in mind when we think. At the same time everything and its opposite some-times require augmentation, intensification, or diminution, so we have *super-, peri-, demi-, semi-;* and words emerge, words of all kinds, so that people can carry on a conversation in English in our hearing and we won't know what they're talking about. Is it still English? It is. *Auto-mobile* is half-Greek, half-Latin, and all English. If the Latin *ipse* means the same as the Greek *auto,* why aren't we driving ipsemobiles? If the microscope helps us see the amoeba, why don't we use a macroscope, rather than a telescope, to peer at the stars? Because we don't merely accept language from our ancestors. We also modify it, thus getting neologisms. The prize-fight term *knock-out* was abbreviated to *K. O.* and then expanded to *kayo.* It's in dictionaries now. Thus *pad* launches the space rocket in one kind of orbit and the beatnik into another. Who was the first man to say *cool, man, cool?* Did *square* descend from *squarehead?* Does a square stand *four-square?* Do your students believe in any connection between *sharp, sharpie, sharpshooter, sharp cry, sharp pain, sharp practices,* and *sharper than a serpent's tooth?* Are these the same words or different?

Will the Latin and Greek of thousands of years ago help contemporary students make themselves understood? How can they doubt it? But simul-taneously they should look at the language being generated today. It's all English.

Your asking the student to put something more clearly may provoke an "Aw, you know what I mean!" or an "I can't put it exactly into words" and thus furnish another opportunity for a vocabulary investigation into how words can tell us what we are thinking about when we find it hard to do so for ourselves. You must persist: "No, I don't know what you mean"; and from this, exasperation may grow mutually in you and your student, as you go on: "How do you expect me to understand, if you can't put it exactly into words?"

This question once placed a student in such extremity that he burst out, "What's the matter, teacher? You stupid?" Teacher was an exceptionally aggressive woman who answered, "What words would you use if I were? Could you? And if you couldn't, who's stupid?" This forced the student into a further retort, "I'll draw you a diagram." But the teacher now began moving in with her greater muster of words, vocabulary, and concept, and sent the student reeling: "You couldn't draw a diagram. You wouldn't know how. You just said so. You haven't the language, the words, or the ideas, so how are you able to draw a diagram?" and went on until the student cried out, "You don't have to be so sarcastic!" And the towel was thereby thrown in.

Students hate sarcasm because this is one battle they cannot ever hope to win. You have the words and the vocabulary on your side. So one-sided is this battle that it is the ultimate in unfairness, universally stated to be so by students and by textbooks on education, but the agreement is less unanimous among those teachers who know a weapon when they see it and who, when they see it, keep it oiled and in shape. They do not care that it is a cruel weapon. It is theirs and no student can use it as well. When all else fails, this weapon will restore the classroom to their control, as respect flies out the window. Vocabulary is to sarcasm as ploughshare is to sword; just as the steel in swords should not be thrown away but converted to humane ploughshares, so should the situational mastery in sarcasm be converted to vocabulary mastery. Use English with full flexibility and resource, and do not infantilize the language. Do not be stilted or juvenile, and do not hesitate to use the most finished and cultivated English at your command. Students will recognize when language is a means of patronizing them and when it reflects your genuine endeavor to give the best of yourself so that they can see what the horizons are. Students are not dismayed by long or unusual words if they see them in purposeful use and in meaningful application. This is as true of the dull as of the bright.

Do they understand the words? Perhaps not. But do they understand that you think well enough of them to speak as well as you can? Yes, even when they ask, "Why don't you speak English?" Sometimes the question is asked good-naturedly, sometimes in desperation because they're honestly trying to follow you and cannot. When the question is good-natured, declare that you're speaking English, even if they can't understand English, and be good-natured too. In the latter situation, with students in desperate case, repeat, restate, and explain for them after you're sure they cannot do so for themselves. Furnish all the additional contexts you can, descending to the lowlands where your students are, the better to conduct them to the uplands. Illustration from context, as in "Billy Jones, who died in service, was awarded a medal *posthumously* after the war," helps avoid misinterpretation and the numerous howlers found in *NEA Journal* and elsewhere. If you define *anthology* as "a collection of literature," a student may want to know if a library is an anthology; seize the error as an opportunity to furnish comparisons with similar words, with synonyms and antonyms. Sometimes the howlers are happy, like the slow reader who mistook *ears-drop* for *eavesdrop,* a deliciously witty error had it been intentional, but the student was pleased that his misreading was a good way of remembering what the hard new word meant.

What of dictionary definitions and word analysis? They are only the beginning, necessary of course, but not sufficient. They must be backed up with illustrations of actual use and context. And your use of English is the most important context of all.

A student teacher reported on a lesson she had observed on the biography of Father Damien, founder of the leper colony at Molokai: "The teacher was so anxious to point out his altruism and courage that she practically omitted the story and wrote a string of adjectives on the board, e.g., *brave, dedicated, persevering,* which, she told the class, described him. The class was bored at this soap opera approach until one boy asked a question that had apparently bothered him. 'How tall was Father Damien?' The teacher hesitated and answered, 'Medium height. Why?' The boy answered, 'How could he live in the huts, since the people were so tiny?' The teacher looked puzzled, questioned him, and the boy explained that he had assumed that the inhabitants of Molokai were leprechauns. So concerned was the teacher with preaching a life of noble sacrifice, that she had neglected to tell them about leprosy."

Your students come to words in a variety of ways. Superb spellers may be opaque to literature and students with enormous vocabularies may be poor spellers. A graduate student describes a Negro boy: "Leon, I am convinced, could not have spelled *help* if he were stranded on a desert island. Yet this boy could read Shakespeare with a sensitivity and perception far beyond his fifteen years. He had read voraciously and had a keen mind for the things he wanted to remember."

Even with so mechanical a matter as phonics, use of conceptualization, contrast, and the matching of comparisons will enliven materials for your slower readers. Thus, write on the board "Put up a *fight* with all your *might* and get it *right,*" and thereafter have students substitute other initial consonants like *l* - - - - and *t* - - - -, for *light* and *tight,* and then compare these with *site, kite, bite,* and *mite;* this array of comparisons reinforces teaching. Extract the *ay* cluster and imbed it in *bay, say, day, slay,* and *pray,* to make "To*day,* I *say,* we *slay* J*ay* and M*ay* and l*ay* their bodies in the *bay,* if they won't *play*." You are not encouraging bloodletting because the slow student knows you are on the prowl for any illustrations you can dig up for him, and he's grateful for it. You've further enlisted his support when you compare *ay* with *eigh,* as in *"Eight sleighs* are arriving by fr*eigh*t." "You *overdo* the delay on the *overdue* bills" illustrates how the contrasting forms, readily available for comparison in the same sentence, clarify the phonics by concept.

Research, Resources, and Techniques

1. In Albert J. Harris' *How to Increase Reading Ability* (Longmans, Green, 1956), note the author's differentiation between corrective reading (group) and remedial reading (individual). An outstanding contribution; an inevitable book if you are interested in this area.

2. Work books for vocabulary improvement and word study abound. Here are some of the better ones:

a. M. M. Mathews' *Words: How to Know Them* (Henry Holt and Company, 1956) is very helpful; contains roots, affixes, and examples of use. A fine reference. For maximum effect use it in conjunction with Radke, below.

b. Frieda Radke's *Word Resources* (Odyssey Press, 1955) offers a good collection of word pairs (on p. 105), which, by matching difficulties, mutually illuminates them—an example of teaching by comparison and contrast.

c. W. Powell Jones' *Practical Word Study* (Oxford University Press, 1952), in Form A and Form B, makes it possible for you to teach from one of the forms and thereafter test on the other.

d. The paperbacks have self-help titles. One example is the Roger B. Goodman and David Lewin *New Ways to Greater Word Power* (Dell, 1955). The effect of these books, self-help though they purport to be, will be beneficially multiplied if you give assignments from them.

3. The motivation to be Tarzan in word study is helped by two articles in *Scientific American* on language derivations:

a. Paul Thieme's "The Indo-European Language" (*Scientific American,* Oct. 1958, p. 63) reconstructs the extinct tongue and the geographic origins of its original speakers by comparing its modern descendants. Fascinating detective work.

b. Similarly, Jotham Johnson's "The Language of Homer's Heroes" (*Scientific American,* May 1954, p. 70) can be used in word study, or in connection with the *Odyssey.* Johnson lists the Minoan words we still speak:

Ending in

—*inth*	—*ss*	*others*	
labyrinth	abyss	asparagus	hymn
mint	colossus	daffodil	wine
turpentine	cypress	cannon	sponge
hyacinth		canyon	sandal
currant		govern	purple

Hence, as we said above, if we still speak Latin, Greek, and languages even older, how would you use such material to motivate a unit in word study? How does Tarzan come in?

4. Numerous articles in *English Journal* deal with this area. Here are two:

a. Lee C. Deighton's "Developing Vocabulary: Another Look at the Problem" (*E. J.*, Feb. 1960, p. 82) is somewhat vague in specific recommendations for the classroom but will help you organize your own thinking on this subject. Especially useful is the distinction between recall and recognition vocabularies. The author recommends the intensive study of a limited list of words rather than the superficial study of a broad one.

b. You will find, in John W. Ragle's "Something Old, Something New, Something Borrowed—" (*E. J.*, April 1956, p. 208) an ingenious approach to teaching vocabulary, in which ample use is made of magazines, newspapers, and detective stories to get suitable vocabulary work. Note the excellent overlap between teaching the mass media and vocabulary work.

Some Tangential Considerations

If present-oriented, students will not want to do too much about vocabulary improvement; if future-oriented, they will. The present-oriented student, chiefly the lower termer, is piqued when asked to find words for what he finds difficult to put into words. Vocabulary and word power do not grow from games and devices but from an environment in which words are used with clarity and appropriateness. The home is one such environment, the classroom another, but most important is the inner environment, where discriminations between meanings are apprehended and sensed, and then these discriminations are sent for shelter and clothing in some word or other. Even if the word is encountered first, the student must awaken within himself the conceptualized meaning, in a preverbal sense, before he attempts to commit the word to his vocabulary hoard. Hence, vocabulary building must be related to concept building, to the need to discriminate, to get at fine differences, as in *continuous, continual,* and *continuing,* or *ingenious* and *ingenuous,* or *affect* and *effect,* or *he lied to me, he fooled me, he deceived me,* and *he persuaded me.* Vocabulary is a consequence of the need to discriminate, and the need to discriminate becomes the inevitable precursor to vocabulary study. (Radke[12] provides materials in this connection.) Even punning has a place, as in "It's not school I dislike; it's the (principle, principal) of the thing." In a parallel way, with slow readers, you can ask, "Which sound does not belong in the grouping?"

    a. Care, bear, scare, spear
    b. Rule, flow, flew, proof, shook, truth.

Or use a rhyming dictionary for additional ideas.

If students are asked to describe the person they'd like most to be, answers will include neighborhood pugilists, Abraham Lincoln, Clark Gable, Albert Einstein, Kim Novak, Eleanor Roosevelt, Antonino Rocca, best friends, and Tony Curtis. If, then, students are asked how much personal change will be required in them to achieve this ideal, answers become difficult to verbalize. The concepts are hard to localize, the vocabulary unavailable, and evidence accumulates that students want to remain as they are. But this is impossible. They cannot impede the passage of days, weeks, and years, or the growth of experiences for which words must be found. Here, for example, are situations and experiences with which they are familiar. What are the words to fit?

    1. You are watching a television program in which the announcer is trying very hard to be pleasant. Somebody ought to tell him not to be so: (a) dominating; (b) ingratiating; (c) photogenic; (d) photographic.

    2. The juke box is on so loud that it causes the walls to rattle and shake. The proprietor complains about the: (a) echo; (b) real crazy tune; (c) reverberations; (d) surface scratch.

    3. You are conversing with a friend in the next seat. The teacher calls you up, in the belief that you are whispering about him, and scolds you because he is under a: (a) misapprehension; (b) dislocation; (c) disillusion; (d) misnomer.

    4. The life guards pull the man ashore. They will save his life by: (a) renascence; (b) resonance; (c) resuscitation; (d) recrimination.

    5. The batter swings, the ball goes far, far out, and the outfielder catches it. The batter is: (a) ebullient; (b) disconsolate; (c) rejected; (d) euphoric. What about the outfielder?

Another form of multiple-choice vocabulary exercise is more suitable for testing than for teaching. Vocabulary teaching is best done in the matrix of actual use.

Another testing device, of doubtful value in teaching, occurs in this Regents question: "Column B contains a group of commonly used foreign phrases. Column A lists meanings of phrases. Write on the line at the right of each of *five* of the phrases in Column B the *number* of the expression in Column A that is most closely related to that phrase."

Column A	*Column B*	
(1) noninterference	(a) nom de plume	(a) ....
(2) confidentially	(b) vice versa	(b) ....
(3) with honor	(c) laissez faire	(c) ....
(4) pen name	(d) per diem	(d) ....
(5) by the day	(e) sub rosa	(e) ....
(6) for each individual	(f) cum laude	(f) ....
(7) the other way around		
(8) unexpected stroke		
(9) against		

These are excellent testing devices but cannot be used in teaching unless ample contextual circumstances are afforded. Vocabulary involves spelling, etymology, and word analysis, but without context and contextual illustrations all else will be wasted.

Without words, we cannot know nor describe what goes on around us. We are blind, deaf, and helpless. Life passes us by, even the school year we are going through. From the opening of the term to the end, you can put vocabulary in realistic circumstances:

1. The World Series (September-October)
2. The Football Season (September-December)
3. The Election Campaign (September-November)
4. Basketball (September-March)
5. Fall and Winter Styles
6. Christmas
7. Why Go to Florida? (November-March)
8. How the Director Improves a Television Drama
9. When the Days Get Longer (January-April)
10. I'd like to Write a Valentine to . . . (February)
11. How This Term Compares With Last (February-March)
12. The First Signs of Spring (February-April)
13. What Congress Has Done So Far (January-April)
14. Spring Training (February-April)
15. Spring and Summer Fashions

16. My Opinion of Family Picnics (April-May)
17. My Friends Versus My Family
18. Why This Summer Will Be Different (April-May)

Finally, research in "recognition" versus "recall" vocabulary proves that we know many more words than we think we know. We understand more words than we use (see above, pp. 147, 152). "Recall" vocabulary, the language we emit in writing and speaking, is considerably less extensive than "recognition" vocabulary, our familiarity with words that come our way; assessments by reliable observers place our recognition vocabulary high up in five figures. Ask your classes to estimate their recognition vocabularies. The figure they give will be far more modest than that of the experts. Why the discrepancy in estimate? Perhaps an experience of mine will be illuminating; I once asked students to look at a blank, featureless brick wall facing the class and to give all the relevant words that occurred to them. After one hundred words had been offered, I wilted and gave out.

Research, Resources, and Techniques

1. Perhaps, in word study, it would be appropriate to turn to older books, like Archbishop Trench's *Study of Words*. Originally published in 1851, it has gone through many editions. Though recent scholarship has supplemented some of its statements, it has not superseded it. By all means investigate this etymological classic. It is an excellent resource.

2. In another old-timer, Emma Bolenius' *Everyday English Composition* (American Book Company, 1917, p. 98), you will, for example, find an excellent assortment of homonyms. These too are still highly usable. Such materials never become dated.

CHAPTER 5

The Teaching of Narrative

Preliminary Consideration I: Mute Inglorious Miltons

When most intimately and privately ourselves—when we dream, in short —we tell ourselves stories in which we stock the stage with creatures, scenery, and happenings of our devising, without command by anybody or anything except our inner needs. We are simultaneously author and audience of fantasies, dreams, daydreams, and nightmares as old as myth and man. The adolescent too is an author who assigns roles to himself, his parents, his friends, his classmates, his teacher in numerous narratives with nobody but himself as audience. *Johnny Tremain, Giants in the Earth, Tale of Two Cities,* and *Silas Marner* compete with a small library of narrative within your students, this classroom of unacknowledged, unpublished authors facing you.

The teaching of narrative begins by seeking mutual accommodations between the published author and your classroom of unwitting ones. Language and verbalization are minimal in these inner narratives in which the author spins the yarn to himself, but in which are other ingredients of the most elaborate novel: characterization, plot, setting, conflict, motive, and mood. Total the output of Simenon, Anthony Trollope, Edgar Wallace— any student in your class has already in his brief span of years told himself far more stories and has utilized narrative devices and techniques too elusive for words. When he finds them in words, the emotions and situations are almost reminiscent—or ought to be.

Students have in the strict privacy of dreamland told themselves stories of abandonment, of being scorned and discarded by everybody, by those nearest and dearest, as in *Silas Marner*; the circumstances in which we sacrifice ourselves for others, whether for strangers or for those we love, as in *Tale of Two Cities*; the rage that has no outlet, the person that can harbor and even nourish a state of rage for years and years, as did Madame Defarge. The adolescent has extensive inner experience with such things. He has dreamed, daydreamed, fantasied, and nightmared them. Narrative of the right sort, imaginatively taught, augments the resources of inner life and illuminates its recesses. You cannot tell a story, if you are Homer or John O'Hara, without touching on inner life, making Homer as contemporary as O'Hara. The travails of Odysseus and the cosmic woes of Ahab thereby become as personal and domestic as Main Line novels or Dead End ones.

Preliminary Consideration II: I. Q. versus E. Q.

The ability to handle these matters has little to do with intelligence. Interest in narrative and need for it are unrelated to intelligence or reading ability. Students in the functioning range of intelligence, with I. Q. of 85 upward, can handle the high school's narrative storehouse—if properly taught —and the narrative needs of the student on the lower end of the I. Q. continuum will be the same as the needs of the student on the upper end, because although I. Q. varies, emotionality does not. Psychologists tell us that the Emotive Quotient,[1] or E. Q., is not shaped like the bell curve,[2] but is strongly skewed, like the ownership of radios in American homes. Everybody's got it, and just about to the same extent. Therefore intelligence and reading ability have little to do with the narrative sense, just as literacy has no connection with grammar. We have already said that an illiterate's language is as ordered as a college professor's (see above, p. 64); similarly, the interest in narrative and the need for it have no relationship to intelligence or reading ability. Even a student who cannot read will want a story read to him, because the viscera are as involved in narrative as is the cerebral cortex.

Unfortunately, we cannot read to our students. They must be launched on reading themselves. Bright or dull, their visceral need for narrative is the same; similar though their visceral needs, their ability to cope with words and concepts varies. The teacher must cherish both variability and similarity. Therefore, whatever the I. Q., E. Q., homogeneity, or heterogeneity of your class, you can pertinently and safely ask your subtlest depth questions. If teaching *Moby Dick* or the *Odyssey* do not hesitate to ask questions like these:

> Can we ever escape, even in the middle of civilized life and comforts, an always encroaching and sometimes pitiless Nature?
>
> When Mom wages her perpetual struggle against dirt, dust, and grime in laundry and dishwashing, how is that related to the struggle of Ahab and the *Pequod* against the sea, or Odysseus' against the warnings of Aeolus and the vengeance of Poseidon?
>
> When we polish our boots, trim our nails, and keep ourselves neat, what are we saying to Nature?
>
> Does Nature intend (as Poseidon intended) to destroy? Did Moby Dick intend to destroy? Or is Nature impersonal? Do you then placate Nature or study her?
>
> Why did Odysseus placate Nature? Why do we, instead, study Nature?
>
> If you were lost in the woods, what could you learn from Odysseus, washed ashore at Scheria, naked and helpless (shortly before he encounters Nausicaa), without food, weapons, or clothing? What would you do to survive? How would you plan? How would you analyze your situation and resources? What would you try to remember? What would you seek first?

These questions have depth and subtlety, but they are not difficult. Therefore we shall take the narratives found in the high school curriculums —*Silas Marner, Tale of Two Cities, Ivanhoe, Giants in the Earth, Huckleberry Finn, Johnny Tremain, Pride and Prejudice,* and others—to indicate the principles by which narrative is taught. These principles are two: suspense and conflict. Throughout we stress their importance.

Preliminary Consideration III: Odysseus Will Be Continued Next Week

Elsewhere we have talked about suspense and the "cliff-hanger" (p. 26) —from which we hereafter drop the quotation marks lest these seem patronizingly supercilious—and continue our analysis of conflict, suspense, and what these are in turn based on, a recognition of clues. The novelist

states his clues almost from the very opening. Proust's *madeleine,* Jerry
Cruncher's rusty fingernails in *Tale of Two Cities,* the allusion to the
stone-pits in *Silas Marner* and to floods and death by drowning in *Mill
on the Floss* are clues which the storyteller plants and to which the teacher
must draw attention. The storyteller cannot do so. Dickens could not—
because the exigencies of art prevent—call our attention to Jerry Cruncher's
fingernails more emphatically than he does. Yet, though inelegant to say
so, these fingernails are the pivot of the novel. Because of them Barsad
is revealed, Carton enabled to take Darnay's place, and escape planned
and consummated. What Dickens cannot do, you must. "Notice!" you say.
"Remember these rusty fingernails! I cannot tell you now, because that
would be giving the story away, but something dreadful and terrible
is connected with those fingernails, something that will cause gooseflesh
to rise in you. Don't ask me to tell. I can't give the story away. Read and
find out."

So, in *Silas Marner,* at the first encounter with "stone-pits" you must
heighten awareness of the clue that George Eliot has given us. You must
draw attention to the words and ask the class what could happen at
flooded stone-pits. As likely as not, students will guess. Their apprehensions
will rise, drama and suspense will enter, and the narrative will begin to
gallop.

Narrative, therefore, must be taught even though the student is his
own home-grown storyteller. One might expect that the interesting narrative, generally popular with students, like *Johnny Tremain,* would require a minimum of explication and teaching, but not so. Of course
Johnny Tremain can get off the ground on its own because it is an
interesting, well-told tale, but you do more than stand by. You must ask
how too keen a sense of deprivation leads to distortion and even to
disaster. Though the student is also a storyteller, and the printed tale
ever so fascinating, deepen it. Intensify suspense and the sense of impend-
ing conflict at every opportunity.

Next, point out contention and conflict where not manifest. Thus in
Giants in the Earth the endless prairie encourages expansiveness in Per
Hansa but causes constrictedness in Beret. Why should the same thing,
the prairie's promise, cause Per Hansa to react in one way and his wife
in a diametrically opposite manner? What basic conflict between them does
the prairie bring to light?

Or, in *Tom Sawyer,* when Tom pays for misbehavior by the whitewashing assignment, present to the class the contention between an imposed duty and the need to shirk it:

> How will Tom get out of the task? Is he the kind of boy who will run away from a task? Will he do it all himself? Is he *that* kind of boy? How can he avoid doing the job and still get it done?

Call it the "prevues of coming attractions" approach, that puts matters in either-or perspective and the class on tenterhooks. Or, earlier, when Tom encounters the new boy in town, and mutual threats are exchanged, you can say:

> How far will they go? Will they talk themselves out of, or into, a fight? What do you think? Who says there will be a fight? Hands, please. Why? Who says there won't be? Why? Will all these words bring on a fight or prevent it? Why?

Thus, you do not rush on to the conclusion but introduce a slow simmer which almost compels students to sneak a look ahead to the next page to see what does happen.

Does this diminish interest or intensify it? By thus dwelling on the narrative's intervening aspects, are we dulling the narrative impact or building it up? Some teachers may feel that this method gives too many hints, thus frittering interest. The contrary is true. Consider the popularity of the Western. The audience knows the good guys, the bad guys, and who will triumph. It knows the end. Hence the end is inconsequential. As *Time*[3] put it, the Western is the American morality play and one always knows how the morality play will end. Being an audience is of greater moment than knowing outcomes, because the storyteller can generally end his tale in any manner he wishes and call his own tune. In a detective story, even corpses have been guilty of the crime, if the storyteller wanted it that way. Clues are protean, pointing every which way, capable of resolution in your way, mine, or the storyteller's. If we guess with the storyteller, we win, but until then the fun is hanging the evidence on the right suspect. We enjoy the reading all the way through, no matter how it ends.

Therefore, you worry unnecessarily about loss of interest if you point up clues like fingernails, stone-pits, and prairies. The end will wait. There's no hurry about getting there; postponement heightens involvement.

The unpopularity of the slow-moving Victorian novel reveals an insalubrious need in modern readers to rush on to precipitate climaxes and an inability to make unhurried love to the patterns of narrative, character, and plot as these open, unfold, and reveal themselves. The old-fashioned novels teach us to take our time. Your students need this instruction.

Preliminary Consideration IV: The Underbrush in the Way

If narrative is vital to us, we resent anything that gets in the way. What gets in the way, chiefly, is the written word. In our earlier discussion of vocabulary (p. 145), we considered the unusual or difficult word. But sometimes even the easy word, when placed in unusual or unfamiliar conjunction with another easy word, causes difficulty. The opening of *Silas Marner* is illustrative of difficult vocabulary impeding narrative interest, whereas the opening of *Tale of Two Cities* illustrates how familiar words, in unusual conjunction, can cause difficulty. Below, we quote both, showing how words get in the way of understanding, whether difficult or easy. From *Silas Marner:*

> In the days when the *spinning-wheels* hummed busily in the farm-houses—and even great ladies, clothed in silk and thread-lace, had their *toy spinning-wheels* of polished oak—there might be seen in districts far away among the *lanes,* or deep in the *bosom* of the hills, certain *pallid* undersized men, who, by the side of the *brawny* country-folk, looked like the *remnants* of a *disinherited* race. The *shepherd's* dog barked fiercely when one of these *alien*-looking men appeared on the *upland,* dark against the early winter sunset; for what dog likes a figure bent under a heavy bag? —and these pale men rarely stirred abroad without that mysterious *burden.* The *shepherd* himself, though he had good reason to believe that the bag held nothing but *flaxen* thread, or else the long rolls of strong *linen* spun from that thread, was not quite sure that this trade of weaving, *indispensable* though it was, could be carried on entirely without the help of the *Evil One.* In that far-off time the superstition *clung* easily around every person or thing that was at all *unwonted,* or even *intermittent* and occasional *merely,* like the visits of the pedlar or the knife-grinder.

The italicized words will be puzzling to a substantial number of students. But even the familiar and usual, when placed in unaccustomed juxtaposition, will get in the way of narrative interest, as in the opening of *Tale of Two Cities:*

> It was the *best of times,* it was the *worst of times,* it was the *age of wisdom,* it was the *age of foolishness,* it was the *epoch of belief,* it was the

epoch of incredulity, it was the *season of Light,* it was the *season of Darkness,* it was the *spring of hope,* it was the *winter of despair.* . . .

How deal with these impediments to narrative? Chase students off to the dictionary? Urge students to guess from context? Paraphrase? Have the teacher do the reading?

The dictionary imposes intolerable delays in allowing the story to unfold. Contextual guessing reduces much of the story to incomprehensible gibberish and is easier for the bright student than the slower one. Teacher-paraphrasing degrades style and allusion to the level of the comic book and loses the richness of literary savor. Teacher-reading is an excellent idea where the teacher reads well, but is frowned upon by many educators because it reduces the contribution that should be expected from the student. What then remains?

We return to the build-up of suspense. Suspense is the secret, suspense derived from clues in the story, that creeps out of *each* sentence as we encounter it, that interprets each word, as we come to it, as contributory to suspense, leading to contention and conflict.

Two Old-fashioned Novels

Let us visit two classes. In one, *Silas Marner* has just been distributed, and the students have turned in their book receipts. So also in a second class, in which *Tale of Two Cities* has just been distributed.

We shall now, on the basis of the principles considered above, describe suitable procedures for teaching both novels. We deal with:

(1) introducing the novel;
(2) the conflict;
(3) the characters;
(4) the setting;
(5) plot and development;
(6) life of the author and other works by the author.

We shall follow this scheme in considering, first, *Silas Marner* and then *Tale of Two Cities* from the first day on which the texts are received until they are finished.

In introducing *Silas Marner* a too-frequent procedure is to discuss George Eliot, her life, her ideals, and her values. The author should be discussed, but not initially. Notice that the outlined scheme places discussion of the author last, after the reading has been completed. The usual preliminary lecture on the life and times of George Eliot is best deferred until the novel is read. The author takes on meaningful flesh and blood after the reading, not before.

How, then, do you begin?

With books before them, and *closed,* ask: "If you are abandoned by everybody you know and love, if those nearest and dearest to you turn their backs on you, and reject you, how would you react, where would you go, what would you do?"

The keynote of the book is abandonment, of Silas by his coreligionists, of Eppie by her drunken mother and weak father—even of Wildfire by Dunstan. Begin with analysis of this keynote, and have students give their opinions. Students have first-hand experience with rejection, both in reality and in fantasy, and here they are experts. They too have imagined the terrors of abandonment.

(Are there other keynotes? Redemption through love is one. If it can be infused with the aspects of conflict and suspense, it too can be used legitimately, but it would seem more appropriate later on, toward the denouement.)

After full discussion, books are opened. You should read because students, unfamiliar with the text, may stumble. An effective reading is of great importance. By effective reading, you best begin the task of pointing up clues, sharpening suspense, revealing and intensifying conflict. At once, however, you come up against the matter of difficult vocabulary:

spinning-wheels	burden
lanes	flax
pallid	indispensable
brawny	Evil One
remnants	unwonted
disinherited race	intermittent

All these in the opening paragraph!

We have promised that suspense and conflict were the solvents for vocabulary difficulty, and the opening paragraph offers an example. As you read—effectively, it is hoped—the class follows in its books, now opened. At the end of the first paragraph you have the class discuss these questions:

Why should a husky farmer (*brawny countryman*) fear a pale, smaller stranger (*pallid, undersized man*)?

What did the mysterious bag contain? (*burden*)

When is a curse harmful? (*Evil One*)

If the small stranger could make *linen* from *flax* by magic, would he let himself be bent under a heavy *burden*?

If you were in a strange country, would you be more afraid of a *brawny* countryman (or use husky farmer, above) or of the *remnant of a disinherited race*?

Which would you be more afraid of, the *wonted* or the *intermittent and occasional merely*?

Observe that the discussable questions are almost as many as the difficult words, with almost a point-to-point correspondence. Vocabulary is elucidated by suspense; guessing from context is thereby helped and thereafter students can be sent to the dictionary to verify their hunches. Suspense, the solvent that makes vocabulary difficulties disappear, infuses the opening, setting, background, character, and situation. Thus we do not expatiate on the Industrial Revolution but hint at dire outcomes, for, still in the opening chapter, the teacher can have the class discuss:

How did factories destroy spinning wheels? Were the people who used the spinning wheels destroyed too?

We move on to Lantern Yard. Two things favor William Dane's duplicity: Silas' epileptic faints, and his complete trust in his friend. But which was the more responsible? Ask this question of students. They will be polarized in two dichotomized groups. Some, generally the more naïve, will hold the epileptic attack chiefly responsible for William Dane's success; the more mature will see that Silas' trust more effectively betrayed him. Does this mean that we are not to trust people? Let classroom debate rage here, then ask:

How long would you remain alive if you trusted absolutely no one— a week? a month? a year? forever? or not even a single day?

We are at Raveloe. Dunstan and Godfrey Cass are arguing. Again we can polarize the class into two dichotomized groups by placing on the blackboard this caption:

Proof That the Weaker Brother Is
Dunstan   *Godfrey*

Some students will give reasons for judging Dunstan the weaker; others will indict Godfrey. On the blackboard list the reasons offered. Which side wins? We cannot determine. We have meanwhile amassed evidence that *both* are weak, each in his own way.

From the evidence on the blackboard, we can now ask the class to discuss:

> Does wealth account for this weakness? (*Teacher:* But other wealthy families show no such outcropping of weakness.)
>
> Does death of the mother account for this weakness? (*Teacher:* But in other families mothers have died and the children, though they have suffered, have not been debased.)

Ultimately, discussion will involve weakness with irresponsibility. In any case, character is beginning to emerge for analysis and study.

Your class is at the conclusion of *Silas Marner*, the scene in which Godfrey and Nancy offer to accept Eppie into their household. Present this situation:

> You come home this afternoon. Outside the house is a beautiful, chauffeur-driven Cadillac. You walk into your house. With your parents are two strange people, a handsome, well-dressed man and a beautiful woman. You are told that these strangers are your true parents who left you with this family when you were very young. They have returned to claim you. How would you react?

Eppie's situation is made more vivid, and simultaneously is used to tap that universal fantasy world in which we wonder if our parents are our true parents.

Possibilities for discussion are numerous. Ask boys, "What would the Squire have done if Godfrey had told his father about his marriage? What would you have done?" And, for girls, "What are the dangers, or advantages, of flirtation from what you know of Mollie, Nancy Lammeter, and Eppie?" Some danger of priggishness is possible here, but can be avoided by the more urbane teacher.

When the reading is complete, you may want to test comprehension. You may request that the class draw a map of Raveloe, or use the following as a quick examination:

> Godfrey Cass married __1__ after the death of __2__ . Meanwhile __3__ has grown up and is being courted by __4__ who is the son of __5__ . Godfrey and his wife have __6__ children so they decide to __7__ Eppie.
> __8__ is found dead in the __9__ with the __10__ that he had stolen from

___11___ . Godfrey tells his wife that he is Eppie's ___12___ . Silas asks ___13___ to decide whether or not to leave him, and this person decides to ___14___ . At the end of the story Eppie marries ___15___ .

In the class studying *Tale of Two Cities,* down the corridor, another teacher is introducing a class to another novel, not mentioning Charles Dickens, or his life, or his childhood, or his opinion of America, but putting the following problems to the class for discussion, problems which are keynotes of the novel:

> Would you ever sacrifice your life for anybody else?
> Which type of survival is more important, to live in the hearts and minds of those you love, though you are physically dead and buried, or to survive physically, and then die, without being remembered by anybody for anything? (Hint: you can use Lou Gehrig as an example.)

Your expectation is that the class will polarize itself into contending factions, so that discussion will arise. The interaction of sacrifice and survival (in the physical sense and in the spiritual) are among the major themes of the novel. Therefore, strike for these, again postponing Dickens' life and other works until this one has been read.

After full discussion, have books opened and again, as in the other case, start reading. Again we encounter vocabulary difficulty, but this time the words are usual enough and familiar enough and simple enough, but they have become difficult in conjunction, where, as in the quoted passage, all the words (except for *epoch* and *incredulity*) are well within the recognition limits of the usual high school class. Here vocabulary is not the stumbling block. Conceptualization is. Once more our difficulty is resolved by sharpening suspense.

Read the opening section, and then ask:

> If things are at the same time best and worst, wise and foolish, believing and disbelieving, light and dark, hopeful and despairing, are they peaceful times or warlike times? Times of good feeling, or of revolution?
> If some people believe the times to be best, while others believe them to be worst, what happens to people who have no opinion?
> Is it possible to have no opinions? What kind of person has no opinions when all around him opinions are leading to revolution, war, killing?
> When do opinions justify revolution, war, and killing?

Similarly, in the opening section, we encounter difficulty in reference, beginning with the time of the story, "the year of Our Lord one thousand seven hundred and seventy-five." (*Teacher:* "How many years ago is that?

The same year as Paul Revere's ride, is it not?") References to Mrs. Southcott and the Cock-lane ghost are bewildering, but let there be no interruption in order to explain these. Explanations are to be found in the *Encyclopaedia Britannica*. An assignment can be given to one or more students to work up a brief report for class discussion on the superstitions of our times and the superstitions of the people in the novel.

We, like Mrs. Southcott, are talking of the end of the world. How different are Jehovah's Witnesses? Does radioactive fallout make Mrs. Southcott's predictions more probable? Is there in us, whether Mrs. Southcott, Jehovah's Witnesses, or diplomat, this chiliastic, millenarian infection which nowadays is given scientific sanction but remains in part Mrs. Southcott's superstition?

The Cock-lane ghost has a contemporary counterpart in a certain Long Island home where things are seen to fly about crazily by the family and the local police, presented on television by Ed Murrow, and written up in *Time*.[4] We are not too different.

We are introduced to the Dover coach. (A map would be helpful to show the route from London to Dover, the Channel, and the route to Paris.) Fast moving narrative closes in on us. Is it a hold-up or not? How can you tell if the unknown rider is approaching at a canter or at a gallop? (Once a teacher was appalled by Puerto Rican and Negro pupils who used their ten fingers and the palms of their hands to hammer out fantastically complicated rhythms on desk tops. The teacher grew older. He learned to enjoy their virtuosity. He asked a class to illustrate the difference between a canter and a gallop, using their palms and fingers. They understood at once what the coachman was listening to.)

Jarvis Lorry, when we first meet him, is uncertain and almost tremulous in the dark, until Jerry Cruncher rides up with his message. Mr. Lorry's "quavering" voice is replaced by "quiet business confidence" as Jerry hands the message to him. Point out here how the mere touch of the message transforms Jarvis Lorry. How will the class interpret this change?

Similarly, our first insight into Jerry's character is his startled reaction to Mr. Lorry's message. We must stress Jerry's statement, "You'd be in a blazing bad way, if recalling to life was to come into fashion. . . . It wouldn't do for you . . . it wouldn't suit your line of business!" In addition, we have the comic description of Jerry's crew-cut coiffure, to be kept in mind when his son appears.

Then comes Mr. Lorry's dozing up the apparition of Dr. Manette, where a series of alternative pictures are presented, which offer choices for class selection. Which way will Dr. Manette react? Subsequently, while Mr. Lorry is waiting for Lucie at the St. George Hotel in Dover, we get a further picture of him in depth; he is an orderly man, but is he also a conscientious one? Shortly thereafter, the architecture of the story rises because we meet Lucie, sensitively and delicately fainting away so that the masterful Pross can come on stage. We must not forget to set the stage because we are soon flooded by a broken wine cask, Gaspard, Defarge, Madame Defarge, and the rest.

Remember that as the clues appear—RECALLED TO LIFE and Jerry's agitated reaction—you must underscore and fix these in the student's focus of attention. Jerry's reaction must not go to waste. The final pages of the novel depend on Jerry's reaction at the very beginning; his way of life and the information it gives him access to make possible Carton's final act of sacrifice.

We have discussed revolutions, the French Revolution, and clash, brigands, uprisings. The background of *Silas Marner* and *Tale of Two Cities* is revolution. In one it is dim, in the other prominent. In both, we want to interest the student in a yarn. Both stories show that hate has lower survival value than love and that self-sacrifice for a worthy end insures survival, rather than destruction. (See Chapter 14 on lesson planning.) Thus, at the end of *Tale of Two Cities,* or even in preparing for the denouement, ask:

> If you dislike or hate anybody, are you strengthening yourself or destroying yourself? In loving anybody, are you strengthening yourself or destroying yourself? Do you live more fully, enjoyably—and longer—if you love or hate? Who lived longer in the hearts and minds of people, Carton or Madame Defarge?

We turn to interaction of character and plot. The message that Mr. Lorry wants Jerry Cruncher to convey is disturbing to the Resurrection-man. Point out this dismay, stress it, urge the student to keep it in mind, thus adding to suspense.

The original trial-scene reference to Carton, as he stares at the ceiling, can similarly be overlooked unless you indicate that the reference is no idle one—though the character seems so. Characters should be compared in their reaction to events whenever occasion offers. Thus you should match Pross and Lucie, Dr. Manette and Mr. Lorry, Carton and

Stryver, Carton and Darnay. Or analysis can concentrate on an individual, when you ask:

> Why should a gifted man like Carton not improve his position? What makes people unable to help themselves when they are fully aware of the causes of their failure?
>
> Would a confirmed bachelor like Mr. Lorry be self-sacrificing or selfish? How does Mr. Lorry prove that some people who live alone must find attachments? Does this prove the need to love people or to be free of loneliness?
>
> Can you reconcile loyalty to an institution, like Mr. Lorry's to Tellson's bank, with warmth, love, and sympathy for human beings? How can Mr. Lorry do so, when he considers himself purely a man of business?
>
> How does Jerry Cruncher, grave-robber that he is, pull the wool over Mr. Lorry's eyes? What kind of woman is Mrs. Cruncher? Is she devoted or stupid for accepting this kind of treatment?
>
> When people are liars, cheats, and informers—as Barsad and Cly are —how do they distort words to give a more favorable impression of themselves? Do they simultaneously try to give *themselves* an improved opinion of themselves? Do villains think of themselves as villains?
>
> What does Stryver's opinion of Lucie and Carton reveal of Stryver? What does Defarge's opinion of Dr. Manette reveal of Defarge? What does Carton's opinion of Lucie and Darnay reveal of Carton?

Or you can direct some questions specifically to boys for the man's point of view on Carton versus Darnay, and others to girls: "If you were Lucie, would you want Carton to visit your home?" To boys: "If you were Charles Darnay, would you want Carton to visit your home?" Or we can analyze the scene in which Barsad visits the Defarges and ask, "How does Madame Defarge show that she is carefully trained to avoid traps? How does Defarge show this?" In brief, how do characters react to events? What does this reveal of them?

We match character with situation and event, with other characters, with opinions of other characters, to enlarge understanding of human behavior, motive, and incentive. Both Injun Joe (in *Tom Sawyer*) and Jerry Cruncher were grave-robbers. Why do we look at them differently? How similar, or different, are the Defarges and Macbeth and Lady Macbeth? Such comparison across books are interesting for seniors who have read both.

Sometimes you will want to differentiate *caricature* from *character,* and you can do so by combining them, getting something like *charicature* or *characature,* or by coining your own portmanteau word. But a caricature like Micawber is truer than a character like Copperfield, Touchstone truer than practically anybody else in *As You Like It,* and Cruncher truer than Darnay.

Lastly, novels have structure. *Tale of Two Cities* covers a period of approximately twenty years—or longer, if we include the flashback in Dr. Manette's letter and Carton's death-scene vision—and we can study the craft of the storyteller as he handles transitions, the polyphony of story-within-a-story, shifts of attention from one character to another: Lucie outside La Force and the wood-chopper; Jerry and Pross hastening their flight and the approach of Madame Defarge; suspense and the cliff-hanger; clues (the rust on Jerry Cruncher's fingers and how it serves to bring Barsad ultimately to heel). The unsophisticated reader merely reads. The more sophisticated reader takes intellectual delight in the mechanism that turns the wheels and the wheels within wheels. The student should learn how stories are told and the techniques by which yarns are spun. Such knowledge does not detract from appreciation, but augments it.

We now cast you in an imaginary drama: We return down the corridor to the first class, where *Silas Marner* is being read. That evening, at a PTA meeting, which you are attending, one of the parents objects to the fact that *Silas Marner* is still taught.

"Why, it's old-fashioned! I read it, my mother read it, and now my boy is going to be bored with it. Why is it still in the reading syllabus? It's dull and has nothing to do with modern life!"

The chairman of the meeting turns to you. You catch a quick nod from the principal that you are to do the job of answering and you think back to the class discussion of that day . . .

When the bell rang, some students had remained to discuss the assignment, to read ahead by themselves and answer questions in their notebooks. "Is it full of hard words all the way through?" one of the students asked.

"Did you find the words hard?" you answered in pretended amazement.

"Well no, not after you explained them," the student replied. "But reading ahead by ourselves, we can't get help from you."

You denied the soft impeachment. "I didn't explain anything. The class did most of the talking and discussing. That's all the explanation there was."

The student nodded. "Because everybody's had ideas on the subject, like when you're younger you want to run away from home, or else you're afraid your parents will leave you, or when they have arguments you're afraid they'll break up, and then what will happen to you? Funny how the same ideas occurred to everybody . . ."

. . . Abandonment. Rejection. These are the ideas in your mind as you rise to face the parent, to describe the lesson that day in an old-fashioned novel that deals with very contemporary problems. Students are interested in the problem of abandonment. It is in their bones. Presented that way, *Silas Marner* is as modern a novel as you could name.

The parent picks up the point. "In that case why not give them the modern examples of abandonment and rejection? I think that would get them even more involved."

You answer pleasantly, "We want them to read the modern novel with perspective; many characters, plots, and situations simply repeat the classics. In *Mill on the Floss* Maggie Tulliver is the original of dozens of heroines in dozens of modern novels. Students will read these modern versions of *Silas Marner* with more understanding because they've read the classic, just as we get more insight into current events if we know American history. *Silas Marner* prepares them to read modern novels."

This dialogue has different endings in different schools. *Silas Marner* is Victorian if a Victorian teacher teaches it, but it can be as modern as Kerouac or Cozzens. Squire Cass is a standard type in the English novel, whether in *Tom Jones, Sense and Sensibility,* or *The Forsyte Saga* and relates to an important Colonel Blimp aspect of British life—and also to George Babbitt. The Brothers Cass make it possible to read *The Brothers Karamazov* with more understanding, or Orlando and Oliver in *As You Like It*. Only poor books are old-fashioned.

Thus Nancy Lammeter at the party is an older portrait of Alice Adams and of innumerable American girls at innumerable parties. Dolly Winthrop is not only a gentler descendant of the Wyf of Bath, but in contemporary avatar is any one of the roles that Shirley Booth has been playing. In fact, in mood and in feeling how different is *Our Town* from *Silas Marner*?

The classics have been rewritten more than once. Cozzens and Marquand restate Thackeray. *Death of a Salesman* is Aeschylean. Joyce's *Ulysses* is indebted to *Tristram Shandy* as well as the *Odyssey*. Jerome Weidman's genre city types draw from *Tale of Two Cities,* as do Baroness Orczy's snobs in *Scarlet Pimpernel*. The "old-fashioned" novel, misrepresented as dull, prepares the student to read the contemporary novel with greater understanding.

Of importance in the classroom is this corollary: The novel is not for once, but for many times. You should be explicit that this is an introductory reading of a famous book, therefore a superficial reading. You should hold out the prospects of deepening and enduring pleasure from a rereading and a re-rereading and many more times that, you hope, because there will be so much not understood the first time that will bring pleasure the second time.

Novels are complicated and lengthy. You cannot fully explore the qualities of a good novel in a few weeks; your basic assumption in planning and teaching the novel is that this experience is the first or introductory one and that the student will have occasion to return to the novel as the years go by. The classroom approach should be a sort of kickoff rather than an *ave atque vale* or once-over-lightly contact, which is why the abbreviated and simplified edition, predigested and decanted into a fake simplicity and lightened vocabulary load, blood-brother and competitor of certain comic books, should be dropped from school purchase lists. Capsule versions are dull for the slow reader and exasperating for the better one.

Where difficult passages in *Silas Marner* and *Tale of Two Cities* are encountered, not omissions but explanations are necessary, and you should (1) bridge with an explanation of your own; (2) indicate that the students are too young, or not ready, by lack of experience or inadequacy of reading level. Observe that this takes you off the defensive and puts you on the offensive.

For example, the opening chapter of *Tale of Two Cities* may be laborious going for some classes and you may wish to omit it, superb opening and setting though it is. Tell a class of the slower type that it may be two or three years ahead of their reading and comprehension level, fill in with an introduction of your own—it's still better than those comics—and plunge directly into the suspense of the Dover coach scene and Mr. Lorry. Simultaneously hold out the promise that with additional maturity, reading ability, and comprehension, the class will return for a rereading of the novel in its unadulterated entirety to gain the increments of enjoyment that rereading of great books bring. A great book is not for once. Construe this as only the initial contact, the curtain raiser, because there isn't much time to do much more. You can discuss: "Has your pleasure in seeing a good movie over again on television been greater, less, or different than the original time you saw it?" The same will be true of good books and good plays.

Passages that become dramatic and deeper on rereading can be offered like tidbits to the class, as movie producers promote anticipation by "prevues of coming attractions." Read them the breaking of the wine cask and the animality that follows, the first meeting of Lucie and Dr. Manette, Jerry Cruncher's denunciation of his wife, the Hundreds of People chapter, the debate between Charles Darnay and the Marquis, or other highly charged scenes. Present these to whet the appetite for reading when they are out of high school, older, more understanding than they can possibly be right now. Leave untaught what is too laborious and what you wish to omit, but tease them with the rewards that maturity will bring to these passages.

Does this approach disjoint? Does it fragment? No. It conveys a *New Yorker* short story feeling, offering a truer sense of life's inconclusive actualities than the well-shaped *Saturday Evening Post* story with the wrap-up ending. Student despair with obliqueness of reference and tortuosity of style never emerges, even in two such difficult chapters as the opening one and "Monseigneur in Town." Urge the better student to attack these in depth. Promise the poorer student a richness of return proportionate to his attempts, attempts that need not be made entirely during this term; more and more will come within his grasp as he grows older and more experienced. You can anticipate that *Silas Marner* and *Tale of Two Cities* will remain in print. Meanwhile let both types of student attack the book, understand what they can, and deepen it for themselves. Also, in both cases, orient them toward future experiences with the novel, as much as with current experiences. What may be difficult to understand now may be much simpler later on and the student should not be embarrassed to indicate, in a memorandum to himself, by chapter, page, and paragraph, what is currently beyond him, not only as a reminder to himself at some future date, but for present class discussion. In this way he can unashamedly confess his boredom here, his interest there, his puzzlement elsewhere, his dislike for the mawkish and sentimental in both these Victorian novels, and his appreciation for Dickens and Eliot at their greatest. The organization of these self-directed memoranda is not simple. They involve the entire critical faculty of the student. In doing so they become valuable in composition and theme writing.

CASE STUDY 10   *Ivanhoe* was still on the reading list, but
none of the teachers had used it for years. The copies were collecting
dust in the book room and the department head, a new broom who was
sweeping accordingly, suggested to the teacher in charge of the book room
that the copies be disposed of. One of the older teachers was horrified at
the idea that this favorite of her girlhood should be thus abandoned. She
took a copy home, read it, enjoyed it, but had to admit to herself her
doubts that high school students of today would be interested in it—
the style was difficult, the characters remote, the problems antiquated.
If so, she asked herself, why had she enjoyed it? As an older teacher,
she had the privilege of teaching an honors class, and she wanted to communicate her pleasure to them, but she would have to take precautions
against the dated characterizations and the desultory development of story.
Working for her were the conflicts of (1) father and son; (2) tyranny and
freedom; (3) protection of the weak and the depredations of the strong;
(4) patriotism and betrayal. These were the values she wanted to come
through. Withal, Sir Walter needed some bulwarks because *Ivanhoe* was
not intended for the mid-twentieth-century reader. The department head
agreed to delay the date of execution; the teacher had the books distributed and told the class:

"I'm sorry you people are so young. It's a great pity. You'll understand
some of *Ivanhoe,* but you're not old enough, yet, to understand more of it.
I was wondering whether to use it with you. First I told myself you were
too young to appreciate all of it, but then I thought that there was a lot
in it that you were ready for right now. I hope I haven't made a mistake.
I sincerely believe you are ready for a good deal of it, enough to make it
worth while to study right now. You know, I could hold off until you're
older but there's no sense in delaying just because you're not mature in
every single, last particular—so here goes. Two or three years from now,
when you reread it, you'll find more in it that you'll understand. So don't
be upset just because you're so young. Be patient."

Note the stress on *being ready, old enough,* and *mature enough,* areas
in which the young are sensitive and defensive. (The same values emerge
in Yeats' "Salley Gardens," p. 106.) The teacher did not stress difficulties
in the book, but alluded generously, charitably, and understandingly to the

forgivable shortcomings of the young reader, thus putting the reader on the defensive, not *Ivanhoe*.

She found the tactic successful, so successful that it went to her head, driving out the good judgment she usually exercised. As the class proceeded in its reading of the novel, occasionally students indicated a lack of understanding; the teacher would nod sympathetically, almost patronizingly. She got into the habit of saying, "You're a little too young yet," instead of attempting some discussion.

One day the teacher was shocked. A student said sharply, "I showed this to my big sister. She's nineteen. She said she didn't understand it either!"

The teacher said approvingly, "I'm glad you're discussing it. What part didn't she understand?"

The crusher came. "All of it!"

Somehow, just at that instant, the teacher's native good sense returned. "Didn't she ever study it in high school?"

"No," the student rejoined.

This was a little better. "Then you'll have to help her out," the teacher said. "You can't expect her to understand the characters, or the background, or the words, if she didn't study it in high school. That's why you're studying it." The teacher turned to the class. "Those who have older brothers and sisters—will you find out if they ever studied *Ivanhoe* in high school? If they did—and only if they did—give them the book, ask them to look through it, and find out if it's as hard now for them to read as it was then."

Of course the outcome was predictable. Reading comprehension improves with age, even if reading rate doesn't. Young adults read newspapers and magazines. The poll of older brothers and sisters showed that *Ivanhoe* was considerably easier now for them than it had been. But, even more rewarding, a few reread it completely for auld lang syne, or because it was still a good yarn, and delighted that it meant more to them than it had before. *Ivanhoe* is still on the shelves in that school.

Research, Resources, and Techniques

1. Sister Mary Felice's "An Approach to Teaching *A Tale of Two Cities*" (*E. J.*, Jan. 1959, p. 31) follows an approach considerably different from the one recommended here. Which do you prefer? How can you combine them?

2. For different points of view on the classics of narrative and their retention in the curriculum:

a. Dorelle Markley Heisel's "Let's Remove the Perennial Hardy" (wonderful title!) in *English Journal* (Jan. 1956, p. 37) feels that *Ivanhoe, Silas Marner,* and *Scarlet Letter* ought to be expunged from book lists. What do your colleagues think? Can a decision be made without regard to teacher quality?

b. Lou LaBrant's "As of Now" (*E. J.,* Sept. 1959, p. 295) is a superb consideration of the tasks of the English teacher. On the highest professional level, this article should improve your integrity of approach and should not be missed. Commit it to your heart. One passage is relevant to the case history on *Ivanhoe:* "The teacher who once said 'I teach this now or else my student will never read this book' must change his thinking."

c. Also relevant to the *Ivanhoe* case history is J. P. Shannon's "The Case of Shannon vs. Novels" (*Clearing House,* Oct. 1954).

d. So, also, is John Dewey's opinion in *Experience and Education* (Macmillan, 1956, p. 49). "The most important attitude that can be formed is that of desire to go on learning."

3. Bearing on some of the points raised here is Stanley S. Cook's unpublished doctoral dissertation, *A Comparative Study of Aims Held by Parents, Students, and Teachers for an English Program in a Suburban High School* (Wayne University, 1955).

Homer Is the Hunted

Why teach the *Odyssey*? Nobody writes that way, thinks that way, or believes that way, some may superficially declare, and among these are teachers who shun Homer because they themselves are superficial. The *Odyssey* is the earliest yarn, unlike the chronicling in the Old Testament. Homer invented the literary devices of climax and crisis. He was the first to use the cliff-hanger, the flashback, and the punch line.

But does the modern reader really care, any more than he cares who discovered fire? Indeed, should he? One has just about enough time to live in the present, especially during adolescence, without troubling about the past. However, most adolescents are tremendously interested in the primitive, in cave man, in early man, in Man against Nature, and even in who discovered fire. The past fascinates them—depending on the teacher! The reason is that the past is part of the contemporary. More, it enriches the contemporary.

We can easily study the literary device of climax and crisis from modern examples, but we can enrich the study of the modern example by transcending time and the thousands of years that separate us from Troy, by posing some eternally interesting questions, and by having full and ample class discussion on problems that men have always discussed and have not yet stopped discussing:

You are living hundreds of miles from home. A beautiful woman is in love with you. She is wealthy. She can give you everything your heart desires. She wants to keep you with her, but you want to leave, to return to your home, your family, your friends. Are home and family that important?

Has anything ever changed your life? If so, was it because of something you did, or what others did, or some combination? Did Odysseus change his life, when he left Calypso's Ogygia, or was it changed for him?

Is homesickness real? Is gravity real? Is love real? When are ideas real and when unreal?

Look around you and determine how much you owe to dead people. The town you live in, the pavement you walk on, the language you speak, the clothes you wear represent building, techniques, weaving, processes, work by which dead people still live. How much do we owe men who lived fifty years ago? One hundred years ago? A thousand years ago? Men who lived during the Trojan War, almost 3500 years ago? Anything? Nothing? How much of what?

In the *Odyssey* you read many strange names, strange places—what does this tell you of the number of men, incidents, and experiences that took place before you were born? Compare the experiences you and all the people you know have had with the kinds of experiences, the numbers of experiences, and the places where these experiences once took place. Which would you prefer? Why should we name places (Utica, Ithaca, Troy in New York State) after Greek cities? Why should we remember these names and places? Why should we remember the multitude of things that happened before we were born?

Suppose everything, everybody, the gods, fate, luck, people, your own friends, were all against you. Could you survive? What would you do to survive?

Orestes killed. Telemachus fled. Was Telemachus or Orestes the more manly? Was Telemachus right or was Orestes? Discuss these questions, remembering that one father, Agamemnon, died at the hands of his rival Aegisthus; the other father, Odysseus, survived to kill his rivals. (For the section on Telemachus' visit to Nestor.)

How can a son grow up to be worthy of his father when the father is absent? What can a father do to make his son grow up worthy of him, when the father is absent? (And when the father is present?)

What do photographs of Greek vases, architecture, and sculpture tell you about the Greeks? Compare your feeling with the feeling in Keats' "Ode on a Grecian Urn"; Tennyson's "Ulysses," "Choric Song," and "Lotos-Eaters"; Edna St. Vincent Millay's "Persephone"; Edwin Arlington Robinson's "Cassandra." All these poems have reference to incidents and people in the *Odyssey*.

Name some Achilles heels. Name some possible Trojan horses. Why is a car called the Mercury? (Or, with *Moby Dick,* below, a Plymouth?)

By such questions you attempt to show how the *Odyssey* is contemporaneous.

Prior to all else is the teacher's understanding. A novel cannot be taught successfully unless the teacher knows it thoroughly, has savored it, and has evaluated it critically. Often students find their own way to literature. How much more thrilling to be accompanied by a teacher who senses that great literature is, of all times and places, not least here and now in this time and place, in this very classroom! Many well-edited school texts are accompanied by discussion and question materials, but these, excellent as they often are, fail of their full effect because the teacher is an unimaginative dullard.

The Greeks never tired of listening to the Homeric tales; neither do we. Freud was occupied with them, as was James Joyce. A modern scientist like Werner Heisenberg thinks they are the best preparation for teaching creativity in science.[5] Too many jaundiced English teachers say, "Maybe so, but try it in *my* classes!"

Let's, using the material provided in this chapter as a springboard from which will dive a teacher unafraid of his charges and excited by the earliest novel we have. We will find a class piqued because it cannot do better than describe a sunrise as "rosy-fingered dawn"; recognizing why Odysseus' men ignored Aeolus' strict injunctions from the occasions they have, with knowledge of the consequences, disobeyed parents, teacher, or their own best judgment; realizing how the incidents in their twentieth-century lives are enriched by the infinity of incidents in the corridors of time that debouch into the contemporary, the pleasant passage of time in ice-cream parlors with other Lotus Eaters, the best combination of persuasion and guile when some modern Polyphemus has them backed against the wall, the unnecessary crowing and boasting that apprises Poseidon of your identity after you have defeated your particular Polyphemus; seeing how greed leads to self-destructiveness in Circe's day as in this, and how the pleasures of Ogygia are never as strong as home sweet home. Or don't they believe any of this?

Let them indicate the passages in the *Odyssey* with which they disagree—and thus learn Homer.

Moby Dick is another novel in the epic style. Humor, humanity, the profound, the documentary are found in Melville's masterpiece. Begin the teaching of *Moby Dick* with a reading and discussion of Masefield's "Sea Fever" and Sandburg's "Young Sea," especially the closing line of the Masefield poem and its meanings. Masefield is saying much the same thing as Melville, especially in the unabridged opening chapter of *Moby Dick*.

However, once beyond the opening, you will find an encyclopedia of whaling, and long sections of nonnarrative and purely expository writing, more an essay than fiction. School editions omit much of this, but there is transitional material that makes for rich class discussion, for which you may want your own unabridged edition:

> Are you a believer in ghosts, my friend? There are other ghosts than the Cock Lane one, and far deeper men than Doctor Johnson who believe in them. (Chapter LXVIII)
>
> After all, I do not think that my remarks about religion made much impression upon Queequeg. Because, in the first place, he somehow seemed dull of hearing on that important subject, unless considered from his own point of view; and, in the second place, he did not more than one third understand me, couch my ideas simply as I would; and, finally, he no doubt thought he knew a good deal more about the true religion than I did. He looked at me with a sort of condescending concern and compassion, as though he thought it a great pity that such a sensible young man should be so hopelessly lost to evangelical pagan piety. (Chapter XVII)
>
> This elusive quality it is, which causes the thought of whiteness, when divorced from more kindly associations, and coupled with any object terrible in itself, to heighten that terror to the furthest bounds. (Chapter XLI)
>
> Oh! many are the Fin-Backs, and many are the Dericks, my friend. (Chapter LXXX)
>
> "Well, then," interrupted Bunger, "give him your left arm for bait to get the right. Do you know, gentlemen"—very gravely and mathematically bowing to each captain in succession—"do you know, gentlemen, that the digestive organs of the whale are so inscrutably constructed by Divine Providence, that it is quite impossible for him to completely digest even a man's arm? And he knows it too. So that what you take for the White Whale's malice is only his awkwardness." (Chapter XCIX)

Literally, there are hundreds of such richly discussable passages in the unabridged edition. Does Melville mean to be mystical? There are passages supporting this hypothesis. Does Melville mean to poke fun at the mystical?

Alternative passages will support this alternative. You can polarize your class into dichotomized groups and gain superb discussion around this major issue. Humor sits side by side with the mystical, the florid with the straightforward, credulity with skepticism. Invite your class to take its choice.

Research, Resources, and Techniques

1. Why not use exciting new discoveries in archaeology to supplement your teaching of the *Odyssey*?

a. George E. Mylonas' "Mycenae, City of Agamemnon" (*Scientific American*, Dec. 1954, p. 72) gives concreteness and actuality to Homer.

b. Emmanuel Anati's "Prehistoric Art in the Alps" (*Scientific American*, Jan. 1960, p. 52) deals with rock carvings in North Italy going back four thousand years, the kind of carvings with which Polyphemus might have decorated his cave.

2. Sam Bluefarb's "The Sea—Mirror and Maker of Character in Fiction and Drama" (*E. J.*, Dec. 1959, p. 501) is especially useful with *Moby Dick, Odyssey,* Masefield, and Sandburg's "Young Sea," and demonstrates how the nautical interacts with narrative and poetry.

3. Marion B. Pierstorff's "Promoting Critical Thought in the Study of Character Conduct in Literature" (*E. J.*, Oct. 1958, p. 422) offers a series of *why* questions. How would you restate these to gain the polarized type of question recommended in Chapter 11? Would this type of question or the polarized question gain greater depth of response? (See Chapter 11.)

Two Popular Moderns

Two novels greeted warmly by teachers and read eagerly by students are *Giants in the Earth* and *Johnny Tremain*. Both are exciting, rich in character, setting, narrative value, and materials for analysis and discussion. They virtually teach themselves and are, in the parlance of magazine editors, "an easy read." The temptation for interest to do the teacher's work is great but must be resolutely withstood.

In *Giants in the Earth,* the prairie offers the same brooding background as the sea in *Moby Dick*. Beret's constricted horror contrasts with Per Hansa's expanded horizons. (However, opportunities beyond character analysis exist. If your school is unit-oriented, immigration, the national strains in American life, local history, natural resources, and even matters of mental hygiene are appropriate.) As characteristics of the Norwegian pioneers, you may write on the blackboard

Initiative
Ingenuity
Fortitude
Courage

and then ask students if these characterize the people now living in your locality. What are the differences between the Norwegian pioneers and the people in your locality? Any? None? What about the new pioneers of the space age?

Compare Beret and Per Hansa to show that Beret, though on the frontier, was not a pioneer and that there may be people now in your community, though not living on a frontier, who are pioneers. Hence, being placed accidentally on a frontier doesn't make you a pioneer. Per Hansa would have been a pioneer even back home in Norway. We can be pioneers in Cleveland, Tucson, Flatbush, or Sacramento. Living on a frontier doesn't imbue you with pioneer spirit.

Johnny Tremain also offers opportunities for the unit and for relationships with American history. The Harper school edition of *Giants in the Earth* offers no teaching suggestions; the Houghton Mifflin school edition of *Johnny Tremain* offers many. In neither case can you stand by passively. Even good books don't teach themselves. You must yourself develop your lesson plans in *Giants in the Earth* and you must actively use the teaching and discussion suggestions in *Johnny Tremain*. In both books interest is not enough. Your job is to help students analyze and dissect, so that reading becomes less the spectator sport and more the participant one. The reader who reads with eyes glazed, mind asleep, mouth open, and adenoids showing reads the popular magazines and tabloid newspapers to become narcotized by words. With *Johnny Tremain* and *Giants in the Earth,* the temptation is to let narcosis rule. Avoid the temptation. These are books to think about. Attack them in depth. Build up suspense. Point up and dramatize the clues. Compare characters (Johnny and Rab, Per Hansa and Beret). This analytic approach makes two interesting books even more stimulating and exciting.

Where teaching suggestions are included in the text, as in *Johnny Tremain,* be sparing in your references to them. Do not tell students to read the assignment and then "answer the question on page so-and-so." Pretend, instead, that page so-and-so is nonexistent and give your own assignment, incorporating the material on page so-and-so. Occasionally a student in idly thumbing through the book may see the assignment you have given duplicated or approximated on page so-and-so. He will not accuse you of plagiarism. Rather he will think that you have done a good job of preparing—and he is not wrong. This material is for you to adapt as much as for students to use. Because students are so caught up in narrative, in conflict, in character clash, in climax, and in other aspects of the yarn, discussion materials in print seem cold and less compelling than narrative in the same print. Therefore, though you use the same discussion and questioning materials on page so-and-so, change the modality of presentation. Mimeograph the materials, write them on the blackboard, speak them as if they originated with you; they will seem fresher than the original and gain greater impact.

Ideas have adaptability. Here is a discussion possibility relevant to the concluding chapter of both *Tale of Two Cities* and *Giants in the Earth*. You ask your class:

"A beggar stops you on the street. He wants a nickel. Would you give it?" Allow discussion. Some may say yes, others no. Here a student will declare his choice depends on the beggar's appearance, there on the beggar's manner.

Restate the question, raising the beggar's request to a dime. Allow discussion. Restate again, increasing the request now to a quarter. Push the amount upward, say to a dollar, or to that point that the class admits is unthinkable.

Repeat and modify. Instead of a beggar the petitioner is a brother. What now is the break-off point? Five dollars? Ten dollars? A hundred? Modify again, this time with a mother or a father. Allow discussion.

New modification: would they sacrifice an arm, an eye, a leg for loved ones? You can point out how insurance companies indemnify for injuries to these organs, reading directly from accident policies. Would they sacrifice for brothers, sisters, and parents, as in eye-transplant operations?

Next and last, under what circumstances would they sacrifice their lives, as Carton did and as Per Hansa did to satisfy Beret's wish?

Units in Fiction

A good story is discussable, opening up perspectives and considerations for fine classroom chat emerging from what we have read—which is as good a way as any of describing the unit. Units arise almost spontaneously from *Johnny Tremain* and *Giants in the Earth,* but the unit is also an opening to teacher-student planning. Let us first consider the unit and then go on to teacher-student planning in narrative.

Remember, in your unit planning, that you are an English teacher, not a social studies teacher. You should not abdicate your special training. *Johnny Tremain* deals with Revolutionary Boston, *Giants in the Earth* with the settlement of the West; you will teach most effectively by involving students with the character of the pioneer in *My Ántonia,* Hamlin Garland, and *Red Badge of Courage* to focus on pioneer Americans in periods of struggle. Economics, history, and sociology should come in small doses. Leave them for other specialists. A unit is not a pretext for superficiality but an opportunity for depth. A unit of *Giants in the Earth, My Ántonia,* and Hamlin Garland will lead to *Roughing It,* Bret Harte, Jack London, Ruth Suckow, " 'Revolt' of Mother," and Conrad Richter. Similarly, *Johnny Tremain* will lead to *Red Badge of Courage,* Walt Whitman, *Caine Mutiny,* the war poems of Siegfried Sassoon (perhaps even Southey's "Blenheim"), John Horne Burns, Theodore Plevier's *Stalingrad, Andersonville,* and so on without end. Such are the morsels for the English teacher to chew on. Your units deal with people, situations, human endeavor, emotions, and the patterns of conflict. Incidentally, a respectable amount of economics, history, and sociology will be learned, to the great comfort of your social-studies-minded colleagues. Try a unit on the untimely demise of the young with "Mary White," *Diary of Anne Frank,* and *Death Be Not Proud*; you will get depth as you've never gotten before.

This conception of English units leads to teacher-student planning in the study of narrative.

The experiences and resources of students are particularly rich on the emotive level, the level to be tapped for successful teacher-pupil planning. You must balance between prying and dull impersonality, remembering that the personal is not always imparted to contemporaries or to you, and is rigorously confined for reasons various and not obvious. Nevertheless, the emotive level is involved in the narrative unit and in English teacher-student planning.

More important, joint planning in no way implies teacher abdication of responsibility, decision-making, observation, or function. You must plan for student planning, as the following instance suggests:

| CASE STUDY 11 | Because of student disorders on public bus facilities, the principal had devoted an entire assembly meeting to public opinion and how the school's reputation was being affected. On occasion, passengers had been threatened and women had been insulted. The identities of students involved did not come to light, but the guidance office was told that the grievance committee of the driver's union was demanding plainclothesmen be assigned to the bus runs during school hours—or so the rumors went that reached the teachers. Students, on the other hand, complained of discourtesies from the bus drivers and of crotchety passengers who forgot that they too had once been young. The principal at the monthly faculty meeting wanted to know what could be done about it, even though he didn't feel that students were altogether to blame. Tempers of bus drivers were apt to get short.

One of the teachers in the guidance program suggested that English teachers might be helpful, which was interpreted by the English teachers as an attempt to redirect the heat from the guidance people to the English department. The feeling was that this too would blow over, but one of the English teachers considered that a possibility for student-teacher planning lurked somewhere around. The meeting went on to other concerns, but the English teacher began plotting a unit on *The War between the Generations,* somewhat related to James Thurber's mythical *War between Men and Women,* this time dealing with differences in age and what these involve, rather than differences in sex.

The more the English teacher thought about it, the more likely an idea it seemed. He had two preparations; in one the class was reading *Ethan Frome,* an unlikely prospect for the idea he had in mind, but the other preparation was reading Schweikert's collection of short stories, in which appeared Sinclair Lewis' "Young Man Axelbrod," Tarkington's "Penrod's Busy Day," Jacobs' "The Monkey's Paw," Edna Ferber's "Meadowlark," and Björnson's "The Father," which gave him precisely the class discussion material he wanted as a common start.

The next appropriate day he reported to the class on the bus incidents that had come to his attention. There was discussion, chiefly second-hand and not well informed. The teacher asked, "What does the phrase *the older generation* mean?" The class knew. The teacher then asked, "What does *the younger generation* mean?" The class knew that too. Then the teacher asked, "What causes the war between the generations?" Here, in the main, students attributed aggression to their elders, and the teacher nodded agreeably and granted that all they said might be true, but then asked a series of questions:

"Do young people sometimes hate older people?"

"Do they try to cut older people down to size?"

"Is your attitude toward the teacher affected by your attitude toward your parents?"

"Is your attitude toward bus drivers affected by your attitude toward parents and teachers?"

"How can a teen-ager act grown up?"

Class reaction was not uniform. Some defended the right of teen-agers to act their age, on the ground that you're only young once, but others asserted that they couldn't be grown up until enough time had gone by and until they were willing to listen to those for whom enough time had, revealing that highly desirable situation in a class, a conflict in opinion. The teacher assigned to one group the short stories which indicated warfare between the generations, "Meadowlark" and "Penrod's Busy Day"; to the other group were assigned stories indicating close ties between the generations, "Young Man Axelbrod" and "The Monkey's Paw." All these stories have other foci: "Meadowlark" deals with vocational aspiration, "Young Man Axelbrod" with intellectual struggle, "The Monkey's Paw" with terror, and "Penrod's Busy Day" with humor. There was danger lest the authors' primary intentions be subverted by the teacher's, but the stories were good enough to pull their own weight and work their own effects. Yet, among these separate effects, the War between the Generations was also recurrent. After both groups had considered that this War had as counterpart Understanding between the Generations, the stories, with their attendant matters of situation, characterization, and plot, were put aside and the class wondered how one could write a short story about teen-agers and adults with a bus as the scene and characters to be selected from students, bus drivers, and passengers they had met. (A relevant note: Barzun says, in *House of Intellect,* "Battle is joined, more or less openly, whenever a group of children invade a public vehicle." [6])

The results were not literature but they were fun. Four stories written by class members were selected by a student committee to be read in school assembly and were enthusiastically received. Other stories were mimeographed and run off for the class to distribute.

Several weeks later the teacher asked if the stories had been useful in mitigating disturbances on the bus. Some students were puzzled; they couldn't see the connection. A few, however, felt that when they got on a bus where the driver was short-tempered they could shrug him off more readily than they could before. Was there a wholesale reform of manners? No. Nevertheless, virtually all the class members agreed that they were more aware of what they were doing when they did it. Self-understanding had grown, even if unaccompanied in all cases by behavioral change.

Research, Resources, and Techniques

1. Otis W. Coan and Richard G. Lillard's pamphlet on the social aspects of fiction gives titles that would be helpful in a core or unit attempt. *America in Fiction: An Annotated List of Novels That Interpret Aspects of Life in the United States* (Stanford University Press, 1956) will give you the materials you need in working jointly with your social studies colleague.

2. For further material on the recent vogue for the novel of business, try these two:

a. Kenneth S. Lynn's "Authors in Search of the Businessman" (*Harvard Business Review*, Oct. 1956, p. 116).

b. Daniel Seligman's "The 'Business Novel' Fad" (*Fortune*, Aug. 1959).

3. Three articles which further illustrate the comparison-contrast principle in teaching literature:

a. John H. Bens' "Teaching Literature in the World of Mickey Spillane" (*E. J.*, Feb. 1956, p. 79) contrasts Shirley Jackson's picture of small-town life in "The Lottery" with Thornton Wilder's *Our Town* and Sherwood Anderson's *Winesburg, Ohio* to find out which picture is truest. This is a good example of the polarizing techniques in questioning which are discussed later (see Chapter 11).

b. James R. Squire's "Individualizing the Teaching of Literature" (*E. J.*, Sept. 1956, p. 314) tells how one group of readers contrasted *My Ántonia* with *The Good Earth* (on the relationship of people to the land); another compared Edgar Lee Masters' "Lucinda Matlock" with Saroyan's "Locomotive 38" (on viewpoints toward life). Thus, in poetry, on the theme of permanence versus change, you contrast Housman's "Loveliest of Trees" and Waller's "Go, Lovely Rose!" This article confirms that you best individualize instruction by multiplying contrasts, comparisons, themes, antitheses, similarities in your materials. You cannot individualize without a wealth of these around.

c. LaTourette Stockwell's "Best Sellers and the Critics" (*E. J.*, Jan. 1955, p. 10) contrasts the novels of Daphne du Maurier with Charlotte

Brontë's, and Miss du Maurier's biographical study of her family with Sir Osbert Sitwell's of his. (Note how Stockwell develops this case history of Miss du Maurier with such comparisons. Why can't you similarly develop classroom lessons?) Such contrasts, comparisons, antitheses, and similarities have been incorporated into publishing ventures in the "Comparative Classics" series of Noble and Noble. How can you teach narrative by comparisons with fiction read versus fiction seen (in movies, radio, and television)?

The Search for Literary Meaning

One cannot predict the reactions of students. You may present a question like this: "If you were about to be like Helen Keller and had three days left to see, what things would you most want to see?" One girl answered, "I would stay home and watch television." Is this answer right? wrong? judicious? in poor taste? It is none of these and all of these. The situation may be so intensely envisaged by the student that the shock and apprehension send her to hugging television as the best delaying action against the oncoming dark in the last few days of sight.

With *Lost Horizon,* if you try "What price would you pay for eternal youth? Would you like to remain forever as you are at this moment?" students may say that they do not have the price to dicker. Faust had an immortal soul. So had Jabez Stone in "The Devil and Daniel Webster" and so too the protagonist in *Damn Yankees,* but is the soul a commodity? If so, is it a marketable commodity? Are souls being bought and sold every day, and not to the devil?

Narrative, therefore, deals with character under stress, so that even animal stories, like *Call of the Wild,* endow the beasts with traits—else where's the story? Yet character delineation and insight into it are complex. If a student says she would pull television around her and cower within the protection it affords, what is she simultaneously telling you about television's meaning for her and thereby about herself? The questions above are good not only because they lead to answers but because they lead to other questions. To develop such questions, you must have a clear idea, reducible to a phrase or sentence (and not much more) of what the author is trying to say in any given passage.

The short story is particularly useful here because it is unitary and thus affords training in extracting the single kernel from which good questions sprout. The fables of Aesop and George Ade have a terminating moral, a gnomic recapitulation. Similarly, you should enunciate briefly, for yourself, the moral of any short story you teach. Read "Masque of the Red Death," " 'Revolt' of Mother," "Girls in Their Summer Dresses," and then determine for yourself, in one sentence, what the author is saying. For example:

"Masque of the Red Death": Not even by revelry can we escape death.
"Monkey's Paw": Wishing will *not* make it so.
"The Garden Party": Not everybody can sympathize with tragedy.
"A Wagner Matinee": Beauty is one means of triumphing over a barren life.
"The Pit and the Pendulum": The incarceration of the mind is worse than the incarceration of the body. (Integrate in a unit with Chekhov's "The Bet" and "Prisoner of Chillon.")

The keynotes above may not correspond with your ideas. Similarly, the keynotes you develop for yourself may not correspond with a student's. All the better. We are not teaching blueprints, but literature.

In the light of your keynote, develop the most challenging, personal, baffling problem you can. Aim for white-hot heat, for impact, and for conflict. The best questions will produce contention and disagreement, in which pupil will be pitted against pupil.

All the possibilities considered so far in teaching the long narrative are contained in microcosm in the short story. In contrast to the novel, where we find—and seek for—dozens and dozens of discussion and appreciational possibilities, we need but one or two for the short story, making it feasible for you to match short story keynotes with parallels in lyric poetry and, as we shall see later, with that other unitary effort, the essay.

Research, Resources, and Techniques

1. Three worthwhile articles on teaching the short story are these:
a. C. W. Breault's "Three Steps to Short Stories" (*E. J.*, March 1956, p. 141) gives actual detailed assignments, with specific instructions to students. Very useful as a guide in literature study.
b. Bernice Freeman's "Teaching Short Stories" (*E. J.*, May 1955, p. 284) is a workmanlike analysis, practical and down to earth, on the teaching of de Maupassant's "The Necklace" and Lagerlöf's "The Silver Mine"; the approach can be extended to the introduction and study of other short stories too.
c. Elizabeth Williams' "Teaching Judgment of Prose Fiction" (*E. J.*, Nov. 1958, p. 495) is especially recommended for the author's unit

on love, greed, and selfish desires (see p. 498 of the article), in which a *True Confessions* story and stories by Katherine Mansfield, Zona Gale, and Albert Maltz, all on the same topic, are compared.

2. There are numerous excellent paperback anthologies of short stories. A collection intended for classroom use is Joshua McClennen's *Masters and Masterpieces of the Short Story* (Henry Holt, 1957). This anthology of high literary value, with top performances by modern writers, is suitable for your more thoughtful students.

3. Dwight L. Burton's *Literature Study in the High Schools* (Holt-Dryden, 1959) is full of interesting suggestions, especially for the non-college bound.

The
Shakespearean
Play

CHAPTER 6

Getting to the Groundlings

Shakespeare is universal: he can be taught successfully to your slow classes as well as to your bright ones. Nobody has dealt more richly with character, poetry, emotions, and understanding—but you know his virtues. What chiefly concerns you is their transmission to the duller members of your flock because you also know that the brighter ones will be less upset by the vocabulary and the conceptual difficulties.

Before you can teach Shakespeare successfully, you must face three requirements:

First, you must know the play thoroughly, almost as well as an actor, and have great parts of it memorized. You must be an expert on the subject of that particular play.

Second, you must be able to act it fearlessly, even if not well. Enthusiasm and intelligent understanding, if coupled with conviction, will gain you a breathless audience. You must be prepared to do much of the reading yourself and therefore to get more fun than you get usually because it's tremendously exciting to do the scene in which Lady Macbeth reads her husband's letter and cry the terrible oaths she does and watch the absorption on the faces in your class, or Jaques' report on his meeting a fool i' the forest, or Cassius' vengeful, bitter account of his saving Caesar from drowning. What magnificent arias these are! Imagine getting paid for singing them! And having a captive audience that must listen until the bell rings! But many teachers fear singing them. Go thou and do otherwise.

Third, have a reservoir of questions that appropriately intensify interest. Good questions stimulate discussion, a matter as vital as the quality of your reading. Precisely because you are a superb reader, the very excellence of your reading may shatter a class, sending it into protective remoteness against excessive emotion. The more powerfully you render a passage, the greater the possibility of emotionally exhausting a portion of your class, which will then seek the harbor of inattentiveness. A class can take only limited doses of a powerful reading before it sends its interests to wandering lest the assault be too overwhelming. Even fine readings have attendant dangers.

Therefore, look around for changes of pace. Give your class an opportunity, through your questions, to react. Particularly if you have floored students with a powerful reading, give them an opportunity to get off the floor, and do so by questions on the material you have just read. Good questions do not dissipate dramatic intensity; on the contrary, they allow students to muster greater resources for the next attack. The better the reading, the better the discussion. The better the discussion, the greater the involvement. The greater the involvement, the more prepared your class for your next reading, or the reading of the cast you select. Good questions allow the change of pace that is one of the secrets of successful teaching.

What can these questions be? The remainder of this chapter analyzes the teaching difficulties generally encountered, particularly with respect to questioning techniques. We cannot treat each play exhaustively because every classroom problem cannot be anticipated, but you should, from the approach here, gain some hints of the problem-approach and how it generates questions.

To repeat, first know your play thoroughly. Second, exult in the opportunity to declaim, recite, rant, or whisper it, depending on the passage. Third, ask the right questions at the right time. If you can fulfill these three requirements, you can teach Shakespeare to the slow as well as the swift.

Do not spend much time on the nature of the Elizabethan stage, especially when it is just as interesting to see how adaptable Shakespeare is to the movie screen. The movies have done so magnificent a job in *Henry V, Julius Caesar, Romeo and Juliet,* and *Hamlet* that one almost feels that Shakespeare might have had the production facilities of a movie studio in mind, so successfully has he been put on the screen. The Elizabethan stage warrants twenty minutes of discussion and not much more. *Henry V* was better mounted by Olivier than ever at the *Globe* or whatever the 1600 stage as Shakespeare described it:

> . . . that hath dar'd
> On this unworthy scaffold to bring forth
> So great an object. Can this cockpit hold
> The vasty fields of France? Or may we cram
> Within this wooden O the very casques
> That did affright the air at Agincourt?

Clearly, he must have had his eye on a Hollywooden O. But even better, he must have known, is reading the text, because here every man, in his own mind's eye, furnishes the perfect cast and setting.

Remember that Shakespeare is a show. He is poet, seer, and character painter, but first and foremost he is theater, and only afterward a word list of unfamiliar vocabulary, or the greatest name in letters, or an excuse for the study of Elizabethan England in core. Primarily he is the curtain going up and, in the words of Margaret Webster, "vital entertainment which will enrich the theater-going lives" of the high school student.[1] Shakespeare is show business or, if not, a dreary and outmoded chore. How do you have the curtain go up and the show go on? What keeps a show on the boards after three and a half hundred years? As an English teacher, do you have the privilege and responsibility of being a stage director, too, of clarifying the structure, motives, action, and stage business, by using gesture, grimaces, and stage movement? Inevitably, if you are putting on a show.

Thus you impart suspense by stopping at the peaks of action, keeping your class simmering by analyzing characters and development for deeper understanding, and asking questions that will generally be of the type: "What's going on? Why? For what reasons? Involving whom? And how, from the text, can you prove what you say?" So you analyze action and motives to that moment, to augment understanding and tension about what comes next and how things will turn out. To increase such simmer, curtains come down. Frequent intermissions are also called for in the classroom, to allow opportunity for speculation and rumination. Interruptions of the right kind are an adjunct to dramatic development; they pour oil on fire, not on troubled waters; they intensify the sense of drama, not calm it. Judicious interruptions by the teacher will sharpen suspense, if they are judicious. Picayune questioning can be resented, because there *is* a show going on;

intelligent questioning that reveals meanings and subtleties not readily perceived by the student will be appreciated.

If you are a good reader, and if you know your play, you will find the fun of reading aloud running away with you. The temptation is great for you to declaim whole gobs of the play, and you rationalize because the class is enjoying the play and simultaneously gaining understanding. Police yourself. Step aside, like the Chorus in a Greek play, on the periphery of action and not obscuring it. Having stepped aside, how do you know the students will move in? First, stop at dramatic high points. Next, let suspense accumulate through the questions you ask. One important way of assuring that students will take over is memorization. Do not hesitate. Assign generous portions. They like it more than they are willing to admit, especially if sound effects enliven the mechanical, droning delivery of too many students. Thus for Antony's forum speech, run a record simultaneously of Beethoven's *Egmont,* or Rossini's *William Tell,* or something of that spirited, pell-mell nature. If music helps enliven dull TV drama, it will enliven dull class memorization work and will give fine excitement to the better recitations. Your job is to sit at the controls and increase or diminish volume, depending on the line and phrase the student is just then speaking. (See Chapter 10, "Speech.")

The savor of words in a Shakespearean play is as important as the meaning. Therefore you should be as concerned with the way a passage tastes as with the meaning. In fact, to insure that a passage is understood, insure that it appeals to the palate of the class. Ask for the over-all meaning of a passage, in addition to the meaning of particular words. If word-meaning is vital to the understanding of a passage, so passage-understanding is vital to word-meaning. When Prospero says,

> Now does my project gather to a head:
> My charms crack not; my spirits obey; and time
> Goes upright with his carriage. How's the day?
> > (*Tempest,* V:1)

not a single word in the passage is strange to the average high school student. Yet "time goes upright with his carriage" is illuminated not by his knowledge of the words but by his understanding of the remainder of the passage.

Students, in other words, get more than you think, if you illuminate by passages as well as by words. Such illumination is part of theater. It enables us to follow opera without libretto, to listen to and appreciate a French star singing songs of Paris, because what is being communicated is a connotative *quality* rather than literal denotation. Your chief care should be for quality and understanding of the passages, rather than for the understanding of words, unless, as in "multitudinous seas incarnadine" (*Macbeth,* II:2) meaning enlarges poetic quality. How do these words, and these words only, convey the precise intention of Macbeth? Challenge students to do better; in this way, defy them into the writing of poetry.

With understanding, your students can go off on their own to do reading assignments. Much of Shakespeare can be assigned to a bright class for home reading, but even such classes must be given hints for self-help in obscure references. Home assignments clarify themselves through a first slow, silent reading and a subsequent reading aloud, but you must hold out a promise of ultimate understanding and gain. Most students, unless they go off to college, will never again open a volume of Shakespeare in their lives. They may stumble into a production at one of the three Stratfords— Connecticut, Ontario, or Avon—but few will pick up a volume for reading, unless they feel comfortable with him because they feel him well within their understanding. Relax them: Shakespeare is not out of reach, he is rewarding, and his meanings can be handled. Like a fine pearl, he gets more luminous with use.

A recent abridgment of *Julius Caesar* states:

> As a result of the difficulty which we have met in the teaching of Shakespearean plays, we have gradually come to the conclusion that these plays in their original form are beyond the comprehension of the vast majority of high school students. We are aware that we are treading on sacred ground, but we are convinced that there is an urgent need for a new approach. Teachers now choose one of two courses: some present these plays to their accelerated or high-ability classes only, feeling that the text is beyond the reach of their other classes; others attempt the dramas with their average groups as well, but are compelled to read to these students and to interpret a majority of the lines for them in order to secure comprehension and some measure of enjoyment of the plays.[2]

A strong, fervid, intense exception is here taken. Your students, even the poor ones, are proud to be reading Shakespeare. They have heard of him. They know his reputation. They are willing to give him a chance. They will both understand Shakespeare and enjoy him if you know the play thoroughly, if you read it effectively, and if you analyze it with them so that problems are presented and suspense is heightened.

Visualization of stage business and stage directions is part of the homework assignment, and you do not assign the mere reading. But students can
only devise stage business and supply stage directions if they understand
the text; this technique drives them to a closer reading. The ways in which
students misunderstand are infinite. Holding them responsible for stage
business and stage direction circumscribes misunderstanding. With the
possibilities of misunderstanding thus limited and pinned down, you can go
on to the deepest drama that Shakespeare offers, the analysis of behavior.

In dramatization, you may hesitate about having different groups repeti-
tively dramatizing the same passage two or three times. Make this competitive. Have the class reward the more effective readers by this adaptation of
television's "applause meter":

1. Mimeograph this:

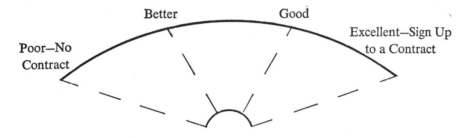

2. Distribute one copy for each of the students who will recite.
3. Have the class black the dotted lines for its verdict.
4. Have a committee sort and rank the class decisions.
5. As usual, be cautious of crooked voting, wherein friends are selected
—the business of the claque. You are justified in weighting judiciously because you are more experienced. Simultaneously, do not deprive your class
of its right to react as an audience; hence, the applause meter.

Remember that you are the audience to interaction between Shakespeare
and your students, rather than the class being audience to interaction between Shakespeare and you, more an occupational hazard in good teachers
than poor ones. The poor English teacher doesn't react to or interact with
Shakespeare. The good one does, and the course of the disease is plain.
Nobody else in class gets a chance to declaim, dramatize, or recite. Does
the class enjoy the performance? Certainly, but only as audience, never as

participant. Nothing can be done about the poor English teacher except make this person more defensive about being poor; but the good English teacher should be warned against confusing the love of Shakespeare with the love of hearing his own voice. Shakespeare is the class's opportunity to audition, not yours, and for each individual in the class to audition himself, as an individual, and to profit by Shakespeare's function as a sounding board for each of us.

Do not depend on your student text edition to teach from; too much is left unexplained. A good desk copy is William Allan Neilson and Charles Jarvis Hill's *Complete Plays and Poems of William Shakespeare* (Houghton Mifflin, 1942). Use it in conjunction with your school's edition.

In reading the remainder of this chapter, be careful not to compartmentalize. Read the suggestions for *The Tempest* and see how much is applicable to *Midsummer-Night's Dream*. Which suggestions for *As You Like It* are applicable to *Merchant of Venice*? Which for *Macbeth* are applicable to *Julius Caesar*? Similarly, after you've read the next chapter on *The Teaching of Poetry*, return to this chapter and see which suggestions for "Kubla Khan" are applicable to, say, Act V of *Merchant of Venice,* or Prospero's last speech in *The Tempest*. Do the last two lines of Robert Frost's "Stopping by Woods on a Snowy Evening" throw any light on Macbeth's *sleep that knits up the ravell'd sleave of care*? Does the closing line of Frost's "The Road Not Taken" help the meaning of *the fault, dear Brutus, lies not in our stars but in ourselves*? or *there is a tide in the affairs of men which, taken at the flood, leads on to fortune*? Does Dylan Thomas' raging against death in "Do Not Go Gentle" throw light on Hamlet's despair over his father's death?

Thus, after you have read the section on the teaching of *Hamlet* and its discussions on modern vernacular, conceptualization, and verbalization, and how these are to be located in the play's language (the same discussion is carried forward in the section "Background Notes—Program Music and Program Poetry"), apply this approach to the particular play you may be teaching. This approach, you will notice, reverses the usual procedures. Instead of reducing the poet's language to the level of class understanding, you take recognizable rhythms, content, and phrasing of everyday speech and send students to the poem (or Shakespearean play) with instructions to find out how the poet states these matters.

As an exercise, apply the suggestions you will find throughout the chapter to *Romeo and Juliet,* not analyzed here because of space limitations.

Research, Resources, and Techniques

1. We'll keep these at a minimum in this chapter, because so much material exists on the teaching of Shakespeare that the research, resources, and techniques repeat themselves. Thus in J. D. Salinger's *Catcher in the Rye* (Signet, 1953, p. 102), we encounter this passage: "I felt much sorrier when old Mercutio got killed than when Romeo and Juliet did. . . . I liked him the best in the play, old Mercutio. . . . he was— it's hard to explain. He was very smart and entertaining and all." You will find the sentiment, not quite word for word, in Owen Wister's *The Virginian.*

2. Similarly, many directors have written on the production of Shakespeare. You may want to compare Margaret Webster's *Shakespeare Without Tears* (Premier paperback, Fawcett World Library, 1957) with Granville Barker's *Prefaces,* to see how stage directors mount a Shakespearean play.

3. A completely different approach is taken in Harold E. Bohn's unpublished doctoral dissertation *Toward an Improved Teaching of Shakespeare in the Secondary School: Proposals Based on Experiences with Graduates in New Jersey High Schools at the New Jersey State Teachers College, Montclair, 1944-51* (Columbia University, 1955).

4. Typical of contributions in this area is Mary Alice Wells' "Appreciation Follows Understanding" (*NEA Journal,* Nov. 1958).

5. For a real treat and a fascinating account of detective work and decoding, read *The Shakespearean Ciphers Examined,* by two brilliant cryptographers, William F. Friedman and Elizabeth S. Friedman, published by Cambridge University Press (1960). Read Mark Twain on the Shakespeare-Bacon controversy to your class. Get their opinions. Then add the De Vere and Marlowe claims. Then show them how the Friedmans knock these claims into cocked hats. Your classes will be excited.

6. One of the finest films ever produced on the techniques of production and direction is by the National Film Board of Canada, *The Stratford Adventure,* which not only describes how the townspeople of Stratford, Ontario, got their festival going, but how Tyrone Guthrie mounts his Shakespeare productions.

Julius Caesar

Before you direct, clarify, and interpret, you must begin. How do you begin *Julius Caesar?*

Ask what year this is. Simple question, is it not? Everybody knows the answer. Then ask, why the particular number? We're in the nineteen-sixties, but from what point are we counting? What happened in Year One? You'll get surprising answers, among them correct ones. With the correct ones, you paint a picture of the world of that time, the massiveness of Rome, the ambition of its citizens, its conquests, the struggle for power among its leading men, and then the war between Caesar and Pompey, two generations earlier, the death of Pompey, and the triumphal return homeward of Caesar. Not until the Renaissance was the world to be as large.

How will Caesar be greeted? Have the class open books to I:1, and *you* begin to read. The opening of *Julius Caesar* is:

> Hence! home, you idle creatures, get you home!
> Is this a holiday? What! know you not,
> Being mechanical, you ought not walk
> Upon a laboring day without the sign
> Of your profession? Speak, what trade art thou?"

Would you accept the following changes?

FLAVIUS: (*Enters, swaggering, like a policeman. Indeed, he is one. The crowd is on the other side of the stage. Frowning and displeased by what he sees, he hunches his shoulders; his head goes forward. He rolls bullyingly across stage, approaches one Citizen, taps him on the shoulder. Citizen turns around curiously. Flavius' thumb jerks backward. He growls:*) Hence! (*Citizen and Flavius glare mutually. Citizen remains unfrightened. Flavius slowly wilts, his eyes waver, and the Citizen turns his back contemptuously on him. Flavius eyes the back of the Citizen up and down, his hand goes out as if to wheel the Citizen around to him again, but then he thinks better of it, flings himself away, coming upstage. As he crosses, his shoulders resume their former swagger. He stops before another Citizen, brave again, and this time flings the Citizen around.*) Ho-o-o-me! (*He follows the reeling Citizen, pushing and kicking, then stops and calls to a Third Citizen, again jerking his thumb.*) You! Git! (*Enter Marullus. Flavius turns to Marullus and spits out the syllables.*) Idle creatures! (*Rolls his eyes heavenward, advances upon the group again, and singles out another individual, poking at his shoulder.*) You! Home! (*Incredulously turns to Marullus.*) Is this a holiday? (*A deprecating sound, Bronx cheer type, from the crowd. Flavius whips around as if trying to catch the culprit.*) Wha-a-a-t? (*Moves forward, the picture of a policeman getting the crowd to move on, throwing and shouldering people aside as he moves into the heart of the throng. Growls at a Citizen:*) Know you! (*Is about to put threatening hands on Marullus, but then recognizes him in time.*) Not! (*Calls out loudly, angrily*) Being mechanical, you ought not appear on a working day without the mark of your profession! (*But, despite the bodies spinning away from him, the crowd does not budge. He is brought to a halt, before the Carpenter. Points a threatening finger at him.*) Speak, sir. What trade art thou?

How much violence does this do Shakespeare? Do these stage directions distort the scene? If you were to stop at this point and ask, "What's going on?" would your pupils' answers show greater or less understanding of the lines than if you read the first version? The second version requires that you act and effectively dramatize. Does it go beyond the permissible limits of interpretation?

Much depends here on your confidence in yourself as an actor and as an interpreter. However you interpret, *you* should read and so effectively that in Marullus' aria that follows, "O ye hard hearts, ye cruel men of Rome," your reading should in itself elucidate, explicate, and almost automatically furnish answers to your questions: "Who is Pompey? Who comes in triumph over his blood? Are the Romans stable or fickle in their political allegiances? Why do people travel for miles to see a parade? What does a parade do to people, whether it's the Pied Piper, the Macy's Thanksgiving Day Parade preparing people to come and buy for Christmas, or a Memorial Day Parade, or the victoriously parading legions of Caesar?"

After class response and discussion, the time has arrived for vocabulary study, explication of the text, understanding of characters, and class dramatization, because the show has been presented and other things, in depth, are now properly considered.

If your reading has been effective, phrases like *intermit the plague* and *light on this ingratitude* become almost automatically elucidated. Where meaning has changed, as the *naughty* in *naughty knave* from the original of wickedness or valuelessness (as in sheer nothingness) to the contemporary soft impeachment of a mother reprimanding a child, your explanations do not take the edge off the show but sharpen it, as the intermission of the modern second-act curtain does. You close the first scene, with

> Who else would soar above the view of men
> And keep us all in servile fearfulness,

on a high note of suspense and threat. What image occurs to them? Hawk? Eagle? Vulture? Sputnik? Keep your class dangling on an emotional and dramatic precipice, as the heroine of the old movie serials was, all week, until the following Saturday afternoon. We have referred to her before and do so here shamelessly because sophisticated drama is built around analogous concepts of suspense.

Let's go on to I:2 and the long, revealing dialogue between Brutus and Cassius. Should you assign so complex a scene for home reading? Yes, provided not only that you have done your homework, and that you know specifically what you want students to get out of the scene, but that you know where to direct them, line by line, for the answers to your questions. Students, given this assistance, will find home assignments in Shakespeare not excessively troublesome.

Specifically, in I:2, the homework assignment should be accompanied by road markers like these:

> Lines 1-10. What's the connection between Caesar's orders to Antony and Calpurnia and the bride who throws her bouquet to the bridesmaids? Do we believe in the superstition? Does Caesar?
>
> Line 9. Would Caesar's desire for children be affected by the crown? If given the crown, would his desire for children be greater or less than before?
>
> Line 18. Is Caesar defying the soothsayer's warning or ignoring it?
>
> Line 46. Have you ever been at war with yourself only to have other people think you were at war with them? What kind of hint does this give Cassius?
>
> Lines 65-78. Does Cassius answer Brutus' question or does he evade it?
>
> Lines 89, 93. Do Brutus and Cassius define *honor* the same way?
>
> Lines 100-15. Is Cassius telling the truth?
>
> Lines 140, 141. Compare with IV:3, 218-22. Which philosophy is correct? Is the "tide" within ourselves or outside ourselves? Are we "underlings" to the stars or in control of our fates? In *All's Well That Ends Well* (I:1), Shakespeare says:
>
>> Our remedies oft in ourselves do lie,
>> Which we ascribe to heaven; the fated sky
>> Gives us free scope, only doth backward pull
>> Our slow designs when we ourselves are dull.
>
> With which passage is the class in most agreement?

Accompanied by these road markers, the students are given the assignment. Difficulties in vocabulary will be partially explained by footnotes in the text, or usually are. When they are not, you must assume the responsibility.

The procedure is similar in assigning I:3. This scene should be visualized for students in making the assignment. Throughout, flashes of lightning and rumbles of thunder punctuate the dialogue. Offstage, sound effects of hooting owls, roaring lions, burning, shrieks are the background to Cassius' plotting and conniving, with the weather not disturbing him a bit.

Again, line by line, students are given their assignments for I:3.

> Lines 3-12. Is Casca the kind of man who dives under a bed in a thunderstorm, or the kind who would like to be out in a boat in the wind and rain?
>
> Lines 15-32. Compare Casca with people who see flying saucers. Are flying saucers real? Do flying saucers have anything to do with fears of atomic war? Did people see flying saucers before they were afraid of atomic bombs? What about flying saucers and invaders from outer space? How are Casca's visions similar?
>
> Lines 33-36. Is Cicero as terrified as Casca? Cicero wrote a book, *De Divinatione,* on fortune telling. From these lines, is the book favorable or unfavorable to fortune telling? Is Cicero afraid or skeptical?
>
> Lines 45-52. Compare Cassius' reaction to the weather with Casca's. How do you explain the difference?
>
> Lines 56-78. Does Cassius feel that heaven is with him or against him? Does he see the storm as warning or as hope?
>
> Lines 80, 111, 112. Is Cassius freely speaking his mind to Casca or is he being careful?
>
> Lines 120-25. Why does Cassius, after seeing Casca's earlier behavior, confide the existence of a conspiracy? Is he wise to do so to a man like Casca? What does this tell you of Cassius' character? Does Cassius plan well or poorly?
>
> Lines 140-65. Why is it necessary to have Brutus in the conspiracy? Why is he so important to its success?

Remember that in every Shakespearean play, not only in *Julius Caesar,* student participation depends on the quality of your questions. In your discussion, allow Shakespeare to lead from strength, in his understanding of the inner mind, in fancy, and in human characterization.

Research, Resources, and Techniques

> Irvin C. Poley's "Drama in the Classroom" (*E. J.,* March 1955, p. 148) offers suggestions for testing comprehension in *Julius Caesar* and for the classroom acting of Shakespeare.

As You Like It

Unrealistic as plots and situations are in television or in the movies, they are no more so than *As You Like It,* where people meet by coincidence in the heart of a forest, a lover fails to recognize the woman he loves, and the unlikely is so piled on the improbable that we are at times urged to believe the incredible. Tightly logical plot lines and absences of coincidence characterize better narrative and drama writing these days; hence much of Shakespeare is almost infantile in the light of modern "realism," a contemporary convention by which the coincidence we encounter in real life we reject in fiction, and hence there is much we reject in Shakespeare.

As You Like It is an extended dream-image, not common-sense reality but some intensification of it, beginning with the sibling hate between Orlando and Oliver. Why do brothers hate?

The explosive opening scene is a restatement of Cain and Abel, Esau and Jacob, Joseph and his brethren, all examples of the intense hate of brother for brother and the expropriation always involved, whether of God's favor or of a father's love. Brother is cast out by brother and deprived of his place at the ancestral hearth.

In the next scene Orlando defeats Charles in the wrestling bout. How likely is it that the talented amateur can ever defeat the professional? Only in fiction does this long shot come through. If so, why are our sympathies with the amateur? After all, the professional has worked at the business. Simple justice demands that he be better. We see the amateur as the underdog, which he is not; he is, rather, the presumptuous upstart. Yet we wish to attain our ends easily, living in our own fantasy world—and the Forest of Arden is precisely that—in which wishing makes things so. Shakespeare, here a soft-minded dramaturgist, has blinded himself to common-sense reality, has drowned himself in a Lethe where improbabilities are heaped on improbabilities—and this is exactly the way we dream that things should be, that the amateurs triumph over the professionals, that tyrants will be overcome when brave men flee from them (see Jaques de Boys' one and only speech, V:4) instead of standing up to them, that beautiful women will fall in love with men on the spot by spontaneous combustion, that men will broadcast their love shamelessly for us if we are women.

Why teach the fantastic and the unreal? Because the ways we delude ourselves, once understood, are less likely to deceive us. Should you therefore teach that the love that Rosalind and Orlando pursue is silly? Love comes by common experiences, passion and tragedies shared together. The love Rosalind and Orlando declare must be worked for. It is an outcome rather than a starting point. Its reduction to absurdity is illustrated in Phebe's instantaneous incandescence for Ganymede-Rosalind.

Similarly, we triumph not as talented amateurs but only after persevering assiduity. Orlando's victory over Charles reflects the infantilism in us.

Then, suddenly, this infantilism shatters into reality. The surface unlikeliness is a subterfuge and the play grows increasingly acceptable, despite its unlikeliness. How can a thing be acceptable though unlikely? By the realities and fantasies of which it is reminiscent. The Duke and his group in the forest are reminiscent of Robin Hood and his merry men. The Forest of Arden reminds us of Sherwood Forest, or the Garden of Eden, and the decent innocence in the bucolic and rural. Jaques' recounting of his encounter with Touchstone ("I met a fool i' the forest") is mirthful antiphilistinism that knocks the hot air out of all the windbags who ever lived, and thereby it reminds us of Wamba, W. C. Fields, Harlequin, and Figaro. So too the love story is as silly as anything in *True Confessions* until we see the complete absence of suspicion in the characters, and thereupon credibility moves in. Orlando and Rosalind are without distrust. (This is also true of Romeo and Juliet, but not of Benedick and Beatrice or of Petruchio and Katharina). The heretofore villainous Oliver, reformed by Orlando's rescue, at once, immediately, and "at first hight" falls in love with Aliena-Celia, coincident with the disappearance of his suspicions of his brother.

You should bring to the attention of your class this pattern of instantaneous incandescence and your doubts about its possibility in real life (except when suspicion is absent, where the lovers are devoid of wariness, and how often does that come about?). Is Phebe right when she says, "Who ever loved that loved not at first sight?" (III:5). How realistic? Very, your class may say. You'll find students less wary than you are about the unmotivated, unplotted, and inexplicable structure and characterization because they are younger, less captious, and more accepting.

More realistic, and well worth discussion, is the hate between Orlando and Oliver, because history offers as many examples of brotherly hate as of brotherly love, as do the ordinary incidents of family living. Sibling rivalry may be as simple as a squabble or as complex as the American Civil War. But who are the brothers involved? Northern White versus Southern White? Or Southern White versus Southern Negro? Answer any way you wish, but the American Civil War elucidates the brotherly hate as noticeable in history as brotherly love, in which the patrimony fought over this time is the authority-figure of a written Constitution. The race problem in America, for the adolescent from the minority group, is quite accurately a drama in sibling rivalry, with the dark brother cast as expropriation's victim. The Negro adolescent requires the morale that this argument offers, that he is a brother treated unjustly and cast out of his father's house. It is good history to say so, and it says so too in *As You Like It*. D'Annunzio said, "The hatred between brothers, that odious hate which, since the creation, breeds secretly at the bottom of human nature to break out at the first discord, more ferocious than any other hate—that inexplicable hostility which exists, latent, between males of the same blood, even though the customs and peace of the birthplace have created between them affectionate bonds. . . ."[3] The adolescent with confused feelings for a sibling knows the emotions in Orlando and Oliver.

Still, despite the evidence of reality in *As You Like It,* we must value the fanciful. The conventions of musical comedy, Westerns, and detective stories require that conventional judgment be relaxed. *As You Like It* is an ancestor of the unlikely opera plot and unlikelier musical comedy story. To ask a class for its ideas on staging and direction, in order to set Shakespeare's loose structure to rights, is legitimate. Your class may well begin to learn the job of the stage director by way of *As You Like It*. For instance, what does Celia do throughout III:2? What pantomime can be developed for her? Or does she sit around throughout the act like a bump on a log, twittering occasionally and nothing else? How can she illustrate the theme of Rosalind's discussion with Orlando? So students climb Parnassus, to see the play's real richness in its verbal play and its flashing dialogue. Along the way we ask questions: Are people as simple as they seem? How foolish is Touchstone? How simple is the simpleton? Or, when people quarrel, how would the "lie seven times removed" (V:4) help avoid quarrels? The passage shows how soft answers turn away wrath, and merits discussion not only because we're studying Shakespeare, but for the sake of getting your students to live more effectively.

Let's return to the explosive opening and your introduction on the first day. How does the curtain go up? Tempestuously. Orlando expostulates with Adam, giving his side of the argument. "It was upon *this* fashion," as if Adam has been urging temperance and Orlando is hotly reminding the elderly retainer of the wrongs done him and the impossibility of further patience or any reconciliation. Oliver's "What, boy!" is accompanied by the raising of a hand, which Orlando coolly seizes with his "Come, come, elder brother, you are too young in this," giving us the first hint of Orlando's considerable physical prowess. As you speak Oliver's "Get you with him, you old dog," you brush and straighten yourself, to show how you have just been released by Orlando.

You, as Oliver, are still ruffled as Charles comes on and you needle the wrestler's dismay. Notice how you can hiss, "I had myself notice of my brother's purpose. . . . It is the stubbornest young fellow . . . a secret and villainous contriver . . ." and so on. Hiss away, all through, meanwhile sly, ingratiating, and persuasive. When, as Charles, you reply, "I am heartily glad I came hither to you," flex your muscles, brace your shoulders, slap your chest.

The acting you do should make explanation easier, even if not superfluous. What complications exist in I:1 are clarified spontaneously by a competent reading. Vocabulary is in great measure illuminated by context, although you should have a vocabulary list for I:1, given with homework assignments. Accompany such assignments with questions and road markers similar to those described in the section on *Julius Caesar*.

In I:2 and I:3 you must go slowly and you must require translations from the original Elizabethan:

> I show more mirth than I am mistress of.
> I will forget the condition of my estate, to rejoice in yours.
> . . . no further in sport neither than with safety of a pure blush thou mayst in honour come off again.

The affectionate debate between the girls on Nature versus Fortune is started by Celia to take Rosalind's mind off her troubles. Rosalind sighs and is dispirited. Celia's heart goes out to her and her attempts to stimulate Rosalind to gaiety become more successful with the entrance of Touchstone. Touchstone's disquisition on the pancakes and mustard offers an opportunity to introduce an exercise in logic:

1. All Cretans are liars.
2. I am a Cretan.
3. Therefore I am a liar.
4. But, if I am a liar, I lie when I say all Cretans are liars.

Is this true or false? Whatever the case, by involving Touchstone in the same parade of logic you have indicated that he is not the fool he is said to be and how his foolery is to be interpreted. It is no fool who says at this point, "The more pity, that fools may not speak wisely what wise men do foolishly."

Have students paraphrase:

> The dulness of the fool is the whetstone of the wits.
> Unmuzzle your wisdom.
> Since the little wit that fools have was silenced, the little foolery that wise men have makes a great show.
> Then shall we be news-crammed.

The remainder of Act I presents no challenges or difficulties beyond those indicated. Orlando and Rosalind have fallen in love, Rosalind, Celia, and Touchstone have fled, so has Orlando, and has your class fled with them or away from them? How can you assure that, when this point in the play is reached, your students too are willingly on their way to the Forest of Arden?

Gaining this assurance is complicated. You will find an attempt to secure it in the section "Program Music and Program Poetry" (p. 230).

Research, Resources, and Techniques

1. Read from the Bible on this matter of sibling loyalty versus sibling rivalry, and show your class how Jacob and Esau ultimately forgave and resumed their brotherly love. Similarly optimistic on racial relations is the article by H. H. Hyman and P. B. Sheatsley, "Attitudes on Desegregation" (*Scientific American*, Dec. 1956, p. 35), which reveals how opinions in this area have become progressively liberalized in the past few years, even in the South.

The Tempest

We want students to interact with the Shakespearean play, and not accept it passively. Before studying *The Tempest* ask which gift they most prefer:

1. being invisible
2. having a million dollars
3. being able to fly by yourself
4. being able to hypnotize others
5. being a mind reader

Despite all these powers, Prospero renounces his life on the island and assumes the responsibilities of men. Why? In this play of revenge, where no revenge is taken, the greatest gift of all is not the revenge his power would permit. He renounces necromancy and its vengeful possibilities for the possibility of being human again and showing pity. Does your class agree this is a wise trade? The Count of Monte Cristo, Du Maurier's Svengali, and H. G. Wells' Invisible Man, involved in revenge and able to wreak it, seek it out. Not Prospero. Instead, he wants Ferdinand and Miranda to fall in love. Though the theme of brother conspiring against brother, as in Orlando versus Oliver, recurs, forgiveness accompanies the theme. Parallel passages on the sibling theme in *As You Like It* can be read to brighter classes.

In the same fashion, the word magic that Shakespeare loves to play with in Antonio's soft subversion of Sebastian (*The Tempest,* II:1) is additionally illustrated if you read Cassius' beguilement of Brutus (*Julius Caesar,* I:2), the magnificent scene between Gloucester and Anne in *Richard III* (I:2), and Iago's gulling of Roderigo in the opening scene of *Othello*. In all these cases, fair words seduce the credulous. These side excursions into similar themes in other Shakespearean plays will afford quick views into the other masterpieces and will also strengthen understanding of the Antonio-Sebastian dialogue in *The Tempest,* II:1.

Remember, however, that understanding also depends on your questions. A question appropriate to I:2, "Why is Caliban forced to curse Prospero, even though he knows he will be punished? Why do we do foolish things, knowing they're foolish? What devil drives us?" simultaneously illuminates Caliban and our own inner selves.

The Tempest is more masque than play. Dramatic conflict never gets off the ground and acting possibilities are infrequent, except in the scenes with Trinculo, Stephano, and Caliban. These are rich and uproarious but, without strict laundering, not too suitable for class use. *The Tempest* is generally supposed the maturest expression of Shakespeare's art and, perhaps for that reason, not the best selection for the high school student, but if the play means much to you, you have the best single proof that you can teach it successfully.

In *The Tempest* let students try to improve on the speeches of Gonzalo in the opening storm scene, or on Prospero's aria beginning "Our revels now are ended," or "What's past is prologue," or Ariel's

> So full of valour that they smote the air
> For breathing in their faces; beat the ground
> For kissing of their feet.   (IV:1)

Unlike the opening of *Julius Caesar,* where you do the reading, the shipwreck scene which opens *The Tempest* lends itself to student dramatization after you have selected your cast and explained it to them. The lengthy scene, I:2, which follows, is preferably read by you because in it the past, the setting, and the important characters are explained. For the opening shipwreck scene drill your cast well. *The Tempest* reads better than it acts, and you will not have much opportunity for dramatic dialogue. At the end of the reading of I:1, ask: "Will they drown or won't they? Why?" Ask also for student opinion of Gonzalo's characteristics. To repeat, the responsibility for I:2 is yours with most classes. Only with a very superior class should I:2 be assigned for home reading. After I:2 has been covered, you may want to give an examination similar to this, to check comprehension:

> Prospero lost his dukedom because of his (brother, father, son, daughter) and because Prospero was too interested in (women, books, liquor, cards). Prospero was put on board a leaky vessel with his (son, daughter, father, brother). Fortunately, they were aided by the sympathetic (Antonio, Sebastian, Gonzalo). On the island, Prospero released the fairy (Sycorax, Ariel, Miranda), who became Prospero's devoted servant, while the ugly and deformed (Caliban, Setebos, Hecate) became Prospero's vengeful slave.
>
> Identify the speakers and the person addressed:
>
> 1. You taught me language; and my profit on it is, I know how to curse.
> 2. All hail, great master! grave sir, hail! I come
>   To answer thy best pleasure, be't to fly,
>   To swim, to dive into fire, to ride
>   On the curl'd clouds.
> 3. Had I not four or five women once that tended me?
> 4. I have great comfort from this fellow. Methinks he hath no drowning mark upon him; his complexion is perfect gallows.

Midsummer-Night's Dream

Midsummer-Night's Dream opens with a scene reminiscent of *Othello* (I:3), where Brabantio protests Othello's wooing of Desdemona. You may want to compare both scenes and then discuss how society must be considered when the purely personal, like courtship and marriage, is contemplated. Should society have something to say about such personal matters? Or is it none of society's business? [4]

With Lysander and Hermia left on stage and with Helena's appearance, you have excellent opportunities for dramatization dealing with matters close to the heart of your teen-agers (I:1). They will need little instruction in what's going on. They know. At the close of the scene, point up Helena's intention of informing Demetrius of the intended elopement. In the following scenes, we are introduced to the two parallel *dramatis personae,* the group around Peter Quince, and the fairy world of Puck, Oberon, and Titania. We swing from broad clowning to exquisite poetry and the fun of it is, as the play proceeds, that they are not as remote from each other as we usually suppose. Puck is of course the ancestor of the Katzenjammer Kids, Peter Pan, and Bugs Bunny of the movie cartoons— a mischievous hell-raiser.

The dispute between Oberon and Titania and its consequence to the peace of the world and of men (II:1) emerge next. The weather, tides, crops, and love have been knocked out of kilter by this argument. Now the four lovers, Titania, and Bottom are affected. Everybody's got troubles, from Puck's eye-wash. Go slowly, here. Though single lines and single words may be difficult for your class, the total meaning is clear and the comedy becomes richer and more hilarious. Throw everybody into the mix-up. Not only should you read, but students should too after they have prepared the lines at home. Do not hesitate to go over passages, because lyricism here is at its greatest. Let your class live with the play in order to learn its music. The play is substantially over with the fourth act curtain because the Pyramus-Thisbe mockery constitutes the fifth act. You can therefore sit a while with the first four acts and savor them with your class. The fifth act, a separate entity, virtually independent of the first four, can be silly or fun, depending how effectively you and your casts act it and the stage properties you have available. A colleague in the art department can help you in making these properties, and they can be a permanent acquisition for your department whenever the play is taught. With properties, the Pyramus-Thisbe episode takes on visual aspects that bring it alive.

Your experiences with *Midsummer-Night's Dream* should prove to you that Shakespeare is not too difficult, on the whole, for your classes. When students encounter "For night's swift dragons cut the clouds full fast,/ And yonder shines Aurora's harbinger" (III:2) and claim bafflement, you can either send them along to the conclusion of the passage in order to gain understanding from the whole, or you can urge understanding from the passage's internal clues, proceeding thus:

What quickly cuts clouds at night?

If night's clouds are cut, what opens up behind and beyond them?

Then what is most likely the meaning of "Aurora's harbinger"?

Similarly, in "gives to airy nothing/ A local habitation and a name" (V:1), the entire passage should bestow understanding on this section. More specifically, how do we give names to nothingness? We do it all the time. Examples, please (p. 41). Hippolyta's reaction here is credence. Theseus' is skepticism. Who is right? Discussion will lead to further understanding of the passage.

In the fifth-act colloquy between Hippolyta and Theseus, you can ask which opinion an older person, say of forty, would be more likely to select, and which a teen-ager. Who, therefore, is younger at heart, Theseus or his bride?

Similarly, if Pyramus-Thisbe is comical and Romeo-Juliet is tragic, though in both the lovers meet death through the same kind of misunderstanding, what makes Lysander and Demetrius react jokingly while Helena and Hermia have not a single speaking line throughout the Pyramus-Thisbe presentation? Do males and females react differently to tragedies of love? Are men more skeptical than women? Similarly, in addition to old-young and male-female dichotomizations, you can bring to bear on suitable passages such polarizations as good-evil, tyranny-democracy, city-rural, familiar-strange, frightening-welcoming, modern–old-fashioned, natural-artificial, educated-uneducated, conscious-unaware, survival-destruction.

The Merchant of Venice

This play's values of bounce, counterpoint, love, loss, and gain should open the hearts and eyes of Jewish and Christian students. It has magnificent acting give-and-take for boys, anguished love acting and opportunities for courtroom aplomb for girls. It minimizes the money-hunger in Christians sniffing out a dowry and maximizes that hunger in Jews seeking interest on their investment. It is an expression of Elizabethan business values that concludes in a burst of glorious lyricism.

The opening scene is best acted in the spirit of a group of men singing "Sweet Adeline" in close harmony. These are Venetian counterparts of Madison Avenue men in gray flannel suits, all young men on the way up, with Antonio the most sober and most successful of the lot. Antonio is sad. He may sense that "wedding bells are breaking up that old gang of mine," and when he asks

> Well, tell me now what lady is the same
> To whom you swore a secret pilgrimage
> That you today promised to tell me of?

you may ask the class how he speaks these lines and if there is any connection with his sadness. Does he growl? Does he speak with difficulty? Is he matter of fact?

In fairness to Shylock, you should point out that Bassanio's wooing of Portia is not untinged with crassness, because a handsome dowry accompanies her: he answers Antonio, "My chief care is to come off fairly from the great debts," and thus shows himself in part a fortune hunter.

As I:1 is of particular interest to boys, so you will find that the dialogue between Portia and Nerissa in I:2 is of interest to girls and that little can be done to interest boys in it, unless they want to find out what girls talk about when men aren't around. Thus I:1 is an opportunity for girls to eavesdrop, and I:2 offers a similar opportunity for boys.

The bargain struck by Shylock, Antonio, and Bassanio, in I:3, is preceded by exchanges of hate and insult. These need not be mitigated in the interest of twentieth-century tolerance. These are strong men with strong feelings. Do not adulterate them. Contempt is as deep in one as hate is in the other, and you should ask your class why majority-minority relations express themselves this way. Shylock is eager to close the bargain. Does he want to become friendly? Or does he see a dim possibility of revenge? We see afterward that he seizes the latter opportunity, but this is after Jessica's elopement and its devastating consequences on him. Ask, just before the trial scene, if Shylock would have been as remorseless had Jessica not eloped. How does Jessica's flight intensify his hatred?

Space limitations prevent detailed examination of the entire play, but the glorious fifth act, one extended epithalamion, will be extraordinarily moving to your sensitive students. Shylock's speech "To bait fish withal" (III:1), Portia's tormented avowal of love (III:2), Bassanio's soliloquy over the caskets (III:2), Portia's "quality of mercy" (IV:1), and other passages beg for memorization. Throughout, possibilities for class dramatization abound.

In the trial scene, Shylock's degradation is riveted down tight by compelling his conversion to Christianity. What kind of Christian does your class think he will make? Is the forced apostasy an act of retribution or of generosity? What kind of trial scene would Shakespeare have written if he were a Jew?

How will you begin *Merchant of Venice*? Experiment with these questions:

Is cheating an enemy more important than being fair? Which protects you more?

Have you ever heard of a fight in which one side was a complete, hundred per cent winner, and the other a complete, hundred per cent loser?

If the businessman is a gambler, is the gambler a businessman?

What gestures in charades would you use for "argosies with portly sail" and "I should still be plucking the grass to know where sits the wind" and "My wind cooling my broth"? (I:1) (See p. 322.)

Are we ever told why Antonio is sad? Can you give any reasons for his sadness? (I:1)

Read Genesis 30. Whose interpretation was right, Antonio's or Shylock's? (I:3)

Which is more reason for causing enmity between Antonio and Shylock, financial beliefs or religious beliefs? Do Shylock's religious customs cause Antonio to hate his financial practices, or do Shylock's financial practices cause Antonio to hate his religious customs?

Does Bassanio want to marry Portia for love or money? (I:1)

How will Bassanio pay back Antonio? Whose money will he use to pay back the "two arrows"?

Is it more honorable to use your bride's inheritance to repay your debts or to loan money at interest?

What special problems does a rich girl have in choosing a husband? Did Portia's dead father help or hinder in making the best possible selection? (I:2)

In refusing to eat, drink, and pray with Bassanio, is Shylock hurting or helping himself in doing business? (I:3)

In his *Occupation: Writer*, Robert Graves says: "Of all the feminine forms 'poetess' is the most suspect. It is used almost invariably in a quarter-gallant, three-quarter-contemptuous sense to denote a woman who longingly aspires to rival man in his most sublime and peculiar province. Of course, many women do accept the word with all its connotations of assured failure. Felicia Hemans was a 'poetess' as Sappho and others have been 'poets.' But, on the other hand, there are men who write poetry of a dull male quality that corresponds with the insipid female quality of the work of poetesses, but there is no male word of offence to correspond. Perhaps we should make one and say that if Felicia Hemans was a poetess, then Southey, Rogers, Leigh Hunt and Company were 'buck poets.'" [5] How would you use this quotation to teach the strong heroines in Shakespeare like Portia and Lady Macbeth? (Also see the discussion on p. 268 on the characteristics of lady biographers.)

Twelfth Night

Just as *The Tempest* stages less well than it reads, so *Twelfth Night* reads less well than it stages. *Twelfth Night* fairly begs to be put on. The more broadly you play it, the better. Duke Orsino's love for Olivia is openly professed, as is Olivia's for Viola-Cesario. There is no subtlety about Sir Toby's drunkenness or Malvolio's posturing.

Nevertheless, paradoxically, because it is so simple and visual it is not a play for a slow class. There are few problems in it and little emotional or intellectual challenge, except for the stage director. *Twelfth Night* has a long history of successful productions but it requires the hand of a professional director for full effect. Therefore, if you are to teach it successfully, you must be prepared to act broadly and with full use of what is known as "stage business." When Feste, the clown, impersonates Sir Topas, or better, when you impersonate Feste impersonating Sir Topas (IV:2), you must alternate between your speaking voice as Feste, and a thin, high falsetto as Sir Topas, thus:

> FESTE (*normal voice, in a sudden low warning*): Advise you what you say; the minister is here. (*falsetto voice, as Sir Topas*): Malvolio, Malvolio, thy wits the heaven restore! Endeavor thyself to sleep, and leave thy vain bibble babble.
>
> MALVOLIO (*desperately*): Sir Topas!
>
> FESTE (*falsetto voice, as Sir Topas*): Maintain no words with him, good fellow. (*normal voice*)—Who, I, sir? not I sir. God be wi' you, good Sir Topas. (*falsetto voice, as Sir Topas*) Marry, amen. (*normal voice*) I will, sir, I will.
>
> MALVOLIO (*urgently*): Fool, fool, fool, I say!
>
> FESTE (*falsetto voice, as Sir Topas, speaking behind his hand, as if speaking from a distance*) Alas, sir, be patient. (*normal voice*) What say you, sir? I am shent for speaking to you.

Visualize *Twelfth Night* not in any stilted fashion, but in high good spirits. In that case, stage the first act opening by having Duke Orsino, as he says, "If music be the food of love, play on" *et cetera,* followed onstage by a group of classmates who are singing some recent love ballad in close harmony, with the accompaniment played by a student who can handle a violin, guitar, or harmonica. Let the group sing, with Orsino sighing and clasping his heart, until some predetermined sour chord causes him to say, "Enough; no more: 'tis not so sweet now as it was before." Orsino continues the aria, apostrophizing the class, and the group softly resumes its music to the end of the scene, singing under the dialogue between Valentine and Duke Orsino.

Before going to I:2, establish for the class that Duke Orsino is in love with Olivia and that Olivia is in mourning.

Olivia is not alone in her mourning. A girl she is soon to meet in strange circumstances, Viola, is being led ashore on the seacoast of Illyria, just rescued from a shipwreck, half-crazed with apprehension for her twin brother. She shivers with cold. She stammers as she speaks, until the Captain's words comfort her. Not only the Captain's words, but the jackets you have borrowed from students to drape around Viola's shaking and chilled shoulders, warm and reassure her, because she has these pulled snugly around her as she says more strongly, "Orsino! I have heard my father name him. He was a bachelor then."

Establish, at the end of this scene, that Viola is bound for Orsino's court, disguised as a young man.

Enter Sir Toby Belch, in I:3, chronically intoxicated and hiccuping, while he chases Maria around the stage, or classroom, as she skillfully avoids him. Sir Andrew comes on, giggling in a squeaky, high-pitched voice. Odds are that unless you can act it well, students will find the scene tediously heavy-handed and the Elizabethan slang difficult to follow and therefore hard to act. Abbreviate it to a point that still allows some understanding of the mischievous Maria, the gullible Aguecheek, and the drunken plans of Sir Toby to egg on Aguecheek toward Maria. Get past I:3 as quickly as you can, and do not feel apologetic.

Thereafter the going is better because in I:4, I:5, and I:6, the delicate fun of the play takes shape. In I:4 remind your class of the story of Miles Standish and John Alden. Is the Duke running a risk in sending a messenger to do his love errands? In I:5, show the chaffing between Maria and Feste, and the thin-lipped, forbidding Malvolio of jaundiced disposition. Feste's lines require discussion, for the word play moves like a rapier and here, unlike I:3, has style. Impart to your students how the word play should be relished; it develops like a geometric theorem, with Feste's triple pun on colours and cholers and hangman's collars, and with Maria's encouragement of him with her "may you be bold to say in your foolery," as she tosses her head in the direction of the household, and snaps her fingers thereat.

Because *Twelfth Night* makes so winning and warming a stage production, you must pay special attention to stage business and to interpretation. When you originally introduce the class to the play, say something like this:

> The play begins with Duke Orsino saying how much he loves Lady Olivia. As I read it to you, determine for yourself if he is foolishly romantic or else deeply and sincerely in love.

Then read the scene. Poll the class on its feeling about Orsino's character. Then have two students read Orsino's lines according to the divergent interpretations. Thereafter, if you like, stage I:1 with the close harmony group described above.

Similarly in I:2 present the alternative interpretations of Viola as weakly hysterical or as bold and determined. Have one student read the lines as if Viola were hysterical. Have another read the lines as if she were making a tremendous effort to contain herself.

In I:3, on the basis of your prior reading, ask the class if Sir Toby is tall and strong, or short and fat, if Maria is pretty or plain, if Sir Andrew is active and posturing, or awkwardly heavy-footed, clumsy, and tripping over his own feet. Have the representatives of divergent interpretations read the lines in accordance with their opinions. Would William Bendix be better as Sir Toby or as Sir Andrew? What of Walter Slezak, Jackie Gleason, Oliver Hardy, Jack Leonard, or George Gobels? For Maria, would they select Ann Sothern, Eve Arden, or Lucille Ball? For Sir Andrew? For Olivia? For Viola?

Your job, with *Twelfth Night,* is to make it straight theater and at the end, when Viola and Sebastian meet, the class should have the same throat-catching leap of feeling that the audience experiences at *My Fair Lady* when Eliza succeeds in saying, "The rain in Spain stays mainly in the plain." *Twelfth Night,* because it is theater, should effect prickles of the skin. You can get wave after wave of them at the encounter of brother and sister.

Macbeth and Hamlet

Here you play with dynamite. Until now we have suggested questions you should ask your classes. Now we suggest that there are questions which are best avoided, and we itemize. Questions like these should never be asked of any class you will ever teach:

> You are out walking. Suddenly you see your mother. She is in the arms of a strange man. They are hugging and kissing. What should you do?
> What would your parents be like if they had never had any children? Suppose you had never been born? Or that you had been born and then died? Would their lives have been the same or different? Better or worse?

Clearly, these questions should never, in any circumstances, be asked. They are too explosive. They are the business of the psychotherapist, not of the English teacher. Yet you deal with precisely these matters in teaching *Hamlet* and *Macbeth*. You may deny this. You may feel that you are concerned with revenge, or ambition, Hamlet's indecisiveness, and the growth of brutality in Macbeth, but not with a child's learning of a mother's infidelity or imagining his parents childless and himself never born.

The *Macbeth* and *Hamlet* taught in high school are not the same as those taught in college, any more than high school physics and college physics are the same. Similarly high school physics is remote indeed from research physics and that is why your colleagues in science are a generation behind the work being done in the colleges and in the laboratories, and why they are being urged to bring their knowledge up to date and why considerable sums are being spent to encourage high school teachers of physics, chemistry, and mathematics to see what has been happening while they have been playing Rip Van Winkle.

Perhaps the English teacher with enterprise and drive should similarly be encouraged to find out how Freud, Jekels, and Ernest Jones interpreted Macbeth and Hamlet and how Granville Barker did in his *Prefaces*. Nobody has as yet said that high school English is as anachronistic as high school physics, but that may be because nobody has yet comprehensively studied the gap in English related to that in science and mathematics, else a blow as startling as sputnik may be required to show how laggard the teaching of high school English is.

For that reason you are well advised not to ask the questions. They are better reserved for college teaching. Meanwhile here are two plays dealing with the most violent of human passions. Let's begin with *Macbeth*.

Your first difficulty is with the witches. The "willing suspension of disbelief" that accepts superstition, to achieve more vigorous jostling by imagination, is the roller-coaster approach, where titillation matters more than good sense. Did Macbeth believe in witches? Of course, and so did Shakespeare, but our students should be taught not to, either here or in *Rime of the Ancient Mariner*. Your job, as an English teacher, is to remove your students from primitivism, ghosts, witches, and cheap, hand-me-down miracles.

Can you do so without weakening the drama?

First, determine for yourself whether the function of the witches is to suggest or to prophesy. Suggestion, if strong enough, molds minds and behavior so that the future becomes predictable; but prediction is not prophecy, any more than suggestibility or gullibility, though they make the future more predictable, are proof of prophecy.

We sometimes see this in parlor tricks, where the magician "forces" us to select a card and then "reads our minds." But, in an even wider area, affecting all society, the advertising campaign in the promotion of new products is the supreme analogue of the witches' role in suggestion rather than in prophecy. We will go into this in greater length in our discussion of the mass media, but here and meanwhile observe how the weird sisters behave like Procter and Gamble after a new soap or toothpaste market.

Procter and Gamble[6] invested several million dollars in a new toothpaste even before it was officially placed on the market as a full-scale competitor of its rivals. This sum was expended in laboratory research, in manufacturing plant, in consumer attitude research, in market testing, and in purchase of newspaper, magazine, radio, and television advertising facilities. Executives at Procter and Gamble predicted the sales volume on the basis of this investment. But the prediction depended also on the suggestibility of the consumer and the amount of money required to force gullibility in toothpaste buyers. Adequate investment in suggestion warranted the prediction. And so Gleem toothpaste was successful. But prediction, even with suitable investment, is not infallible, as Ford's experience with the Edsel car shows.

Macbeth, however, *was* suggestible. The weird sisters could thereby predict, but, though prediction looks like prophecy, it isn't. The weird sisters think they are witches, so does Macbeth, and so does Shakespeare. We know they aren't. We don't believe in witches. How then do they prophesy? By gullibility and suggestibility.

The dread and terror are thereby intensified. You and your class can reject the weird sisters' supernatural pretensions, but this does not diminish the even greater horror at the suggestibility within Macbeth that allows them to predict. But, an equally suggestible student may protest, how did they know he was to become Thane of Cawdor? To ask the question implies suggestibility in the questioner. In asking the question, he too is as suggestible as Macbeth and Shakespeare, and you ought to ask the class if this is so. We today are not too far from suggestibility ourselves. On the basis of this suggestibility advertising flourishes. Now to the play.

Ask (in a squeaky, high, tremulous voice, and as if your dentures are wobbly):

> When shall we three meet again?
> In thunder, lightning, or in rain?

and then answer yourself in a gruff, thick, basso profundo:

> When the hurlyburly's done,
> When the battle's lost and won.

And then add, crisply, and in a businesslike fashion, looking out at the sky through the classroom window and checking it against your wrist watch:

> That will be ere set of sun.

Behind your hand meow like a cat, and then answer in the First Witch's tremolo: "I come, Graymalkin." Again, behind your hand, croak like a frog, and then in your gruff bass announce: "Paddock calls."

Leave the weird sisters there. They are not the drama. The human beings are—people who are obscured at once by vocabulary, characterization linked to unfamiliar characters, and structural inversions (*of the revolt the newest state; knowledge of the broil as thou didst leave it; doubtful it stood*). Why do they speak this way? They are breathless, they speak in short gasps because they have just left a battlefield and outcomes are still uncertain. Here are some stage directions that capitalize on this. The asterisks represent a deep gasping breath, one asterisk per breath. Between asterisks speak rapidly and breathlessly. Lean on the desk, as if in deep fatigue:

> DUNCAN: What bloody man is that * ? He can report * * *
> As seemeth by his plight * * of the revolt * *
> The newest state * * *
> MALCOLM: This is * * the sergeant * *
> Who * like a good and hardy soldier * * fought
> 'Gainst my captivity * * * Hail * ! brave friend * !

> Say to the king * * * the knowledge of the broil * * *
> As thou didst leave it.

Read the Captain's speech similarly, taking frequent pauses for breath and between pauses speaking rapidly. Fight for air, until you come to "For brave Macbeth—well he deserves that name" and here speak in a longer, flowing, sustained paean and without any further signs of distress, because the Captain is glowing with admiration and has temporarily forgotten his wounds.

After Duncan orders the Captain's wounds attended to, and before the entrance of Ross and Angus, have students tell you what is going on. They should identify Duncan, Macdonwald, Malcolm, and Macbeth. They should be able to report how Macbeth has saved Duncan's throne. Ross and Angus confirm the Captain's report of Macbeth's bravery. Stress, at the end of the scene, the despoilment of Cawdor and the transfer of the title to Macbeth.

Thus you have set the stage in a specific fashion. You have taken a text which has few stage directions—or, in professional lingo, stage "business"—and have behaved like the director you truly ought to be. Now, for the remainder of the play, give your assignments and roadmarkers so that students are sent ahead on their own to do the reading and, with instructions, to be prepared to give accompanying stage directions and stage business.

Thus, with what gestures of kicking and handwaving does the First Witch say, " 'Aroint thee, witch!' the rump-fed ronyon cries"? And with what gestures of rowing and paddling "But in a sieve I'll thither sail"? With what turning of the backside "I'll give thee a wind" and with what lifting of a leg does the First Witch retort "I myself have all the other." Too ribald for a high school class? Quite likely. Such improprieties are perhaps better reserved for the professional production. Here are questions more decorous:

> Of whom does Banquo ask, "How far is't called to Forres?" If of the witches, with what gesture would he call out?
> With what gestures and stage business do the witches greet Macbeth?
> Read "My noble partner you greet," etc., with suitable stage business. Is Banquo mocking or serious?
> Devise gestures to accompany the witches' hailing of Banquo that will contrast with their earlier hailing of Macbeth. To whom will they be more respectful? How will this affect the differences in the way they hail the two men?
> Is Macbeth pleading or commanding when he says, "Stay, you imperfect

speakers, tell me more"? If pleading, how would he gesture and move? How if commanding?

After the witches vanish, do Macbeth and Banquo remain still, or do they move rapidly around the stage in search of them?

Is Macbeth complimentary or thoughtful as he says, "Your children shall be kings"? Does he shake Banquo's hand? Or does he clasp his hands tightly behind his back?

But we need not seek to clothe understanding in gestures and stage business, no matter how appropriate. When Ross and Angus appear on the heel of the witches' disappearance, and Ross reports, "As thick as hail came post with post," the student will not gain understanding unless he understands *post with post,* meaning news, not fence posts. Understanding can become dramatic. In the quartet scene of Ross, Angus, Banquo, and Macbeth (I:3), such understanding can cause students' scalps to rise, their skins to prickle, and set goose flesh scurrying over them:

> What is the interpretation of "The greatest is behind" (1. 121)?
>
> Does Banquo, in "That, trusted home, might yet enkindle you" (1. 123, 124), scoff at the witches, or does he plead with Macbeth not to take the predictions too seriously? Is Banquo taking the predictions seriously? Or does he want to forget the encounter with the witches? Compare what is going on in Banquo's mind with what is going on in Macbeth's mind.
>
> What are the *two truths* (1. 130)?
>
> For what does Macbeth say, "I thank you, gentlemen" (1. 132)? What have they done that he should thank them?
>
> What is the horrid image (1. 137)?
>
> Describe the surmise that smothers function in Macbeth (1. 144). What was his "single state of man" before (1. 143)?

Turn now to Duncan, a man of complete and abounding trust and generosity. There is not a scintilla of suspicion in him. He has faith and complete goodness. He is sunny, kind, large of heart and mind, and a saintly man. Portray him so.

By what right? Because you are the head stage director. When he asks, "Is execution done on Cawdor? Are not those in commission yet returned?" he is sorrowful and regretful, not vengeful. Malcolm's answer is gentle, placating, comforting. With the entrance of the quartet—Macbeth, Banquo, Ross, and Angus—Duncan's goodness rises to a summit and is overwhelming. The man is all kindness and decency. He rubs the tears of feeling from his eyes (1. 35) in "My plenteous joys" when he appoints Malcolm as his successor. Take out your handkerchief. Dry your eyes. Blow your nose. And smile, meanwhile, like the most beneficent of men. Into this burst with sudden hoarseness, "The Prince of Cumberland! that is a step on which I must fall down, or else o'er-leap," and say it as you are bowing, your head down, withdrawing respectfully from your king, backing away and your eyes downcast.

The remainder of the act is borne to a climax by Lady Macbeth and climax it is, leaping from extreme of violence in her "Come to my woman's breasts, and take my milk for gall," to Duncan's almost cloying "This castle hath a pleasant seat," to Macbeth's despairing "I have no spur to prick the side of my intent," but here Lady Macbeth is the prime mover throughout.

Though the lines are climactic, you should not rush. Stop off for arias that should be memorized: "Glamis thou art, and Cawdor," and "The raven himself is hoarse," and "If it were done, when 'tis done."

Thus you get *Macbeth* off and running with the class as jockey and yourself in the stands.

Tyrone Guthrie, that distinguished stage director, has written "Why and How They Play Hamlet,"[7] pointing out that *Hamlet* is like a Rorschach inkblot; everybody interprets his way.

The Ghost, for example, can stir your class for the wrong reasons, like Dracula in a horror movie. But how can you teach *Hamlet* without the Ghost? If we don't believe in ghosts, Hamlet also begins to wonder about what he has seen:

> The spirit that I have seen
> May be a de'il, and the de'il hath power
> T'assume a pleasing shape—yea, and perhaps
> Out of my weakness and my melancholy
> (As he is very potent with such spirits)
> Abuses me to damn me.   (II:2)

And he says later to Horatio:

> Observe my uncle. If his occulted guilt
> Do not itself unkennel in one speech,
> It is a damned ghost that we have seen,
> And my imaginations are as foul
> As Vulcan's stithy.   (III:2, 80)

So the apparition may be the dead king's ghost, or some evil inner weakness in Hamlet luring him to destruction. Neither the Ghost nor the play-within-a-play is satisfactory courtroom evidence. The strongest evidence against Claudius issues from his own actions: his inability to pray for forgiveness and his despatch of Hamlet to England. Don't waste time on the Ghost. It's only an Elizabethan convention to get the more basic drama going.

How do you begin study of *Hamlet*?

You cannot ask the question basic to *Hamlet* and to the splendid French film *The 400 Blows* ("You are out walking. Suddenly you see your mother. She is in the arms of a strange man. They are hugging and kissing. What should you do?"), but you can modify:

> A boy finds out that his mother is a cheat and liar. This boy is in love with a girl. How will his feelings for the girl be affected or changed? Or won't there be any effect?
>
> Who is more likely to believe in ghosts, a happy man or an unhappy man?
>
> On the condition in Denmark and Marcellus' speech, "why such daily cast of brazen cannon, and foreign mart for implements of war," you can ask: Are most people interested or indifferent when a national crisis occurs? Does it make any difference to you what happens in the Congo or in Korea?
>
> If a number of people report seeing a ghost (or flying saucers), is society happy or troubled?
>
> Because *Hamlet* is not the original contact with Shakespeare and is generally taught in the last year of high school, after students have had experience with at least one Shakespearean play, ask: What difficulties do you expect to face in reading *Hamlet*? What rewards do you expect to get out of reading it?
>
> Many people consider *Hamlet* the greatest play ever written. If so, what should it be like if you are not to be disappointed in it? What do you have a right to expect?

Such questions are useful before you begin the play. Now you have them open books.

The changing of the guards with which the play opens is not difficult. You can do it, or have your students do it, with smart salutes, heel-clicking, and the port-arms or present-arms type of military exercise. Then comes Marcellus' speech, "Horatio says 'tis but our fantasy." Here's where your troubles begin, and here's a suggestion.

Reverse the curse of our generation, the comic book or abridged version. Write out the four sentences below on a slip of paper. Before the period begins, give it to a student with legible handwriting to put on the blackboard: "Horatio says *we can't see straight*. He won't *believe* about *this thing* we've seen twice. So I *asked him to come* and *wait* with us. If the *thing* comes, maybe he'll *admit* we saw it and speak to it."

Have students select the equivalents to the italicized words in Marcellus' speech, so that *can't see straight* is matched with *'tis but our fantasy*, *believe* with *belief take hold of him*, *this thing* with *this dreaded sight*, *asked him to come* with *entreated him along*, *wait* with *watch the minutes of this night*, *thing* with *apparition*, and *admit* with *approve our eyes*. In Bernardo's speech immediately after, you can have another student write on the blackboard, "Let me bend your ears," and ask students to find its equivalent in the passage, which is, of course, "Let us once again assail your ears." Instead of reducing Shakespeare to the vernacular, you have done the reverse; you have begun with the vernacular and found its parallel in the lines of the play. You are ascending toward Shakespearean language, poetry, and imagery; you are not descending from it. Thus "When that star had just about reached where it's shining now," becomes Bernardo's "When yond same star that's westward from the pole had made his course t' illume that part of heaven where now it burns," and the class must match vernacular with Shakespeare.

Of course, you will have to agree with them—because they will bring the matter up!—that the paraphrase is easier than the original. No doubt about it. But, once having matched the vernacular and the Shakespearean and having achieved the sense of the passage, which means more? Allow the Shakespearean version to soak in for some minutes. A considerable minority, at the least, will assert that the Shakespearean presents the same idea in greater depth, with more overtones, and with greater power.

Enter Ghost, saying nothing, and disappearing, still saying nothing. Is the Ghost there to warn the country of some danger? So Horatio and Marcellus believe. Certainly the Ghost warns of danger—but what kind and from what source? Fortinbras (Armstrong!) is the least. Tell the class that the dangers are so horrible that you would rather not discuss them yet.

In keeping the class dangling, you are, as artfully as Shakespeare, unhurriedly developing the plot. We only now meet Claudius, who comfortably and in no rush at all despatches his plenipotentiaries to the Norwegian king. That business concluded, Laertes and Polonius enter the discussion. We still amble at an *andante* pace. We have met half the cast, much action has gotten under way or been discussed, and the hero has yet to speak. Not till then will we get an inkling of the main plot line.

Discuss the imagery of Claudius' opening lines. Which is stronger—mirth in marriage or dirge in funeral (to change the lines somewhat); delight or dole; the contracted brow of woe or remembrance of ourselves? No answer is necessary, though discussion is, because with a hypocrite like Claudius an answer is hard to come by. But the issue must be opened up and the class must *now* learn that Claudius has married his dead brother's wife. Therefore, why does Fortinbras hold a "weak supposal of our worth"? Is this related to the marriage with Gertrude? Discuss this before Claudius turns his attention to Laertes. Go on to character analysis. Is Laertes obedient and dutiful—or like Hamlet? Does Polonius stand high with the King or low, that Laertes needs permission both of father and King to return to France? If the father is valuable to the King, how would the King regard the son? After discussion, turn to Hamlet.

"Kin," "kind," and "too much i' the sun" introduce us to Hamlet and they offer evidence enough, before you go further, to have the class compare him with Laertes. Is Hamlet as tractable? Clearly not. Is he forward in response because he is Prince and heir apparent? Or for some other reason? We are about to find out.

Hamlet is black within and without. Does he look the world in the eye? No. With "vailed lids" he seeks his father in the dust. He sighs deeply ("windy suspiration of forc'd breath"), his eyes are wet ("fruitful river in the eye"). Have students find the textual equivalents for the deep sigh and the wet eye and compare his outburst with the sweet temperateness of Gertrude and Claudius, who seem so gentle, so understanding, and who apparently have so much of the right on their side. Build up this sweetness of their expostulations and how seemingly unreasonable Hamlet is until you come to the aria "O that this too too solid flesh would melt" and especially his "But two months dead!"

That should be the shocker. Maybe Hamlet is right in his revulsion and in his prediction, "It is not, nor can it come to, good." Whether you read the passage, or students do, make it strong, violent, upsetting, disgusted, so that you almost retch with "Fie on 't! ah, fie!" and you pull at your collar as if needing breath and your gorge rising. Act, act, act.

Again match contemporary language with the textual equivalents:

> "I'd just like to go up in smoke," and "O that this too too solid flesh would melt,/ Thaw and resolve itself into a dew!"
>
> "God doesn't want us to commit suicide," and "that the Everlasting had not fix'd/ His canon 'gainst self slaughter."

"Sun to shadow," and "Hyperion to a satyr."

"The more you eat, the more you want," and "As if increase of appetite had grown/ By what it fed on."

And so on. In matching contemporary language with Shakespearean equivalents, students will increasingly agree that feeling and thought are less deeply plumbed in everyday language.

Horatio, Marcellus, and Bernardo enter, and disparate plot elements consolidate. The Ghost is not news to us, though it is to Hamlet. The going here is not difficult and can be dramatized by students if alerted a day ahead to prepare at home. Preparation should not only include study of the passage, but possibilities of stage business, gestures, and movement. (Bernardo, for example, has no separate speaking lines, Marcellus barely two. If students have no suggestions as to stage directions or stage business, you can take their roles.) Hamlet, at first suspicious, fires questions at Horatio, whose answers persuasively diminish Hamlet's skepticism as they increase his horror.

Have class discussion, with books put away, on Hamlet's feeling that *foul deeds will rise.* It's time to catch a bit of breath, look around, and review how far you've come, because we are about to deepen the ultimate horror and pity of it—we are about to meet Ophelia. Before you do so, a quick review is appropriate on Claudius, Gertrude, Polonius, Laertes, Hamlet, and the political situation in Denmark. After that, you're ready for her.

Stress Ophelia's sweetness, her compliance to Polonius, and the way she is caught between faith in her lover and love for her father. How is she to decide? How would your class decide? She denies emotion and accedes to reason, or Polonius' kind of reason (which ultimately unhinges her reason; but that's none of the class's business yet). Polonius gives reasoned advice here, much like Chesterfield writing to his son. Is it good advice that Laertes gives to Ophelia, Polonius to Laertes, and then to Ophelia? Are they being helpful and solicitous, or interfering? How should a young girl behave when a prince and heir apparent comes awooing? Why should the father and the brother be against the courtship? What makes them believe that Hamlet will never marry Ophelia? Does the class agree that Hamlet is that dishonorable? Or, in imputing dishonor to Hamlet, do Laertes and Polonius reflect their own values? Is Hamlet crooked and devious, or are Laertes and Polonius?

Leave these questions fully discussed but unanswered. They are better that way.

In the confrontation of Hamlet and Ghost, intone, as in Gregorian chant, but *sotto voce,* the "Angels and ministers of grace defend us!" and then, having uttered the prayer, explode into "Be thou a spirit of health or goblin damn'd" and the rest. Augment horror as far as bearable. It's legitimate, but how can you simultaneously teach your students to reject superstition? Ask them, "Suppose all this was told Hamlet by a real, live person instead of his father's ghost. Would he believe the story or resent it?" Another question: "Why does Hamlet walk away from the place where the Ghost speaks? Does this mean he is afraid of the Ghost or that the evidence against his mother and Claudius is proved?" Another: "Hamlet tears himself out of the hands of Horatio and Marcellus to pursue the Ghost. Is he courageous or pulled by a power greater than himself?" Another: "Describe the stage action, gestures, and stage business when the Ghost says 'Swear!' " Another: "Why does Hamlet swear Horatio and Marcellus to secrecy but never tell them what has transpired between the Ghost and himself?"

After you have given them the undiluted impact of Elizabethan superstition, analyze why, just as astrology was a precursor to astronomy and alchemy to chemistry, ghosts and supernatural visions are today explicable by psychiatry and psychology. The Ghost will not predispose your students to the supernatural prevalence of witches more than they already are, but the ghosts of Caesar, Banquo, or Hamlet's father offer an opportunity for discussion of the nature of horror and pity.

Would Hamlet have felt more horror if he had dreamed what the Ghost told him? We cannot stage *Hamlet* without Hamlet, but can without the Ghost and retain all the horror that the Elizabethan audience got. Now the situation can be imagined in a variety of ways. Suppose Hamlet's father had killed Gertrude and married another woman? Would Hamlet feel the same way about the surviving father and the new stepmother? Suppose, instead, that Hamlet had been a girl? Consider the diagram:

Is the situation that Hamlet and Orestes face (Situation I) worse than the situation faced by the children of Henry VIII (Situation IV)? Which is more nightmarish? Do the girls agree with the boys? Just as theatrical asides and soliloquies reflect how we talk to ourselves, so ghosts do not

HAMLET IS A

Survivors	Man	Woman
Mother and	I	II
Stepfather	Hamlet	
	Orestes	Electra
Father and	III	IV
Stepmother	Absalom—II	
	Samuel 13, 14, 15	Children of Henry VIII—Elizabeth I and Mary I ("Bloody Mary")

exist but the horrors they reflect do; some patterns of horror are presented in the diagram.

In this diagram, which of the four cells draw the votes of the girls and which the votes of the boys? Do sex-linked differences in horror exist?

Shakespeare and the Sugar-coated Crutch

Shakespeare never contemplated having you and your class as audience, even though he had a fair idea that he would be read far after his time. He has been effectively set to music by Mendelssohn and Verdi, to movies both silent and sound, and to comic-book versions. Shakespeare is very big in audio-visual.

Especially rewarding are the recordings, after the class has read the text. Do not use the recordings until you have gone over the entire play and your class understands it. You will have to put aside almost two class periods for the recordings. Have the class follow the play with books open, like an opera-goer with his libretto. Wherever possible, conclude the study of Shakespearean plays with recordings and with the class reading along.

Thus you get the show on the road, or on the boards, with an audience prepared to know what's happening. Your students are now a knowledgeable audience for any of the Stratfords, for Olivier's filmed *Henry V* and *Hamlet,* for the M-G-M *Julius Caesar,* or, best of all, for their own reading, given occasion, need, or opportunity, the rest of their lives. They will not need comic books or audio-visual aids.

An educational film producer has developed a sequence of films on

Hamlet designed to run for four class periods, a considerable portion of the time allotted to *Hamlet* in most classes. The films come equipped with a commentator (an excellent means of sparing students the responsibility of interpreting and understanding for themselves), who offers a prefabricated discussion on Shakespeare's motives and drama. It could all be read in a book. Undoubtedly the films will do a better job than the poorest English teacher—what wouldn't?—and a far worse job than the capable English teacher.

Of course not all English teachers are capable of teaching Shakespeare successfully. Hence the major task of the educational film is to mitigate the worst effects of the poor English teacher and to supplement the endeavors of the master teacher. The master teacher increases interaction between student and text. Only after this interaction should students, either bright or mediocre, be exposed to audio-visual adjuncts.

Audio-visual aids have a venerable history and go back to Egyptian picture-writing. Picture-writing gave way to the written word because the written word is the most efficient way known to man of symbolizing, teaching, and remembering. That's why many people get deeper drama out of Shakespeare read than Shakespeare seen and feel as intensely hammered by a reading of Shakespeare as by a Maurice Evans or Laurence Olivier production. The primitive audio-visual approach is no substitute for private, inner visualization and imagination. For example, audio-visual materials are useful in more elementary concepts; in teaching conic sections, a model of a cone or a diagram is helpful; an illustration or model of subatomic or molecular structure is helpful to a point; thereafter it's limiting, even impeding.

The educational film producer's *Hamlet* cannot overcome the effects of the poor teacher, because nothing can. In *Hamlet,* the best audio-visual aid is the master teacher who can act, ask stimulating questions, read effectively, and involve the class. Packaged merchandise, like films, closed-circuit television, recordings, and teaching machines, are for the more readily understandable circumstances of learning. *Hamlet,* however, is not readily understandable. The *realia* of a cone helping the mathematics student understand conic sections or a Tinker Toy helping the chemistry student visualize molecular structure work because they are handled and manipulated by the student. But an educational film on *Hamlet* that is merely a filmed lecture remains a lecture, even if on film or on videotape. The high school student is a poor audience for the lecture method.

Research, Resources, and Techniques

1. How does the Melancholy Dane do with the bright students and with the slow ones?

a. William Fidone's "An Above-Average Class Studies *Hamlet*" (*E. J.*, Nov. 1956, p. 470) says the bright did well. Why shouldn't they? The class was bright and the teacher capable. Nothing should go wrong and it's no miracle they enjoyed the play. Read the article and see how the lessons went.

b. For an interesting comparison, read Priscilla M. Zink's " 'Hamlet' —Caviare to the Generals" (*E. J.*, Jan. 1955, p. 37), which shows how *Hamlet* is of interest even to a slower, non-college-bound senior class.

2. Charles Calitri's "Macbeth and the Reluctant Reader" (*E. J.*, May 1959, p. 254) gives you the author's pointed comments on the Underground Library, making this article significant for anybody who wants to enlist in the Teacher's Underground (p. 285 below). More important, you'll find here some excellent questions that you can use in teaching *Macbeth*.

3. For sensible discussion on the shortcomings of the filmed version of *Hamlet* produced for classroom use by Encyclopaedia Britannica, see Patrick D. Hazard and Mary Hazard's "Juilliard, Jazz, and the Golden Gate Bridge" (*E. J.*, Sept. 1959, p. 347).

4. *Time* (July 4, 1960, p. 60) proves that Shakespeare is still playing to full houses.

The
Teaching
of
Poetry

CHAPTER 7

Background Notes—Program Music and Program Poetry

You have heard that the relationship between poetry and music is close. Not always. Evidence exists that poetry and music are antithetical, or, more precisely, that one tries to invade the other's domain. Thus, Tchaikovsky wrote the *Romeo and Juliet* overture, Mendelssohn the incidental music to *Midsummer-Night's Dream,* and Verdi operas of *Macbeth, Othello,* and *Falstaff.* What is called "program music" is an attempt to tell a story, or paint a picture, with tones, notes, intervals, flats, sharps, harmonies, melodies, and the composer's tools of the trade, so that we get a narrative effect or a visual one, as in Beethoven's *Pastorale Symphony,* or Debussy's *Sunken Cathedral.*

Similarly, Swinburne's "Garden of Proserpine," the "sprung verse" of Gerard Manley Hopkins, Tennyson's songs from *The Princess* are samples of musical values in poetry.

In teaching poetry, you sometimes have to divorce words and music or silence one or the other. Ignorance of words does not impair the satisfaction in music. On another level, the explosive emotions of Donald Duck are not communicated by words but more effectively by squeals, snorts, and squawks. Therefore words are not necessary to the communication of emotion by the human voice. Words can, indeed, blur the emotional message.

Emotion is conveyed by stress, accent, rate of speech, loudness, intonation, inflection, qualities that are musical rather than verbal. Have a student practice saying, "Honest, boss, I didn't mean to make a mistake. But you told me I'd recognize him by the way he was dressed," until the class agrees that the statement is spoken realistically. Then have the student use the same quality of voice, stress, accent, rate of speech, etc., in saying:

> Believe me, king of shadows, I mistook.
> Did you not tell me I should know the man
> By the Athenian garments he had on?
> *Midsummer-Night's Dream,* III:2

Have a girl practice, "I can't choose by myself. The way I was brought up, I'm not allowed to decide. I'll have to marry the way my father wants. Otherwise, prince, you'd stand as good a chance as anybody," until the class again agrees that the statement is read realistically. Then, with the same qualities of voice and delivery, let her say:

> In terms of choice I am not solely led
> By nice direction of a maiden's eyes.
> Besides, the lottery of my destiny
> Bars me the right of voluntary choosing:
> But if my father had not scanted me
> And hedged me by his wit, to yield myself
> His wife who wins me by that means I told you,
> Yourself, renowned prince, then stood as fair
> As any comer I have look'd on yet
> For my affection.
> *Merchant of Venice,* II:1

Or have students compare

1. Look out the window!
2. Look out! The window!

to determine what causes the differences in stress and then have them say Antony's "Lend me your ears" as in 1 and then as in 2. Most students use 1, but Marlon Brando, in the movie *Julius Caesar,* used 2.

Notice that this involves an approach different from the usual paraphrasing, which occurs *after* the student has encountered the passage, has read it, and has been told to "put it into your own words." In the variation here recommended, you, the teacher, first determine the words in which a contemporary student houses his emotions, then force him to practice the words until greater habituation with words in the presence of the class occurs, and then rehouse these emotions in the poet's words. First, a public statement of emotions in words recognizable by students and class; then, a public statement of the same emotions in poetic and unfamiliar language. Throughout, these statements, whether in words familiar or unfamiliar to the class, are publicly practiced and publicly witnessed. Suppose you assign, "You remember where the primroses in the woods are? Where you and I used to stretch out and schmoose?" so that students get the proper notes of reminiscence and inquiry into their voices, and then have them read, with the same intonations of reminiscence and inquiry:

> And in the wood, where often you and I
> Upon faint primrose-beds were wont to lie
> Emptying our bosoms of their counsel sweet. . . .
> *Midsummer-Night's Dream,* I:1

The meaning of the words, the delicacy, and the poetry come all the more inevitably because the Shakespearean passage is based on the student's recognition of his own experiences. Then, as poetry should, it accentuates the emotional recognition and the student's prior experiences. The music of rate, pitch, intonation, volume is the same, but the words are different.

Teaching Two for the Price of One

Elsewhere we have said that, next to spelling, poetry is the easiest thing in the English curriculum to teach. We shall now try to prove this.

The first suggestion in reducing the difficulty of poetry is to find a well-matched, relevant mate to the poem you plan to teach, another poem of a similar theme that will keep your poem company. You will find it easier to teach "Ozymandias" if you simultaneously teach with it Holmes' "The Deacon's Masterpiece" or MacLeish's "You, Andrew Marvell" because all three have a common theme, the passing and evanescence of mortal things; "Miniver Cheevy" with "Richard Cory" because of the common theme of flight and escape; Wordsworth's "Westminster Bridge" with Whitman's "Crossing Brooklyn Ferry" and Sandburg's "Chicago" because of the common theme of urban life and the values of men in city living; Frost's "Mending Wall" with Edwin Arlington Robinson's "Firelight" because both treat incommunicability of feeling; "Sir Patrick Spens" with Byron's "There Is a Pleasure in the Pathless Woods," from *Childe Harold's Pilgrimage,* for poetry of the sea; Tennyson's "Crossing the Bar" (with its peaceful acquiescence to death) and Dylan Thomas' "Do Not Go Gentle into That Good Night" (quite the opposite!).

Or try a gimmick by matching *out of.* From Dylan Thomas' "Ballad of the Long-Legged Bait" there is this:

> Out of the urn the size of a man
> Out of the room the weight of his trouble
> Out of the house that holds a town
> In the continent of a fossil. . . .[1]

Compare it with Whitman's "Out of the Cradle Endlessly Rocking" or with "Out of the bosom of the air" from Longfellow's "Snow Flakes."

Compare Bret Harte's "Crotalus" and Emily Dickinson's "A Narrow Fellow in the Grass" with D. H. Lawrence's "The Snake" for explicit detail versus indirect imagery in herpetology. Abraham Lincoln is the bond between Whitman's "O Captain, My Captain," Vachel Lindsay's "Abraham Lincoln Walks at Midnight," Masters' "Ann Rutledge," Witter Bynner's "A Farmer Remembers Lincoln," and Benét's "Nancy Hanks." Interactions between nature and man unite Sandburg's "Fog," Wordsworth's "Daffodils," Shelley's "To Night," Sandburg's "Grass," and two Shakespearean sonnets: "Full many a glorious morning have I seen," and "Like as the waves make towards the pebbled shore."

Or try, as a poetry unit, *Crazy over Horses,* in which you teach "How They Brought the Good News from Ghent to Aix," "Paul Revere's Ride," "Charge of the Light Brigade." To appeal to the girls in the class, add Browning's "The Last Ride Together" for a combination of romance and horsemanship. Similarly, on war, combine Browning's "Incident of the French Camp" with Byron's "Sennacherib," Macaulay's "Horatius at the Bridge," Southey's "Blenheim," the poems of Siegfried Sassoon, and recent others. These ideas are not revolutionary; they are the mildest extensions of groupings found in such anthologies as those edited by Auslander and Untermeyer.

Have you, in choosing two or more poems to teach simultaneously, multiplied your difficulties by two or more—or cut your difficulties at least in half? The latter, because the opportunities to compare, contrast, and mutually reflect the two enlarge your resources.

In specific illustration, how would this approach apply to Robinson's "Richard Cory" and "Miniver Cheevy"? Why should you want to conjoin the two? Both deal with character. In one case, a man surrounded by wealth and position kills himself—one kind of flight. In the other, a man projects his dreams and fantasies backward—another kind of flight. In both, you have an example of the greener grass on the other fellow's side of the fence. You have a comparison of two sorts of retreat. Consider that Richard Cory's neighbors ". . . worked, and waited for the light,/ And went without the meat, and cursed the bread," while Miniver Cheevy "grew lean while he assailed the seasons." Does this mean that Richard Cory's neighbors and Miniver had something in common? If Miniver Cheevy was born too late, did Richard Cory die too soon? Miniver cursed the commonplace, but Richard Cory "was always human" when he talked to the commonplace townspeople. How were they the same? How were they different? Then, for a clincher, you can tie both poems to Poe's "Eldorado" to find out what Miniver's Eldorado was and what Richard Cory's was, why our sympathies go out to Richard Cory and are withheld from Miniver.

Do this and you will be teaching poetry. Press your students for their interpretations of *child of scorn* and the *mediaeval grace of iron clothing* in "Miniver Cheevy" and *imperially slim, glittered when he walked,* and *cursed the bread* in "Richard Cory." Be prepared for a combination of astutely insightful answers and the silliest ones—sometimes from the same adolescent. One student pronounced it Chevvy. Another said that a child of scorn was the child of Mr. and Mrs. Scorn, and when asked to interpret "He mourned Romance, now on the town," said: "Things aren't what they used to be. Everybody's going steady now." Some of these errors are perfectly acceptable. It is more important to take a silly answer seriously than to reprove or correct; more basic issues are involved. Thus the student who mispronounced it Chevvy was in a hurry. He was corrected and rushed on with his contribution. The child who thought Miniver was the offspring of Mr. and Mrs. Scorn was corrected by another student who pointed out the difference in surnames. This cleared the way for another student to say that Miniver was the child of people who scorned him, or else Miniver was scorned by those around him, which drove him in consequence to turn to the past—not an untenable interpretation. We will discuss the way to accept interpretations in the next section, where we consider the teaching of obscure poetry. Meanwhile, you will find that the important thing is to get students into the habit of reading closely, to encourage them to form the habit of staying with the poem in order to extract the juice from it, not to prove how much wiser you are than they.

Have you driven over Brooklyn Bridge, or the George Washington Bridge at dusk? Have you ever seen your native city, or town, or your home, from a distance? Can you describe what it looks like? What makes it different from other cities, or towns, or homes? New York, London, Chicago are different. According to Whitman, New York is one kind of city. What does "Crossing Brooklyn Ferry" say? Chicago is still another kind of city, says Sandburg, so you have "Chicago" to compare with New York. What do these have in common with the London of Wordsworth's "Westminster Bridge"? And how are they different? And where does *The Deserted Village,* Goldsmith's Sweet Auburn, that loveliest village of the plain that never quite made the grade, come into the picture of major municipalities?

Similarly, you can compare Southey's "Battle of Blenheim" and Browning's "Incident of the French Camp." Here you have the common theme of the glory of war and the stupidity of it. If Southey is right, how can we in peacetime encourage the bravery and loyalty—desirable virtues surely —that wartime nourishes? If Browning is right, is man doomed ultimately to exterminate himself because leaders will sacrifice everything and everybody to remain in power? Suppose the boy had lived, after delivering the message to Napoleon. How would he resemble old Kaspar? Why do dictators do well when people don't question? How does the absence of questioning injure democracy? What kind of questions would *you* put to old Kaspar? To the boy who fell dead? To Napoleon?

This kind of comparison between poems can lead you to the albatross in *Rime of the Ancient Mariner* and Poe's Raven because a symbolized ornithology is common to both and Poe's bird of death can be compared to Coleridge's bird of spirituality. Or you might want to compare Coleridge's poem with itself: How likely is it that a person on his way to a festive occasion would allow himself to be detained by a seedy old character? It *is* unlikely. But is the Wedding Guest perhaps stopped by something in his mind's eye, on the very portal of the wedding festivities, and does he see himself as an old man when life-in-death will have become death-in-life? In other words, is this an interior dialogue between the Wedding Guest and his interior self, the Ancient Mariner, a situation in which a man in the midst of joy and gaiety suddenly feels the future chill of the yet to come and his self to be? What does the class think? Is the poem about two men, or about one man talking to himself? Try these questions:

Is it realistic that the Wedding Guest would stop?

If not, what is it that stops the Wedding Guest in his tracks on his way to a joyous occasion?

Is it an actual Ancient Mariner he sees, or himself years from now?

Is this, therefore, a dialogue between two people, or is it an interior dialogue, with Wedding Guest and Ancient Mariner *one* person? Is it a soliloquy of a young man who sees himself years hence as an old one?

Rightness and wrongness of answers are not the important matters here. More important is the habit of interpretation, of the attempt at still deeper reasoning that such discussion achieves. You should therefore seize gratefully upon the obscurities in the poetry you teach, not avoiding them, because there lie your richest teaching possibilities. As Herbert Read says in his especially valuable essay "Obscurity in Poetry": "Obscurity in poetry cannot be regarded as merely a negative quality, a failure to attain a state of perfect clarity. It is a positive value, but more, it is a whole series of such values. . . ." [2]

Thus, in "Ozymandias," you should dwell on "the hand that mocked them and the heart that fed." Of whose hand and heart does Shelley speak—the sculptor's or Ozymandias'? Or ask about a hand mocking—how could a hand mock? On what did the heart feed? Or did the heart mock and the hand feed? Do heart and hand feed in the same way?

Did Richard Cory *glitter when he walked* because he wore a lot of jewelry, or didn't he have to wear any jewelry at all to glitter? Was the glitter internal or external? Kind or harsh?

Miniver Cheevy *assailed the seasons*. Because he didn't like the weather? Or hated the passing of time? Because he was getting older? Because the seasons stood between him and something?

In "The Raven" why does the bird of death alight on the symbol of wisdom?

In "Mending Wall" where are the ultimate walls? Between the fields of Frost and his neighbor? Or in the heart and mind of Frost's neighbor, effectively walling off parts of himself from other parts of himself? Does the wall between the fields symbolize a wall within one of the two men? If so, which one?

Many years ago, a young English teacher gestured to illustrate the walls within Frost's neighbor, within the neighbor's heart and mind, by drawing first an imaginary vertical line and then an imaginary intersecting horizontal line over his heart and over his forehead to show how internally compartmentalized Frost's neighbor was. A student asked belligerently, "Ain't you talkin' against the Christians that way?"

The young teacher was puzzled but suddenly saw that he had inadvertently made a sign like a cross over heart and forehead. "Because it looked like a cross?" he asked, to make sure.

"That's right," the student replied.

"That's not what I meant," the young teacher answered. "I meant to show how the neighbor's heart and mind were separated by fences." The student nodded, mollified, but the young teacher suddenly assumed the mantle of belligerence the student had dropped. "Can the sign of the cross also divide people? Can it also become a fence? What must you do to make sure the cross doesn't do so?"

Recently a truly great American poet was subjected to a television interview by a college professor who had spent much time analyzing the poet's work. After listening sardonically to the professor's pronouncement and interpretation of what he must have had in mind when he wrote the poems, the poet, in full view of the television audience, made it clear that the pedant ought to have his head examined. The thoughts that were alleged to be in his mind were completely new to him. This was the first time he had ever heard of them, to the coast-to-coast discomfiture of the professor. The poet said he had no patience with people who tortured and distorted the simple, plain, unadorned meaning of his words. At the end of the show, the audience was left with the feeling that the professor got on by dissecting the ideas of his betters, having none of his own. The poet was asking for an end to interpreters, wanting nothing to get between the poem and the reader.

True, the program's professor was a pedant, but his presence indicated that poetry is not read the same way by all readers. It is read and interpreted differently by different people, so that the reader's personal history inevitably is added to the poem and its meanings no matter how the poet deludes himself that his work is simple, plain, and unadorned. If poets think so, they know less about their own work than others do—a frequent state of affairs. Proust points out that we know only the passions of others. Some interpretations make more sense than others, college professors can interpret wisely as well as stupidly, and poets can be as unaware of what they are saying as we are when we speak informally to friends. The important poem has implications that the poet knows not of. He cannot know everything of what brought the poem forth, as Shakespeare said in Sonnet 103:

> And more, much more, than in my verse can sit,
> Your own glass shows you when you look in it.

Therefore, interpret. You have as much right to interpret the poem as the poet to insist that the meaning is clear and straightforward. It may not be, and the last person in the world to take as authority is the poet himself. But do not be pedantic in your interpretation. Invite your students to formulate their own interpretations and match yours against theirs.

Obscurity in poetry—and its consequence, interpretation—therefore should not be avoided but sought out. The poet should not deny its presence nor the teacher apologize for seizing on it.

Here's an example from Emily Dickinson as it appears in the Auden and Pearson anthology:

> Farther in summer than the birds,
> Pathetic from the grass,
> A minor nation celebrates
> Its unobtrusive mass.
>
> No ordinance is seen,
> So gradual the grace,
> A pensive custom it becomes,
> Enlarging loneliness.
>
> Antiquest felt at noon
> When August, burning low,
> Calls forth this spectral canticle,
> Repose to typify.
>
> Remit as yet no grace,
> No furrow on the glow,
> Yet a druidic difference
> Enhances nature now.[3]

What do you make of it? What is the *minor nation* that is *farther in summer than the birds?* What is the *spectral canticle* that typifies repose? This extraordinarily evocative poem compels dozens of interpretations. The author's students admit its loveliness and its simultaneous meaninglessness. When they are well baffled by the poem, they are introduced to the stanzas omitted in this version but found in Johnson's edition of the complete poems, numbered as stanzas 3, 4, and 5:

> 'Tis audibler at dusk
> When day's attempt is done
> And nature nothing waits to do
> But terminate in tune.

No difference it knows
Of cadence or of pause
But simultaneous as sound
The service emphasize,

Nor know I when it cease,
At candle it is here,
When sunrise is, that is it not.
Than this, I know no more.[4]

Dickinson titled it "My Cricket" and Colonel Higginson thought of *Insect Sounds,* and at once the pattern falls into place. Students recall their associations and interpretations and begin to apologize for them. They need not. They are as correct as the poetess and her correspondent. One student saw the *minor nation* as the goblins in "Rip Van Winkle" and the *unobtrusive mass* as their ritualized game of ninepins. This interpretation is as tenable as Emily Dickinson's. Nevertheless, interpretation should not be wildly free-wheeling but should be validated against the poem. Thereby interpretations undergo refinement and are not discarded out of hand as absurdities.

The Narrative Poem

You can find in writers as diverse as J. N. Hook and Gilbert Highet the statement that the good teacher has a bit of the actor in him—if not the ham. Better, let's call you a bard. You are, among other things, a storyteller who can break their hearts, and because you have a story to tell you can't help but win their attention. What are the stories?

A woman died to save her lover. A wonderful story, called "The Highwayman," but what's the setting? And who ever heard of a wind that was a *torrent of darkness*? What does the moon look like when it's a *ghostly galleon tossed upon cloudy seas*? What does a road look like when it's a *ribbon of moonlight*? Dwell on these things because this is poetry as well as narrative, and then get on with the tale. Stop at "dark in the dark old inn-yard a stable wicket creaked," to ask how can something creak dark —is it a good sound or a threatening one?

With the appearance of the redcoat troop check on how the soldiers could have been informed, and what Tom the ostler had to do with it. Do not neglect the repetition in the fourth line of each stanza. It is intended to hold you back and stop the onward rush of narrative. Therefore hold back and ask what effect it has. Does it help taste the lines better?

However, because you, as bard, have a story to tell, do not dwell too long on these matters; get on with the tale. Read the final two stanzas in a hushed, barely audible voice, almost as if you are telling a ghost story around a campfire. Discuss with the class why these two stanzas are printed in italics. What effect does this convey?

Narrative poetry should have punch. "The Haystack in the Floods," for example, arouses terror and pity from the first stanza. Your class will have to reconstruct the picture from the evidence of the two lovers in flight from the medieval French court, betrayed, captured, he slain, she spurning dishonor to be returned to Paris and death, or madness. The poem is touching and tragic. Why not teach "The Highwayman" and "The Haystack in the Floods" as a unit? How interestingly they contrast! Notice how "The Highwayman" much more readily lends itself to choral reading than "The Haystack." Why should this be so? What do meter, rhyme scheme, and prosody have to do with greater adaptability to group reading in one case than in the other? In both poems the lovers perish, but in which one is death more touching and affecting? Is it because in "The Highwayman" the story is told to us, but in "The Haystack" we must furnish and reconstruct part of the story? Which way of telling is better?

Do not let your definition of narrative poetry become too constricted. Anything that not only tells a story, but allows your students to create a story, constitutes a narrative poem. Thereby much of *Spoon River* becomes narrative poetry, "My Last Duchess," "Sir Patrick Spens," "Young Lochinvar," and sonnet sequences like *Modern Love, Sonnets from the Portuguese,* as well as Frost's "Witch of Coös" and Tennyson's "Rizpah."

How does crime affect family structure? How does a crime committed by an individual reverberate throughout the family? Compare "Witch of Coös" and "Rizpah" by teaching them as a unit. By setting one against the other, you can compare the role of the mother in maintaining family structure despite the fracturing influence of a crime on family cohesiveness. Set both poems against the medieval "Edward, Edward," comparing the role of the mother in all three poems. Top it off with Sidney Lanier's "The Revenge of Hamish" for the picture of another mother's plight.

In "Sir Patrick Spens" you have a hidden tale to unfold, of a court plot to get rid of a knight by sending him to sea in the dead of winter. What is the plot in "Skipper Ireson's Ride" and "The True Story of Skipper Ireson," and how to match both against "Sir Patrick Spens"? This coupling of narrative poem with narrative poem enables you to bring out poetry, values, concepts as you never could by teaching one poem in isolation. Of course, you must be sure that the narrative poems you couple this way have at least one theme in common, and this requires imagination—poetic imagination—in you. There's much in Robert Frost that you can match with Browning. Both men tell stories in terms of character. A prim trimness characterizes Tennyson and Edwin Arlington Robinson. Amy Lowell's "Patterns" sits well with Christina Rossetti's "The Convent Threshold."

Similarly, you can match the narrative poem with certain short stories. Similar themes are found in "Prisoner of Chillon," Chekhov's "The Bet," and Poe's "The Pit and the Pendulum." Katherine Mansfield's "Garden Party" goes magnificently with William Blake's "On Another's Sorrow," as does "The Monkey's Paw" with Frost's "Home Burial." In William Faulkner's "Bear," Sam Fathers says: "A bear or a deer, too, has got to be scared of a coward the same as a brave man has got to be." And in Robert Frost's "A Hundred Collars," Lafe says:

> I'll knock so fashion and peep round the door
> When I come back so you'll know who it is.
> There's nothing I'm afraid of like scared people.
> I don't want you should shoot me in the head.[5]

In Faulkner's story, the father quotes from Keats' "Ode on a Grecian Urn," not at all a narrative poem, but a poem most relevant to the Faulkner story, and Robert Frost's "Bear," also low in narrative weight, has a relevance to the Faulkner story of the same name. Is this a unit? It is, very legitimately.

Why should the story be cast in poetic form? Why didn't the poet tell his story in prose, straightforwardly, the way regular people talk? You will answer that "it sounds better that way. It's more effective." But don't ask them if they agree, because they may not and very bluntly too. Yet it does sound better but not for reasons that are easily determined, though you can illustrate something of what you mean by recordings that your teen-agers are familiar with, in which ballads both old and new are sung by Belafonte, the Weavers, Oscar Brand, and other popular singers and folk-singers. Try singing prose, and see how far you get!

Because the rhythm and rhyme of most narrative poetry are clear-cut, you can relate the narrative poem to the study of rhyme schemes and scansion. Prosody answers the student who wants to know why the poet can't say his say the way regular people do. Why should the poet impoverish the story? He wants to enrich it by concentrating it in a planned frame; the frame plans for the same sound at the end of each line and, within each line, for the same rhythmic bounce. To achieve this is extraordinarily difficult, as your students will see when you assign the first line of a limerick and defy them to write one. You remember that the rhyme scheme of the limerick is AABBA. Give them some samples and turn them loose. Can they tell a story in five lines, as the limerick so often does, while still keeping the rhyme and rhythm pattern? Give them examples from Lear or other sources, and then put on the board:

> There was a young man from Ghent . .
>
> There was an old man from Japan . . .
>
> A student who came from Quebec . . .

Although this is best done with a bright class, students can do a surprisingly funny and competent job. Results are astonishingly expert. Furthermore, by the use of combining forms and suffixes in line endings, for example, -*graph* in *autograph* and *telegraph,* you can integrate rhyme schemes with word study (see p. 147).

But a limerick is almost primitive compared to the more subtle interplay of rhyme and rhythm in the Spenserian stanza and the sonnet. Illustrate iambic, trochaic, anapest, and dactyl from poetry, and so too dimeter, trimeter, tetrameter, pentameter, hexameter. But better yet show these stresses convey feeling even in prose:

He's square. He's a square. (In which case is he above-board? In which case an ordinary dullard?)

I won't I won't! (Do iambic and trochaic here help distinguish, by accent alone, and so spare us additional words?)

Why not? Why not? (Which is gentler and more persuasive? Which more aggressive?)

Listen to this. Listen to this. (Which is the more urgent? Where is the listener more important? Where the message?)

The Lyric Poem

The lyric poem is a feeling-sharpener. It is like a magnifying glass, or microscope, which enlarges a particular aspect of thought or emotion. Do not confuse the lyric poem with a song. It isn't, though it can become one, but only to intensify the feeling, or enlarge it, or magnify it through music. Generally, you only confuse the issue by relating the lyric poem to song. Not sound, but idea, symbol, and emotion are the important notions to keep in mind when teaching the lyric poem. Until your students identify this central core, you have nothing to talk about. This identification is your first order of business. Good poems sharpen feeling. All poetry has lyricism, but a lyric poem attempts little beyond lyricism, on the unspoken assumption that that is quite enough for one poem to handle. What is being sharpened, enlarged, or magnified? The answer is primary in teaching lyrical poetry.

What is to be enlarged in Wordsworth's "Daffodils"? The poem is about the memories that enrich loneliness. Before beginning the poem ask your class: "What's it like to be surrounded by your friends when you want to be by yourself?" Get what mileage you can out of this question and then go on to its mate: "What's it like to be lonesome when you want to be with friends?" Again get discussion. Finally, ask: "Is it greater unhappiness to be surrounded by your friends when you want to be by yourself, or to be lonesome when you want to be with friends?" Do not allow these motivating questions to overmotivate because you want to get on with the poem. While the discussion has been going on, you have put on the board *lonely as a cloud, inward eye, bliss of solitude, pensive mood.* (If possible, have a daffodil or jonquil at your desk. There are students who don't know what a daffodil is!)

Read the poem while students follow from their copies. Then ask: "How can a cloud be lonely?" After they have made their attempts, probe for what is meant by *inward eye.* Do they have inward eyes? How does the inward eye function? How does the inward eye increase the pleasures of being alone (*bliss of solitude*)? Why is it as important to keep our inward eye open when we are alone, as our outward eyes open when we are with others? Wind up this consideration by having students read the poem.

We have taken the first step. We have sharpened, enlarged, and intensified feeling. We now take the next step—doing the same with a second poem that has some relevance. Let's, as an example, take Frost's "Tree at My Window":

> Tree at my window, window tree
> My sash is lowered when night comes on;
> But let there never be curtain drawn
> Between you and me.

Vague dream-head lifted out of the ground,
And thing next most diffuse to cloud,
Not all your light tongues talking aloud
Could be profound.

But tree, I have seen you taken and tossed,
And if you have seen me when I slept,
You have seen me when I was taken and swept
And all but lost.

That day she put our heads together,
Fate had her imagination about her,
Your head so much concerned with outer,
Mine with inner, weather.[6]

Frost too is talking about an inward eye, but here the eye sees an internalized world of conflict. Does it help the internalized conflict to see an
external parallel? Approach an answer by having your class discuss: "When
you are unhappy, or in trouble, would you want the weather to be stormy
or pleasant? Which kind of weather would you prefer when you are
happy?" As before, see what discussion emerges. Then ask: "When are
your thoughts clearer, when you are happy or when you are troubled?
Which makes for clearer thinking, happiness or sorrow? Which makes for
deeper thinking?" Then read the poem. You'll want to know from them
why Frost lowers his window, but not his window shade; then, why is the
shape of the tree like the shape of a cloud; then, why are both like the
shape of a dream; then, why should the shape—or shapelessness—of a
dream shake Frost to the point where he is all but lost; then, why "Fate
had her imagination about her" when she put Frost's head and the tree's
"vague dream-head" in such close proximity; finally, what is *inner weather*.

Now let's couple "Daffodils" and "Tree at My Window." Both poems
deal with inner experience and its reality. To Wordsworth, memories are
as real as actualities; so, to Frost, are dreams. This is the concept that must
be sharpened, enlarged, magnified, and intensified. The thesis of both poems
is that the inner world can be as shattering as the outer world. Do your
students agree?

They may not. Students may deny, as one did, that introspection is
desirable. The direct quotation: "I don't think it's so good to keep thinking about yourself all the time. You can go punchy that way." The student
was absolutely right, but the student teacher was not prepared to accept
dissent from the opinions of such worthies as Frost and Wordsworth, a

position that proved only that the process of feeling-sharpening had gone on further in the student than in the student teacher. Many reputable psychiatrists would agree with the student rather than the student teacher, proving that the process of feeling-sharpening may well take a direction opposite to that recommended in the poem. Rejoice when it does so.

Luckily, not all student teachers are so rigid in their interpretation of poetry. Quite another type of student teacher was leading a discussion of "Richard Cory" when a student said, "Did he put a real bullet through his head? Couldn't the poem mean that he put an imaginary bullet through it?" The author was in the room at the time and can report that the glow on the student teacher's face was transfiguring. The words tumbled out of her: "Wonderful! What made you think of that? That's a marvelous idea!" This student teacher had a feeling for poetry and for people. She had motivated the lesson by asking the class, "Has anybody here committed suicide recently?" Students looked at one another, helpless grins on their faces, but finally light broke through and hands went up as the class realized that in one way or another, as Wilde said, every one of us kills a little bit of ourselves each day. We're always committing partial suicide.

Poetry must be read slowly and watchfully; poetry is not suitable for reading-rate speed tests where you have the volume in one hand and a stop watch in the other.

Just as narrative poetry leads more naturally into prosody, rhyme scheme, and accentual pattern, so lyric poetry leads more naturally into the figures of speech. The football team that *goes to town* or *carries the mail,* the *screwball,* the girl who is *way out in left field* are figures of daily speech that bring us up to the minute and make us snappy, hep, and socially acceptable, so that *chickened out, he's a square, he got hooked, out of this world, in orbit, fanned on three straight pitches, farmed out to the bush leagues, up the creek without a paddle, I don't get it, you don't send me, beefed up, he's the end from Endsville,* reflect the teen-ager's social postures and social acceptance. Teen-age language is as involved in figures of speech as Christina Rossetti's silence that *spoke like thunder* or Dickinson's soul which can *close the valves of her attention like stone.*

Ask your class if it perceives any relationship among tough talk, tough-minded talk, and the way figures of speech contribute to both. Because poetry is richer in figures of speech, poetry is tougher-minded than daily talk—when it is good poetry. The fierceness in Whitman's "Respondez! Respondez!" depends on the image:

> Let a floating cloud in the sky—let a wave of the sea—let growing mint, spinach, onions, tomatoes—let these be exhibited as shows, at a great price for admission!

But it also depends on how deep we allow the image to cut. We generally are afraid to. The personification in Donne's "Death Be Not Proud" can be conveniently labeled, as can simile, metaphor, metonymy, and the other figures. But more important than the labeling is the way figures can hurt, please, frighten, or delight us, if we allow them to do their work and don't turn away because we fear them. Thus, certain poems of Emily Dickinson, a gentle spinster who can terrify worse than Dracula or Frankenstein's monster, bring us as terribly close to death as any thoughts of our own. Hardy's poems are a reminder to your students that their dreams and ambitions, and yours too, are an even bet to come to dust.

CASE STUDY 12   The student teacher was a tall, attractive, soulful looking brunette, with a resemblance to Audrey Hepburn. Let's call her Miss Hepburn. She presented herself to her college instructor, Professor Methods, for help in preparing a unit on Carl Sandburg that Mrs. Regular, the co-operating teacher, had asked her to handle.

Miss Hepburn was nervous. The class she was to meet was unimaginative, hard to move, disorderly when Mrs. Regular was out of the room and indifferent when she was around. Miss Hepburn had selected "Chicago," "Fog," "Grass," "Lost," "Cool Tombs," and several others from the somewhat dated Monroe and Henderson anthology *The New Poetry*.

"These go off in several directions," Professor Methods said. "Why do you want to teach them? And don't tell me it's because Mrs. Regular assigned them."

"To show something about rough and tough people," Miss Hepburn replied.

"What's the something you want to show?" Professor Methods pursued, seeking the specific.

Miss Hepburn thought and then said, "That they're in trouble if they're not sensitive."

"Sensitive to what?" Professor Methods demanded.

"To as much as sensitive people are. Sandburg talks about death, cities, and music as if he had as much right to the subjects as Edna St. Vincent Millay."

"But he doesn't sound like Millay. What's particularly Sandburgish about his roughness and toughness when he writes about death, cities, and music?"

"He's tender at the same time."

"Then what's the relationship between his tenderness and his roughness and toughness?"

"He's protective."

"Pull it together for me."

"Roughness and toughness don't matter if you're tender, and you're protecting something with your roughness and toughness."

"Make it simpler."

"Toughness has a responsibility to protect the tender."

"All right. How would you show that with 'Chicago'?"

Miss Hepburn went quickly through the poem and pointed at "Bragging and laughing that under his wrist is the pulse, and under his ribs the heart of the people."

"Good. Now what about 'Grass'?"

She shook her head disappointedly. "The whole poem's about it, but I don't see anything specific and you're always insisting on specificity."

"I'm not *that* difficult!"

"You should hear your students!"

Professor Methods gave up. "Look at the last word, and tell me what occurs to you."

" 'Work'?" Miss Hepburn frowned in thought. "The grass can work like a laborer or like a nurse."

"Good! Is the grass repairing the old or building the new? Is it working like a laborer or like a nurse?"

On the day appointed, Professor Methods sidled surreptitiously into the rear of the classroom, trying to be the invisible man and knowing that within a few minutes the class would forget his presence even if Miss Hepburn couldn't. (See p. 340 on behavior under supervisory fire.)

It wasn't the first time Professor Methods had visited. He remembered some of the students. One in particular was interesting, a tall young man in tight levis, with a high, gleaming pompadour and long sideburns. A girl some seats away was caught up here and there by her clothes to accentuate bust and buttocks. That was the kind of class it was—youngsters anxious to get on with the business of being older than they were. Furthermore, there were several retarded readers in the class.

Miss Hepburn had three sets of mimeographed poems:

Group A: (1) "Fog" (2) "Lost" (3) "The Harbor"

Group B: (4) "Chicago" (5) "Prayers of Steel"

Group C: (6) "Four Preludes on Playthings of the Wind" (7) "Grass" (8) "Cool Tombs"

She distributed them and said, "In front of you is a puzzle. I'm going to divide the class into three groups and see which group furnishes the best answer to the puzzle. Read your group of poems silently. When you are finished, write in your notebook a brief description of the kind of man the poet is."

Naturally, since the cards had been stacked, the students reading from Group A did not agree with Group B or Group C. A few in Group A thought the poems were written by a woman. All in Group B thought the poems were written by a man. Group C thought the writer was terribly pessimistic, which amazed the readers of Group B.

Group A seemed to feel that Sandburg was a lover of nature. Group B felt he was a lover of cities. Group C felt that he was very sad because he wrote about death and destruction. Miss Hepburn said, "Let's find out what kind of man he is from the poems, even though they're contradictory. Just the people in Group B—where does he say in "Chicago" that he's *proud* of his city? Just the people in Group C—where does he say in "Four Preludes" that he is *scornful* of people who live in cities? Just the people in Group C—look at the last word in "Grass" and tell us how he wants the grass to work. Does he want the grass to work as a nurse works or as a butcher works?"

From Group B, after some pulling, came the line: ". . . so I turn once more to those who sneer at this my city, and I give them back the sneer. . . ." [7] From Group C:

> . . . . even the writing of the rat footprints
> tells us nothing, nothing at all
> about the greatest city, the greatest nation,
> where the strong men listened
> and the women warbled: Nothing like us ever was.[8]

At this point came the surprise, and the paradox. In all three groups students complained that there were considerable areas they didn't understand, though they had given the right answers. Wha. were Austerlitz, Ypres, and Verdun? How is Chicago the hog butcher for the world and the stacker of wheat? Where are the doors of cedar and the panels that are strips of gold? And numerous other content questions indicating that though students can hunt down specific answers to specific questions, they do so through a pathless wilderness of strange words and meanings.

The boy with the sideburns and levis asked, "Could we have the other poems too?"

"Of course. I've got enough to go around," Miss Hepburn said, and distributed to all three groups the two sets that had been withheld from them. Nobody had to tell Miss Hepburn that she had them moving well. *They* had pointed out to her that they wanted additional information, and that they were interested in seeing the poems that the other groups had been given.

After distribution, Miss Hepburn read "Chicago" and then asked: "How can the poet be proud of a city that's wicked, crooked, and brutal?"

The girl with the shape raised her hand. "That's only at the beginning, but at the end he says it's got a heart too."

"Where?" the student teacher inquired.

"When he talks about the pulse being under the wrist and the heart is under the ribs. Isn't that what he means?"

"Yes. Chicago has slaughter-houses, and factories, and grain warehouses." Not only Professor Methods had an eye for the poem's key phrases. "But most important is its heart and its energy. Does he say the same thing in the other poems?" Armed as they now were, they were directed to "Four Preludes" to compare the life and death of cities.

Time did not permit much more, but the class, so indifferent and aloof at other times, was completely involved. Mrs. Regular later told Miss Hepburn that the class had gone far beyond anything it had accomplished before.

The next day Miss Hepburn met with Professor Methods to analyze results. Miss Hepburn was pleased. "I forced them to defend a point of view against the others. They were fighting each other. Also my playing hard to get made them curious about what I was holding back."

"But isn't it wrong for a teacher not to put all her cards on the table? Isn't it trickery?"

"Maybe, but they were more interested. And it wasn't trickery either.

I presented them with the contradiction in Sandburg that wasn't a contradiction after all. I wasn't cheating."

"I agree. It was generalship, not cheating, and tactics, not trickery."

Simplicity versus Clarity

Simple poetry does not necessarily have clarity. Equations in nuclear physics have simplicity but are not clear. Simplicity is not synonymous with clarity or understandability. In fact, advanced science compresses its statements to a simplicity that is the antithesis of understandability. The economy of statement in a scientific formula leads to complexity simply stated, which is not the same as understandability.

In teaching poetry for outcomes of clarity and understandability you may lose the scientist's simplicity of utterance, because the human beings that poetry deals with cannot be reduced to simplicity as a mathematical or scientific statement can. Be satisfied if you gain understanding and clarity; do not aim for the stereotyped and falsely simple. Poetry cannot be reduced to an equation, because such reduction ends in the platitude and the cliché—in other words, the stupid.

Let's take Coleridge's *Kubla Khan* to see how we can impart clarity, but not simplicity, to it.

We must first ask ourselves why our students should learn *Kubla Khan*. Is it beautiful? Certainly. Esthetic? Of course. But so are other poems and we want to find out why we should teach, and our students study, this particular poem. Suppose we begin by saying that Coleridge here attempts to organize a fantasy. Is this of importance to your class? Very much. Consciousness is devoted to this job. To get order, logic, and sequence out of our fantasy life is of minute-to-minute importance. John Livingston Lowes showed in *The Road to Xanadu*[9] that Coleridge's fantasy has basis in actuality. Kubla Khan was an historical person powerful enough to decree the building of a stately pleasure-dome. So there are elements of objective experience in the poem, imbedded though they are in the matrix of dream and fantasy. In *Kubla Khan,* you want, as your specific aim, to show how real a dream is.

But what kind of *real* do you want to define? You don't know yet. That's what you will get from your students. Suppose you ask them; in asking properly you establish your motivation. Your motivation will go something like this:

Does our imagination work more when we are awake or when we are asleep? (Accept all answers.)
Who dreams more about clothes, the model or the housewife?
Who dreams more about money, the rich man or the poor man?
Who dreams more about food, the hungry man or the full man?
Who dreams more, the man who has or the man who has not?

Notice that you are setting up connections between fantasy, deprivation and need, and satiation. You have one last piece of motivational business to transact before going on to the poem. Ask:

Is it possible to think without using your imagination? Is it possible to sleep without dreaming?

Again, accept all answers and then read the following quotation from William Dement's article "The Effect of Dream Deprivation" in *Science:*

. . . Dreaming appears to be an intrinsic part of normal sleep and, as such, although the dreams are not usually recalled, occurs every night in every sleeping person. . . . Since there appear to be no exceptions to the nightly occurrence of a substantial amount of dreaming in every sleeping person, it might be asked whether or not this amount of dreaming is in some way a necessary and vital part of our existence. Would it be possible for human beings to continue functioning normally if their dream life were completely or partially suppressed? Should dreaming be considered necessary in a psychological sense or a physiological sense or both? . . . A certain amount of dreaming each night is a necessity. . . . If dream suppression were carried on long enough, a serious disruption of the personality would result.[10]

Ask for reactions to this quotation and do not comment, but go on to say, "We're going to read a dream. As in all dreams, the poet remembered some parts and, when he woke up, forgot others. We want to see what he remembered and what he forgot." Begin with "In Xanadu," and then stop. "That's a real place and Kubla Khan was a real man," you ought to say, and then read the first five lines.

Ask: "What color was the pleasure-dome?" Can they guess the color from the words? In the author's experience, most students will see the pleasure-dome as white. When he has asked why, the answer often has been in the sound quality of st*a*tely and s*a*cred. Conversely, instead of asking them to pinpoint the source of the image in the sound, the author has asked them to create an image from the sound, as in pleasu*r*e, whe*r*e, sac*r*ed, *r*ive*r*, *r*an, th*r*ough, cave*r*ns, and measu*r*eless; from these sounds, was the pleasure-dome noisy, quiet, or humming?

But Alph is in part a synthesized name, unlike Xanadu and Kubla Khan, which are historical names.[11] It's a made-up name for a made-up river. A dream-river, a sunless sea, and caverns measureless to man are the kind of scenery you meet in dreams. How would a sacred river look? Muddy, clear, slow, rapid, broad, or narrow? Does it have boats, swimmers, bridges? Do people do laundry in it? Throw garbage in it? Enlist the aid of the *Encyclopaedia Britannica,* and have students look up Ganges, Nile, Tigris, Euphrates. What makes rivers sacred?

If you found yourself alone in caverns measureless to man, would you feel frightened or thrilled? If you were standing on the shore of a sunless sea, would you look around or get away as fast as you could? Here, you go in the direction opposite to Coleridge—not reducing fantasy to words, but encouraging fantasy to emerge from words.

Then Kubla Khan protected it with ramparts and lookout points. Were the walls and towers needed to keep out enemies or to make his friends comfortable? That's one of the things the poet may have forgotten when he woke up. Was the author standing within the garden, and on a level with it, or was he viewing it from above, from a height? He saw the brightness reflected from the sinuous rills. Where must he have been standing? But then he describes incense-bearing trees. Did he forget, when he awoke, the promenade he had taken that intervened between seeing and smelling? If so, what could have happened on the promenade that took him from one place, where he could see *gardens bright with sinuous rills* to where he could smell *many an incense-bearing tree*? So also the sharp transition to the *forests ancient as the hills* makes us wonder if he could see the forests from where he stood in the garden, or was another promenade necessary? Were there people he met on the way? What were they doing? How did he greet them? Did he have companionship?

You may object that you will be reading things into the poem. You are doing nothing of the sort. You are giving each of your students a try at reconstructing the dream that Coleridge claimed to have had. More important, you are giving them a chance to organize their own fantasies on the basis of the material that Coleridge has so kindly furnished.

Blackout and quick dissolve as we are suddenly transferred from the *sunny spots of greenery* to *that deep romantic chasm which slanted/ Down the green hill athwart a cedarn cover,* and passage from sun to shade, almost as if the *forests ancient as the hills* quickly reminded the dreamer of *a savage place!* that lurks underneath our most sedulously cultivated and formal gardens; instead of sun we are now beneath a waning moon, *haunted/ By woman wailing for her demon-lover.*

Ask: Why the rapid transition from sun to shade, from pleasantness to terror? Does this happen in dreams? Is it natural for our fantasies to take this quick, inexplicable turn? Are love and hate, fear and faith, courage and cowardice, similarly united in us, as the savage place which the dreamer calls both holy and haunted? How can that be? Which is it?

To repeat, accept all answers. Do not police a student's fantasy. One girl was reminded by *woman wailing for her demon-lover* of the behavior of certain of her sex with respect to juke-box idols, and maybe she was as right as if she had mentioned Vathek or some other figure out of a Gothic novel.

Fast thick pants has been confused with trousers, and no harm, but the picture of a geyser-volcano is dramatic. In one line violent, the sacred river in the next is serene; another sudden switch and it sinks in *tumult to a lifeless ocean.* Upheaval and peace; peace and then the somberness of *a lifeless ocean.*

Opposites are conjoined throughout. Kubla hears *ancestral voices prophesying war.* The sacred river's tumult is not loud enough to prevent him from hearing it. Will Kubla go forth to war, despite the *dome of pleasure,* or will he stop his ears with *the mingled measure* and take his ease? Is it less or more manly to remain in Xanadu? Does Xanadu represent inaction or contemplation? Accept all answers!

If a student interprets Alph as the river of existence with its violent eruption from *caverns measureless to man* symbolic of birth, the *meanderings with a mazy motion* symbolic of living, and its sinking in *tumult to a lifeless ocean* as symbolic of death, do not reject this interpretation as far-flung. A psychoanalyst wouldn't do better. *A sunny pleasure-dome with caves of ice* is no longer *a miracle of rare device;* it is known to anybody with a shack in the country and an accompanying deep freeze. To Coleridge they were opposite; to us they are complementary. How many of the other opposites in the poem are similarly complementary?

The *damsel with a dulcimer* offers both vision and sound. Which is clearer in the remembrance of the dreamer? The vision persists, but the sound is lost. Which is harder to recall, when we awaken from dreams, what was seen or what was said? Safer, says Coleridge, not to recall too much of what we dream. We will be called madmen by those around us, because we will be unfitted for our waking hours, even though we will have power to build, within ourselves, our own pleasure-domes. *Ancestral voices prophesying war* are all around us, summoning us to competition with others, to breadwinning, to the combat of the market place, to duty, to social responsibility. Opposed to these voices—or perhaps complementary to them—is the *music loud and long* which builds *that dome in air*.

Ask: Does music have structure, like a building? Does music too offer us boards, nails, girders? What kind of edifice does poetry build? What kind of edifice has *Kubla Khan* built, not in Xanadu, but in our minds?

Unlike the physicist or mathematician, you cannot get elegant, trim simplicity from *Kubla Khan* but you can get clarity and understandability. You can multiply your effects by conjoining *Kubla Khan* with Poe's "Haunted Palace." Space forbids a detailed analysis of Poe's allegory of the body, the soul, and death, but both poems have enough contrasts and similarities for you to match one with the other.

Other suggestions on the teaching of poetry will be found in Chapter 14, "Lesson Planning."

Research, Resources, and Techniques

1. Criticisms, anthologies, and evaluations of poetry are too numerous for listing, but two examples of how such books can help you in your teaching are:
   a. Randall Jarrell's *Poetry and the Age* (Alfred A. Knopf Vintage paperback, 1955), especially its outstanding discussion on Robert Frost;
   b. Max Eastman's *Enjoyment of Poetry* (Scribner, 1928) for values that should govern in the study, analysis, and writing of poetry. The Eastman book also has fine chapters on the naming process, a matter that we discussed in Chapter 2.

2. Howard Creed's *"The Rime of the Ancient Mariner:* A Rereading" (*E. J.,* April 1960, p. 215) deals with the background considerations, interpretation, and teaching of this poem.

3. A British analysis has been published by the Incorporated Association of Assistant Masters in Secondary Schools, *The Teaching of English* (Cambridge University Press, 1957). See p. 123 of this work for a rather original approach to "Sir Patrick Spens," in which miming of ballads, or charades, is described. The section is informative about the approach used in Britain.

4. Georgia Christopher's "Literature and the Beginning Teacher" (*E. J.,* Sept. 1959, p. 321) spells out the hazards that will face you when you attempt poetry. It's all true, but there's a happy ending. The author finally

declares that the enjoyment of poetry depends in great measure on the teacher's approach—but, unfortunately, does not tell us too explicitly what the better approaches ought to be. Otherwise, a good statement of the perils that the beginning teacher faces in teaching poetry.

5. Roy C. McCall's "Taking Literature Out of Cold Storage" (*E. J.*, Jan. 1955, p. 30) reveals how important in the teaching of poetry is the ability to read aloud and to do so well. In addition, he claims that another difficulty is assigning poetry beyond the student's level. But would a fine reading bring "My Last Duchess" (suggested as difficult by Professor McCall) within comprehension range, or would it remain too difficult even with a fine reading? Hence, can you divorce difficulty level from the teacher's reading, or must the former be evaluated in terms of the latter?

6. How remote is poetry from practicality? Read Peter Drucker's article in *Fortune* (May 1952) on the importance of poetry and short-story writing in training for industry.

7. Michael Yatron's "Carl Sandburg: the Poet as Nonconformist" (*E. J.*, Dec. 1959, p. 524) should be read in conjunction with Case Study 12, on the Sandburg unit.

8. If you are doubtful that the more hard-boiled students can become interested in poetry, read Charles G. Spiegler's "Report on a 'Tough' School," in *The New York Times Magazine* (Nov. 24, 1957, p. 25). This is a generous, understanding description by a teacher who knows first-hand of the needs and problems of the not-so-difficult difficult school, a vocational school in this case, and of the rewards it offers to the teacher who is willing to put forth effort. You can teach poetry in such schools.

9. Frederick S. Kiley's "Served on a Black Platter" (*E. J.*, Nov. 1956, p. 483) deals with popular songs and their relation to the teaching of poetry. (See earlier reference in Chapter 2, p. 43.)

CHAPTER 8

Essay, Biography, and Drama

Teaching the Dull but Respectable

Some forms of literature offer climaxes, excitement, and quickening of pulse beats. Poems heighten feeling, and so do novels. But the essay's merit is uneventfulness. Sometimes it tilts over into narrative, as in the first part of "Dissertation on Roast Pig," or the tragedy of "Mary White," the melancholy of "Dream Children," or the last days of Robert Scott[1] in Antarctica. In biography events occur without climax. In the essay, ideas occur, but occurrences do not. These characteristics of essay and biography make harder going for you.

Let's begin with the teaching of the essay, whether personal, literary, biographical, or other. The essay presents a point of view, an issue, an attitude, or an evaluation. Note these terms. Note also what their debatable aspects are. For example, in "Dissertation on Roast Pig," one of the central ideas is serendipity: we sometimes blunder into a delicious repast where we expected ashes. Another: invention and progress successively peel away the unnecessary, so that we do not, after a while, burn huts to roast our meat. But are these ideas true? Voltaire's Candide and Zadig reaped ashes instead of roast pig. In building automobiles with fins and chrome, are we progressively stripping down to essentials, or are we building unnecessary huts around our basic transportation needs? Does stream-lining speed us up or encumber us? Is it truer that roast pig emerges from ashes or that roast pig turns to ashes?

Therefore teach the essay by the issues that the essay raises, without attempting to attack the essayist's point of view or the opposing one you have counterposed. Essays are deceptive. Even the personal, ingratiating one that doesn't seem to have a debatable issue anywhere in sight will have one lurking there, never fear. If you can't locate it, don't teach the bore. Identifying the issues is somewhat more difficult in the gentle essay —and essays tend to be gentle in tone—and easier in the modern, tough-minded essays.

Little can be said about the structure of the essay because of the variety that characterizes—or fails to characterize—this literary Proteus. More important is the attitude of your pupils toward literature that doesn't tell a story or heighten an emotion. No climactic discharge, no denouement, no closing couplet winds up the feeling. The essay is more like a chat, a one-man bull session, beginning somewhere and ending somewhere else, and often indecisively. All you can ask is that it be interesting and worth the time. Your problem comes when it is and when your students think it isn't.

For example, you have located the issues in the essay to be taught; you have counterposed possible antithetic points of view. These are ready to serve, but you must set a chatty, bull-sessionish atmosphere, reflecting the feeling-tone of the usual essay: gentle, unhurried, and discursive, with goal outcomes less important than the getting there. How can you achieve this? By employing a paradox, by starting a quasi-fight, because the chatty bull-session thrives best in the atmosphere of debate.

We have mentioned that it is half as difficult, or twice as easy, to teach two poems at a time as one, by pitting one poem against another. Do the same with the essay. The gormandizing and smacking of the lips—the appeal to sheer orality—in "Dissertation on Roast Pig" can be juxtaposed to Don Marquis's "Eat, Drink, and Be Merry for Tomorrow Ye Diet."

Juxtapose the opposed: Stephen Leacock's "Oxford as I See It" and Cardinal Newman's "The Idea of a University"; Max Beerbohm's "Going Out for a Walk" and Hazlitt's "On Going a Walk"; "Mary White," about having lived and died, and "Dream Children," about never having lived at all; Helen Keller's "Three Days to See" and Robert Louis Stevenson's "Aes Triplex," where the conflict deals with hoarding and treasuring each passing moment, or living lavishly. You will find students taking one side or the other.

There is an entire section in Leslie Fiedler's *Art of the Essay*[2] called "As Europeans See Us," in which the image of America and Americans is contrasted with the European image. Match this with the material you will find in Charles B. Shaw's paperback called *American Essays*.[3] Match H. L. Mencken's "Sahara of Bozart" with John Kendrick Bangs' "Southern Hospitality," for a contrast in regionalism. Inject conflict into the gentle art of essay reading. Achieve chattiness in your classroom discussions by providing issues and strife.

Emerson's "Self-Reliance" and Orwell's "Shooting an Elephant" disagree on how unaffected we ought to be by the opinions of others—or do the two agree? Dean Swift's *Bickerstaff Papers* and Benjamin Franklin's "The Titan Leeds Hoax" (which you will find in the Shaw volume) are on exactly the same theme—the exposure of the frauds of astrology, though Franklin's was written years after Swift's magnificent satire and really plagiarizes it. Your brighter students will enjoy both and see anticipations of Thurber and S. J. Perelman tied into this possible unit "Satire in the Essay."

One large headache: you will be teaching the essay from some anthology. Your class will not have convenient access to such useful collections as John Lincoln Stewart's *The Essay*, John Ashby Lester's *Essays of Yesterday and Today*, Andrew Thomas Smithberger's *Essays British and American*, and the Margaret Bryant collection.[4] These furnish an adequate reservoir of the opposing ideas you need, but you will not have enough copies for your class. How, then, can you needle the class into contention when you have but one well-intentioned book to work with? Here are some springboards for conflict that lead to the chatty bull-sessions you want, the groupings you will find in the typical essay anthology:

> Places and regions, like New York, Paris, Puerto Rico, San Francisco, the Grand Canyon, and the Tennessee Valley, are gravitational centers around which clouds of essays stream in orbit. Thus, around the American South, you group Bangs' "Southern Hospitality" and Mencken's "Sahara of Bozart." Similarly, group Rupert Brooks' "Niagara Falls" (in his *Letters from America*) with Paul Goodman's "Our Visit to Niagara" (in Pocket Books paperback *Discovery #6*).
>
> In sports, you can match Heywood Broun's "Dying for Dear Old ———," and the A. J. Liebling sports stories in *New Yorker*, with sports page editorials.

Your anthology will present a point of view on science. Contrast the anthology's essay in this area with recent magazine articles on the same topic in *Reader's Digest, Saturday Evening Post,* or *The New York Times* Sunday magazine section. What opposed values can be juxtaposed on radioactive fallout, on the scientist's responsibility to society, on pure research versus applied research?

Your anthology will have a piece or two on fashions, clothes, art, taste, or on the change in these since the author was a boy. Shaw's *American Essays* has Agnes Repplier's "Opinions," a gentle, diffident piece, and a lineal descendant of Steele and Addison. Compare it with Swift's "Meditation upon a Broomstick" or "Modest Proposal."

The Repplier essay can also be usefully compared with E. B. White's "How to Tell a Major Poet from a Minor Poet." In the first, classification is delicately avoided; in the second, it is satirized.

A grouping of people can include biographical essays as diverse as Mencken's "Valentino" and Gilbert Highet's "The Old Gentleman" and the way in which they can be compared with book reviews of recent biographies.

Hobbies can be broken down into subgroupings—Fishing, Conversation, Dogs, Coin Collecting. Thus for fishing you might select a grouping to include Stewart Edward White, John Muir, or John Burroughs. For dogs you might compare the gentle treatment of Eugene Fields' "Other People's Dogs" with the savage revenge of Francis Parkman in "The Ogillallah Village" (from *The Oregon Trail*).

Social and political issues dealt with in your anthology can be integrated with recent articles in *Harper's, Reporter,* or *Fortune.* You will almost certainly find something in your anthology on movies, newspapers, and the mass media. Though Leslie Fiedler's *Art of the Essay* has an excellent selection of essays in this area and will be helpful for contrasting materials if your school library or local library has a copy, the representative in your anthology can be more readily contrasted with current happenings in the newspapers and magazines.

Another topic almost inevitably encountered in your anthology will be Education. Perhaps you fear that the Whitehead paperbacks, the Chesterfield letters to his son, Montaigne, and even Dewey may be too difficult for your students. In isolation they might, but in comparison and contrast they won't. Show what the issues are; then ask your students which viewpoint is more palatable. In starting a fight, the difficulties disappear and the intellectual heavyweights become suddenly more understandable. Show how ideas compete, and you can even use essays reserved for the college level.

Your anthology will have something on Wit and Humor. Thus Shaw's *American Essays* has two essays on this, Charles S. Brooks' "On the Difference between Wit and Humor" and Frank Moore Colby's "The Pursuit of Humor," which you can tie in with *Mad,* Sid Caesar, Mark Twain, and *New Yorker* cartoons.

But this amassing and collecting of materials to supplement your one lonesome anthology of essays is only the beginning. Let's assume that you have done your homework. You know the essay you will teach. You have set up opposing points of view. You have juxtaposed the opposing points of view. You know where these other essays can be located. It now remains for your students to pursue these other essays, not so conveniently at hand as your anthology is.

Don't send them after titles. Send them after answers to questions raised by the essay you are studying in the anthology. The titles they are pursuing should represent other viewpoints, other sides of the argument. Do all you can to raise arguments, lest you become beguiled by the archness and coyness of certain essays. Essays tend to be mild, but you want contentiousness. Where essays are strong and vigorous, as the best ones are, all the more to your purpose. Louis Kronenberger's *Company Manners*[5] is a collection of one man's essays that you can use in a variety of groupings, as you can Orwell's collection.[6] Both have bite. Let their bite be felt, not reduced to genteel nibblings. The hotter the fight over issues in your class, the more your students will depart from the anthology's *table d'hôte* and learn an *à la carte* independence of judgment from paperback collections of what *one* man says, or how an article in *Saturday Evening Post,* or a profile in *New Yorker,* or a lead piece in *Saturday Review,* supplements or makes hash of the essay in your particular anthology. But you must know where to send them. You must know the resources of the essay beyond the handful in your anthology. You must know that a certain section out of Barzun's *Teacher in America,* or Riesman's *Individualism Reconsidered,* or a chapter of Koestler will fit in nicely with the sample in your anthology.

You have no alternative, else the essay may become the dullest bore you've ever had to teach, refined and respectable, but dull, dull, dull.

Now push further. You have stressed contention in the essay—but the essay has a special quality of reflectiveness too. Of the issues raised, what would earlier writers have said? How current, indeed, are those issues raised in *The Tatler* and *The Spectator* and by Sir Roger de Coverley! How interesting to compare Montaigne's "Of Cannibals" with Margaret Mead's paperbacks on New Guinea! Does not the *Saturday Review,* in its special supplement articles, repeat Sir Francis Bacon? Isaak Walton and Stewart

Edward White, though centuries apart, are saying much the same thing. You want students to pursue, through contention and agreement, the recurrence of important ideas through the years.

Finally, you want your students to express their own points of view, after they've read a half-dozen essays, past and present, pro and con, on the same thing. How do they feel? Let them express themselves and write their own opinions, and what do you know? They'll have written an essay too!

Afterward, discuss with them how study of the essay helps one carry on a conversation. Did their study give them hints on how to talk with others? What did it teach about carrying on conversation easily? Can students better analyze what they talk about, over and over again, tediously and *ad nauseam*, with friends? Can they list what they do not talk about? What in the essay can enrich their talk, the talk they are more bored with than they suspect?

Research, Resources, and Techniques

1. Essie Chamberlain's *Essays Old and New* (Harcourt, Brace, 1934) contains some essays not readily available, including Santayana's "On War" as well as Francis Bacon's "Of Riches," "Of Studies," "Of Friendship," and "Of Truth" and makes it possible for you to match the venerable with the up to the minute.

2. The anthology by Leo Hamalian and Edmond L. Volpe, *Essays of Our Time* (McGraw-Hill, 1960), has a more difficult selection, intended for the college level, but don't be frightened and don't restrict your choices to your brighter students. Match ideas and don't be too concerned about vocabulary level.

3. Jay E. Greene's *Essays for Modern Youth* (Globe Book Company, 1960) groups the selections around themes like "On the Playing Field," "Science in Today's World," "The Air Age," "Enjoying Music and Art," "Exploring Books and the Theatre," "Adventuring in Business and Work," "Putting Leisure Time to Use." Around twenty such themes and keynotes, Greene has formed his interesting, modern anthology.

Lives of Great Men? Don't Remind Us!

We forgive the biographer far too much because of his subject. After Weems wrote of Washington, and lied about him too, generations of children were forced to submit to Weems for Washington's sake. Your book-storage room contains biographies without merit or interest, purchased only because the author wrote about noteworthy people. Other biographies are as stirring as any Western or suspense story. Helen Keller's autobiography, Anne Frank's *Diary of a Young Girl,* Gunther's *Death Be Not Proud,* De Kruif's *Microbe Hunters* are fun to teach because they are naturally exciting. Unfortunately, you may be stuck with some weak, pallid imitations of De Kruif. You cannot transcend the spirit of the biographer, no matter how soaring the person written about. Teaching the life of Shelley from an uninspired biography will be uninspired too, despite Shelley and no matter how excellent your teaching. In no other area of literature are you so much a prisoner of the material to be taught. But if the material is good, like the samples above, the material will carry the teaching as much as material can reasonably be expected to. The pity is that so many excellent biographies are available and not purchased. Some peculiar hazard accompanies school purchases of biography. With so many interesting selections possible, the dull nose their way into purchase because choice is governed by the person written about rather than by the writer.

Unlike the essay, which should be read for itself alone, the biography offers opportunities for research, references, allusions, analysis, history, and independent study. You will not want to miss these opportunities. These exist in biographies of sports heroes, famous scientists, or an interesting family group, and they can be pursued in an unassuming paperback or a portentous hardcover tome. Biographies will deal with struggles against men or against the forces of nature. In the course of these struggles, traits of honor and integrity will be exercised, sometimes in the face of great adversity and temptation. Remember that the student makes the investment in research, not you. You must be the persuasive broker who brings student and biography together, to show the profit reaped from using biography as a springboard into research and independent study. What are the ways of persuasion?

Because these are real people who have actually existed, so have their problems had real and actual existence. Your students have problems, some of which they are willing to talk about and some not. Whether mentionable or not, problems remain problems until surmounted.

> Are your students' mentionable and unmentionable problems as significant as those in the biography?
> What resources and talents do these people have by which they surmount

problems? Do they have social and family connections? What personal ability do they exercise? Is this ability inborn or acquired through hard persistence? Is it worthwhile expending resources, talents, and abilities? Is it only worthwhile to expend resources, talents, and abilities if you have them, or will anybody, whatever his range of these, find it equally worthwhile to exercise them?

How does one make one's life interesting? How do you find interesting things to do? Are our lives dull because of the things that fail to happen to us or because we do not know how to make them happen? Do we become interesting persons because interesting things happen to us or because we do interesting things to things? What are the things around us? How can we make them more a part of us?

What mistakes can we make in trying to raise the interest possibilities in the things around us? How are wrongdoing and crime mistaken ways of gaining interest in things around us? How can we avoid wrongdoing and crime in the course of making things interesting?

Does the person in the biography work better with others or by himself? What kind of people did he enjoy being with? What kind of people offended him? Did he need people or ideas for inspiration? Did he do best when co-operating or when competing?

When in doubt, seize the bull by the dilemma. If major merits of the biography are research and independent study, how can you make these relevant? For example, in Macaulay's "Essay on Addison," a passage occurs:

> At the beginning of the year 1704, the state of parties bore a close analogy to the state of parties in 1826. In 1826, as in 1704, there was a Tory ministry divided into two hostile sections. The position of Mr. Canning and his friends in 1826 corresponded to that which Marlborough and Godolphin occupied in 1704. Nottingham and Jersey were, in 1704, what Lord Eldon and Lord Westmoreland were in 1826. The Whigs of 1704 were in a situation resembling that in which the Whigs of 1826 stood.

Any self-respecting edition of Macaulay's biographical essay would have identifying material and footnotes, naturally, but would these help or further confuse? The names are unknown to you as well as to your students. Too bad, but you must push further, beyond the names, to the issues involved. What are they? How do they resemble party splits in America today, when wings of the Republican Party have more in common with wings of the Democratic Party than with their own party? The names change. The Marlboroughs, Godolphins, Nottinghams, and Jerseys of one generation, and the Cannings, Eldons, and Westmorelands of another, in telling us of party loyalty and party splits, inform us of

Northern Democrats, Southern Democrats, Rock-Ribbed Republicanism, and Liberal Republicanism of our day, and even of communist "left-wing infantilism" and "right-wing opportunism." The unknown names are therefore worth the research and independent study you must insist on, not for the sake of the names and dates of the past, but for the way they illuminate some aspects of the present and the way party politics go, whether Thucydides describes them or Harold Ickes. Indeed, your students will inevitably find the names unfamiliar, whether mentioned by Macaulay, Thucydides, or Ickes. You must teach so that the *ideas* gain greater familiarity and so that students do not think the names and dates a chore but an extension of experience.

As Macaulay compares past and present, as Plutarch compares his subjects (Aristides with Cato, Demosthenes with Cicero, and so on), as Ickes compares his own judgment with the judgment of others, so the student must set up comparisons and contrasts wherever he can. He should compare the author and the protagonist, the protagonist with other characters in the biography, the setting with alternative settings, the values with other values, the people in the biography with the people he knows, the opportunities in the biography with the opportunities the student has heard about, the people the student knows with whom the character would get along best and worst.

The student must learn something factual, because biography is factual. If the student backs away from Shakespeare, Whitman, or Dickinson, you can do nothing about it because there is no disputing tastes and because some respectable people have also backed away from them. You can't accuse a student of criminality if he begs off from *Hamlet* or "Respondez! Respondez!" or "The Bustle in a House"; they may be magnificent but not for him.

Biographical study is another matter. You are not asking students to feel or empathize, but to *know*. If they feel and empathize, all the better, but biography is real and involves knowledge. Knowledge, in turn, requires involvement. How do you gain this involvement?

First assort your recommendations by groups. Observe these classifications:

> 1. *Sports and Athletes:* in addition to Tom Meany's *The Magnificent Yankees,* Jim Brosnan's *The Long Season,* and biographies of Babe Ruth, Lou Gehrig, Christy Mathewson, Walter Johnson, you have sports biographies in *Saturday Evening Post, Sports Illustrated,* and other magazines.

Bob Considine and Bill Slocum have written the prize-fight biography *Dempsey*. Some of the "Profiles" in *New Yorker* deal with sport figures.

2. *Missionary Physicians:* here see *Tom Dooley's Story*. Norman Cousins' *Dr. Schweitzer of Lambarene*, Dr. Victor Heiser's *American Doctor's Odyssey*, Dr. Wilfred Grenfell's *Adrift on an Ice Pan*, and numerous others. Physicians have written stories of their lives in South America, the Tennessee mountains, India, Alaska, and many elsewheres, thereby forming a convenient grouping around which to classify your recommendations and assignments.

3. *Negro Leaders:* for many years Booker T. Washington's *Up from Slavery* was alone, but now you can add James Weldon Johnson's *Autobiography of an Ex-Colored Man*, Walter White's *A Man Called White*, Carl Rowan and Jackie Robinson's *Wait till Next Year*, Richard Wright's *Black Boy* and many others.

4. *Actors and Actresses:* to attempt more than the sketchiest hint of a list would be foolhardy. Billie Burke and Cameron Shipp's *With a Feather on My Nose, Talking through My Hats, A Star Danced*, Guthrie McClintic's *Me and Kit*, Cornelia Otis Skinner's *That's Me All Over*, Sheilah Graham and Gerold Frank's *Beloved Infidel*, Lawrence Langner's *The Play's the Thing*, and dozens after dozens of others offer interesting and illuminating possibilities.

5. *Politics and Government:* Gunther's *Roosevelt in Retrospect* and his biography of Albert Lasker; Eleanor Roosevelt's *This I Remember;* Catherine D. Bowen's *Yankee from Olympus;* Martha MacBride's *Young Hickory*; Irving Stone's *The President's Lady*; John Kennedy's *Profiles in Courage*; Jim Bishop's *The Day Lincoln Was Shot*—give an insight into political thinking that we can get from this area of biography. Compare the Ickes and Frances Perkins biographies of Franklin D. Roosevelt, for example, to see how the same story can be told in two different ways.

6. *Overcoming Disabilities:* though representation in this area is more limited than in the classifications above, you have Helen Keller's *Story of My Life*, Louise Baker's *Out on a Limb*, Hector Chevigny's *My Eyes Have a Cold Nose*, Ted Husing and Cy Rice's *My Eyes Are in My Heart*, and Marjorie Lawrence's *Interrupted Melody*.

7. *Religion:* again you have ample materials, as in Kathryn Hulme's *The Nun's Story*, Monica Baldwin's *I Leap over the Wall*, David Daiches' *Two Worlds*, and church-approved biographies.

8. *Adventure and Risk:* you'll have no trouble with such a listing as Sir John Hunt's *Conquest of Everest*, Maurice Herzog's *Annapurna*, Norgay Tenzing and James Ramsey Ullman's *Tiger of the Snows*, Lindberg's *Spirit of St. Louis*, Thor Heyerdahl's *Kon-Tiki*, and other biographies of discoverers and explorers.

9. *Family Life:* this area of biographical writing has seen Frank Gilbreth and Ernestine Gilbreth Carey's *Cheaper by the Dozen*, Clarence Day's

Life with Father, Charles W. Thayer's *Bears in the Caviar,* Dorothy Canfield's *The Bent Twig,* Pamela Moore's *Chocolates for Breakfast,* and others.

10. *Science and Medicine:* aside from the De Kruif *Microbe Hunters,* and its successor, Greer Williams' *Virus Hunters,* you have Bernard Jaffe's *Crucibles,* Mrs. Fermi's *Atoms in the Family,* Eve Curie's *Madame Curie,* Arthur Hertzer's *Horse and Buggy Doctor,* and Helen Clapesattle's *The Doctors Mayo.*

11. *Social Work:* classics here are Jane Addams' *Twenty Years at Hull House,* Jacob Riis' *The Making of an American,* and Lillian Wald's *The House on Henry Street.*

12. *Writers and Literature:* you can group here by novelists, poets, playwrights, journalists, or other subdivisions, and still have materials to spare because you have lives of Dickens, Marchette Chute's *Shakespeare of London,* Trevelyan's *Life of Macaulay,* Carlyle's *Essay on Burns,* and biographies of Hemingway, Faulkner, Robert Frost, James Joyce, in such profusion that you must set up walls against the flood of material.

13. *Teaching and Education:* your profession is represented by Mary Ellen Chase's *A Goodly Fellowship,* and by others like Elizabeth G. Vining's *Windows for the Crown Prince* and Bliss Perry's *And Gladly Teach.* Isn't it too bad that more teachers haven't written about the lives of great teachers? Still, you have the story of "Copey" of Harvard—but that may be above the heads of your students. Unfortunately, this is one of the skimpier classifications.

In addition you have *Who's Who, Living Authors,* and the *Encyclopaedia Britannica.* You have biographies from *Saturday Evening Post* and the biographies that have won Pulitzer prizes. You have—and classify these as you will—*Under a Lucky Star,* Sandburg's *Always the Young Strangers,* James Barrie's *Margaret Ogilvy,* Catherine Marshall's *A Man Called Peter.* You have thousands and thousands of lives to deal with, but you must group and assemble these.

Biographies are classifiable, and should be, to appeal to the parallel grouped interests in your students. Gilbert Highet in *The Art of Teaching* argues persuasively that students fall into types and this classification of biographies argues that some classifications will be more appealing to certain groups than others.[7] Students are interested in biographies dealing with juvenile delinquency (Rocky Graziano's *Somebody Up There Likes Me,* and Walter Bernstein's *New Yorker* article in the "Reporter at Large" section for September 21, 1957, pp. 129-59, called "The Cherubs Are Rumbling"), financial success (Bernard Baruch), and persuading others (John Gunther's biography of Lasker).

If biographies can be typed into groups, and if students can be typed into groups, your job is to match the biography with the student so that type calls out to type. This in turn requires that you know the materials available and the classifications into which your students are most likely to fall. Classify your students with the highest probability that John will prefer this kind of biography, Daniel that, Mary the other, and Joan still another. You've got to know your customers. You cannot get them interested in biography unless you do.

Suppose, however, that you have one biography to teach, rather than a set of groupings that you're assigning for outside reading. For example, De Kruif's *Microbe Hunters* is to be taught to this variety of types, some of whom are interested in science and others not. In the fashion of Plutarch, you can assign the class to the reading of the section on Spallanzani and on Leeuwenhoek, asking the class to contrast the characters of the two men and to judge which—the Leeuwenhoek type or the Spallanzani type —is more decisive in the growth of science. Next, were their characters reflected in the kind of discoveries they made? Is the kind of discovery an outcome of the nature of the man who makes it? In asking this question you are involving not only the students interested in science, but those interested in the play of character.

But there are still other students, less interested in science and in the nature of men than in themselves. Of them ask: was Spallanzani's life more interesting to live than Leeuwenhoek's? If one was more peaceful and the other more exciting, do they opt for peace or for excitement? Do the girls in your class agree with the boys in your class?

Another approach is to pique your students with a problem that is only solved by reading the text. Present this: you have a droplet of water crawling with organisms smaller than the head of a needle. How would you get one and just one of these microscopic organisms off by itself? De Kruif tells us how ingeniously Spallanzani did so. Before you send them off to the text, give them the problem to stew over.

Or, before you send them off to read the chapter on Leeuwenhoek, pique them with Zeno's paradox of the race between Achilles and the tortoise, to get them thinking of the smallest things there are.

> Achilles and the tortoise raced. The tortoise wagered that, though Achilles was twice as fleet, he would never catch the tortoise. Because Achilles was fleeter, the tortoise was given a four-foot handicap. The race began. Achilles ran the four feet to the starting line, but the tortoise, half as fleet, had by that time run two feet beyond. Achilles ran the two feet, but the tortoise had by that time run one foot. Achilles ran the one foot,

but the tortoise was now half a foot ahead. Achilles ran the half-foot, but the tortoise was a quarter-foot ahead. By the time Achilles ran a quarter-foot, the tortoise had run one-eighth of a foot. Thus, Achilles never catches the tortoise, according to Zeno's paradox. Yet we know, from observation, that he should. How will your students resolve the paradox? The answer is that Achilles will catch the tortoise four feet ahead of the starting line, but the paradox *never allows Achilles to run the full eight feet* (four feet to the starting line and four feet beyond).

Present the paradox but do not furnish the answer. Small as Leeuwenhoek's animals were, there are things still smaller. How small can you get? They may be able to recite the names of molecules, atoms, electrons, and entities smaller yet. What happens to the time dimension then? We split time into seconds, milliseconds, microseconds, millimicroseconds, and nannoseconds, which is the thousandth part of a millionth of a second. Is not this too short a time for anything to happen? For what can this infinitesimal offer time enough?

Therefore, establish classifications in the biography that involve the varieties of students in your classroom. You must set up contact points between the book's classifications and the classroom's, between the values you stress and the questions you ask.

Thus, on the basis of sex classifications, you can ask: "Do boys understand other people better than girls do? Do men or women have more intuition into character? Who's smarter about other people, a boy or a girl?" See Donald Cox' "Do Women Make the Best Biographers?" for one point of view.[8] Your class will enter interestedly into this debate. You can extend it and ask, "Would boys or girls make better M.C.'s on *This Is Your Life*?" (See pp. 212-213.)

Because the biography deals with real people and with actual occurrences, you may ask an excess of fact questions and misconstrue the actual for the factual. The actual is not inconsistent with the judgmental. The judgmental question (or the pivotal question, or the polarized question—both discussed later, p. 345) is the contact point between classifications in book and in your classroom. The judgmental question does not seek facts from the text, but assumes awareness of the facts in the text. The answers it seeks build on the facts but are not limited to the factual; they are judgmental. How can you ask such questions?

CASE STUDY 13 *

The student teacher enjoyed the arguments between the English chairman and the co-operating teacher. Both had been colleagues for a long time, and, the student teacher gathered, had once been friends before the chairman's promotion had come between them. The co-operating teacher was somewhat envious and the chairman, recognizing the situation, was gentle.

The student teacher was unusually competent. The chairman offered the young man a position as a substitute teacher for the following term. The student joyfully accepted. In the final week of student teaching, the co-operating teacher reviewed his achievements and shortcomings, complimented him on the appointment, and said, with the chairman listening, "I hope you'll be happy and I hope it's what you want. Ten or twenty years from now you don't want to have any regrets."

The chairman grunted, "Some people have regrets no matter what happens."

The teacher retorted, "I'm sorry to this day I didn't go into law."

"I've got my law degree too," the chairman said. "I'm not sorry."

"You're a chairman. I'm not," the teacher said. "Did you think you'd remain a teacher this long when you began?"

"Nope," the chairman said frankly. The student heard them simultaneously reminiscing and transmitting the wisdom of the race, as the chairman turned to him: "In the thirties it was as good as being a doctor. Teachers in this system on maximum were getting $4500 a year, in hard money. You could go to Europe, run a car, and have a place in the country."

The teacher chimed in, "The money was good and the law looked like a hard pull, so we played it safe and stayed put. Teaching got the cream of the college graduates then, which is more than I can say for today's college graduates. The cream's going elsewhere. Be sure you know what you're doing."

The chairman expostulated, "Why can't he find a good life in teaching? We were proud as hell when we began!"

"It meant something. What does it mean today? I don't want it on my head that I talked a young innocent into a job he'll regret when he's

* Adapted from the term paper of a former student who must, for obvious reasons, remain anonymous.

my age and *he's* ready to retire. We're not making the same money we made then, and we're not receiving the same students either. He ought to know what he's getting into."

The chairman said to the student, "Don't listen to this old windbag. He's not as bitter as he sounds. Ask him about Joe X. Joe X was a classmate of ours and the finest English teacher we ever knew. He didn't want law. He wanted to write, but he just never found the time, so all through the thirties he coasted on the good money in teaching and never got around to that manuscript, just as we never got into law. After the war he went into business with his brother. Instead of returning to teaching, he made money, lots of it."

The teacher carried on. "Last winter he came by, for auld lang syne, and we all went for a drink. We got pretty high and started thinking about the old days. Did you ever hear of Owen Johnson and the Lawrenceville stories?"

"No," the student said.

"Good heavens," the teacher groaned. "The ignorance of the young these days! From Brian de Boru Finnegan, and the Superiority of the Superlative over the Comparative, Joe X derived the idea of the Irresistible Force, the Immovable Object, and the Bottomless Pit."

"Let me tell it," the chairman urged his colleague. "You've heard what happens when the Irresistible Force meets the Immovable Object—nobody quite knows. Now imagine what happens when the Irresistible Force meets the Bottomless Pit."

"It just keeps going," the puzzled student answered the two gaffers.

"Exactly. Joe said that, in questioning, he was the Bottomless Pit and his students the Irresistible Force. He'd draw them on with question after question. His classes would seethe with thought, even his slow classes. We'd try to imitate him, but being the Bottomless Pit isn't easy. It's too tempting to give answers. You've got to keep backing away all the time, holding out tidbit questions that will keep the class coming toward you, like a shark after bait. But it's got to be real bait. Good questions mean you know your material and everything relating to it. Good questions come hard."

The teacher broke in. "In the army, he had been receiving letters from us and from his wife that things were getting tougher in teaching and that the money wasn't so good because defense workers were making far more. We all were taking jobs after school for extra money and because our families were growing. By that time Joe had three children. His wife moved in with her mother and took a job. When Joe came out of the army, he went to work for his brother, whose factory had grown with war orders. Joe figured that the Bottomless Pit worked in teaching and perhaps could in business. The factory was in pharmaceuticals. After Joe spent three months learning their manufacture, marketing, distribution, and advertising, he doped up a series of questions. Asking the right questions was difficult, but he finally got a half dozen, like 'Why do you use such-and-such a percentage of gross sales for your advertising budget? On what basis do you stick to this percentage?' "

The chairman interrupted, "From a creative teacher to a creative businessman, and all because of the Bottomless Pit. He wasn't telling his customers; he was asking them."

The teacher said, "You're glossing it over because you're short of substitute teachers next term."

The chairman, well practiced in being goaded, took it in stride. "The Bottomless Pit will help, but it takes time to learn that questions make you more the master of your classroom than statements. But what questions? Some are weak and others are powerful. How do you differentiate? You'll only know when the Irresistible Force—students, I mean—keep coming after you, unable to stop answering. Joe learned that a stock of the right questions—not the right assertions—can make a man's fortune. In the same way, it can make the creative teacher, the kind who at the end of the day bounces out of the school building while the others are slouching out. A stock of the right questions can make you happy in your work."

The teacher said heatedly, "Classroom questions are easy compared to the questions you ask a taxpayer about a salary increase. He's already calling me a Bottomless Pit!"

But the more effective the questioning and the richer the student answers, the more imperative to establish way stations of recapitulation and summary. An exciting and stimulating lesson can get out of hand unless, periodically, you take time out to highlight and wrap up the discussion to that point. Biography offers so many varied points and facts that such summary is especially important if we are to remain aware of the threads in the life we are studying. In more general terms we discuss the techniques of summarizing in the chapter on lesson planning (p. 406).

The Bottomless Pit can be a trap, a teasing technique in which the student accelerates in ever-increasing frenzy, and then, fatigued by his exertions, relapses into the doldrums, unless you take time out, as judicious parents do when their children are carried away by the spirit of play, to slow them down awhile. Well-placed and well-paced summarizing enables students to stop and catch breath, organize thinking, and make appropriate notes in notebooks. Furthermore, because good questioning always has a goal, frequent summaries will designate the way stations toward the goal.

One major goal in teaching biography is the self-understanding that comes from the understanding of others. Just as one hoped-for outcome of study of the essay should be an understanding of good conversation and greater ability to share easily and gracefully in conversation, so an out-come of biographical study is this hoped-for insight into self and others. Just as we learn from the essay that people will listen if you have some-thing interesting to say, and that they'll willingly offer attention without being forced into it, so we learn from the biography that we are not alone in our unhappiness, our troubles, not even in our strong sense of indi-viduality. We are more like other human beings than we like to think, humbling though it is to the strong sense of individuality within us.

The well-studied biography gives us the techniques of inner exploration. Exploring the Upper Amazon is far easier than exploring the Inner Self. Darkest Africa never presented greater obstacles than Murky Me. As we have said, you are not trained in psychotherapy and are not to pursue it in your classroom, but you are well within your legitimate domain in getting your students to see how complicated human motives and human behavior can be.

Research, Resources, and Techniques

1. Dwight L. Burton's "Teaching Literature to Our Youths Today" (E. J., May 1955, p. 274) contains good suggestions on questions for lit-erature study (one or two are a little vague and general), some very sound ideas in teaching biography on the differentiation of fact from imagination, and some worthwhile suggestions on the unifying theme in literature study. A very good article.

2. Carl Bode's "The Buxom Biographies" (E. J., Feb. 1955, p. 65) re-lates biography and historical fiction and shows how the latter becomes respectable reading; they are mutually interacting, so that the reading of one encourages the reading of the other.

3. What happens when an interested student wants more material on the subject? For example, a student becomes interested in the life of Leeuwenhoek from his reading of *Microbe Hunters*. You can send him to A. Schierbeek's *Measuring the Invisible World: Life and Works of Anton van Leeuwenhoek* (Abelard-Schuman, New York, 1959) for additional information on the same subject, but you should also lead the student to a comparison of biographers, matching De Kruif with a more scientifically reliable parallel, Greer Williams' *Virus Hunters* (Knopf, 1959).

4. In case you think that biography deals with stuffy people only, here is a partial list of biographies run in *McCall's Magazine,* and announced in *The New York Times* for August 18, 1960: Fred Astaire, *Steps in Time*; Anthony Eden's memoirs *Full Circle*; Gerold Frank, *Zsa Zsa Gabor*; Moss Hart, *Act One*; Kate Smith, *Upon My Lips a Song*; the Duke of Windsor, *Windsor Revisited*; Keenan Wynn, *Ed Wynn's Son*; Maurice Zolotow, *Marilyn Monroe*.

5. Learned T. Bulman's "Biographies for Teen-Agers" (*E. J.,* Nov. 1958, p. 487) demonstrates the thoughtful sifting that *English Journal* does for you. This is a guide for you to follow in assembling materials on the teaching of biography.

6. Stanley B. Kegler and John S. Simmons' "Images of the Hero—Two Teaching Units" (*E. J.,* Sept. 1960, p. 409) is an unusually practical article on biography, with fine teaching and questioning suggestions. Imperative reading.

Matching Biography and Essay

Wherever possible, integrate. Are you persuaded by now that teaching two related poems is easier than teaching one and that teaching two related essays is easier than teaching one? In the same way, the simultaneous pairing of a biography with a related essay will augment the interest in your class. An illustration offered earlier, "Mary White," *Death Be Not Proud, Diary of Anne Frank,* and "Dream Children" carries the central theme of untimely death of the young, or the young that never came to birth, giving you the opportunity of comparing and contrasting essay with essay, biography with biography, and essay with biography. The theme is sad and cannot be pushed too far with the adolescent.

On the other hand, you can match a biography of a sports hero with Heywood Broun's "Dying for Dear Old ———." You will find no difficulty in matching biography with a relevant essay. The match will add grace and lightness to biographical analysis, avoiding dry pedantry.

Because biographies are more extended than essays, more than one related essay may find a home in the context of the biography you are teaching. That old standby, De Kruif's *Microbe Hunters,* can be related to dozens of essays on science and scientific method in *Harper's, Reporter,* and *Fortune,* or, if you object to magazine articles as Joseph Wood Krutch did in "No Essays—Please!" [9] you will find numerous paperback collections of essays by Whitehead, J. B. S. Haldane, and others.

In your lesson plans for biography, supplement the major themes in the life you are analyzing with essays that bear on the themes and with related composition topics. Paired topics like "The Happiest Day of My Life" and "The Saddest Day of My Life" may not always prove successful when assigned without context, but when assigned at high points and low points in the biography, they gain from the reading. A topic that might die on its feet in other circumstances may catch fire because it emerges from a dramatic point in the biography. Try, when events in the biography appropriately call for it, topics like these:

> My Narrowest Escape
> The Most Important Lesson I Ever Learned
> The Time I Felt Like Crying
> The Hardest Job I Ever Had to Do
> How I Learned about Human Nature

Back up these composition subjects with related readings in *Reader's Digest,* which is full of such topics, and other popular magazines. Keep on the alert for composition topics and periodical reading that emerge from the material in the biography.

Poetry offers less opportunity for integration with biography because biography is literal while poetry is rich with overtones, yet some poems are appropriate, as George Meredith's "Lucifer in Starlight" is to sputnik, or his "Melampus" to a biography of Fermi or Einstein, and, of course, there are the eulogies of Whitman and Melville on Lincoln.

Biography stimulates vocational and avocational interests. Boys will be interested in sports heroes, and girls in actresses or ballerinas. Bernard Baruch and Albert Lasker will attract boys planning business careers, and girls a *New Yorker* profile on a famous couturière. More than one famous career has been sparked by the reading of biography and more than one student has had his fuzzy vocational plans clarified by the study of biography. Teen-agers wander in a sea of vocational aspirations and opportunities. Biography opens up the sound choices available. Nothing contributes more to a satisfactory life than enjoying one's work. Biography shows that a man who loves his work finds irreplaceable satisfactions. Furthermore, biography shows how opportunities are created, rather than passively accepted. It supplements the findings of aptitude testing and vocational counseling that not one specific job will make for a satisfactory life, but that a variety of possibilities exist for satisfactory job adjustment.

Enhance these possibilities with relevant essays and magazine articles. Keep a roster of appropriate essay titles that will fit into the right places and events in the biography. Assign composition topics that tie essay and biography together.

Remember that biography, although realistic and actual, can also be dramatic. Fictionalized fact, historical fiction, biographical movies, and fictionalized biographies are more popular than the knowledge and information aspects of biography. Interpretation and your own—and your students'—version of might-have-been is altogether legal, provided that it does not tamper with fact; actually, it is unavoidable because all the facts will never be in. Exhumation of what Lincoln, Napoleon, Beethoven, Cézanne, and Nefertete actually thought and felt will never be complete. Therefore, once your students know the facts, encourage them, on the basis of the facts, to interpret and set their opinions against the author's and against authority. A bright and beautiful senior once said Lincoln's face had greater sex appeal than any she had ever seen. This reminded another girl of a resemblance between Lincoln's face and Sinatra. Meanwhile the boys sat by brooding because hooting at Sinatra is permissible but not when paired with Lincoln. The bright and beautiful senior guessed that there was a difference and the Sinatra fan said there wasn't; one of the boys said that the bright and beautiful senior had read it somewhere because it didn't sound original and did sound familiar. The bright and beautiful senior denied anybody else had ever thought of it. Interpretation? Why not?

Beware sanctimonious biography. The goals and values that compelled the elder Rockefeller to set up the Rockefeller Foundation, Carnegie to make his bequests, a convicted slot-machine racketeer to send his children to college, a former rum-runner to endow numerous benefactions, and the British habit of knighting pirates like Henry Morgan and Francis Drake, should be neither beatified nor damned. Men's motives are complex. Too many school biographies, like campaign biographies, puff the safe virtues. What did the man's enemies say?

Only so can you assure yourself that well-considered goals and values, rather than fake ones, will be dealt with in your class. A desirable out-come of the study of biography is the growth of integrity in the student about his goals and values, and a stronger sense that he can enunciate them and maintain them.

Drama

Many methods texts combine the teaching of modern drama with the teaching of Shakespeare, but the problems in Shakespeare are not those in modern drama. The vocabulary in modern drama is simpler, plot structure and characters familiar, and situations more recognizable. Shake-speare presents other difficulties; the vocabulary, diction, and poetry are unusual and unaccustomed. Hence the separation.

Drama speaks more directly to your class than does most narrative fiction. The staples of the secondary school syllabus in drama include *Our Town, Winslow Boy, Death of a Salesman, Pygmalion, Elizabeth the Queen, Glass Menagerie, Admirable Crichton, Harvey, Strife, High Tor, You Can't Take It with You, Life with Father, Cyrano de Bergerac, Emperor Jones, Beyond the Horizon, Barretts of Wimpole Street, I Remember Mama,* and they range in a wide spectrum from realism to fantasy to romance to genre. Despite this diversity, modern drama shares common qualities. Plays have dialogue, entrances and exits, curtains, stage directions, and conflict. They are built on action and excitement. They have a typical, stylized arrangement. They can be read rapidly. Generally the vocabulary in plays is less taxing than the other literary materials you assign. The contemporary student has sufficient contact with films and television to translate print into speech. In fact, the brighter students will often finish an interesting play at home in a single sitting, without waiting for assignments from you.

Only an extraordinarily poor teacher can wreck the interest in a play that was on Broadway, made into a movie, thereafter put on television, made a fortune for its author, and had audiences in the hundreds of thousands. In the nature of things, such an endeavor is interesting; only incredibly inferior teaching can ruin it. Therefore, expect your students to enjoy reading plays. Your major roadblock is elsewhere, in visualization and interpretation.

Plays are meant for acting, for talking aloud to audiences. Here play and student part company. How painful to see teen-agers struggling less with lines than with themselves when they are before a class! Though self-conscious, they want to act well. They want to speak the lines with assurance, to stride easily and gesture freely so that the class will listen with interest. They can't. How can drama help?

Fortunately, modern drama does not indulge in lengthy monologues but in rapid-fire interchange. Use this crackle of dialogue to give your students the fluidity and self-assurance they want: have them speed up their pace in dramatic reading, generally far too slow; if a word is missed, let it lie and keep them ploughing ahead; as their partners in dialogue finish, and their lines begin, let them come in at once, rapidly, as they do in conversation, unless the stage directions order otherwise. Stage presence is gained simply by keeping the lines going and getting aboard on time. Memorization is not necessary, but knowing the lines well enough to get them off quickly is.

Thus in Salinger's *Catcher in the Rye,* Holden Caulfield describes Lunt and Fontanne: "When one of them got finished making a speech, the other said something very fast right after it. It was supposed to be like people really talking and interrupting each other and all. The trouble was, it was *too* much like people talking and interrupting each other." [10]

Student gestures and stage movement are stiff, without the stiffness of the highly formal Japanese kabuki or Chinese theatre. This formal stiffness is as difficult to attain as the loose flow of Western theater tradition. Show how both looseness and formality require practice and how either is more appropriate to different characters and sections of the play. Then have one of your better student-actors imitate you. Then get another, then a third, then a fourth, in descending order of ability, to get students imitating one another, rather than you, and get the play out of your hands and into theirs. Thus they will be deliberately copying either Oriental formalized patterns or Western informal flow, contrasting stateliness and looseness, for themselves rather than for you.

Next, student-actors should talk to others of the cast and not to the class, to one another and not to their seated classmates. If they persist in this amateur actor's habit of addressing audience rather than cast, scatter the actors around the four corners of the room; do not draw them up front. With the voices of the *dramatis personae* coming from all points of the compass, the class feels itself more a part of the play, less an audience, and, itself becoming involved, reduces the painful shyness in the more withdrawn of your actors.

Have the self-conscious ones turn their backs to the class. If shy students refuse to do their share of acting, allow them to remain at their seats, so the knee-knocking will be less conspicuous. Sit with these students. Read the lines together with them. Allow them to read silently. Prompt them. You may never get them to face the class, though they will want to do so. Maybe some subsequent teacher will be successful. You will at least have set the foundations. Your students will be eternally grateful for getting them out of their shells, fight you though they will.

Our earlier discussions on interpretation and understanding of poetry, narrative fiction, the Shakespearean play, the essay, and biography are applicable to the play and need not be repeated here. Analysis of character, plot, and development in the play is as in novel and short story. However, because language in a modern play is so familiar, its full meanings are likely to slip by and the analysis may overlook the richest poetry and overtones in the plainest prose.

For example, consider the first act exchange in *Death of a Salesman* between Willy Loman and his son: Willy: "Bernard is not well liked, is he?" Biff: "He's liked, but he's not well liked." The word *liked* has many overtones, as do the words *attention* (Linda: "Attention must be paid.") and *important* ("Your father's an important man."). Significant aspects of the play lie behind these familiar words and you cannot let them slip by. Willy Loman's use of *well liked* tells us volumes about Willy and about the basic philosophy of the play. Many plays have memorable lines of this kind, lines which have a peculiarly theatrical and even contemporary eloquence. Thus, from "What will Mrs. Grundy say?" in the 1798 *Speed the Plough,* to "Hey Flagg, wait for baby!" in *What Price Glory?* to "Is no bank account!" in *I Remember Mama,* ringing lines climax the drama, however unremarkable out of context; in the plays they come through like bolts of lightning and afterward become everyday speech. Skin prickles and scalps rise when Emily says in Act III of *Our Town,* "Oh, Mama, just look at me one minute as though you really saw me. Mama, fourteen years have gone by. I'm dead." The words are simple and tear so hard!

But you must be similarly watchful about sounds. The first act closing of Shaw's *Caesar and Cleopatra* with its stage directions for Cleopatra's "great sob of relief" depends on the same wordlessness as Lady Macbeth's sleepwalking sigh, "Oh, oh, oh!"—sheer sound moving our hearts because it recapitulates prior suspense. Eliza Doolittle sets the stage by a completely different "Aah-ow-ooh!" in the printed version of *Pygmalion,* with each sound typical of the play and reflecting its feeling.

Illustrate this qualitative difference in sound either by your acting or by recordings and films. The printed version cannot convey the feeling, so you must. Thereafter discuss how the playwright's skill brings action and characterization along to such a point where only a sound is needed to give us as perfect understanding as words could. Indeed what words could possibly substitute for Lady Macbeth's sustained sigh as she wrings her hands, or for Eliza Doolittle's "Aah-ow-ooh!" or for Cleopatra's great sob?

Be watchful. The clarity and simplicity of modern dramatic writing may deceive you, unless you read alertly with your ears as well as your eyes, and unless you visualize the two-dimensional printed page in terms of the three-dimensional stage and the fourth dimension of time in pacing and tempo. If you do, any play you teach will offer the same opportunity of word-eloquence and sound-eloquence.

Do not permit your students to remain obedient readers, responding to images on the flat printed page in a flat way, instead of to cues of images in plural dimensions. Thus, in the opening of *Our Town,* the Stage Manager speaks explicitly, stage business is explicit, time and place are explicitly given, and even the nature of the play's technique is given ("First automobile's going to come along in about five years." "There's Doc Gibbs. . . . Doc Gibbs died in 1930."), but this explicitness does not diminish the need for students to set up in their own minds cues about visualization and imagination. If the Stage Manager's "The morning star always gets wonderful bright the minute before it has to go," is the play's keynote, tell them so. How, then, should the lines be spoken? How should the Stage Manager stare at the morning star before he goes upstage, as the directions order him? Casually, sadly, kindly? Not only must students visualize the concurrent breakfasts of the Gibbs and Webb families as separate and parallel, but also the rapid-fire crackle and increase of pace, as Emily Webb and George Gibbs make their preparations for school. In the Stage Manager's long speech, devoid of stage directions, where he says, ". . . we're going to look back on it from the future," how would your class have the Stage Manager move? How would they have him speak— loudly, softly, ironically, pityingly—and where? When Dr. Gibbs, later on, tells George: "Here's a handkerchief, son," what has George been doing while Dr. Gibbs talks to call forth this remark?

If every student in your class has dead ancestors, relatives, and friends in Heaven, how are the deceased looking at him? Similarly, meanwhile, we're seeing dead people. When Rebecca sits beside George, remind the class that Mrs. Gibbs dies at Rebecca's house; we've already been told so. When Rebecca describes the strangely addressed envelope, is it fun or eternity speaking? Let students compare Rebecca's lines with the Stage Manager's lengthy mid-act speech, where he says, "Well—you people a thousand years from now," to contrast the infinities of space and time in which the play attempts to move with our minute-by-minute behavior. Does eternity make our activity petty or precious?

These lines, and the considerations that should accompany them, could easily slip by. Go behind the transparent simplicity of the language to reveal the deeper meanings. The Stage Manager himself says so: "You've got to catch it between the lines; you've got to *over*hear it."

Thus, plays are easy to read but hard to understand. Don't underestimate the challenge of visualization. The combination of flashback-narrator-actor in *Our Town* makes visualization imperative. *Glass Menagerie,* where Tom Wingfield introduces the play and acts as one-man Greek chorus and participant in the drama, similarly requires projection by the reader beyond the two-dimensional printed page. The same demand is put on the reader in *Death of a Salesman.*

Not only the complications of contemporary stage techniques make visualization imperative, but the need to analyze character. Amanda Wingfield and Willy Loman are cut from the same jib, anchored by dreams and euphoric because anchored. Amanda's "Oh, we're going to have a lot of gay times together! I see them coming! Mmm, just breathe that air! So fresh, and the moon's so pretty! I'll skip back out—I know where my place is when young folks are having a—serious conversation!" and Willy's "I see great things for you kids, I think your troubles are over. But remember, start big and you'll end big. Ask for fifteen. How much you gonna ask for?" must be integrated with Willy's shuffle and Amanda's flutter. In visualizing shuffle, flutter, and talk, you enter choreography. When Amanda Wingfield spreads the newspaper and sits down on the landing, conceive it as a tiny dance. When Willy plops down, it's a dance too, although the choreography is different. The choreography thereafter illuminates character.

If stage techniques and characterization in *Glass Menagerie* are reminiscent of *Our Town,* and if aspects of *Death of a Salesman* are reminiscent of *Glass Menagerie,* a common impulse must infuse all three. Does this common impulse infuse other outstanding plays? What can it be?

It's show business. Fine plays can be commercially successful, like Shakespeare. Show business gathers many people together at the same time in socialized activity; the rituals of theater-going deserve class discussion.

People dress up for the theater, but not necessarily for the movies. Why the difference? Why, furthermore, do people usually buy tickets in advance for the theater, but not for films?

Why do films have continuous performances, not interrupted by intermissions? Why do theatrical performances have intermissions between acts? Do intermissions detract from interest or add to it?

Do newspaper reviews affect decisions to see films? The fate of a Broadway play is decided by the New York drama critics, not by advertising, but a heavy promotional and advertising investment in a film may make it successful. What makes the opinions of drama critics crucial in a play? Why are film critics less decisive in the success of a film? How can the theater-goer defend himself against the extremes of marquee advertising, which quote unfavorable reviews out of context to lure the audience inside?

Would students prefer films to local amateur theatrical productions? To local summer-theater professional productions? Why? (Incidentally, you ought to be an unpaid publicity agent for any local theatrical groups, amateur or professional.) To school productions?

Why is the Broadway stage less sexy than films have recently become? Why is the Broadway stage cleaner than many paperbacks? Do the critics have anything to do with this?

If Broadway plays are expensive to produce, and if a play represents a fantastic financial gamble, and if funds are required from numerous contributors ("angels"), how is the quality of the play affected? If organized groups are approached for benefit showings, how would this affect the quality of a play? If theater-going is expensive because costs are high, are plays aimed at the ordinary audience or the audience that can afford to pay? Can the ordinary audience these days afford to pay?

Do novels and stories survive better than plays? Do they retain interest longer? Are Shakespearean revivals successful because they are popular or because they are subsidized? How would you modernize an old play? By costume or by language?

How is acting affected by scenery? Does the proscenium stage require the same kind of acting as theater-in-the-round? How does preparation of the film actor and stage actor differ? Do modern improvements in stage lighting and decor modify acting (Stanislavsky and The Method)? Why do we reconcile unionized stage hands and cold cream with our sense of theatrical reality, but cannot with the Greek chorus and the Elizabethan aside and soliloquy? How much of theatrical reality is a matter of fashion?

To avoid having play-reading degenerate into a spectator sport, you must continuously stimulate response, opinion, reaction, and assessment. Give assignments that will involve these. One teacher, with Rachel Field's one-acter *The Fifteenth Candle,* assigned topics which, after modification, are applicable to most plays:

> If you (the student) do not approve of the ending, rewrite the dialogue, changing the end.
> Write a short scene or descriptive passage, showing Rosa five years later. (Or Amanda Wingfield or Biff Loman.)
> Write a paragraph in defense of Mr. Vedetti, Rosa's father. (Or attacking the philosophy of *Our Town.*)

Awaken all the conflict and clash you can, analyze the deceptively simple language, give dimension to gesture and choreographic value to stage movement, and you can have as exciting a production as the original Broadway opening!

Research, Resources, and Techniques

1. Philip A. Coggin's *The Uses of Drama* (George Braziller, 1956) is a survey, historical and contemporary, that has useful hints for classroom discussion.

2. Ina Honaker Herron, in "Changing Images of the Small Town" (*E. J.,* Dec. 1958, p. 537), wonders if people in small towns are nicer than in the big, big city. Thus *Our Town* values can be compared with Mencken's "Sahara of Bozart." See the John H. Bens reference, p. 186.

CHAPTER 9

The Mass Media

Furniture of the Modern World

We are bathed in a sea of sights, sounds, and words, manufactured, designed, and planned for the money in them and made evil and dangerous by your aloofness from them as something unclean. A cheap juke-box tune, a stupid suspense show on television, or a sexy paperback cover is no more to be avoided than an illness, and you can no more flee your classroom than can a physician or a surgeon flee his office. He learns what he can from these things, and so should you.

Unfortunately, some people want you to flee—some parents, some cautious administrators, and your narrower colleagues. As these words are being written, a teacher in the Southwest is having trouble because she recommended *The Catcher in the Rye*, J. D. Salinger's distinguished novel, to her classes. And in *Time:* "Pointing a finger at Schoolteacher Franklyn Olson, 23, the justice of the peace intoned: 'Young man, your crime is as serious as if you had given them marijuana cigarettes.' Olson's crime: assigning five schoolboys in Thomson, Mich., to read *The Stranger*, by France's late Nobel-prizewinning novelist Albert Camus. Olson's sentence: a \$100 fine and 90 days in the county jail. . . ." [1] No physician would tolerate having a layman diagnose or prescribe (though the layman is justified in discussing the merits of socialized medicine), and one wonders how justified is the parent who prescribes curriculums. English is particularly vulnerable to such side-line prodding, partly because some teachers are weak in the public-relations aspects of their work, and partly because prejudice and bigotry do not automatically disappear with parenthood. You cannot do anything effective in the mass media without a good community

283

to work in and without an administrator well soaked in the values of English. The remainder of this chapter assumes this kind of administration and community. Read it, but remember that you cannot crusade or risk your job. You cannot, as an individual, do what must be done by teacher organizations; work through them to upgrade the professional level of teaching so that it will be as unthinkable for parents or community to tell you what to teach as it is for you to interfere in the patterns of home and family. You must, in other words, wait until teachers are professionals and not community baby-sitters.

Enlightened communities and good administrators encourage you to plunge into the mass media, to present the best of modern novels to your students, whether hardbound or paperback, the good television and radio programs, the good show tunes and folk songs, the magazines and newspapers. We have more than we have time to digest. True, television can be improved, but the crowded English curriculum has scant room for television even at its present level. The English edition of *Scholastic* and "The Public Arts" section of *English Journal* give you advance notice of the more desirable shows; alert your students to these.

Publishers' Weekly, Saturday Review, and the book sections of *The New York Times* and *New York Herald Tribune* will keep you abreast of the better paperbacks. Have you ever read *Variety*? This show business magazine, without being crass, gives you the financial background of show business, publishing, and journalism. You cannot tell where you will encounter meaty material for your English classes. Many years ago, Gilbert Seldes, in *The Seven Lively Arts,* seriously analyzed the comic strip *Krazy Kat* as an art form. More recently, Al Capp's *Li'l Abner* and Walt Kelly's *Pogo* have received the same respectful attention from critics. You cannot, therefore, condemn comic books out of hand. Some are trashy, but responsible writers, reviewers, and professors will defend *Li'l Abner* as powerful, imaginative satire. If you accept *New Yorker* and *Punch* cartoons, you cannot do less with *Pogo*.

How much of the newspaper's material comes from its own reporters? How much is merely a reprint or handout from an enterprising public-relations organization? Your students should read newspapers, not passively, but as active, interacting readers, watchfully, sniffing for propaganda and tendentious editing, and mindful of the story's source. When well read —and this is more important than their being well written!—newspapers can be tremendously informative. So, too, can magazines. The American who knows how to read newspapers and magazines is as well informed as any citizen in the world. The teen-ager in your classes wants to feel the contemporary throbbing within him, so much is he a creature of the here and now. You can help him live more richly in the present by teaching him to discriminate among the kinds of newspapers and magazines clamoring for his attention.

The remainder of this chapter considers how you can put the mass media to work in your classes.

Research, Resources, and Techniques

1. Robert B. Heilman's "Literature and Growing Up" (*E. J.,* Sept. 1956, p. 303) illustrates by his "push-pull" method and his "forbidden-fruit" techniques how you can function well in the English Teacher's Underground.

2. Harry E. Hand's "Sex in the Modern Novel—A Teaching Problem" (*E. J.,* Nov. 1959, p. 473) attempts to solve a headache: How do you draw the teeth of Kinsey's findings? Can you tranquilize adolescent sex interests by avoidance? How should people like Freud be discussed in a high school class? How can you discuss Oedipus, Electra, etc., and still not cause a disturbance? What about the bald sex-talk in *Time* and the ever-increasing sexiness of *Life* and the *Saturday Evening Post,* periodicals which appear in school libraries?

3. We made earlier reference (Chap. 6, p. 229) to Charles Calitri's "*Macbeth* and the Reluctant Reader" (*E. J.,* May 1959, p. 254), but his comments on the Underground Library have relevance here too. How can the Teacher's Underground make constructive, educational use of the Underground Library? What are the possibilities of an alliance?

Journalism

Begin with a newspaper . . . and a ruler. Have your students measure and compute the percentage of newspaper space devoted to advertising. Thirty per cent? Forty per cent? Fifty per cent? Or more? How does it depend on the day? Why should Sunday newspapers be more loaded with advertising than weekday issues? Why should food advertising be especially heavy on Thursday, and real estate and automotive advertising heavy on week-ends? Is the amount of space devoted to advertising excessive? If newspapers are reluctant to lose advertising revenue, does this affect the way newspapers report news?

Most newspaper men and editors will heatedly deny that they take direction from the advertising department of their newspaper or slant news to satisfy the advertiser. This is undoubtedly true in many instances. Witness the case of cigarette advertising. Unquestionably, cigarette manufacturers, who had formerly placed much of their advertising in newspapers as compared with radio and magazines, withdrew it from newspapers devoting space to the carcinogenic possibilities in cigarette smoking. Naturally, the newspapers were pained to lose advertising revenue, but they continue to feature news dealing with smoking and cancer.

If newspapers refused to yield to pressure from advertisers here, they have competed mercilessly with the other mass media for advertising revenues in other cases. They have castigated radio and television in a competitive bid for the advertiser's dollar, as the following article from *Advertising Age* indicates:

DAILIES HAVE OWN
PAYOLA, OVERPLAY
RADIO'S: SWEENEY

NEW ORLEANS, Dec. 4—Kevin Sweeney, head of the Radio Advertising Bureau, this week warned newspapers that radio might begin to strike back if they continue to "overplay" the broadcast payola story.

In a speech before the advertising club here he called payola the "most overplayed newspaper story of the year." He said payola in radio didn't represent more than the "tiniest fraction of 1% of the music played.

"We suggest to the newspapers which have overplayed the payola story that they resist their competitive urge to needle broadcasters every day, because they might get more than they bargained for," he continued.

"Radio is no longer the tame pussy cat of the '40s. We are unwilling to be shoved around without cause, to cast down our eyes and say, '*Mea culpa*' when a couple of bright young men take money to play records. We are more likely to lash back at our friendly competitors in print saying, 'Tidy up your own payola situation.'

"Clean up the society page, where the ugly duckling daughter of the department store owner appears every time she sips a cup of tea. Clean up the police news situation in many cities, where a leading retailer has to commit first degree murder to get on Page 1—something unimportant like drunken driving scarcely gets him a line. Clean up the automobile page, the sports page, the real estate section and amusement pages, where so-called news stories are allocated strictly on a trick-or-treat basis.

"Payola is a news story. It belongs in every newspaper, tv newscast, and radio newscast, but in proportion to its importance, and only where it's news," Mr. Sweeney asserted.[2]

Newspapers have run stories on the investigation of ethical-drug manufacturers by Senator Kefauver's Congressional committee. Ethical drugs (drugs sold by prescription) are advertised not in newspapers but in medical journals, so that newspapers will freely air the pricing policies of their manufacturers. But these same newspapers will be less likely to air the pricing policies of proprietary drugs (drugs sold without prescription), which do advertise in newspapers, and still less likely to air the pricing policies of cosmetics manufacturers and large department stores because a heavy proportion of newspaper advertising revenue derives from these sources.

Newspapers are not being dishonest, but realistic. Your students should not read newspapers cynically but with awareness. If they want an objective story about department-store operations, they should not consult newspapers but magazines, because magazine advertising revenue does not depend on department stores (except for a few specialized magazines like *New Yorker*). If *Readers' Guide to Periodical Literature* or *Industrial Arts Index* show no magazine blasts against department stores, your students can gather that here, certainly, is one aspect of the economy that would face up favorably to Congressional committees. In this fashion your study of the mass media contributes to alert and discriminating citizenship.

On the other hand, newspapers are sometimes bought for their advertising, rather than for news articles, editorials, or columns, so advertising itself can be studied for examples of smart and persuasive writing and illustration. Advertising can have literateness and artistry. People on Madison Avenue have published novels and poetry, have had plays produced, and have had one-man shows. Astuteness in the top agencies ranks with that in most college faculties, though scholarship may not. The brains on Madison Avenue are working—or conniving—every second of the time, and these brains are superb. Their products are worth the scrutiny of your students. Layout, captions, copy are outcomes of canniness and much research into the habits and characteristics of the consumer. They are not accidental or idly arrived at. They are the distillation of ability with intentions upon your pocketbook. See Martin Mayer's highly readable *Madison Avenue, U.S.A.*[3]

Have your students follow newspaper advertising, for example, the kind placed daily by large retailers. Do rival department stores advertise the same way? Do they aim at the same public? Do they give different images of themselves from day to day, or do they present a persisting, unvarying image? If you snip out the name of the advertiser and ask students to guess whose advertisement it is, guesses will be better than chance when students have had experience reading advertisements. How can they spot the identity? What is there about message, type, layout, illustration that lets the reader pierce the anonymity? Do newspaper advertisements for the national advertisers, like General Motors, Ford, Chrysler, stress different images; for Procter and Gamble, Colgate, Lever; for General Foods and General Mills; for Shell Oil, Socony, and so on?

An interesting device used by advertisers is the "split run," in which alternative advertising is used to see which of two ads is more successful in attracting the consumer. *Printers' Ink,* an advertising trade magazine, has collected a series of these dual advertisements under the heading *Which Pulled Best?* The world of advertising copy is a legitimate source of reading materials, vocabulary, and image-study. These *Printers' Ink* analyses of successful and unsuccessful campaigns and James Woolf's analyses in *Advertising Age* of superior and inferior advertising can be of great informational value to your classes.

T. S. Matthews, in *The Sugar Pill,*[4] analyzes newspaper reading as a compulsive habit. His point is that newspapers must appear every day, even if there is no news, because of contractual advertising obligations and not because anything important has happened in the last twenty-four hours. Matthews' point is generally applicable to the casual newspaper reader, whose newspaper reading is a matter of routine, but is less relevant in the reader who has a purpose in his daily purchase. This purpose for purchase may vary from the race-track gambler who wants his daily form sheet, to the broker who wants to know daily stock quotations, to the housewife who wants to keep up to the minute on recipes and household hints, to the teen-ager following the *Charley Brown* comic strip, the sophisticate following *Li'l Abner* or *Pogo,* and the crossword addict. The more specific the purpose of newspaper reading, the better. Your students should be taught this, because the more specific the purpose, the more rewarding will newspaper reading be. Else, as Matthews says, it becomes compulsive routine.

This purposefulness is the reader's best defense against assaults on his opinions and points of view. Most newspaper stories are not born in the newspaper office, but are received from the news syndicates, from governmental agencies, and, most important, from public-relations officers paid by private groups, corporations, and individuals who have an ax to grind.

Newspapers are vehicles for propaganda. The *couturière* and the food manufacturer have public-relations people (or press agents) trying to get free space on the woman's page, and the prize-fight manager, the theatrical agent, the corporation are providing press releases, known as "handouts," to the appropriate editors.

A sometimes dreadful picture of the work of the public-relations man is given in *Professional Public Relations and Political Power* by Stanley Kelley, Jr.[5] Public-relations men often guide corporate policy. Thus, to gain favorable opinion, A. T. and T. attempts geographical distribution of its stockholders, not wanting geographic concentration. An intimate knowledge of public opinion and how it is manipulated controls this policy.

Kelley discusses the manipulations of a California public-relations firm called Campaigns, Inc. in behalf of public utilities companies, the Republican Party, and the American Medical Association, and he claims that public relations has become more important than bossism or lobbying, that nothing can withstand a favorable climate of public opinion, and that this climate can be molded through the voter's different roles and his multigroup affiliations. The outcome is centralization. Local ties have become weaker as the nation has grown more mobile, with the consequent weakening of local loyalties and even of the local political boss.

As a specific example, Kelley gives a fascinating account of medical economics, the politics of physicians, and the way in which the American Medical Association mobilized nationally to defeat the Truman health-insurance bill. Throughout the nation, doctors exerted pressure on their patients who were political and opinion leaders, on druggists, and on retail store owners in their campaign against "political medicine." Doctors mobilized behind the campaign of 1945 in New York chiefly by letter writing—and you can show your students that politically sophisticated people are not averse to letter writing!

Even more unsettling, in what Kelley calls the "merchandising of doubt," was the Maryland campaign to unseat Senator Millard Tydings. The campaign on behalf of Tydings' opponent, Senator Butler, enlisted the support of Joseph McCarthy and materials provided by him included faked photographs and an "opinion" survey.

With respect to presidential campaigns, the work done by public-relations men is even more significant, even if undercover. They analyze public opinion very carefully, considering, for example, whether the stay-at-home vote is chiefly Democratic or chiefly Republican, or whether it is similar to the voting population. Political planning is incredibly minute and delves deeply into the relationships between local voting patterns, local mass media, and media research (a term explained below). Hence the major advertising agencies are important because they can release trained manpower to the party and the candidate of their choice and can pre-empt choice time spots on radio and TV for the favored candidate. Friendly sponsors give up their choice time spots to their side—chiefly Republican. In national campaigns, Democrats have had difficulty enlisting open support from advertising agencies.

Hence, Kelley concludes, the public-relations man is more than a technician. His knowledge of the mass media—and the way you and your students read newspapers—makes him important in council and in decisions. Public relations thus becomes related to the tendency toward centralism and to the drift toward national leadership as opposed to local leadership.

Do your students feel somebody's gaze on the back of their necks? If they're reading newspapers, somebody's reading *them* simultaneously. Much of what they read in newspapers has been planted there by public-relations men who work for others, and on behalf of others, and who are eagerly watching to see what is forming on the surface of men's minds or below the surface.

John Crosby describes the attempts to assess what the public is thinking, and how research into the thinking of the public and the consumer takes up the time of those experts who simply must know what people want, prize, or think they need. Hence the numerous "market research" campaigns. Observe the lingo, reported by Crosby, that has sprouted among advertising people who want to find out how the customer thinks:

> Let's drop this down the well and see how big a splash it makes.
> Let me take a temperature reading on this and I'll get it back to you.
> Let's guinea pig that for size.
> Let's flow feathers around the room.
> Let's run it up the flagpole and see who salutes.
> We'd better get down on our hands and knees and talk to the consumer.
> Let's follow it and see what it eats.
> Let's put it on the radiator and see if it melts.
> Let's bury it and see what grows.

So your students are more laboratory specimens than they suspect. Units in journalism that omit this fact are presenting half the picture

Do not conclude that your students are helpless in a goldfish bowl, impaled on the coldly measuring eye of the public relations manipulator. Nothing could be further from the truth. Provided that newspapers are read purposefully and that action emerges from purposeful reading, the work of the public-relations man can be in a sound, democratic direction. Your students should learn that newspaper reading is only the beginning, that they should be pleased and displeased by what they read, not merely passively accepting. They should learn how to write letters to the editor, to congressmen, to officials.

If they want to know your opinion on the issues of the day, answer delicately. On debatable issues, present all the relevant points of view. When students badger you for your position, fight them off. You have no right to take even indirect advantage of your situation as their teacher, despite their sweetest persuasion. Indeed, your opinion partially and sometimes more than partially, especially if you are respected by them, may shut them off from contending approaches. Do not take unfair advantage of your place as the classroom's chief opinion leader.

Unfortunately, newspapers are becoming fewer and the survivors are not always the organs that an operating democracy deserves to have. For this reason, the weekly news magazines supplement the materials that the daily newspapers furnish. We shall discuss this problem later, in the section on magazines.

Should you be a scold about sensational journalism? No. First, it will do no good. Second, the sex and criminality that so richly embroider some newspapers actually occur. Third, journalistic sensationalism is part of newspaper tradition; your job is to help students assess it, not to condemn it. Do not ask as a reformer, "Which newspaper has more respect for its readers, the good newspaper or the sensational one?" but as if you are seeking information. Newspapers are in business. If there were no profit in publishing them, they would not be issued. From the bloody circulation wars of the first decade of this century, when Hearst fought Pulitzer for newsstand space with the aid of goons and strong-arm men, newspapers have used both honorable and shady means of remaining in business.

Read this discussion material to your class: "Gang warfare between newsboys and truck-drivers of rival papers occasionally developed. The war of 1910-1914 between employees of the *American* and *Tribune* in Chicago, marked by murder and mayhem, taught thugs the possibilities of the gang warfare that developed later in that city, and furnishes the most crudely vicious episode in the history of circulation contests." [6] If, as this quotation suggests, newspaper circulation wars led to Capone, and if these wars seem over, how do newspapers compete for circulation these days? Comparing the number of newspapers in your community today with those forty years ago, has peaceful competition been less or more deadly than violent competition?

In New York, for example, one newspaper, the New York *World-Telegram,* represents the amalgamation over the years of *The Sun, The Globe, The Mail, The Telegram,* and *The World* (morning and evening editions). What responsibility does this put on surviving newspapers to report fairly all social, political, and economic points of view? Do newspapers succeed in maintaining this fairness? Do they need to or can they be indifferent to it? Are they responsive to alternative points of view?

Can the one-newspaper town or city be certain of objective news reporting? Does it matter much to the typical citizen of such towns? Do Canadian and British newspaper readers read the same news as American readers?

If Presidential elections since 1932 show that newspaper political preferences do not reflect the final returns, does that mean that citizens do not read editorials, or do not trust them, or have other reasons for neglecting editorial advice? Or are Presidential election returns an unfair and atypical measure of the faith placed by most people in their favorite newspapers?

In asking these questions, avoid cynicism; aim for aware understanding. Newspapers need readers. You can't believe everything you read in the papers, nor do responsible newspapers want you to; but there's much you can believe. The American who wants to be well informed can be more easily than any other man in the world, thanks to the American newspaper, with all its faults, provided that the reader can read between the lines and can assess freedom of the press.

For example, effective newspaper reading requires awareness of the techniques of news-gathering. Newspapers not only sell news; they also buy it from news wholesalers, otherwise called news syndicates. The Associated Press, the largest of these wholesalers, is a co-operative venture, while the other major syndicates are affiliated with large newspapers or newspaper chains. Therefore, if syndicates also peddle comic strips and columnists, so that a newspaper can publish almost exclusively on what it buys from outside sources, what responsibilities does the local newspaper —the news retailer—abdicate? What responsibilities become more acutely its domain? Has the local newspaper assumed these responsibilities? How does this reflect on local news coverage and local public opinion?

Your students should be able to identify syndicate initials—AP, UPI, NANA, and accompanying datelines and by-lines—for recognition of the news wholesaler and news origin. Further, if these stories from far-away are attributed to "an informed source," "a reliable source," or "a source close to the White House (or Quai d'Orsay, or Downing Street, or the Kremlin)," how do you decipher these phrases? Is this a code by which the writer warns the reader to be cautious or credulous? Would a name be more dependable? If so, why isn't the name given? Was the story "leaked"? If so, why? Was it leaked to give information or to tease it forth? These questions arise daily in connection with major and minor stories. The detective work fascinates students.

Students generally know that the front page is the most important one and that the right-hand column contains, in the editor's judgment, the most important story of the day and the left-hand column the next most important story. But how does the editor arrive at his judgment? If two local stories on man-bites-dog and dog-bites-man come in, your students will recognize that the first is the more important. But if man had bitten dog in Pakistan and dog had bitten man in front of City Hall, the first becomes greatly reduced in importance. Also important for editorial judgment as to newsworthiness are: Whose dog was it? Who was bitten? Lassie and President Roosevelt's Fala would affect editorial judgment as to importance.

But, because editors do not always agree on the importance of the stories they run, accounting for right-hand placement in one newspaper and placement elsewhere in another newspaper, invite your students to match their judgments against the judgment of the editor. Do they agree that the right-hand story of the day is the most important one? If they do, what reasons can they give? If they disagree, for what reasons? What are the personal, social, economic, political, and historical reasons for selecting one story as more important than another?

Which stories are "handouts" planted by public-relations people and which stories are paid for by the newspaper? Does a governmental or corporation press representative uniformly try to get stories into the newspaper? Or does he, under other circumstances, try to keep stories out of the newspaper? Does the newspaper reveal that its source was a public-relations man (or press agent)? Is the source disguised or revealed?

Structurally, the news story, unlike the short story, has its climax at the beginning, accounting for the newspaper lead, or opening paragraph, with information that answers the reader's Who? What? Why? When? How? Remaining paragraphs expand on these, with the least important material coming at the tail end of the story in a steady decrescendo, with little lost if the need for space forces cutting at the end. Effective newspaper reading requires close attention to the opening paragraph, and attention progressively attenuating with succeeding paragraphs. Show students that the experienced newspaper reporter tries to overcome the rigid lead form with a variety of stylistic devices, in order to reconcile the requirements of interest and informativeness.

If the school newspaper is your responsibility, at least one of your classes should help you share this responsibility; it is demanding enough for you to be spared at least one teaching assignment. You will need time to proofread carefully, to dash to and from the printer's, and to soothe ruffled feathers among faculty and students.

Research, Resources, and Techniques

1. Frank B. Jacobson's "Two Ring Circus in the Mass Media" (*E. J.*, May 1955, p. 280) describes a newspaper unit for two different groups. In one, newspaper reading and analysis were stressed; in the other, writing. Thus the same material can be given various stresses, depending on the group's ability.

2. T. S. Matthews' *The Sugar Pill* (Simon and Schuster, 1959) states that newspaper reading, like all repetition compulsions, is obsessive and hence a mark of neuroticism. He argues that we read newspapers not because something has happened but because we have to think it has. Are as many things going on as newspapers say?

3. Martin Mayer's *Madison Avenue, U.S.A.* (Pocket Books, 1959) gives an excellent view of the mass media in action. See p. 162 of Mr. Mayer's interesting and informative book for an instance of how newspapers can sometimes resort to blackmail in efforts to get advertising. Would they be similarly inclined in getting a news story?

The Magazine

Like the newspaper, the magazine must appear regularly, even when nothing important or interesting happens. Again, like the newspaper, the magazine has seen some notable contractions and expansions in the last half century. *Time* has succeeded *Literary Digest*. The Crowell stable of magazines has disappeared (read Theodore White's *View from the Fortieth Floor* on how a magazine dies). The *Saturday Evening Post* keeps an eye on *Life* and *Look*. *Reader's Digest* now accepts advertising. Where newspapers are limited in what they can lend the English curriculum, magazines offer great richness, variety, and appropriateness.

Know what magazines your school library receives, and what is in the back file. We have already discussed one use to which the author had occasion to put the magazines in the school library (p. 121). Although American magazines do not exert the influence on American political thinking that they did in the days of the muckrakers—even *Time, Newsweek,* and the weekly journals of opinion, right and left, do not do so—they are tremendously influential in matters of taste, home furnishing, hobbies, and amusement. They are generally easy to look at. They are a fine way to introduce your students to the essay, to fiction, to poetry. They are less intimidating than books. They are contemporary without being unsettling. What are the possibilities in magazine fiction and in magazine articles for your classroom? Let's first see what's doing in magazine fiction.

Do your students prefer romance, suspense, Westerns, society, adventure? They can step right up and help themselves. The range of quality is wide. Much magazine fiction is repetitive and highly patterned. The *Saturday Evening Post* represents one pattern in fiction, and the *New Yorker* another, the former highly structured, the latter directionless, but each has maintained its recognizability and differentiability for decades. *Saturday Evening Post* fiction has found its way into the classroom more frequently than *New Yorker* because it has more action—a result of the feeling among teachers that the more action, the more interest, although this is truer of the junior high school class than of the upper half of high school, where brighter students are quite ready for *Harper's, Atlantic,* and *New Yorker*. In addition to bulk subscriptions to *Scholastic,* you can get special student-subscription rates to most of the magazines mentioned. During adolescence it is pleasant to have mail coming into the house addressed to one's self. Magazines have a well-defined personality, and their fiction reflects this personality. Thus, send them off to the school library's file of back-issue and current magazines, let them sample the magazines they prefer, and then have them make arrangements for the magazines of their choice to come into their homes on a regular basis, as subscribers.

Some organization of their magazine reading in fiction is necessary, else you will be encouraging fiction reading for narcosis rather than for discrimination. In the women's magazines, for example, much of the fiction is of the soap-opera type, but side by side with it is excellent narrative. Teach students that the same magazine, in the same issue, may have low-level and high-level reading. What constitutes the difference? Similarly, some Westerns are mediocre and others excellent. The difference between a *Shane* and the average rootin'-tootin' Western should be analyzed in connection with oral reports or more formal reading reports. Extra credit is more deserved by the student who scouts the magazines for worthwhile fiction than by the student who dutifully completes a routine reading of assignments from you. One shows enterprise, the other compliance. Enterprise is further assured when the student compares good magazine stories with poor ones, or, better yet, good ones with other good ones of the same type, so that a Luke Short and Ernest Haycox Western are compared. Such masters of the short story as Roald Dahl and Irwin Shaw are well within the range of your better students.

Above all, this attack on the contemporary in fiction makes your classroom reading of Dickens, Eliot, Sinclair Lewis, Hardy, or Rölvaag all the richer. Fiction becomes a key to life, an answer to the problems of living, rather than a retreat from them—as reading can too often be. Though this widening of understanding is gained from all good fiction, the contemporary in good magazine fiction has a special savor particularly appreciated by those creatures of the contemporary, the teen-agers in your class.

Sanction fiction not primarily intended for the classroom, but not to the detriment of the other fiction you must treat; it has possibilities, say with weak readers, that classroom reading cannot match. Surrounded by advertising, illustration, and greater informality of format, the magazine story comes to the weak reader with the promise of excitement that the story bound in hard covers, or even in paper, cannot offer. Hence, one of the more important initial roadblocks, apprehension about the reading challenge, is surmounted. The story has a picture, which helps, and captions that present the central situation.

When the weak reader encounters difficult vocabulary, his notebook should have not only the unfamiliar word, but the contextual sentence. Can he guess word meaning from the context? The weak reader will go at magazine fiction with greater confidence than at the hardbound or paperback narrative. This confidence is as important as any measurable reading gains, because you may get none of the latter, but much of the unmeasurable former. Nonetheless, despite the nice pictures and the attractive format, see that the weak reader keeps a notebook of the unfamiliar vocabulary that his magazine fiction reading presents and that this vocabulary is imbedded in the sentence in which found.

Similarly, your bright students should pasture in *Atlantic, Harper's, Partisan Review,* and *New Yorker,* discussing in class what problems and situations their fiction deals with, again because you want to control the reading and because you want them to read with purposefulness.

Finally, magazine fiction can be a spur to class writing of narrative, and not only in your creative writing classes; the style is familiar and up to the minute, a relevant model for many students.

The magazine article is as rich a teaching resource as the narrative, almost too rich to manage unless you have a program in mind. One such is the speech program (p. 324). Whether you assign topics for oral discussion, or students select their own, have them go through *Industrial Arts Index,* or *Reader's Guide to Periodical Literature,* for magazine articles that bear on the topic. The diversity of opinion that they encounter should encourage them to develop their own opinions. The reading of magazine articles should include diverse points of view, and, even before they begin reading the magazine articles, they should know that disagreement is the rule, rather than the exception, and that for every point of view represented in *Reader's Digest, Time,* or *Saturday Evening Post,* they will find a contending point of view in *Saturday Review, The Reporter, The Nation,* or *Bulletin of the Atomic Scientists.*

In this way, the comparison of magazine articles offers an elementary lesson in research techniques and in the locating of resources. Magazine articles repeat themselves; take as an example the magazine with which you should be familiar, *English Journal.* *English Journal* repeats itself roughly every three years, so that you will find articles on *Macbeth,* on functional grammar, on vocabulary spelling, on new ways to teach spelling, and the entire range of English, over and over again, giving enormous overlap from one bound volume to the next. For virtually every article in *English Journal* for the period 1957-60, you will find a matching counterpart for the period 1947-50. Why, then, isn't the 1947-50 set of *English Journal* simply reprinted? It is, in part, but then new considerations emerge, so that a recent article on *Macbeth* is not the same as another published ten years earlier, nor this year's articles on modern poetry the same as earlier articles on the same subject. On the other hand, *English*

Journal cannot escape from the recurrent necessity of publishing articles on *Macbeth* and modern poetry unless it goes out of business. So, over a period of time, articles on the same subject will reappear not only in *English Journal* but in any magazine published. Hence the repetitive typology of the magazine article and its rewarding resources in teaching research techniques.

Against this, we can set the timeliness of the magazine article. Articles on sports, entertainment, fashion, home design, and politics must necessarily be current. Recurrent typology versus current timeliness simultaneously characterize the magazine article, certainly no deterrent to excitement in research.

Just as magazine narrative offers models for classroom narrative writing, so the magazine article offers up to the minute models for descriptive and expository writing. *Popular Mechanics, Sports Illustrated, Holiday,* show how professionals handle description and exposition. No matter what may interest a student, he will find a magazine to enrich that interest and articles to extend it. If he wants not only to describe and explain that interest to others but to explore it for himself, he will find adequate materials in magazines.

This interest may lead to the desire to write for publication. Your school magazine, if you have one, is a good practice arena. People get paid, and sometimes rather well, when they get themselves published.

Research, Resources, and Techniques

1. Helen Thornton's "English for Technical Students" (*E. J.*, Sept. 1955, p. 343) states: "Magazines appeal to the student because they seem adult material, and, as such, provide a link between school and the life outside which he is soon to enter." Unfortunately, the remainder of the article holds the possibilities of vocational and technical students too low. They can be challenged more than this article indicates.

Television and Radio

English Journal and *Scholastic* will help you ahead of time with both radio and TV. What is coming up the coming week that will supplement your work in English? Both offer you logs of the desirable. That's just the beginning.

One way or another we get our vitamins, if not from foods, then by prescription. Similarly, one way or another we must get our dosage of narrative and narrative symbols. Once upon a time we got it from bards; these days, through mass media. We need stories as we need vitamins. Television is the latest device for giving us our daily dosage of narrative, relieving us of the necessity of getting narrative through the written word. Of course, it lacks the taste of the written word just as vitamins lack the savor of food. It affords us the basic minimum essentials, but the pity is that, unlike vitamins, television could offer far richer fare. Meanwhile, how can you use it?

Most English teachers do not take advantage even of the best that television offers. One understands why they do not waste time on the worst, but enough of the useful is available for television programing to be more significant in your teaching, and there is time for you to plan. Not only do *English Journal* and *Scholastic* recommend suitable programs in advance, but so do *Cue* and the Sunday newspapers.

However, some students may not have television in their homes nor access to a set. Your television viewing assignments can therefore be only suggestions, or else you must have ready alternative options to the viewing assignment. Television has not yet reached the stage in American civilization that radio has. Not every home is equipped with it, and you cannot penalize those students who are without it.

But because all students have had experience with movies, either on television or in that old-fashioned place, the movie theatre, you can use the motion picture to sharpen appreciation of television by assessing the contributions of author, actor, director, and producer. For what are these people receiving credits? Consider the function of the camera, as an example, when a character in a television play, or in a movie, walks from the extreme right to the extreme left of the scene. The camera can accompany him ("dollying"); or can follow him, remaining fixed at the extreme right as he walks to the extreme left; or can await him on the extreme left as he approaches it from the extreme right; or can remain in the middle of the scene rotating and keeping the character fixed and in focus as he approaches from the right, passes, and goes on to the left. Do you get the same feeling in all four cases? In the first, the character remains the same size; in the second he diminishes in size as he departs; in the third he increases in size as he approaches; in the fourth he gets larger as he approaches and smaller as he recedes. Do these constancies or alterations in size have an effect on the viewer? If so, what is the effect? Although we have presented some simple cases of camera placement and have omitted matters of camera angle and other resources available to the cameraman, you can demonstrate how the camera alone can affect the emotional values of a scene. Such complexities as camera angles, "dollying-in," "dollying-out," and "panning" can enable a clever director to tell the story virtually by the camera alone.

What is the director's role? A character makes an entrance. Hastily? Slowly? Buoyantly? Dejectedly? The author has presumably specified one or the other in the script, but how many ways are there of entering hastily? What specific way of entering hastily throws further illumination on the character? What way of entering hastily moves the plot forward? Would an old man's haste be the same as a young woman's? Would a young woman in love enter hastily in the same way that a young woman fleeing a loathed suitor would? In how many ways can the hero lean forward to light the heroine's cigarette? In how many ways can she inhale the smoke? In how many ways can he meanwhile look at her, look at his fingertips, or look at the wall? The author cannot set down in his script exactly how an eye is to waver, a mouth to twitch, a hand to point, how much time these are to take, nor can he indicate precisely the pacing and tempo with which the next speech or business is to follow.

But the script is the author's and the basic development is his. He is at the beginning of things, as the actor is at the culmination. We have already indicated that *The Tempest* is difficult to act and magnificent to read, whereas *Twelfth Night* stages magnificently and is difficult to read (p. 213). The same author has not given the player any acting responsibility in the first and has done so amply in the second. Shakespeare seems to have been writing more for the reader in *The Tempest* and more for the audience in *Twelfth Night*. When the audience is kept in mind, the actor has an opportunity to fulfill *his* task. Fine acting is truly an art, although dependent on direction, camera work, and authorship. When the latter three combine effectively, the framework is set for the fine actor to show how powerful a contribution can be made.

Now to the junk. Only Grade C movies can match the depths to which television has sunk in some Westerns, mystery, horror-suspense, and family-situation shows. They are routinized, because they must be. They are vehicles for the sales message—generally for "small ticket" items like cigarettes, cosmetics, or breakfast cereals. Nevertheless, they are worth your attention because the physician learns by dissecting a diseased cadaver and so can you. Be objective as you dissect. Don't call names or invoke artistic values. They are out of place. These are examples of crass commercialism pretending to be nothing else, so deal with them on their own terms.

First, draw attention to the necessity for music. Have your students imagine that exciting ride of the posse without background music. Many students do not realize that music builds tension, as in the silent movie with the pianist banging at the "William Tell Overture." A listening assignment in which they describe a television scene of the posse galloping with music and without, will show how part of the drama never peeps over the rim of consciousness, and how silly the scene would be without music to sugar-coat it. The more sophisticated teen-ager knows this and, after watching *Peter Gunn,* goes out and buys the record of the show's music; this indicates the beginning of ability to dissect and may lead, let's hope, to the maturity of an adult who, having seen the Russian film *Alexander Nevsky,* purchases Prokofieff's adaptation of the sound track or who buys Leonard Bernstein's music for the film *On the Waterfront.*

Have students time the show. How long—to the second!—does the show run? Why is the length of the show governed with meticulous exactness? What would happen if the show went over by eighty or ninety seconds? Why does it *never* run over by that much? What part of the show was compressed, or expanded, because of this? How long do the middle commercials run? How long do the end commercials run? Do the students consider themselves a good audience for the products being advertised? Or is the advertiser wasting money on them?

Turn to plot development. Do they watch the show to see how it will end, in anticipation of the unexpected, or to reassure themselves that it will end as expected? They can identify the good guys and bad guys almost from the beginning; they know the good guys will triumph; so is it an uncertain conclusion that interests them, or is it a foregone conclusion? What would their reactions be next week, if the good guy lost and the bad guy won? Would they accept it? Wouldn't they believe there was a mistake somewhere? Would they write a letter of protest?

Consider character portrayal. Here you cash in shamelessly on the need of television producers to hop aboard a bandwagon. When *I Love Lucy* was popular, family-situation comedies sprang up. Westerns bred more Westerns. *Peter Gunn, 77 Sunset Strip,* and *Hawaiian Eye,* virtually interchangeable, are brewed from *Thin Man,* Mickey Spillane, and *Dragnet,* in indistinguishable recipes. Does this similarity mean that the audience wants the same show or the same characterizations, or that it is hard to be original and easy to pick the brains of a rival producer? How do the faults repeat themselves? The virtues? Do students enjoy these characters because they remind them of people they know, or because—precisely the opposite—they are reminiscent of absolutely and positively nobody they know or are likely to know?

Be specific here. Take a group of three heroes of Westerns, or three heroes of suspense dramas, or three bumbling housewife-heroines and, mentioning names, ask for differentiating qualities of the three in any of the groups, say of the private eyes in *Peter Gunn, 77 Sunset Strip,* and *Markham.* What do we mean by stereotypes? Give them the word and the definition. Ask: Are plot and character as packaged as the sponsor's product? When products are packaged uniformly, must character be packaged as uniformly? Why are characters in Westerns packaged so uniformly? In suspense shows? Does U. S. Steel package its characters as uniformly as Kellogg's Corn Flakes? Does this uniformity of characterization originate in the inability of the writers to think of anything new, or because it's too risky to change the package? What is the effect on the audience to have corn flakes for breakfast, lunch, and supper?

Let's go on to even grimmer matters. Television's top programing comes when you and your students are doing other things. People with active interests will not give attention to television when it is at its best—Sundays. Those rainy or snowy Sundays that keep us at home cannot be counted on to furnish you systematically with materials for classroom use. But do what you can to bring this meritorious Sunday programing to the attention of your students; use these materials in as significant a setting as you can furnish.

Closed-circuit television is another matter, beyond the scope of this book, because the direction taken in your school system is difficult to determine. Remember, though, when well presented, closed-circuit television enlarges your responsibilities and does not relieve you of them.

Radio, like television, provides a certain amount of superior material— panel discussions, documentaries, and lectures. Whet the appetite of your students for these programs. A mere announcement of them will be less useful than a short discussion of the matters they will deal with and the debate involved. Religious matters, political matters, problems of youth, education, sex education, family relations are all available for appropriate class discussion. Set the framework of questions that need answering and then mention some typical radio programs, on FM and AM, that will help in securing answers. In other words, again, be aggressive in plowing up problems for your class to inspect. Radio these days offers a rich menu. Sharpen their appetites for the cuisine.

Most important is radio's musical offering. Folk singing and balladry are reaching deeply into young people's lives. Music publishers of popular songs know that their most important single public is the teen-ager. Bring the top show tunes to your class. Not only has the American musical comedy contributed to world music, but the lyrics of these musical comedies show humor, ingenuity, and understanding of human nature. They are more than gags tied to ditties. They are treated with respect by critics like Brooks Atkinson and Louis Kronenberger and well merit class discussion. Don't apologize for "Come to Me, Bend to Me" from *Brigadoon,* "Eldorado" from *Candide,* or "A Puzzlement" from *The King and I.* Musical comedy has traditions and patterns that are worth studying. The pattern is seen in Gilbert and Sullivan and Rodgers and Hammerstein.

Note the similarity in themes in:

(1) "The Bum Won" (*Fiorello!*), "Fugue for Tinhorns" (*Guys and Dolls*), "I Am So Proud" (*The Mikado*).

(2) "I'm Not at All in Love" (*Pajama Game*), "Many a New Day" (*Oklahoma*), and "Were I Thy Bride" (*The Yeomen of the Guard*).

(3) "Another Op'nin', Another Show" (*Kiss Me, Kate*) and "There's No Business Like Show Business" (*Annie Get Your Gun*).

(4) "Eldorado" (*Candide*), "Glocca Morra" (*Finian's Rainbow*), "Bali Ha'i" (*South Pacific*), "Brigadoon" (*Brigadoon*).

(5) "Adelaide's Lament" (*Guys and Dolls*), "I Cain't Say No" (*Oklahoma*), "In Vain to Us You Plead" (*Iolanthe*).

(6) "Think of the Time I Save" (*Pajama Game*), "Tomorrow Morning" (*Destry Rides Again*).

(7) "Name Dropping" (*Bells Are Ringing*), "Ascot Gavotte" (*My Fair Lady*), "Spurn Not the Nobly Born" (*Iolanthe*).

(8) "Jubilation T. Cornpone" (*Li'l Abner*), "My Mother's Wedding Day" (*Brigadoon*), "After Sailing to This Island" (*The Gondoliers*).

(9) "Wouldn't It Be Loverly?" (*My Fair Lady*), "Something's Coming" (*West Side Story*), "Braid the Raven Hair" (*The Mikado*).

(10) "Show Me" (*My Fair Lady*), "Marie's Law" (*Fiorello!*), "On the Day When I Was Wedded" (*The Gondoliers*).

In tracing the genealogy of musical-comedy ideas, you give depth to the theater. Lerner and Loewe borrowed from the English musical comedy stage in "With a Little Bit of Luck" (*My Fair Lady*) and went back to

"Tell Me, Pretty Maiden" from the American *Floradora* for their "Wouldn't It Be Loverly?" It doesn't hurt our feeling for Shakespeare to realize that Falstaff, Dogberry, and Sir Toby Belch are very much alike as characters, and that they in turn have a common ancestry in Rabelais' Gargantua. Radio makes these theater experiences available to your students.

Ask: How do songs get written? Is it better to write the words first, and then the music, or the music first, and then the words? Which came first in "America" (*West Side Story*)? What about a song in which the rhythmic beat is less marked, as in "Pore Jud Is Daid" (*Oklahoma*)? How does a song writer get his ideas? Note how simple phrases furnish the start for very effective songs, phrases which students use unthinkingly but which give the song writer his start: "Just You Wait" (*My Fair Lady*), "What's the Use?" (*Candide*).

Research, Resources, and Techniques

1. An editorial on educational television, "Have Magic Screen, Will Travel" (*Science,* March 29, 1957), indicates that some science programs do not serve a teaching purpose. The Bell Telephone films *Our Mr. Sun* and *Hemo the Magnificent* are especially singled out.

2. "Adapting Literary Materials to Television: Part II," edited by Louis Forsdale (*E. J.,* Jan. 1956, p. 18), considers television technique in writing, acting, directing, and camera work.

3. Patrick D. Hazard's "Behind the Tinsel Curtain" (*E. J.,* March 1956, p. 134) offers practical suggestions on teaching appreciation of television. In addition to some good ideas for classroom work, there is a brief note on teaching understanding of the teen-ager's purposes in reading comic books.

4. Frank and Audrey Hodgins' "Teaching Guide for *Richard III*" (*E. J.,* March 1956, p. 138) helps you prepare students to watch a television production. You can, on a less ambitious scale, teach more aware televiewing by using the approach in this article, which, briefly, shows them what to watch for.

5. Hidden among the recommendations of James J. Brunstein's "Ten Uses for Commercial Television in the English Classroom" (*E. J.,* Dec. 1958, p. 566) is a valuable idea: television offers a common experience to strong and weak students; here both groups share.

6. For a comparison of varying points of view on the uses of television, read Milton A. Kaplan, "Television Drama: A Discussion" (*E. J.,* Dec. 1958, p. 549).

7. For administrative considerations, read *The Superintendent's View-*

point on Educational Television, Region 1 Conference of the NAEB. Thomas Alva Edison Foundation, New York, 1959.

8. C. S. Steinberg's *The Mass Communicators* (Harper and Brothers, 1958) gives you one reason why television is so much more popular among your students than reading: "TV has given the illusion of direct contact, of man speaking to man" (p. 8). How can you impart this illusion to reading and to all the other aspects of the English curriculum?

9. Miriam Goldstein's "Humanities through Television" (*E. J.,* April 1960, p. 250) shows that television teaching is no stronger than the age-old problems it presents. If so, why use television to present these problems? Or is the average English teacher too incapable of presenting these problems in the absence of technological aids?

10. Think about this quotation from *Teaching by Television* (Office of Reports, Ford Foundation, 477 Madison Avenue, New York 22): "Television is not a panacea that will cure all the ills of American education or solve all its problems. It has been described, and rightly so, as the most important new educational tool since the invention of movable type, but like the textbook the new medium is essentially just that—a tool. Like any tool, it can be misused or badly used. But if it is wisely and imaginatively used, television can play a major role in broadening and enriching the education of American students at all levels of schooling." Therefore, we still need wisdom and imagination, two very scarce commodities to come by, even among teachers.

11. How the commercial media can be used in teaching is illustrated in *English Journal* (Oct. 1958, p. 520), where the well known *Father Knows Best* series is brought into the classroom.

12. Does this strike you as a contradiction? *The Educator's Guide to Free Tapes, Scripts, and Transcriptions,* by Walter A. Wittich and Gertie Hanson Halsted, published by the Educators Progress Service, Randolph, Wisconsin, costs $5.75.

Films

Time was when the legitimate theater produced hundreds of plays annually on Broadway, and touring companies ranged the provinces. Although Ibsen, Shaw, Hauptmann, and Strindberg were contemporaries of the late nineteenth- and early twentieth-century flowering of theater, they were more than outnumbered by the Bronson Howards and Samuel Shipmans, so that most plays did not deserve to survive and didn't.

The theater was not killed by choking on its own mediocrity. Indeed, the theater never quite died. Instead, it was replaced by the silent movie with its own storehouse of mediocrity, in which lurked an occasional Réné

Clair, G. W. Pabst, Eric von Stroheim, and Charlie Chaplin. The silent movie too could have gone on forever, not at all the worse for its banality and bad taste, had the sound film not replaced it and continued the tradition of making money with stupidity. The sound film could have gone on eternally, unchanged, had not television taken its place, with television's own kind of mediocrity, stupidity, banality, and bad taste, always excepting the occasional John Ford, Sergei Eisenstein, John Huston in sound film, and the Paddy Chayefskys and John Frankenheimers in television. While the machinery of mediocrity grinds out its potboilers, sparks sometimes fly off and the sparks prove more enduring than the potboilers.

Your job requires encouraging the sparks and destroying the potboilers, but your teen-agers remain the chief group that continues, with unabated interest, to patronize the movies. Adolescents always were their one best audience, and they continue to be—and not always for the best movies, as *I Was a Teen-Age Frankenstein* proves.

In our discussion of television (p. 299) we spoke of the roles of the cameraman, the director, the author, and the actor. This analysis is also appropriate to your teaching of film appreciation.

Most high schools have sound-film equipment that you can set up in your classroom and a central film repository that you can use. Know the film well before you present it to the class, because you can then plan in advance when to stop the film for discussion of the fine points of acting, writing, direction, or camera work that call for special attention, and of such matters of technique as continuity, graphic values, background, and setting.

Be sure that shades are in working order so that outside illumination can be effectively shut out. Unfortunately, on fine early autumn or late spring days, the result is a stuffy classroom; fine weather is not conducive to an agreeable audience. Schedule your film showings, therefore, for late autumn, winter, or early spring. The worse the weather, the better the reception your film will get!

Also, the better the film, the more battered with use. Check with your repository to see if two superb documentaries, Pare Lorentz' *The River* and *The Plough That Broke the Plains* were ever available, and if so, whether they are still in condition to use. Possibly not, as may well be the case with two useful films, both starring the late Ronald Colman, *Arrowsmith* and *Tale of Two Cities*. Though more than a generation old, these films are still compelling because a good film does not age. Huston's *Treasure of Sierra Madre,* if you can get it, will thrill your audience as it did the original audiences.

Your school may have an audio-visual squad, responsible for setting up the projector and threading it, but learn to use the equipment yourself. It frees you from the schedule bookkeeping that so often inhibits teachers from more liberal use of film resources.

The film is threaded, the shades are down, and you are ready to throw the switch. Lights, camera, action? Not yet. Tell the class briefly what the film is about, what is particularly interesting in it, what they are to look for. Start the film and run it. Do not hesitate, when good judgment advises, to stop the film and discuss material that deserves emphasis. Students may fume because you are interrupting the show, but it's more than a show that they're there for. Let them fume until you make your point. You want them to get a sense of the depth and planning that goes into the good film.

For that reason, too, the good film deserves discussion and analysis after the showing. Prepare yourself for this discussion as fully as you would for any other lesson. Do not depend on the entertainment value of the good film to spare you the necessity of preparation and thought.

Perhaps the chief point in teaching the film is that you elucidate the effort and planning a good film requires. The good film reflects a high state of technology and of artistry. The good film is viewed without pain because of the pains that went into it. The good film is a complex endeavor. The more knowledgeable your students are of these complexities, the more enjoyment will they derive from the good film.

The use of a "shooting script" will make this complexity somewhat clearer. The shooting script spells out how scenes are to be acted and indicates in detail camera placement, lens focus, expressions, gestures, and flow of motion. The shooting script is the raw material, on paper, that is translated into the film we see.

In teaching appreciation of the film, depending on the film of course, be mindful of such specifics as:

1. Setting and lighting.
2. Placement of the cast in a scene.
3. Use of mood music and sound effects.
4. Gestures and business.
5. Continuity of scenes.

6. Use and manipulation of cameras.

7. Quality of writing. How much of the film is attributable to the author?

8. Pace and tempo. How much of this is attributable to the director?

The rapid slide of the movies since the advent of television has diminished their sociological force, except in the case of teen-agers. What is this sociological importance?

Ask your students how often they attend movies. Then ask whether they are affected more in group behavior or in individual behavior by what they have seen. Have movies had any effect, or no effect, on them and on their friends? When they leave the movies feeling excited, and they meet people who have not come from the movies and are not excited, does the heightened feeling in them make it easier for them to get along with these people, or more difficult, or isn't there any difference? Do movies make them more discontented with life, or more contented? Are they more satisfied with what they have, or less satisfied, after they've left a particular movie? Does it depend on the particular movie, and if so, how? Why do their systems seem to need the shock of a horror movie? How do movies help organize their lives? Disorganize them? Is it better to go to the movies after you've taken care of your responsibilities, or before, to take your mind off your troubles? Has what they've seen in movies made them more able to deal with other people, or less able? Such questions individuate sociology.

Other questions illuminate esthetics. Which is more difficult to produce, the realistic movie with documentary qualities, or the romantic movie in which imaginativeness is exercised? Is *Marty* more difficult to write and direct than *Gigi*? What is the truest movie they have ever seen? What is the saddest? What is the funniest?

Some years ago I undertook an experiment which indicated that we are more affected than we realize by the movies we see and the books we read. I asked a group of 285 high school students to write compositions on:

(1) The Best Movie I Ever Saw
(2) The Worst Movie I Ever Saw
(3) The Best Book I Ever Read
(4) The Worst Book I Ever Read

Half the group wrote compositions on (1) and (2), and the other half wrote on (3) and (4). For both groups, I measured the number of words written in approval and in disapproval and also measured the frequency of occurrence of self-reference words (I, me, my, mine), negative words and affixes (no, not, never, neither, nobody, none, dis-, in-, de-), the impersonal pronoun *it,* the copula *was,* prepositional phrases, the conjunctions *and* and *but.* I found:

(1) more is written in approval than in disapproval;
(2) self-reference words increase in disapproval;
(3) negative words increase in disapproval;
(4) the impersonal pronoun *it* increases in disapproval;
(5) the copula *was* increases in disapproval;
(6) prepositional phrases decrease in disapproval;
(7) the conjunction *and* decreases in disapproval;
(8) the conjunction *but* increases in disapproval.

These results showed that language habits are causally ordered. Tracing these causes is baffling but the world of words is as rational a world, as subject to cause and effect relationships, as is the world of chemistry and physics. Language structure is changed by differences in emotional situations. The war cry, the talk of lovers, and the oratory of the politician variously affect the structure of discourse. Even when the speaker is most conscious of his audience and the need to establish communication with it, this awareness does not extend to the frequency of prepositional phrases, conjunctions, copulas, negatives, or impersonal and demonstrative pronouns. Students in this experiment were certainly unaware that such shifts were occurring in their patterns of discourse.

The movies we see affect us, whether we know it consciously or not. Your students see the movies they need to see. Why do they need to jitter and quiver in a horror movie? Do sexy movies tranquilize them or torment them further? Ask: Why torture and torment yourself? Is it fun to run a fever that dislocates everything else in you? Is it fun to seek to be out of control?

Movie makers have been called "dream merchants" and movie studios factories of fantasy. The dreams and fantasies they manufacture must be powerful indeed to cause the annual expenditure of hundreds of millions of dollars, the group aberration of fan clubs, and the individual compulsion of the fan letter. Are any of your students involved? What's the conversation like when they discuss some idol? Has any friend (not they, of course!) written a fan letter? What was in it and why was it written? Would they rather more people wrote fan letters to the star that day, or would they prefer their letter to be the only one the star received that day? Are there some people to whom they would show the fan letter and others to whom they would not? Are the people who write fan letters the same as people who do not?

Films, more and more, are dealing with crucial political problems of our time and can be used in class discussion. *On the Beach* is one such effort, on which Joseph Turner commented editorially in *Science:* "These ideas are powerful and the viewer is much affected, yet he leaves the theater with the feeling that he has been moved more by what he has brought to the film than by what the performance itself accomplished." [7] This interesting point can be considered by your class in connection with many controversial films. Are we affected by a prior something in us, or by what the film by itself does to us? And, in fact, this consideration applies to fiction and poetry.

The film as art and the experimental film can be truly challenging experiences, with a range from *Moonbird,* to the Mr. Magoo cartoons, from Jean Cocteau's *Blood of a Poet,* to the Ingmar Bergman *Seventh Seal* and *The Magician,* to the Mike Todd *Around the World in Eighty Days,* and the old but still contemporary Serlin, Steiner, and Van Dyke *The City.* If your school is within convenient reach of a large urban area, you can learn when and where such films can be seen under noncommercial auspices. Art museums, bookstores, colleges and universities will be the more likely clearing houses for this information. Thus in the New York City area, the Museum of Modern Art, the New York University library, Teachers College, and the YMCA are useful.

Research, Resources, and Techniques

1. Richard Braddock's "Films for Teaching Mass Communication" (*E. J.*, March 1955, p. 156) samples the films on publishing (newspapers and magazines) and production (movies). Note that this information runs only to March 1955, but the techniques haven't changed much since, so that the article is adequately contemporary.

2. Let's not forget that old standby, the H. W. Wilson Company's *Educational Film Guide,* chief source for the educational film.

3. George Bluestone's *Novels into Film* (The Johns Hopkins Press, 1957) indirectly shows how the English teacher and the script writer share many problems. The adaptation of fiction to film (or videotape) parallels the analysis and teaching of fiction in the classroom. Read the

book; your interpretations of narrative may be helped by the difficulties faced and surmounted by the script writer.

4. Is realism more creatively challenging than fancy? Was Falstaff more difficult for Shakespeare to sculpture than Prospero? Was Shaw's Alfred Doolittle more complex a literary creation than Jack Tanner? Here is Shaw's opinion: "The comparison between Falstaff and Prospero is like the comparison between Micawber and David Copperfield. At the end of the book you know Micawber, whereas you only know what has happened to David, and are not interested enough in him to wonder what his politics or religion might be if anything so stupendous as a religious or political idea, or a general idea of any sort, were to occur to him. He is tolerable as a child; but he never becomes a man and might be left out of his own biography altogether . . ." (from the Epistle Dedicatory to *Man and Superman,* Penguin Books, p. xxxi). Therefore, what is literary truth? What is the truest movie scene your students have ever seen? What is the saddest? What is the funniest?

The Paperbacks

Earlier we suggested that this chapter be read only by those teachers who work in an educated community with courageous administrators. Those employed in Mississippi, Alabama, Georgia, San Jose, California, or Miami, Florida (see *The New York Times,* June 26, 1960, E7) will have to work through the English Teachers' Underground, surreptitiously. In school districts where Salinger's *Catcher in the Rye,* Hemingway's *The Sun Also Rises,* Wolfe's *Look Homeward, Angel,* Saroyan's *Human Comedy,* and Huxley's *Brave New World* are removed from reading lists by prurient parents and timid administrators, you, like all missionaries, must do the Lord's work for conscience' sake without risking your job. Go underground; in some school districts the best teachers are there.

Periodically, have these books with you. Discuss them without recommending them. Allude to them as exciting, outstanding, important, without urging students to buy them. Say how important it is for you, an English teacher, to keep in touch with significant literature that illuminates people and situations. Tell them that you cannot accept these titles in book reports because they are on the local Index, but that these books are widely known and widely sold—in inexpensive editions readily available. By such means, even if you teach in Mississippi, you can tell students about Faulkner, who comes from there, Eudora Welty, Tennessee Williams, Steinbeck, Camus, or Hemingway.

If not in so delicate a situation, paperbacks extend your resources. But approach them with discretion. Too frequently good things come in lurid covers, and you will regretfully be compelled to back away. You are in a strong position, far stronger than you may suspect, to ask publishers to do a responsible job of jacketing. You should not hesitate to write that you cannot, unfortunately, use a particular title, much as you'd like to, because of the bad taste it comes wrapped in. Paperback publishers are becoming wiser. There is less tendency to distort the contents of a good book with a completely irrelevant dishabille.

Paperbacks emerge when they are still timely. Publishers seek promotional tie-ins with movie versions and television adaptations, while the titles are conversation. Furthermore, because of the contemporaneity of the format, even the classics seem fresher in paperback. You can recommend titles in paperback that would seem formidable to students in hard covers: *Great Expectations, Return of the Native, Mill on the Floss, Lord Jim, Man and Superman,* modern and classic short stories, the great essays, the finest poetry, are informal and more palatable. They can be slipped into the pocket or pocketbook, read on the bus, on the beach, underlined, used hard, passed on, or accumulated for an attractive, inexpensive library.

For these and certain other reasons paperbacks have cut into the magazine business. The reader sometimes wants a more prolonged experience with the material he reads. He wants to live with it for a while. He doesn't want to be distracted by contiguous advertising, contradictory though this seems to earlier comments in this chapter on newspaper reading (p. 287). For serious reading, nothing substitutes for a book. The paperback allows a student to sip the Pierian spring without that deep drink better saved for his college years or for later maturity. Magazines do not have the same seriousness about them. They do not offer the opportunity to become immersed in a unitary experience for a period of time. Their editorial policies and their self-image do not permit them the range of type and style that books afford.

Although paperbacks are easily accessible, a reading program based on them should not be loose. Do you limit student reading by organizing it? Your outside reading program is a program; it is programmatic; it is not haphazard. You want to know what your students are reading, and you want them to state their reactions to what they are reading. We have already discussed the qualities of a desirable reading program (p. 133). To these should be added the classroom paperback library, based on the "swap" or exchange of books among students. Encourage it on the basis of full-dress book reports or more informal reading reports. Appoint a class librarian who will supervise the bookkeeping involved. Make your personal paperback library available for classroom circulation. It means something extra for a student to read a book that *you* have read and that *you* own.

If you are on the mailing list of paperback publishers, post this promotional material on your bulletin board. Point out that the publishers have timed the release of certain titles to coincide with release dates of films based on the books, or on other events of public interest.

Capitalize on the timeliness of the paperback by relating news events to stories that are timeless. A girl can break up a romance for reasons as diverse as Becky Sharp's or Maggie Tulliver's. Fast-talking crooks in the police court are described at greater length in the Mr. Jingle of *Pickwick Papers*. Throw ideas, problems, and news events at your students. After you've done so, tell them of the books that treat of these matters with far greater richness, all available at convenient drug-store, stationery-store, or bookstore counters. This, of course, is an aspect of the "keynote" notion presented in the section on outside reading (p. 133).

The use of paperbacks in the schools has been studied with depressing results by M. Jerome Weiss for the National Council of Teachers of English. Teachers seem ignorant of the multiplying resources of paperbacks and comparatively few plan for use of paperbacks in their teaching. The paperback is an inexpensive means of stretching the school's budgetary dollar, but administrators, like teachers, show a woeful ignorance of how paperbacks can be an excellent adjunct to the school's teaching materials.

Research, Resources, and Techniques

1. Two articles by David Zamchick have appeared in *English Journal* on this topic:
a. "Problems in Paperback Publishing" (Dec. 1958, p. 483) deals with certain profit-and-loss aspects of paperback publishing and reasons for the disappearance of the lurid cover.
b. "Paperback Buying Patterns" (May 1960, p. 336) discusses relationships between intelligence, sex, and paperback purchases, as well as the teacher's function in encouraging suitable purchases.

2. Robert Shostak's "Meet Me at the Fair" (*E. J.*, Feb. 1959, p. 83) describes a Paperback Book Fair held under school auspices.

3. To reduce the complications in shopping for paperback titles for a class at a time, get in touch with *Scholastic,* sponsor of Reader's Choice, 33 West 42 Street, New York 36, N.Y., a buying service for teachers seeking to expand paperback use.

Business Background to the Mass Media

Because of the materials that flood from the newspapers, magazines, radio, television, films, and paperbacks, your students can rapidly develop a great big open ear and open mouth, too agape as audience to be active as responders. They must defend themselves against inundation and learn to formulate their reactions and express them. In one sense, this is fighting back against the mass communicators, but in a larger sense it maintains the integrity of their own individual personalities.

Nobody has sensed this more clearly than William H. Whyte, Jr., who, with the editors of *Fortune,* wrote *Is Anybody Listening?* [8] Every teacher of English should step forward and be one of the Anybodys listening to Whyte. The book is a battle cry to a heightened democracy in action, to a stronger citizenry, to Americans who assess the mass media besieging them and act on that assessment.

Business leaders concerned with secretaries who can't spell and with Americanism, democracy, and responsible citizenship on the job and in the community haven't analyzed what they want. What constitutes Americanism? Is it the pledge to the flag at assembly? Is it the belief in a two-party system? Is it the belief in free enterprise? Or is it a sense of glory you find in Walt Whitman?

At what critical point does profit-seeking become corner-cutting? If for every plaintiff you have a defendant, and if for every plaintiff's interpretation of the Constitution there is a defendant's interpretation, do you not in effect have two Constitutions, one espoused by the plaintiff and the other by the defendant, and reflected in majority and minority opinions of the Supreme Court, going back to Hamilton and Jefferson, strict construction versus loose construction, States' rights versus centralism, engendered by litigation which is in turn engendered by self-interest?

When your students talk about defending the Constitution, ask them which one they are talking about, to evoke a keener willingness to abide by the law, whatever the interpretation. If you want your kind of interpreter in office, how do you determine your kind of interpreter? How can you trust a candidate's promises? How can you assure faithfulness to promises?

When citizens ignore what they read in the newspapers, and vote for a Roosevelt or a Truman, or ignore their leaders, as when union members vote Republican, what is the voter suspecting in newspapers or in union leadership? Are your students' duties as citizens discharged when they vote only once a year? In what sense should they be voting throughout the year? Is this too fatiguing when citizens have matters of their own to be attentive to? Or does this attentiveness to year-round public politics make citizens more effectively attentive as well to their own private concerns?

Is listening to people the same as asking questions? The pollsters ask questions and thereby surreptitiously bury issues, choices, and alternatives. In asking: how will you vote? what will you buy? do you like this kind of package? what is your preference as to Brand A versus Brand B? polls often go wrong because questions have been prematurely put before enough listening has been done. The Edsel car and the 1948 elections are possible examples of questions unwisely substituting for listening.

The mass media depend on mass audience reaction. This reaction can be predicted within fairly sharp limits, so that we know rather well how many people will tune in their television sets on Monday nights, as compared with Sunday nights, as compared with Friday mornings, and how many copies of *The New York Times* will be sold on Monday as compared with Friday, or the ratio of newsstand circulation to subscriptions for *Life* as compared with *Look* as compared with *Saturday Evening Post,* and the relation of Brand X advertising appropriations with Brand X sales. We would not have the mass media without mass response. Response, however, is not self-expression, and when predictable response becomes infused by the unpredictables of self-expression, we again have the Edsel car and the 1948 elections.

To use the mass media in your classroom without having concurrent channels for self-expression nourishes passivity, and worse, the most damaging consequences that a free citizenry can suffer; the mass media can become the modern counterpart of bread and circuses unless you accompany their use with assessments, appraisals, compositions, reports, and class talks. Your students must get a *participating sense,* else fancy talk about communication (chiefly from the top down) is mass persuasion and mass propaganda, with clods as outcome, made literate to consume more acceptingly and to follow somebody's orders more efficiently.

Americans are given more channels to express themselves than they take advantage of. Approximately half of the eligible population votes. Even fewer participate in primaries. Still fewer ever take pen in hand to write to their legislative or Congressional representatives. Psychologically, this is defeating for the social, economic, and political leaders of America, and expresses itself in contempt for the mass mind and in the rewards in making money. Money itself fails to satisfy and we get the spectacle of Harrimans, Rockefellers, and Kennedys turning to politics in an effort to get into the game.

In this game, your students will for years be on the sidelines, as law clerks, medical internes, soda jerkers, department-store clerks, typists, or college undergraduates. What can make the game as much fun for them as for the participants? First, they must feel part of it and not divorced from it. Next, your students must sense the presence of a team, social, economic, political, or moral, on one side or the other of the fence, which they can cheer. Which team do they look forward to joining? It's not their present team, the team of teen-agers they know now. The team will be new, the members of which they haven't met yet and cannot avoid meeting any more than they can avoid growing up. If they cannot avoid growing up, if they cannot avoid being five years older five years from now, and cannot avoid the duties and responsibilities they will face then, what groups or teams will be of most help in facing these duties and responsibilities? What are the "farm teams"—the baseball term for minor league teams that prepare and train immature players for major league baseball—that they can join now if they are future teachers, physicians, lawyers, auto mechanics, factory hands, or housewives?

The most important farm team is the English classroom. The English classroom should deal with popular ideas and complex ones, with fatuous ones and inspired ones; remember that simplicity is not attained by short words and sentences; simplicity is a complex thing.

Thus, if an employer wants to use the house journal to encourage loyalty among his employees, exhortation and sweet reasonableness, however simply stated, will not be enough unless provision is made for the employee to express himself without penalty. If he cannot do so in the employer's house journal, he will in mimeographed handbills circulated outside the factory gates or in the columns of the union's newspaper. The readable is not necessarily the believable. If you gain credulity without understanding, and adherence without awareness, you approach the totalitarian.

How do your students gain belief, understanding, and awareness? By becoming truly involved in democratic processes. The mass media are not incompatible with quality and humanity. More willing to learn Shakespeare than they know, and more interested in spelling, punctuation, and grammar than too many English teachers will grant, students cannot be taught house-journal Shakespeare, or house-journal spelling, punctuation, and grammar, whether in the classroom or by closed-circuit educational television.

Will quality and humanity emerge if you ask: "You are given your choice between the Lone Ranger's horse Silver, or a new convertible. For what reasons would you choose one or the other? Which would the junior high school student be more likely to choose? Which would the high school senior choose?"

Or: "You win a television prize and are offered a choice of a trip to Europe or a new car. Which reasons would govern your choice?"

Answers will be more original than you are prepared to hear, even though the questions are based on the crassest stereotypes of the mass media.

The mass media in your classroom indicate that you are not afraid to let the outside in. When your bulletin board has cartoons from *New Yorker* and television schedules of important viewing dates from your local newspaper, when you have taped current book jackets and *Saturday Evening Post* covers and theater programs all over your classroom walls, when you are regularly scheduled for film showings with your colleague in charge of audio-visual—and he is grateful because you are building up his volume of activity—when your students are swapping paperbacks and you are accepting book reports on the proper ones, then you have set the stage for students not passive in face of the powerful top-down pattern of communication in today's society, but for students and citizens who are prepared for two-way communication.

Another kind of group organization, your classroom, will reflect you. Will it be pyramidal, with you at the apex, or will it be circular, so that students can feel themselves as effective personally as their fellows? Though the group organized like a pyramid is more efficient, the circle is more satisfying and morale building. Do you want task efficiency or morale effectiveness? In the long run, where diverse tasks are undertaken—as in your classroom—the pyramid's efficiency breaks down. Be democratic; encourage two-way communication; it works best not only for examination purposes at the end of the term, but also in the gratitude students will feel for you after the term is over. They will be better prepared for life.

Research, Resources, and Techniques

1. "The Anti-Scientific Attitude," by Bernard and Judith Mausner, in *Scientific American* (Feb. 1955, p. 35) deals with the interaction between science and public relations. Fluoridation of town water in Northampton, Massachusetts, involved community relations, public relations, attitudes toward science, the mass media, and small-town thinking.

2. Muzafer Sherif's "Experiments in Group Conflict" (*Scientific American*, Nov. 1956, p. 54) describes how group friction in a boy's summer camp was experimentally synthesized and how the variables of group co-operation and competition were manipulated. Has direct bearing on your classroom management.

3. Hans Gottschalk says in "English Augmented: Diversity or Depth?" (*New York State Education*, Dec. 1959): "A characteristic offshoot of accelerated specialization lies in the already astounding augmentation of our general vocabularies and in the proliferation of many new 'dialects' or specialized vocabularies. The latter already outgrow the ability of English teachers to master them." Do you think it necessary for the English teacher to master these new vocabularies? If you do, how can the mass media help?

4. Everett C. Smith, in "Industry Views the Teaching of English" (*E. J.*, March 1956, p. 122), tells why industry is trying to break into your jail and why it is trying to communicate with you and your students, to free you of the imprisonment of time and place, discussed in Chap. 1.

5. You will find a general discussion in *Using Mass Media in Teaching English* (Bureau of Secondary Curriculum Development, New York State Education Department, Albany, 1960).

6. Eckhard H. Hess and James M. Polt's "Pupil Size as Related to Interest Value of Visual Stimuli" (*Science*, Aug. 5, 1960, p. 349) illustrates the amazing inquiries made by advertising agencies. This experiment, inspired by a well-known advertising agency, deals with changes in eye-pupil size; psychologists and physiologists know that the pupil dilates with increase of interest. Thus the pupil of the eye of a cat will enlarge when it smells food, the pupil in a man will when seeing the photograph of a partially disrobed human female, and the pupil of a woman when seeing the photograph of a partially disrobed man. The authors of the article say that neither in man nor in woman is enlargement as great with the photograph of a member of the same sex.

With this information the advertising agency measures pupil dilation in a woman shopper in a supermarket, without the customer's knowledge.

As the shopper goes up and down the aisles, her eye is now and then caught by attractive packaging. Which packages are more attractive, on the evidence of pupil enlargement? Which less? On this information, the agencies attempt to improve packaging of their products.

Is this intrusive? Do you think class discussion on this would be related to the opinion-molding carried on by the mass media? What do your students think?

7. From an editorial in *Science* (Nov. 18, 1960): "One need watch television only briefly to learn that scientific instruments, phrases, and symbols are being used—and misused—to promote a wide variety of products. If the listener reacts as the advertiser wishes, he smokes the cigarette chosen by 'more scientists and educators' than any other brand, dresses his hair with the preparation that does not evaporate in a solar heater, shaves with the blade that 'engineers' call a 'scientific break-through,' and then, for he probably needs it, takes the pill recommended by 'three out of four doctors'. . . . For scientists [this din of pseudo-scientific chatter] has two meanings: (1) science is a useful sales gimmick, now apparently on a par with endorsement by a pretty girl; and (2) the public, including children, is given a false and misleading impression of . . . scientific work. . . . What can be done? . . . We can protest and we can ridicule."

Interpretation: show your students how to make pleasure and displeasure felt in the offices of the mass media.

8. In the same way that William Whyte's description of communication patterns in American business, American group relations, and American leadership coincides with communication patterns in your English classes (*Is Anybody Listening?* [Simon and Schuster, 1952]), so J. A. C. Brown's *The Social Psychology of Industry* (Penguin, 1954) shows how industrial communication has been successful and how you can use these patterns of successful communication in the classroom.

CHAPTER 10

Speech

Demosthenes Is on the Telephone

Students don't always want to come to the front of the class to speak to others; they want very much to sit at their seats and talk their heads off, and they can do so all day long. Why are they so relaxed and easy at their seats, and trembling for their lives when in front of the room? Any teacher knows that people are unwilling to express themselves, especially in classrooms. The easiest and most relaxed experiences of the curriculum in English become the stiffest and most artificial.

Consider telephone conversations. Lessons on the use of the telephone seem an insult to the normal intelligence—illiterates use the telephone—but call students up front to illustrate the materials that your local telephone company has developed for classroom use and you will see embarrassment, terror, and other states of mind that sanction any device which gives students exercise in the hazards of public appearance.

On the other hand, according to Plutarch, Demosthenes himself might have had trouble talking over the telephone. Demosthenes had an urgent personal need to speak effectively, to protect himself; his inheritance had been squandered by executors of the estate. "Demosthenes, who, first venturing upon oratory for the recovery of his own private property, by this acquired ability in speaking. . . ." [1] Similarly, for students to speak effectively is of considerable personal importance. Students agree. They want to be in command of their powers of expression, but they anticipate trouble.

They must do as Demosthenes did. They must practice in private, away from prying eyes. Plutarch describes Demosthenes' privacy: "Hereupon he built himself a place to study in under ground . . . and hither he would come constantly every day to form his action and to exercise his voice: and here he would continue, oftentimes without intermission, two or three months together, shaving one half of his head that so for shame he might not go abroad, though he desired it ever so much." [2] Pushing privacy thus far is unnecessary, but public effectiveness is best gained by private practice. "In his house he had a large looking glass, before which he would stand and go through his exercises," [3] with nobody looking on.

This private practice must have the physical accompaniments of gesture, tone, and inflection. "It is told that some one once came to request his assistance as a pleader, and related how he had been assaulted and beaten. 'Certainly,' said Demosthenes, 'nothing of the kind can have happened to you.' Upon which the other, raising his voice, exclaimed loudly, 'What, Demosthenes, nothing has been done to me?' 'Ah,' replied Demosthenes, 'now I hear the voice of one that has been injured and beaten.' Of so great consequence toward the gaining of belief did he esteem the tone and action of the speaker." [4]

If Demosthenes had so much trouble learning to speak effectively, have patience with your students. Plutarch's description is a useful guide. Demosthenes was driven to speech work by financial desperation. You can similarly goad your students to speech work, not by financial desperation, but by deprivation in some other area. Remembering their reluctance to speak in public, you must determine the things on which they feel strongly, the areas of controversy without answers. Can a wrestler beat a boxer? Are the better teams in the American League or the National League? Is a vacation at the seashore better than a vacation in the mountains? Is Belafonte better than Presley? Should a girl's education concentrate on marriage or on a career? Is co-operation or competition the best way of handling Russia? Should one try to dress neatly or comfortably? Is eighteen too young to vote? Who needs group approval more, the teen-ager or the adult?

Abstain from furnishing answers. Direct students to sources and resources which offer the raw material for answers, but be wary of furnishing answers yourself.

Speech work is most interesting to speaker and audience when it attempts to persuade. Earlier, in discussing oral book reports, we mentioned the augmentation of interest when students attempt to persuade, or dissuade, others to read, or from reading (p. 144). All speech work should have this quality. This, in turn, requires that the audience be on its guard.

Discussion can be formless, wrecking possibilities of debate, unless preparation, that private matter of materials, gesture, tone, and inflection, reduces the risks of embarrassment. The student must protect himself against the faces and grimaces, the sly attempts to get him to laugh and lose control of himself, by memorizing his outline, his gestures, and his voice inflection, before coming before the class.

Sanction the use of the mirror at home, the bathroom or bedroom mirror, with door closed, not as encouragement to narcissism, but as an exercise, without anybody around, in persuading the group. Let your class practice looking at the mirror at home, door closed, with the full knowledge that this is the face, these are the gestures, these are the expressions and intonations of voice that the class will see; your students will be giving their powers of fantasy control, exercise, and direction. Fantasy aiming at actuality is your intention and theirs.

Show them the little details that may never have occurred to them, that gesture, like voice, has intonation. The old-fashioned books on declamation illustrated the varieties of gesture available to the public speaker, like high, low, and middle plane gestures, or front, oblique, and lateral plane gestures, and the hand forms divided into supine, prone, index, clenched, and vertical.[5] We tend to sneer at such cataloguing these days, but your student will be more respectful when you show how they can be related to the quality of voice, to Indian sign language, to the hand-talk of aviators as they describe flight patterns, and to ethnic differences in gesture as described by Efron.[6] Hitler latched one thumb over a gun belt, and quick-draw men in Westerns latch both. The poolroom shark uses "body english" and the golfer "follow-through." What do these varieties of gesture express? When a virtuoso pianist (like Glenn Gould) grimaces as he plays, is he showing off or can't he help himself? The body, as Demosthenes knew, is intimately related to meaning and can supplement it for greatest effect. We said it before and it's worth saying again: many a true word is spoken in gesture.

Speech begins with silence, so, to teach speech, you must teach silence. Charades are a way of doing so—communication through gestures. How, for example, through charade-gesture, would your students express:

> The boy stood on the burning deck.
> I bought the cheese, the meat, but not the bread.
> It never rains but it pours.
> Love makes the world go round, in circles.

Set up teams of three or four each, and have these teams compete. Your students will gain a fluidity of body movement and of gesture. Have them observe the ways in which gesture reflects personality.[7]

The Manners of the Court

Let's compare two great orators, Hitler and Churchill. Hitler was a torrent. Churchill was slow. One gave you no time to think. The other gave you, and himself, all the time needed. The ratio of silence to speech is far greater in Churchill than in Hitler. One was effective in a sick, hysterical, and paranoid society. The other was effective in a democratic, cerebrating society. Which do you prefer?

If speech is partly silence, and if communication in silence can be taught by charade gesture, our next consideration is consideration. The poor speaker wants his audience to have consideration for him. The good speaker wants to show consideration for his audience. The poor speaker requires courtesy; the good speaker extends it.

Courtesy implies power, as contrasted with servility. Courtesy can also be contrasted with civility, the manners of the free citizen. If courtesy is the manner of the court, and servility the manner of the serf, and civility the manner of the free citizen, which of the three shall the student in a democratically run classroom adopt when he stands before the class?

Courtesy and servility imply an unequal distribution of power, but civility implies an equal distribution. Which to adopt? The decision is not straightforward. Much depends on the speaker. Is he shy? Then let him cultivate an excess of manner, going forward beyond the usual to a formality, a studied posture, a stiffness of delivery in which patterned speech, gesture, and attitude form a protective bulwark of courtesy behind which he can quake unseen. Is he self-assured? Then he can be fluid in speech, flexible in gesture, relaxed in bearing, receptive to others and to the instincts in himself. He can be authoritative without being authoritarian, strong but not overpowering. He will be able to laugh at himself even as he laughs at others. Is he bumptious, an attention-seeker, a lover of the limelight? Let him cut himself down to size by servilely bowing and scraping, by deferential obsequiousness. The choice of courtesy, civility, and servility depends on the type of student.

One type will say "Let's not," arm forward, palm out, holding off the matter. Another will say the same words fist clenched, arm pounding. A third will wring his fingers as he says so. Gesture, therefore, also reflects the three manners and interacts with them. Adolescents do not always know what to do with their hands and feet. Some will lean on the front desk, others will back away to the blackboard, others will look down at the floor. Meanwhile their pals will be surreptitiously grimacing at them, hoping to reduce them to helplessness. Remember that the student in front of the room is a target not only for himself, but for his fellow-students who would love to see him break down—these his closest friends! One sign of weakness in the speaker and the pack will close in.

Therefore you must give the pack some responsibilities. Speech work involves not only the speaker, but the audience as well. The others are not on vacation while someone else is addressing them, but are held to the task of active listening and positive response. Response should be chiefly to the speaker's matter, not his manner. The directions of response should be indicated before the speaker begins. How, when you may not know the speech beforehand? Certain questions can be standard whatever the speech; on these the audience should be expected to respond:

> What is the most important idea?
> How else would you stress the most important idea?
> With what idea would you state your disagreement?
> Of what do any of the ideas in the speech remind you?
> Name one idea that should have had more stress.

Naturally, if you know beforehand of the material to be discussed, you can be more specific in your directives to the audience. These demands upon the listener simultaneously put the speaker on his toes, because he knows the audience will be attentive. They spare him the embarrassment of an indifferent audience or an audience trying to get him to laugh. If anything, be even more rigorous in your requirements of the audience than of the speaker. Two or three such speech lessons and the class will know that it must be on its toes and that speech work does not mean a respite for all in the class except the one designated victim; that all are in the same boat.[8] This brings us to the next matter.

The Group as Speaker

Anybody can learn to speak to an audience, even the slow student. Intelligence has no relationship to public speaking; look at certain public officials, TV announcers, politicians, and sales people. Making sense is not the issue here; it is the ability to get up, look around at a sea of features, and not be uncomfortable. Your brightest and most sensitive student may suffer a thousand spiritual deaths in facing his classmates; your dullest may look forward to the experience.

Group speaking helps both extremes. Debates, panel discussions, and committee reports are examples of such group speaking. They require much preparation and had better not be spontaneous. Do not be deceived by radio and TV panel discussions, with their apparently free-and-easy air. The participants are generally experts; if not, the moderator must be unusually skillful. You can take your classroom lead from such programs as *Youth Wants to Know, Dorothy Gordon's Youth Forums,* and similar programs. The topics selected for discussion on these shows will be of interest to your class panelists.

At the beginning, appoint yourself interviewer so that when conversation flags you can pick it up with a judicious question or a provocative statement. Make specific assignments to your panelists so that they can be prepared to protect themselves against the points that another panelist may bring up. Again, do not let the class lapse into the doldrums while the discussion proceeds, but advise the others that they will be questioned either by you or by members of the panel.

Keep abreast of the latest panel techniques that the avid promoters and audience-hunters of television create. They are extraordinarily fertile in these frameworks for group discussion, far more so than you have time to be. Be shameless in the way you borrow their techniques, even to the title, and you will find that this added fillip of the contemporary gives the discussions a lift out of the stale.

Although at the beginning you have appointed yourself chief interviewer, relinquish this post as soon as possible to a succession of chairmen. Successful chairmanship requires an alertness and skill taught with the rules of parliamentary procedure, and a talent for maintaining control while forwarding discussion. Chairmen may sin by monopolizing the discussion or by letting it become disorderly; have your chairmen police the discussion without either dominating it or sitting by while it rages.

As the class gains competence, raise the level of group discussion. You will be amazed at how far classes can go, if the topic is meaningful. Topics that are occupying Congress, the United Nations Assembly, the local Chamber of Commerce, or conventions of scientists not only are appropriate but will get fascinated attention in panel discussions; they are not over the heads of your classes.

In addition to these structured topics, you can have fun with unstructured ones—the kind known as socio-drama. Here you have neither preparation nor planning, but an unrehearsed display of spontaneity:

"The doorbell rings. You answer it. A man wants you to buy a subscription to a magazine. He says he is working his way through college." Cast of two, the magazine salesman and the customer.

See Helen Jennings' *Sociometry in Group Relations* for additional suggestions.[9]

The Electronic Audience

Of course, in speech work, you should use the tape recorder wherever you can, because though speech work aims for the ears of others there is a lovely narcissism in hearing the sound of one's own voice, however unfamiliar. The technologically up-to-the-minute tape recorder reflects the ancient need to admire ourselves. Watch the faces of your students the first time they hear the sounds of their own voices on tape, the pleasure and intentness accompanying the incredulity: the voices are theirs and they sound this way to others! Nevertheless, they listen with the closest attention to something within themselves; like some of our greatest speakers, they begin to listen to themselves even as they speak to others. Good speakers are narcissistic. They are in love with the sound of their own voices. The tape recorder teaches your students to learn to love the sound of their own voices. Tape recording is inexpensive. You can erase and erase, but don't do so in the presence of your narcissists; you will be erasing part of them. Narcissism on this level is completely normal, a sense of self and a feeling of comfort with one's own identity.

But the tape recorder also is therapeutic. It exposes defects in enunciation and articulation, making them clear to the speaker. Encouraging self-analysis, the tape recorder also strips away spurious self-love, and speech defects become clearer than by any other means. The student cannot deceive himself, because the others will assure him that this is truly how he sounds.

Focus the tape recorder on one student at a time or on the panel. You cannot, with the usual equipment, do better than pick up students within a six- or eight-foot radius of the microphone, but within this radius you can record a half-dozen students at a time and get the voices with fair clarity.

Because the tape recorder is inexorably objective, have your students put their best foot—or voice—forward, lest they become hopelessly dejected about the recorded results. In discussing the class newspaper, we mentioned the self-love of students seeing their names on the mimeographed sheet (p. 118), but there you can edit when their products might cause embarrassment. You have no opportunity for such kindnesses here. Therefore warn students to speak as well as they can. Students will take this additional care when the recorder is beamed at them. They will be more self-conscious but less self-effacing, less likely to break into helpless grins, especially if they have prepared. Furthermore, the audience treats the experience with more respect. In brief, use the tape recorder in as many circumstances as you reasonably can.

The tape recorder and phonograph record offer another resource: the sounds of John Gielgud, Robert Frost, Carl Sandburg, Siobhan McKenna, and other bards and actors contrasted with recordings of the same passages done by your students. Have your students record their readings of Frost on tape, and then compare Frost's reading with theirs—and don't hold Frost's reading up to them as the perfect one. You may well have students in your class who do a better reading than the author, and when you have such students tell them so.

Speech Work Never Stops

Speech work integrates with everything you do. The charade gesture described above can also be related to word study and illustrate the differences in *skip, run, walk, strut, amble, stroll,* and so on (p. 86).

Argumentation and debate are obviously related to "The worst enemies of democracy are the educated rich," compared with "The worst enemies of democracy are the uneducated poor." They are also related to sentence fragments and sentence structure (p. 84):

> What made him do it? (complete)
> What made him do it. (fragment)
>
> This way he can see the problem. (complete)
> The way he can see the problem. (fragment)
>
> Who is there? (complete)
> Who is there. (fragment)

In composing and arranging their reasons for one's being a complete sentence and the other a fragment, students must organize their thinking and present their thinking so that others in the class see and understand, an important part of speech work.

Speech work relates to classroom management; individual instruction, best in theory, may cause uninvolved students to become indifferent and restless. How to reconcile? Thus the particularly shy child will participate in choral reading in small groups of four to six—so effectively that he may become a leader in choral horseplay! Generally, choral work in speech allows the individual to come forward and the group to become involved.

Should students stand or sit when reciting? What constitutes class courtesy? These matters, discussed later (p. 353), are aspects of speech work too.

Even mental hygiene and guidance on teen-age problems constitute the agenda of your speech programs. They are usually handled by classroom panels in the TV pattern.

The tendency of student criticism to become student cannibalism, which requires preparation for responsible listening as well as for responsibly prepared speaking, was avoided by one teacher who asked students to imagine that they were wealthy manufacturers wanting their product to be well advertised by a radio announcer. The classroom was an audition room. The students had to try to sell themselves by their delivery. The class was to determine which announcer was to get the job and why.

Robert Erman shows how the business letter can be integrated with speech work on the job interview to help the student analyze his equipment and preparation for business and to indicate the kinds of interview that the student can anticipate. As Erman describes them, "It can be the rambling informal type, where the interviewer is untrained; or the pattern type, where the questions are pre-determined and the answers evaluated; or the follow-up type, usually held after the employee has been on the job for a short period of time; or the directed type, wherein the interviewer introduces topics in order to get the applicant to speak; or even the undirected type, during which the applicant is allowed to talk on and on. Regardless of its nature, however, our pupils must be prepared to meet such an exigency head-on." [10] Both business letter and job interview illuminate the student's weaknesses and strengths as he seeks employment and tests the hospitality of the job market. Here, also, socio-drama occurs as you or one of the students role-play the interviewer while someone role-plays himself.

Speech work often proceeds on two levels, conscious and subconscious. Be prepared for what the American Management Association describes as the "hidden agenda":[11]

> In a given group meeting there may be a stated agenda which the group is working on; however, individual participants may have their own private goals and points of view which they may be trying to get across in subtle ways. These unstated goals are called "hidden agenda." If the executive [or teacher!] is successful in obtaining a permissive atmosphere many of these hidden goals can be brought out into the open and dealt with.

Almost always, you will find these "hidden agenda" operating in your speech work.

Diction and Quality

Your work has been made considerably easier since *My Fair Lady* popularized Shaw's *Pygmalion.* Follow the recording with the paperback edition of the musical-comedy script, and you may supplement with Tanner's lines in the second act of *Man and Superman:* "This man takes more trouble to drop his aitches than ever his father did to pick them up. It's a mark of caste to him." But then drive the lesson home. *My Fair Lady* was of course a prodigious success in the theater, but how many of its audience went home thereafter and profited by Shaw's profound teaching that in becoming more aware of our speech we become more aware of ourselves?

Shaw never meant to say that perfect diction makes perfect people of us, but he did mean that the human voice is capable of making elegant sounds, of being pleasant both to speaker and listener—and this without any false straining after snobbism or upper-class speech. If Eliza Doolittle makes the social grade by altering her cockney patterns, her father does too by resolutely retaining his. You need not reform regionalisms or ethnicisms in the diction of your students. Listen to our political leaders on radio or television; hear them reflect their geographical origins, whether New Yorkers, Mississippians, Hawaiians, Californians, or Bostonians, to a national audience. These are the leaders of our country and no one of them attempts Oxonian English. Do not try it in your class either. If the cockney drops his h's the Oxonian drops his r's; if the Bostonian drops his r's and broadens his a's, the New Yorker drops his final g's and broadens his o's.

Diction does not mean a common standard of good English, but common musical values in speech, good quality of voice, clarity of enunciation, a love for and an interest in the way our own words come out of our own mouths. Neither tough speech, affected speech, nor slovenly speech evidences any such interest. Tough diction and affected diction are more concerned with effects on the hearer. Slovenly diction is in retreat from both hearer and speaker. Without the slightest alteration in regional or ethnic tendencies, your students can alter the musical and tonal qualities by sounding better to themselves. We make a conscious effort to sound better to ourselves when we sing. We make no such effort when we speak. Because we do the best we can with our voices when we sing, have your students sing to the tune of "You are lost and gone forever. Dreadful sorry, Clementine," the similarly scanning "How d'you do? I'm pleased to meet you. And the weather is just fine," and then, retaining all the voiced quality of voice, the vibrations in the vocal chord, and the relaxation in the chest, but omitting the variations in pitch and rhythm of the song, have them repeat the greeting as if they were being introduced. In the same way, match "Way down upon the Swanee River" with "I'm seeing a movie tomorrow"; or "When I was young I used to wait on master, and give him his plate" with "If you're not ready, then I'll go, right now, before the snow." Have them fit the syllables of the synthesized sentences into the tunes they know; let them sing the synthesized sentences and then speak them with all the vibration and resonance that singing requires. Point out to them that they sound better without sounding conspicuous. You will find excellent materials in recent textbooks on speech.[12]

Research, Resources, and Techniques

1. Jane Britton's "Let Them Talk—The Community Will Listen" (*E. J.,* March 1955, p. 159) suggests some topics for classroom panel discussions and shows how these may have socially useful results. Interesting.

2. A reminder—when you read poetry, or when students read poetry, have the class follow from its own copies. See the chapter on poetry, pp. 230-255.

3. Jotham Johnson's "The Changing American Language" (*Scientific American,* Aug. 1955, p. 78) is interesting and humorous in its discussion of shifts in American pronunciation. Thus, in upper New York State, pronunciation would be "Put on your colt and we'll go for a roll in the bolt," for "Put on your coat and we'll go for a row in the boat," but that's no surprise for anybody, like you, who's read a linguistic atlas. The examples in the article will be amusing for your class.

4. Ruth E. French's "Planning Speech Training for All Youth" (*E. J.,* Sept. 1956, p. 328) considers some speech programs and resources—including films on how to speak on the telephone.

5. Robert C. Pooley's "The English Teacher's Preparation in Speech" (*E. J.,* April 1956, p. 181) points out that you will not be truly effective without speech training and that an excessive number of English teachers do lack this training, with resulting ineffectiveness and unhappiness both to students and to teacher. Why be unhappy? Why not train yourself in speech effectiveness?

6. Since in this chapter and elsewhere we have been hinting that listening is as important as talking, here is a useful source:

a. Stanley B. Kegler's "Techniques for Teaching Listening for Main Ideas," *E. J.,* January 1956, p. 30, says that part of your work in speech is teaching how to listen. Hence an important part of speech is keeping your mouth shut and your ears open.

b. Donald P. Brown's unpublished doctoral dissertation *Auding as the Primary Language Ability* (Stanford, 1955).

7. From Grant Mauk's "Speak Up" (*E. J.,* May 1955, p. 290): ". . . include a unit in speech, a unit in talking before a group, in your course outline. Every student you have will thank you for it. They know that the ability to speak well is necessary to the full development of their personalities, to their success in any business, and to their happiness as students in the immediate present." Though short on actual, specific suggestions for teaching speech, this article is long on well-warranted enthusiasm. The attitude, approach, and values are recommended to you for stiffening your approach toward the refractory and shy student.

8. If you are interested in how neurology and speech interact, read that very important book by Wilder Penfield and Lamar Roberts, *Speech and Brain Mechanisms* (Princeton University Press, 1959). Also, Kurt Goldstein is an important source for the psychological origin of speech disorders, in his *Language and Language Disturbances* (Grune and Stratton, 1948).

CHAPTER **II**

Teaching
Effectively

Contra Highet

The purpose of this book is to get you to be an experienced, effective teacher sooner than you would otherwise be. Effective teaching involves matters beyond mastery of content and grasp of English; there is a methodology to teaching. Some people deny this and write books against courses in methods and books on methods, but in so doing, they write excellent methods books themselves. One such instance is Gilbert Highet's *The Art of Teaching,* a very fine book on teaching methods, which states its opposition to teaching methods. A point made by Highet is that teaching is not a science but an art.

This, however, leaves an important question unanswered. If teaching is an art and not a science, then how much technique, technology, methodology, and science go into art? A considerable amount. The history of art shows that art is not haphazard and is highly methodological. The very notion of form and composition is evidence of the artist's methodological approach to art. Improvements in scientific techniques made the pianoforte hammer and string possible and thus made Chopin possible. Study of the chemistry of pigment, paint, and oil in the Renaissance made Italian and Dutch art possible. Modern painting is an answer to the discovery of the camera, and modern music is a response to sounds never heard before, the sounds of traffic, riveting machines, railroad wheels, and the rhythms of the oscilloscope. The forms of literature inevitably reflect modern science and technology.

332

Teaching *is* artistic, rather than scientific; therefore, like all arts, it includes elements of science and methodology. The assumption that your classroom is a reasonable microcosm of a reasonable universe, that what goes on in your classroom is not haphazard or accidental but can be explained, if we have enough information on the underlying events, borrows from scientific method. If a man crosses the street at a velocity of X miles per hour, and if an automobile comes down the street at Y miles per hour, we can predict the point at which vehicle and man will meet. The man will be taken to the hospital and he will tell the doctor he had an "accident," but how much "accident" is it if we were able to predict the occurrence? There are no "accidents," really. An "accident" is something we weren't wise enough to foretell. It's much like what the physicist calls "noise" in an electronic circuit, the haphazard that emerges when we are not able to control everything because we don't know enough.

The purpose of a textbook on classroom methods is to reduce the "accident" and the "noise." Gain the feeling that ultimately everything in your classroom is understandable, no matter how wildly inchoate it seems. Whatever is going on has a reason—therefore don't panic but try soberly to determine what the reasons are.

Research, Resources, and Techniques

> Morris Kline's "Projective Geometry" (*Scientific American,* Jan. 1955, p. 80) relates Renaissance Art and projective geometry. Which do you think came first, in this interaction of mathematics, art, and technique?

On First Walking into a School

You will begin your teaching career by being a poor teacher. You will continue to be poor until the end of the first year. You are not alone; you are typical. Everybody who ever taught began by being poor at first— your supervisor, your principal, your superintendent, and every one of your colleagues.

You will be recognizably and obviously poor. Not only will your colleagues sense it, but your students will testify to it from first-hand experience. If you are discharged from your post, it will not be for teaching inability but for some graver reason, like inability to get along with others on the faculty (see Case Study 15), or unwillingness to follow instructions, or stupidity, or unprofessional conduct, but not, your first year, for inability to teach.

Why, after education courses, methods courses, student observation, and student teaching, should you not walk into a classroom and take over completely and with full control? What good are courses if they do not supply this ability? Education courses cannot make a silk purse out of a sow's ear (p. 16), nor a good teacher out of a poor one. They can reduce the poorness in the poor teacher and sharpen up the good teacher, putting a higher polish on him than he would otherwise have. Expect no more of education courses, or education texts, or life.

Why are you so poor at first? Because you haven't yet lived through the repetitive, routinized cycle of the school year. Experience the first full cycle and most of your troubles are over. Trying as the first year is, it's the worst and it ends. You'll survive it. With the first day of the second year, you remember the clerical forms and the routines that must be followed, and as you begin to be reminded that you've been over this course before, you're home.

Meanwhile, the first year, the paper forms, the clerical routines, the tight scheduling are bewildering. Find yourself an indulgent older colleague, latch on like a leech, and learn forms, routines, and schedules as rapidly as you can. Your apprenticeship will be over all the sooner.

Strangely, there is some relationship between mastery of clerical forms and mastery of classroom disciplinary problems, but it remains inexplicable to the author. At about the same instant that you begin to anticipate what paper forms and timetables are coming around the corner next, you suddenly find yourself able to relax in the classroom, more the master of classroom climate. Get the hang of the piddling, unimportant, time-consuming, energy-wasting paper work as soon as you can, and put it behind you so that you can handle it without excessive thought or irritation. The generalized sense of competence that you will get will transfer into the classroom too.

CASE HISTORY 14*   When her older child was ten and the younger six, her husband, who had just begun to establish himself in law, was killed in an automobile accident, and she had to go to work. She

---

* Adapted from a student's paper. Names omitted for obvious reasons.

had never taught beyond her student teaching and a term immediately thereafter, but she found a situation as an English teacher in her community. She was a conscientious mother and it was a wrench to leave her children and to split her loyalties between home and job. She tried to get home as soon after school as possible because she felt her primary allegiance was to her children rather than to her students. She consoled herself that she had evenings and week-ends with her children and resented the preparation that cut into her time with them. However, she cautiously covered her tracks so that her supervisor would not suspect excessive corner-cutting. Nevertheless, her teaching was poor. She knew she was capable of far better work, but she would not divert any time from her home and family.

But things were slipping from her control at home too. She had always been a calm and pleasant mother, yet her temper was getting as short with her children as it was with her students. The pressures of being a mother and a teacher simultaneously were wearing her down.

She had become friendly with a young woman in Social Studies, who had recently married. This young woman was also cutting corners, not because she had children, but because she had a husband to be trained and a new home to furnish.

At their lunch table were other new teachers. Among them was a physics teacher who had left a career in engineering at a salary almost twice his present one, a bubbling, vital, enthusiastic man in his early thirties, who explained, "They had hundreds of us at drawing boards in one large room, and I wasn't using my education or my training. I was more like a clerk in a large department store. That's as far as I was ever going. In four years I hit my maximum. After four more years, I was still making about the same. I could have changed jobs but it would have been the same problems over and over again; my wife and I talked it over. It wasn't engineering as I had been told about it in school and read about it in fancy want ads. I thought engineering would be creative. It wasn't. It was a nine to five job. Teaching is different. You can take problems home with you."

At first, the two women didn't believe what they were hearing, but as time went on they learned he was serious. The three met at an in-service course, which the women resented because the younger wanted to write a novel one of these days and the older because it took one afternoon away from her children. The man leaped into the course with vigor and interest; it was the portal to advanced work.

The older woman, lonesome for adult company, invited the man and his wife and the younger woman and her husband to her home. When the man and his wife arrived, the older woman told them that the younger woman had telephoned that she would be delayed. Her husband, an accountant, was tied up. Meanwhile, the three talked, and the older woman commented on the man's energy. "Is he that way at home?" she asked.

The wife answered, "He has more energy now than before."

"When I leave school, I'm just ready to start a day's work," the man answered.

"Teaching takes everything out of me," the woman said.

The man laughed. "You're leading two lives, two separate and distinct lives. You're a teacher and a mother. I'm leading one life, and one life only. I'm a teacher around the clock."

The wife answered, "You don't have a house to run too."

"Nonsense," the man answered. "I help with the house, the shopping, and the children as much as any husband I know. I'm doing more around the house than I ever did when I was in engineering. The difference is I'm having fun."

"Fun?" the woman exclaimed.

"Sure. Teaching stimulates me. It doesn't fatigue me. I walk into the school sleepy and I walk out alive."

The wife said, "He's going ahead for his doctorate. He never felt like doing that before."

"You bet!" He leaned toward the woman, as the doorbell rang. "Don't split yourself in two. You could be a better teacher because you're a mother, and you could be a better mother because you're a teacher. If you'd only see them as supplements, not in opposition!"

The younger woman and her husband came in, escorted by a thoughtful look on the older woman's face, and the conversation resumed with the older woman's explanation, "I'm split in two. I'm a split personality, half-mother, half-teacher. That's what's wrong with me, but I can't help myself because I've got to make a living."

After introductions, the younger woman demanded that the man stop picking on their colleague. "Her home is more important than her job. Being a conscientious mother is more important than being a conscientious teacher."

The man shook his head. "She can't be a conscientious mother unless she's simultaneously a conscientious teacher. She won't pick up her home responsibilities by dropping her teaching responsibilities. They'll suffer or improve in a direct linear relationship." The women looked blank.

The husband explained, "He means they go together."

The man nodded. "You'll never have a rich home life if you don't have a rich teaching life. You've got to be problem-oriented, not time-off-oriented. I've heard you girls talk at the table. You come in Monday and count the days till Friday-Thank-God. Comes Friday and you mourn that you've only got forty-eight hours till Monday. Comes September and you count the days till vacation. Comes vacation and you tick off every day until you get back. From the very first day you start teaching, you plan on retirement."

"You remind me of an announcement I have permission to make," the younger woman said. Her husband smiled. "I'm going on maternity leave."

Congratulations and When's? followed, and the man resumed, "What's wrong with teaching isn't that there are too many women in it, but that the women aren't women all the way. You shouldn't be half-teacher and half-mother, but all woman. You're going to have a baby. That's wonderful, but it should make you a better teacher. Motherhood should improve your teaching."

The older woman broke in, "It sounds fine, but when I'm preparing supper and getting my own children ready for school and cleaning up week-ends, I don't have the time to get lesson plans ready."

"It's not time," the man said. "It's guilt. I've listened to you. You feel guilty about not being home. If you'd stop feeling guilty, you'd have time. Your experiences at school would make you a better mother, and your experiences as a mother would make you a better teacher. I went into teaching not because it was easier than engineering, but because it was harder. I was looking for problems, not for time off. If I ever get my doctorate, I'll be prepared to handle bigger and bigger problems. There's nothing more poisonous than not enjoying your work, and there's nothing more enriching than enjoying it."

The husband said, "I agree." He turned to his wife. "Maybe the best way to get your novel started is by doing your lesson plans. You're always kicking about them. You don't do them, and you haven't started your novel either."

The conversation went on to other topics. After her guests had gone, the older woman cleaned up. Standing the kitchen sink, she reviewed her male colleague's appraisal. Guilt? Partly. But she was still in mourning, long after she was required to be. It was time she stopped being half-mother, half-teacher, and became all woman again. Widowhood didn't mean she was bereft of womanhood, nor that she had to skimp on being a teacher and a mother.

She put away the dishes and sat down to her lesson plans for the coming week.

Research, Resources, and Techniques

1. J. N. Hook said of some English teachers in "The National Council Looks Ahead" (*E. J.*, Jan. 1955, p. 1): "I fear there are some who merely go through the requisite motions in order to draw a paycheck. They regard their work as routine labor; they must be in a certain place at a certain time and say certain things and write certain marks on certain papers. They have no more interest in improving their teaching than a ditch-digger is likely to have in digging a more artistic ditch. . . . On Friday at four o'clock they sigh in relief and then spend Saturday and Sunday in a fog of fear that Monday will come again."

2. Two contributions, somewhat parallel in their thinking:

a. Joseph Mersand's "English Meets the Challenge" (*E. J.*, Feb. 1960, p. 61) recapitulates the situation in high school English and points up the need to be tough-minded and hard-headed in your faith as an English teacher.

b. Similarly inspirational is Robert C. Pooley's "The Professional Status of the English Teacher" (*E. J.*, Sept. 1959, p. 309). This outstanding evaluation should be read with the Lou LaBrant lead piece in the same issue.

How to Look around a Classroom

You know how important eye movements and eye fixations are in reading. The reading expert can tell from your eye movements how efficient a reader you are. Your class, facing you, is also expert in eye movements and can tell from the way your eyeballs move in their sockets whether you are in control of yourself, whether you are therefore in control of the class, whether you are uncertain, or whether your wavering eyes only mean you are fishing for ideas or someone to call on. The class has taken no course in this area of human knowledge, because this is protoplasmic and instinctual. (See page 46.)

The reading expert wants you to scan the printed page with a minimum of fixations and in a smooth, rapid, onward swoop. Do you scan a class-room the same way? Not quite. Fixations are sometimes desirable, as is a slow, gradual, unhurried sweep of the students in front of you. Regressions in eye movement, so undesirable in reading, may be fine in letting the class know your eyes are all over the place, and as your eye goes back to one student, or a couple, who may need this minatory prodding into alertness.

Just as lip movements in reading are undesirable because their twitch-ing slows you down, so you want to cultivate a relaxed set of mouth and facial muscles as you look at your class.

Let eye movement reveal composure in you, especially in you because you are an English teacher. Your colleagues may not admit it, but, as an English teacher, you are top man on the totem pole of the faculty hierarchy. More is expected of you in the way of cultivation and breed-ing. (See Chap. 13, "The English Teacher's Colleagues," p. 389.) Culturally, you are monarch of all you survey because you survey more than any of your colleagues do, and, when you survey your class make it look like that—but survey like a true monarch, one with breeding and cultivation, not like a tyrant or martinet. Your eye movements should be wide and ample, not furtive, narrow, or hurried. They should have proper pace, tempered tempo, and stateliness. They should not shift hurriedly back and forth with every commotion on the periphery of vision.

When a student recites, should you look at him, or elsewhere? If so, where else? Or is it rude not to look at a reciting student? Not necessarily. He may feel fidgety if you do and to move your glance elsewhere may be a mercy. Try it several ways, in several circumstances, and see what results you get.

When you call on students to recite, the natural tendency is for you to look at them. Try, instead, looking at the class—and have the student do so too. One student teacher explained the effectiveness of the procedure (looking at the class instead of the reciter) by the class feeling that they were under scrutiny, and that the teacher was keeping an eye on them while the recitation proceeded. Perhaps, but it is equally possible that the class feels that the teacher is also listening and is a coparticipant. Whatever the explanation, the practice of looking at the class and having the reciter do so too is an excellent occasional variation in eye movement.

Another variation deals with informality and gaiety. They become you, the English teacher, provided they are not giddiness, instability, or weakness. Thus, you should learn the techniques of shutting one eye at a time, known as a wink, and its variations. Flicker one eyelid with almost imperceptible speed and it can mean understanding; accompany it with a nod of the head and it can mean approval; prolong it and it means quizzical inquiry or even disbelief. You haven't said a word meanwhile, but a world.

Or what of rolling your eyes back so that the whites show and you seem to be looking at a point in the ceiling? That might indicate thought or consideration of some point raised. But to do so and meanwhile rock your head from side to side? That might seem like astonishment. Widen the lateral swing of your head and it might mean incredulity even to pain.

Be expressive. Be ocular.

Classroom Discipline

In great measure, your disciplinary problems are a function not of students, but of worry about what your superiors will think and of your imagination working overtime.

Imagine these situations:

You walk into your classroom. In the back of the room two students are talking, laughing, and looking at you. What is your reaction? Too frequently you will almost spontaneously think that it's you they're talking and laughing about. At once, you become offended. But perhaps they weren't talking and laughing about you. Suppose, instead, their talk and laughter dealt with something completely unrelated to you? Would your reaction be the same? What, therefore, makes you leap the gap into imagining you are involved?

A disciplinary situation arises in the classroom. Students may be brawling, or restless, or talking when they should not, or they may be just generally noisy. To what extent is your reaction an outcome of what is directly there before your eyes? To what extent an outcome of an imaginary situation, the inner image of the school principal walking by your room at that particular instant and unfavorably taking notice of the disturbance?

Do not mishandle a situation because of fear of what your principal might say, *if* he were to walk by just then, or what others might, if they were looking on. Handle the situation without superimposing the opinions of imaginary witnesses or supersupposing that unseen they are looking on disapprovingly. Suppose your principal did walk by. Would he prefer to see you quaking at what he might have to say or sure in your ability to manage the class? Would tolerance of the noise level be evidence of your control? Or intolerance of it?

Thus, a contributing factor to your failures in classroom control is somebody who isn't there and your apprehensions about what he would say if he were. A contributing factor to your successes in classroom control is not being paralyzed by him, whether he is present or absent.

Become friendly with your supervisor and your principal. Do not confuse bootlicking with friendliness, and do not confuse friendliness on the job with the friendliness of friends. You must differentiate these three. Do so on the work-and-problem basis of your day-by-day experiences and you will find that your superiors are as interested in improving your professional importance and contribution as you are. In fact, they are sometimes lonely for a chance to help!

CASE STUDY 15   In a graduate workship, Problems in Secondary Education, the term was drawing to a close. At one of the last meetings, the timid but attractive student burst forth: "I won't be at my school next term, I'm afraid. I don't think my contract will be renewed. My department chairman is a woman and she's not pleased with me. She doesn't have any complaints about my work, she says, but she doesn't approve of my professional relations with other people. I haven't been pushing and I've tried to keep out of her way. I like the school and the students like me. I want very much to stay. I don't know what I did that was wrong."

The young woman was almost in tears. She had contributed thoughtfully, if not forcefully, to the workshop, and seemed thoroughly devoted. She was a graduate of a good Roman Catholic institution, expressed herself well, and was respectful of the approved values in English without being stuffy.

A purpose of a workshop is to provide answers wherever possible. The other students looked expectantly at the instructor. The instructor studied the young woman. He had been favorably impressed by her. She was a decent young woman and well bred. She was brighter than her retiring, deferential manner indicated. She was still a bit too young to be called a lady, but in time she would have the self-assurance, given professional achievement, that a true lady has, and a true lady in a classroom is a precious thing and rare.

"I agree with your chairman," the instructor said. "You're scared of her, aren't you?"

The young woman had a lovely complexion, lovely teeth, and a lovely smile. The smile just then wavered on the edge of a good cry. She nodded. "She frightens me."

"You want your contract renewed?" the instructor asked.

"Very much," she answered. The class was listening. The instructor had to put up an answer or shut up.

"I'll make you a promise," he said rashly. "I'll guarantee you renewal of your contract if you do as I say. Beginning tomorrow, when you meet your chairman in the corridor, smile at her, and chat with her. If you don't find her in the corridor, stroll into her office your free hour, sit down, make yourself comfortable, and chat, chat, chat."

The roses in the lovely complexion began to fade. "About what?" she trembled.

"About the discussions we've been having in the workshop—except this one—or about Paris fashions, or about a book you've just read, or about an article in the newspaper, or how you admire the dress she's wearing and you meant to talk to her about it and where did she buy it? or can she recommend a good hotel for vacation—chat, chat, chat!"

At the following week's meeting of the workshop, the young woman was asked to report on her personal experience with teacher-supervisor relationships. She smiled, nowhere near tears this time. "Everything's all right. She's a lovely woman. We're getting along just fine. There'll be no trouble about renewal."

The instructor shuddered. He had gambled on the lines in *The Gondoliers,* where the two kings say:

> But the privilege and pleasure
> That we treasure beyond measure
> Is to run on little errands for the Ministers of State!

and had assumed that principals and supervisors treasure beyond measure the companionship that their teachers withhold from them. It's oftener true than false.

Notice that in this section on classroom discipline we are not only discussing your relationships with your students, but with your superiors. Your attitude toward your superiors contributes toward your success and failure in classroom discipline. Though your superiors are not actually present when you face a classroom disturbance, they are effectively and unnecessarily put into the picture by your imagination. Strangle your imagination! When you encounter a classroom disturbance, nobody, no principal, no supervisor, will be looking over your shoulder.

Generally, principals and supervisors are better people, as a group, than teachers. Teachers are not so experienced, sophisticated, understanding, or responsible. You will get better advice from your principal and supervisor than from your colleagues. Principals and supervisors have larger and more generous perspectives. They have been around more and longer. They are usually not so narrow. Are there exceptions? Yes. Some principals are petty czars, but petty czars in administrative and supervisory posts are fewer than in the classroom. How many are in the classroom? Too many. Therefore, in your care and feeding of supervisors, learn tact. Learn how to smile in a friendly, not ingratiating, fashion. Do not become paralyzed and do not fawn. Ask for advice.

Meet classroom disturbances with alertness, not apprehensiveness. Encounter your superiors with true warmth, not as a toady or a lackey. React to your students with curiosity, not suspicion. Get to know them. The more you know them, the better you control them. Who's the "them"? Your student and your superior, both. Both contribute to your disciplinary headaches, one overtly, the other covertly.

CASE STUDY 16   A young woman reported to a graduate class: "I was at my desk chatting with some students and three boys stood in the doorway, cursing like mad and using the filthiest language they could. Cleverly, they weren't shouting. They were almost whispering, but just loud enough for us to hear everything. I got more and more embarrassed and pretended not to hear, but their voices grew louder and I couldn't pretend any more, because I'm not deaf. I told them angrily they ought to be ashamed of themselves. At once, they became apologetic, and said they were sorry and didn't know I was listening. I ordered them along, and as they went down the hall I heard them guffawing. They had succeeded in getting the rise out of me they wanted. What could I have done?"

The experience, the graduate class decided, was not isolated. Others had had similar experiences. Some felt the teacher had no alternative, a few thought that she should have continued to ignore it, and some agreed with the suggestion that she should have sent their names down to the office. One remark was particularly interesting: an anecdotal record be kept of such incidents, along with the names. The instructor asked, "How would you go about it, and what's the purpose?"

The suggestion for anecdotal records had come from a handsome young man who had originally intended to become an actor, had majored in speech, but had found himself detoured into the classroom. He was in the bottom half of the group and didn't seem too well endowed with brains. He explained: "I took a course in tests and measurements last term and the professor described anecdotal records on kids. He said that you should keep them and that incidents like this are good for anecdotal records for the cumulative record."

The instructor waited for more, but there was no more, except a weak smile. The instructor said, "So far, so good, but it's not far enough. An anecdotal record is as verbatim a report as you can make and as good a picture as you can take, but what do people behave like when you take their picture? It depends on the camera. With a movie camera they'll move around and grimace. With a still camera, they'll stand still. They'll conform to the camera. They'll pose suitably. When kids are in the corridor, cursing at each other, but not at you, to see what reaction they can provoke you into, you can quell the disturbance in one way or another, by reprimanding them or just frowning at them or else by valiantly ignoring them, but how realistic is that when they know you're hearing every syllable? But there's another way, and that's taking a picture of them. Suppose you were to open a notebook and write as accurate an account as possible of the comments, curses, and behavior. Notice how you're administering a taste of their own medicine. They're not cursing at you. Oh no, not a bit! They're taking every precaution not to. At the same time you're taking a picture, and if they're in the field of vision, they put themselves there; you didn't." He asked the young woman, "What would have happened if you had silently taken out a notebook and pencil and had started to write everything they were saying?"

Somebody in class interrupted. "They would have run like thieves."

The young woman nodded. "They would have been too scared to guffaw.

Or maybe not. Maybe they would have demanded to know what I was doing. They might even have got indignant."

"Of course," the instructor said, "but you wouldn't have been helpless any more. You'd be calling the shots, not they." He turned to the handsome young man and said. "Keeping records isn't a passive matter. Anecdotal records can be a means of classroom control. If the class knows you keep anecdotal records on behavior not only for the cumulative record card in the principal's office but as a means of objectifying their behavior on paper, they'll conform to that kind of camera and modify their behavior too. Anecdotal records and behavior records, seen that way, are another way of classroom management. Keeping records means keeping control."

How to Ask a Question

Of course you must ask factual questions to check on information. Such questions are simple and straightforward, and they present you with no intellectual challenge and your students with no opportunity to exercise judgment.

Judgment questions cut two ways. They reflect your judgment and offer the student a chance to parade his. Throughout we have offered examples of such questions and now suggest an approach that may help you develop your own. The approach is philosophical and goes as follows:

Thinkers as diverse as Hegel, who wrote on dialectic opposites, Morris Raphael Cohen, who expounded the philosophic principle of polarity, Plato, who presented dualism as a way of explanation, and modern mathematicians like Norbert Wiener, who have reduced—or elevated—computation to binary digits,[1] propounded the basic notion of mutual exclusivity, which goes under the name of Information Theory, wherein things are or aren't, go or come, affirm or deny, are absent or present, are either or or.[2] Cherry says: "What distinguishes news from propaganda? What is the difference between competition and conflict? Why does society continually split into two, like the two opposing teams in a game: capital and labor, the two parties of stable democracies, the two sides in war, believers and infidels? Within each side there is sense of cohesion, loyalty, and rectitude. Our side is wholly good, the other wholly evil. Is such dualism inherent in the way we think?"[3]

Perhaps yes, perhaps no, but I know no better questions than those that drive students to one alternative or another, with no possible compromise in between, questions that exact a polarizing effect on the class, that present two sides, only one of which you can take. Here are examples of these polarized questions from former student teachers describing their original experiences with polarized questions:

1. The problem of the thought question versus the polarized question is much like the controversy in psychology between directive and non-directive therapy. . . . The advantage of the polarized question is that it allows for divergent responses and, moreover, gives the class some inkling of what is going on in the mind of the teacher. For example, if the teacher asks, as I did, "Who is the more pitiful character, Godfrey Cass or Silas Marner?" the students may choose either one so long as they provide reasons for their selection. Moreover, they know that the teacher feels that both of these characters are pitiful and that therefore there must be incidents in the book to support the choice. However, if the teacher were to ask, "What trait does Godfrey have in common with Silas?" the class may spend the entire period rejecting characteristic after characteristic and never get anywhere.

When I was teaching *A Tale of Two Cities,* I asked the class, "What is the most outstanding characteristic of Madame Defarge?" I received responses varying from "She is always knitting" to "She raises her eyebrows whenever one of the Jacquerie enters the room." However, when I followed this up with, "Who was more vengeful, Madame Defarge or her husband?" I received numerous excellent responses which really probed deeply into the natures of these two individuals.

. . . In poetry I have found it almost invaluable when comparing two poems with similar themes. For example, in one lesson I asked, "Do Poe's raven and Coleridge's albatross serve to reveal something about the nature of the chief characters in these poems?" No response. Complete silence prevailed. Then I reworded my question: "Which reveals more about the main character in each poem, the raven or the albatross?" Once I had let the class know that they both do reveal something, the entire class was prepared to supply me with revelations.

But it isn't always magic. When I asked a class that had just discussed "Westminster Bridge," "If Wordsworth were alive today and had to travel from New York to California, would he walk or take a plane?" one eager student replied, "He would walk because he would probably say that flying is for the birds."

2. The question "When did Columbus discover America?" is a fact question and calls for a memorized date. [See p. 355] However, the question "Whose discovery was more important because of its influence on the United States, Columbus' or Balboa's?" requires knowledge of the places discovered, the dates of the discovery, and the significance of the discoveries.

I asked a bright ninth grade class reading *Julius Caesar,* "Who was more honorable, Caesar or Brutus?" I was amazed at the answers I received. Even the quietest students were eager to be heard. Many students felt that Brutus was because he acted in good faith and tried to do what was right for Rome. Some added that Caesar was a power-mad individual who would have acted like a dictator.

But others believed Caesar to be more honorable because he built up Rome by conquering other lands. A few students said that Brutus had broken one of the Ten Commandments and therefore was not honorable, no matter what motivated him. The class response was excellent. They enjoyed the discussion.

Another question worked with my eighth grade class. We were discussing the TV production of *Green Pastures* and I asked them which character they liked better, De Lawd or Noah.

The reactions came in hard and fast. Many students did not like De Lawd because he forgot about the people on earth and let them fend for themselves (thought-provoking for the teacher!). Others did not like Noah because he was too interested in "material" things. They were referring to the kegs of whiskey he took with him.

3. It's a form of dichotomy. The polarized question leaves the student with the necessity of making one of two distinct choices. He must choose either A or B. However, to ask such questions a teacher must have a rich background in English and of the materials at her disposal. When teaching spelling, the teacher can point out the differences between words—*ie* versus *ei,* and *affect* versus *effect*—so that the "thin line" may be seen.

My aim in teaching Joaquin Miller's "Columbus" was to show that courage and determination are necessary in the face of danger and that man must have the courage of his convictions. My polarized question was that the student should imagine himself in a space ship, with five other men, on a journey to the moon. At a point halfway up, what feeling would be dominant—to continue upward with the spirit of adventure and the motivation of curiosity? or to return to the safety of the earth with the motivating feeling of responsibility for the safety of the men? The class was in an uproar. They were forced, by the nature of the question, to take only one choice of the two which were given. They offered reasons with enthusiasm. Students disputed students. The atmosphere was electric.

On another occasion, my aim was to increase vocabulary and to use more vivid words. I motivated with your illustration from Whorf and the number of separate words that Eskimos have for our one word *snow*. I asked why this should be so, and students saw readily that survival had much to do with it. I wondered, aloud, how this would apply to our own civilization and language, and how many words we have for *automobile*. We listed *bus, hot rod, Chevrolet, Oldsmobile,* and then I asked my polarized question, "Do these fine discriminations among words help more in survival in primitive people or more in civilized people?" Naturally, after the dust settled, I had no trouble summarizing on the necessity of discriminating between words, choosing words carefully, and drawing fine distinctions between them.

I have asked them to distinguish between *outstanding* and *gigantic,* how words can mean different things in different contexts, and so on. I have asked, "When you don't use long words in conversation, is it because you don't remember them or because it embarrasses you?" The class responded with diverse opinions. More than one gave examples of times when a long word would have clarified the conversation but was withheld for fear of embarrassment.

The drawback is that such questions necessitate a thorough knowledge of English materials. A teacher must know what makes the pupil tick, and the characteristics and problems of the child.

4. I have used this method with great success. The students were alive and responsive; I didn't feel quite like God spouting dogma from on high, and everyone came away thinking—including myself.

A very innocent lesson dealt with an inconsequential short story, Irving's "The Devil and Tom Walker." But when the bell rang, the class was divided into two camps and a furious battle was raging. The issue: was Irving moralizing or satirizing? Well! To these students, imbued with a zealous feeling as to what is good and evil, this became a call to arms, and a learning experience emerged which warmed the heart. All came away with an understanding as to what dogmatic "moralizing" is, what a satire is, as well as the knowledge that a writer does not necessarily write to teach or preach but may aim to entertain.

Huckleberry Finn lends itself to this approach because Twain has for each character another who stands in opposition: Huck and Tom; Jim and Pop; Miss Watson and the Widow Douglas; each is the opposite side of the same coin. At the question, "Who is the more imaginative, Tom or Huck?" the class became involved in an analysis of both boys and eventually came away with an understanding of Tom as a "romantic, literary gent" and of Huck as a sensitive, imaginative poet.

A teacher I observed got a good lesson out of the question, "Who is the more tragic figure—Ophelia or Eustacia Vye; Hamlet or Clym?" At present I am preparing *Giants in the Earth* and I think that questions like "Who is the more sensitive, Beret or Per Hansa?" "Why should Beret have broken down while the others were hardly affected, especially since Beret had a family—which gave her a more secure hold on life while most of the others were childless?" will lead to thinking on the part of the students and result in good discussions.

5. It uses the competitive feeling among students to good advantage. The flame is kindled and the heat diffused among the students themselves, rather than between the students on the one hand and the teacher on the other. If the discussion gets very heated, students cut each other's throats, rather than that of the teacher.

Opposite and contrasting ideas are presented over which students may hassle. Because of the tendency to take sides and take a stand on an issue when two opposing viewpoints are presented, this technique can effectively capture the interest and maintain eager class discussion. The student uses reflective and original thinking in explaining why he chooses one side of the polarized question rather than the other.

In Aldrich's "A Struggle for Life," where the man reacted in a certain way because he thought that he had been entombed for a number of days, when, in reality, he had been in the tomb for two hours, I asked the students which was more important: the reality of the situation or what the man *thought* was the reality. "Thinking makes it so" and "mind over matter" were discussed; even the anticipation of blind dating and taking difficult tests were brought into the picture.

I have found that the polarized question should be used only with previous knowledge pertaining to the question. The question should not come out of thin air.

With O. Henry's "A Municipal Report," I asked, "Would you have done the same thing?" and did not get the heated discussion I expected. All the answers were, "Yes, because . . ." The reasons were good and I was surprised that the students were capable of such astute thinking, but there were no takers for the opposing view. I was the only one who would not have done the same thing. I misjudged the justice-kindness-legal values of the students. But after I gave a lesson on Wilbur Daniel Steele's "Footfalls," I asked the students which murderer they sympathized with more, the hero of "Footfalls" or Uncle Caesar of "A Municipal Report," previously read. There was silence as the students thought about it. As I looked about the room, I realized that they were truly contemplating and perhaps searching their own souls. As the hands shot up, the bell rang. The students, bursting to be heard on their sympathies, walked out of the room discussing the question. I was smiling within, that the students were so aroused that they left the class thinking. One student even approached me after class and asked my own opinion.

While I was observing a lesson on Ambrose Bierce' "Horseman in the Sky," the teacher asked why the Civil War was such a terrible war, and students said that the horrible thing was the separation and alienation of families due to the animosity they held for the other's ideals. This idea was applied to the story. It occurred to me that "Which war was more terrible, the Civil War or the First World War?" would have resulted in the same eventual answer, but, probably, with more eager discussion.

In teaching Poe's "Eldorado," my polarized question turned out to be a rhetorical one. "Do you think that this implied that Eldorado was unattainable, or do you think it could be reached by *riding over the mountain?*" Nobody suggested that Eldorado was unattainable, and the discussion went on *how* to attain it, rather than on whether it was attainable. The discussion was good, but I learned a lesson which might be of help to other teachers—be careful not to turn your polarized question into a rhetorical question, except when the rhetorical question suits your purposes.

The instances I have discussed have been with a bright group, true scholars and, more often than not, self-motivating. With them, maybe the outstanding results of the polarized question do not show a true picture. Let us look at students on the opposite end.

With the "general" class, students who rarely have much in the way of inspiring class discussions, the polarized question takes them out of their shell of silence. It gives them something to work with, something on which to base an opinion, something pulled down from the clouds of the abstract. A story was read on the topic of "going steady." The duration and intensity of a "first love" was pitted against that of a later, more mature love. The variety of opinions surprised me. These kids had thought of things that never entered my mind. This seemed to be one of the few times when the students actually were eager to give their opinions.

On the other hand, the same class had read a farce play and then a comedy. The following polarized (?) question was asked: "In which play were the characters more real and more important?" There were a few takers, but only the students who usually volunteer. Nobody else was aroused. I analyzed the failure of the question and I think the phrase *real and more important* does not polarize. The phrase is vague and should have been more specific, so that I could have something specific to get them fighting with each other. The phrase *real and more important* didn't send them to the North Pole or the South Pole. It just didn't send them!

I've had them fighting over fragment sentences and aroused their competitive feeling by putting the fragment on the blackboard and asking, "Is this a name with an action missing, or an action with a name missing?" (p. 62).

In my workbook a sentence like "For a change, my brother is doing (well, good) in school" gave me the idea for a polarized question when I wouldn't let them make a choice but I wanted them to figure out which word outside the parentheses was being described. Once they saw that the verb was being described and not the subject, the rest was easy.

6. In teaching *The Valiant,* a short play by Holworthy Hall and Robert Middlemass, one question that met with enthusiastic response was "Does a man have the right to set up his own moral standards of right and

wrong, or does it depend on what others think in society?" Some students felt that if every human being acted as he wished, the result would be sheer chaos, whereas other students felt that people ought to decide for themselves, leading to a debate on whether or not man is intrinsically good, whether or not each man acts for the good of all society, or just out of purely selfish motives. A discussion on the "goodness" and "badness" of human nature ensued; it was really very exciting.

In the same play, I asked if it was braver for James Dyke, the hero of the story, to die like a martyr, without revealing his true identity, or to reveal his identity and thus face the shame of being branded a murderer by all who knew and loved him. A debate followed on cowardice versus bravery, and what constitutes bravery. The class never agreed, but we did have a stimulating and thought-provoking discussion. I am beginning to realize how important it is for a teacher to pose a question, drop it into the hands of the children, and then gradually step out of the picture.

When teaching Hawthorne's "The Minister's Black Veil," I asked the class whether they agreed with the author when he states that all people wear intangible veils. "Do we really want to know one another, or do we prefer to have other people, with all their emotions, keep their emotions hidden behind a façade?" We had a marvelous difference of opinion. Another was "Do some people wear dark sunglasses to disguise themselves or to call attention to themselves?" I found students still discussing the questions after the bell rang. Most of the students felt that people *do* know one another, but some of the others challenged this, and said, "No one ever really knows anyone else!" They talked about if people were basically lonely—it was a good discussion. Nobody relinquished his point of view.

My co-operating teacher conducted a dynamic discussion on *Pygmalion* and Shaw's conception of "middle class morality." When Alfred Doolittle refuses money from Henry Higgins because he would become a victim of "middle class morality," the teacher asked, "Is a man with a great deal of money liberated or imprisoned by his wealth?" The discussion went on to the obligations of the poor and the duties of the rich to the rest of society. Sometimes students went off on tangents, but I don't think that was a drawback. They were interested, they were excited about Shaw's play, they were defending various points of view, and they were learning how to discuss a complex problem in an intelligent manner.

I am setting up questions that deliberately provoke the discussion of antithetical ideas, but students shouldn't think that a classroom discussion means an opportunity to lash out, personally, at their fellow students.

Research, Resources, and Techniques

1. How the English teacher, more than any other teacher, runs the risk of being a stuffed shirt is discussed in G. Robert Carlsen's "English and the Liberal Arts Tradition in the High School" (*E. J.*, Sept. 1955, p. 323). The ignorant and unthinking snobbishness that teaches for wrongly valued outcomes—especially in the English teacher—is a real concern.

2. Edward J. Gordon's "Levels of Teaching and Testing" (*E. J.*, Sept. 1955, p. 330) clearly explains the questioning process, the levels of difference in questioning, and the way fact questions can be elevated to thought questions. An article deserving of close reading if the questioning process baffles you.

3. See the Marion B. Pierstorff citation (page 180).

4. The fighting issues in English today, on the basis of which you can improve your polarizing techniques in questioning, are considered in Helene W. Hartley's "English in a Community of Conflicting Interests" (*E. J.*, March 1960, p. 149).

Thumbs Up on Hands Down

Life isn't a glowing bed of roses once you have perfected your questioning technique, or perhaps is, with thorns. New problems arise, once your questions send your classes into paroxysms of eagerness to answer. For example, which do you do first, ask the question or call on the respondent? Most experienced teachers will ask the question first and then designate the respondent, explaining that if you first call on the student, the others will relax because they feel the heat is off, for the time.

But even this general rule has its limitations, particularly when your class is on the edge of its seat with eagerness to tell you, and students are calling out, unable to repress themselves. Then you may find it necessary to reverse orthodox questioning sequence and call on the student before you ask the question, as a signal to the overeager others that your selection of respondent is made. However, in most situations, the sequence is question stated and then respondent designated. With questions of the thought kind, allow enough time for thought.

You have asked the question, you have allowed a brief pause for thought, you have identified the student who is to answer, the student has answered, and then—horrible, horrible!—you repeat the student's answer. You have sinned, or at least committed an error typical of the inexperienced teacher. Do *not* repeat student answers! Do you feel that the others in the class did not hear? Then have the student or a classmate repeat for the sake of the others. Do you feel that the answer needs stressing? Call on another student to stress the answer needing repetition. Be watchful of this insidious fault, often committed unconsciously; it slows down the lesson and deprives it of its forward momentum. Experienced supervisors object to the habit because it looks as if the teacher is stalling or at a loss for thoughts or words. It may not be so. You may be repeating for what you consider highly meritorious reasons, but these weigh less than the push, the drive, the head of steam you lose when you repeat student answers. Guard against this fault.

Or you ask a question and a student asks you to repeat because he didn't hear. Don't do it. Have a student repeat for you. Similarly, if you ask a question and a student says he doesn't understand, do not yourself re-phrase; ask a student to rephrase for you. This simultaneously puts the question in simpler terms and enables you to check on how well your meaning is getting across to the class. If the student, in repeating for you, fails to capture your meaning, and if another, then another, similarly fails, you will know that your question was vague originally and that you your-self must rephrase. Do not take this as a blow. Indeed, your supervisor will recognize that you are in control not only of the class but of yourself and that you know how to check back on yourself as well as on the class.

Classroom situations are best handled in their own terms. A student had the habit of raising his hand and snapping his fingers to attract the teacher's attention—a most distressing habit. The teacher asked the student repeat-edly to stop, but the student persisted and, when reprimanded, pretended to be apologetic, claimed forgetfulness, and continued. The teacher's level of tolerance was reached one day when she asked a question and among the volunteers was the finger-snapper, back at the old stand. The teacher asked that all hands be lowered except the finger-snapper's and to him she said, "Keep it up until I tell you to stop." In a minute cramps set in and perhaps permanent paralysis of the finger-snapping muscles because he never tried it again. Cruelty? No—simply yielding in the direction of the pressure like a wrestler, or rolling with the punch like a boxer.

Should the student rise when answering? For what purpose should he arise? To show deference and respect to you and the class? By all means, if you and the class feel it necessary. But suppose the others in the class don't feel it necessary? Then it's you who feel the need of respect and deference, and that doesn't sound well. Students don't care whether their reciting classmates show them respect or not. Should you want to formalize the circumstances of recitation that way, you run the alternative risk of stiffness, but if you like a stiffly starched classroom, there is nothing wrong. You can be not only a good teacher but a democratic one under formal classroom procedures. Conversely, you can be the worst kind of autocrat whose students cower in their seats and never get to their feet.

Generally, students are heard more clearly over the room, they are more likely to think through their answers, they gain experience in addressing groups, when they get to their feet and answer. These are reasons having nothing to do with respect and deference. They are simply practical. You will have students who are reluctant or defiant about getting to their feet. Don't order them up. Ask the students in the remoter corners of the room if they are able to hear the answer of the reluctant or the defiant one; check on their hearing by having them repeat the answer of the reluctant/defiant one. Present reluctant/defiant one with the alternative of speaking up more distinctly or getting to his feet. You want them on their feet not for reasons of respect or deference, but only for the sake of improved audibility.

You can have a trimly run classroom with students who respond from a sitting posture, so, sitting or standing, your classroom will reflect you. You don't want looseness or indifference. You want attentiveness. You want learning. You also want to find out your supervisor's preferences and to be guided by these preferences, until your supervisor has observed you long enough to respect your classroom controls. The superior supervisor wants attentiveness and learning and knows that they can be gained whether the student stands or sits.

The student has answered. He has failed to make the correct answer. You have your choice. You can reprimand him; you can correct him; you can call on another student to correct his answer. In the first two choices you involve yourself; in the last choice you involve another student. It's always better to involve students rather than yourself; hence, select the third option under most circumstances. There will be exceptions, chiefly occasioned by your own bad temper; you will on more than one occasion find yourself losing your temper. Resign yourself to it, but don't be self-indulgent about it. You should object to it in yourself as you object to it in others, but you are human and prone to the weaknesses of the flesh.

Students can be stupid or unprepared, but neither justifies a sense of personal affront. As often as possible, when student answers fail to hit the mark, move other students into firing position.

As a hypothetical instance, you ask a student when Columbus discovered America (p. 346). He answers, "1776." What should your reaction be? Do you say, "Wrong!" Or do you suspend the immediate passing of judgment and feel yourself piqued by curiosity that another significant date in American history was substituted? Should you be saying to yourself, "Stupid idiot!" or rather, "What was in his mind to give that answer?" In one case you cut yourself off from any further inquiry, but in the other you continue to leave the channels of communication open between yourself, the student, and the remainder of the class too.

Similarly, there are ways in which you can say "Wrong!" You can say it and damn the student in his own mind and in the minds of others; or you can say it and invite the others to share in the righting of the Wrong.

The wrongest answer you ever will get has a tincture of rightness about it; we have no measure of absolute zero in psychology, and we have not reached it in physics. Be careful with "Wrong!" because you are untenably saying that you have finally hit on -273 degrees centigrade in human affairs. You, then, will be as wrong as the student. Psychometricians, those statisticians who are involved with measurement and evaluation in the areas of sociology, psychology, and education, have not evaluated for themselves what zero is in measurements dealing with human beings. The student who gives you 1776 where 1492 ought to be has some reason for claiming partial credit. It may be minuscule and barely visible to your eye, but, like all subatomic evidence, it bears investigation. Call the others in the class to patch the answer before you condemn with "Wrong!"

Another student answers. The answer is again indistinct, but this time the student is standing and you cannot invite him to raise himself out of his seat because he has already done so—but there he is, articulating poorly, muffling his syllables, and you are faced with another choice. You can approach the student, the better to hear him, or you can depart from him, turning your back on him, interposing distance to get him to speak up, and putting more students between you. Which is preferable? Generally the latter choice. The student, as you depart, will put volume into his voice, will call out to you, and in doing so will engage more of the students. He will not be speaking to you alone but to the group, which you have augmented by thus putting more and more space between you. Do you want a student to speak up? Do not approach him. Instead, retreat from him. (See p. 26.)

Should the teacher move around or stay in front of the room? No unitary answer is possible, except the generalized It Depends. If a student is reciting at the left side of the room, you ought to float over toward the right; if the student recites from the right side, float toward the left. If the class is having a fiery discussion with students belaboring one another in furious proposal and rebuttal, remain wherever you are, as motionless as you can be.

After a series of questions and answers, a point has finally emerged, a salient point in the development of the lesson. Are you to state it or should the recapitulation of the development to that point be made by a student? If the student can state the point effectively, fine; if not, yours is the job of summarizing what has gone on. Students like to know that four, five, or six nutshells can summarize what has happened. If the students can verbalize these nutshells, you are well assured that you have communicated with them; but if they cannot, then you must do the verbalizing for them. Certainly, at least twice during the course of most lessons, you should be able to look back and see what terrain you have covered. Just as experienced wilderness travelers blaze trees and look back over the landscape they have traversed to avoid getting lost, so you should make provision somewhere along the middle of the lesson for recapitulation. So also at the conclusion of the lesson. Thus you provide a midway summary and a terminal one.

Therefore, you keep your eye on the clock. You want to be sure that the bell doesn't ring before you've had a terminal summary. You've got ground to cover, you've got a certain amount of time allotted to the ground, and you've got to be mindful of the ground and of the time it takes. How do you keep your eye on the clock without making it too conspicuous? The question may sound foolish, but recollect your own feeling when you've seen a speaker looking at his wrist watch. In any case, it's less conspicuous to pass both wrist and watch before your eye than to pass your eye over the watch. Certainly, as experience mounts, you'll gain the professional know-how of the experienced New York taxi driver who turns off the avenue just as the changing traffic lights leave the other drivers waiting while he speeds along the intersecting side street in time to pick up the next green light at the parallel avenue. You too will perfect the instinct that tells you two minutes before the bell strikes that it's time to wind up and summarize.

Research, Resources, and Techniques

1. In Marion Zollinger and Mildred A. Dawson's "Evaluation of Oral Communication" (*E. J.,* Nov. 1958, p. 500), the flow charts show you how your lessons can be rated by a supervisor. Avoid figure 2; teach according to figure 3 for best questioning and discussion outcomes.

2. The democratic classroom is dealt with in Arnold Leslie Lazarus' "Guards for Our Future Security" (*E. J.,* Sept. 1955, p. 347). Its desirability is shown, but *not* the difficulties of attaining it. Democracy in a classroom sounds absurdly simple and altogether praiseworthy, but it is almost impossible to attain without backbreaking work and outstanding ability. Only a master teacher can run a truly democratic classroom; only mature students can contribute to it. It's not for the mediocre teacher or the callow student. It's not a simple matter of kind hearts and good intentions.

When the Best Laid Plans Bring Forth a Mouse

Both Highet[4] and Hook[5] agree that the good teacher is part ham actor. We have softened the impeachment by saying that the good teacher is also part bard. If so, consider:

Typically, you will be teaching four or five classes, with two preparations. You have prepared an excellent lesson. You walk into your first preparation. Things go well, as they should when you prepare a good lesson. Then you meet the second class, and, with the same preparation, the lesson falls on its face. Why? Or perhaps the situation is reversed. The first class dies on you, but when you meet the second class, the lesson takes fire and soars. Again, why? Why should not the same preparation work equally well with both classes?

Several reasons can be operating. One of your preparations may be with the class you meet just before the lunch period. The students are hungry, ravenous as only growing teen-agers can be, and the best planning in this circumstance is faced with almost insuperable obstacles of metabolic needs. It's not the planning, but the hour. The last period of the day, on a sunny, pleasant afternoon, presents other obstacles. Students are restless, and they've had a day of it. On the other hand, the first period of the day finds students still sleepy, complaisant, easier to handle, with disciplinary problems at a minimum. They haven't yet worked up steam, so that though they're easier to handle, they're not so responsive as you'd like them to be. This situation reduces problems of class management, but it also reduces what you can get out of them.

Meanwhile, here you are with a well-prepared script in your hand, but the production isn't going as you planned. Now is the time to analyze what the good actor does. The good actor doesn't depend only on the lines he has been given. He works himself into his role even before he goes on stage, and you, in the same way, must work yourself into your role every time you put on your preparation. You cannot depend solely on your plan, thoroughly prepared though it is. As an actor projects his lines across the footlights as if the hundredth time was the first, so you must work yourself up every time you put on your lesson. This doesn't require your eyes in a fine frenzy rolling, but it does mean suiting yourself to your material every time you put it on. Some kind of action is required of you, sometimes understated, sometimes provocative, sometimes teasing and baiting, sometimes electrifying. But whatever the material in your lesson plan, act accordingly. The show that you put on can be muted or excited, but you must put on a bit of a show to get the lesson moving in the direction you plan. This takes energy, thought, and time. You will find these well invested in the return you get in school and after school. You will be stripping yourself of the ineffectuality that characterizes too many teachers, and in exchange gaining strength, purposefulness, and a sense of power not only in your professional life but also in your private life, where it matters just as much.

Use of the Blackboard and the Mimeograph

The blackboard can be useful not only to students as you summarize the major points of the lesson, but also to you as you clarify for yourself the development of the lesson. Use the blackboard freely and in an orderly fashion. It will help you as much as it helps students. If you've ever seen photographs of scientists at work at places like the Institute for Advanced Study at Princeton, you'll remember them at work not with pencil and pad, or at their desks, but standing up, chalk in hand, before a blackboard. The blackboard helps clarify thought.

Many teachers at the beginning of a lesson write the lesson's theme, or aim, or intention, or topic, on the board, so that students know what the major note of the hour is to be. This is similar to the former practice of the TV performer Jack Paar, who had some saying, or aphorism, or wisecrack, written on a blackboard for the audience to react to. Not a bad idea for you to adapt or modify. (In addition to your lesson's keynote on the board, why not have students bring in comments, dialogue they've heard, apothegms or wisecracks, and write these on a corner of the board you have reserved for them and these? You'll get representations from Sahl to Shakespeare and Paar to Pope.)

Assignments should be on the board, usually, before the beginning of the hour, so that students can start work immediately at the bell. If assignments are lengthy, you should have them written out on paper; give the paper to a student and have the student copy it on the board. In fact, whenever possible, have students do this blackboard work for you. Material put on the blackboard acquires a special urgency. If important enough to be put on the blackboard, it is important enough to be incorporated into notes, and note-taking should be taken seriously, especially by students preparing for college admission. The blackboard will schematize the work for your students.

As the lesson progresses, and as you summarize each step, you ought to put this way-station, or subsummary, on the board. These accumulate, so that the end of the lesson sees an impressive list, worth transferring to notebooks.

The blackboard pointer endows you with status as the riding crop does a European army officer. For some obscure psychological reason, your pointing effectiveness is multiplied by the pointer. If you want to stress anything written on the blackboard, the pointer has more power than your index finger. The eyes of your students will follow the pointer more readily than your finger. The pointer helps in explanation. Use it freely. It's your riding crop, not meant for use across the backs of the poor, cringing natives, but as a symbol of leadership that has a clear sense of direction and is on its way there. Nothing is more ridiculous than a riding crop attached like a vestigial remnant to the hands of a nincompoop. A riding crop has a purpose; so has a pointer. Use it well, not stupidly.

The blackboard is a resource for you; it is likewise a resource for your students. When at work at it, they are lifted out of the blank anonymity of the class. The reluctant/defiant student mentioned earlier who is refractory about speaking from the front of the room will do so with alacrity

if despatched to the board with a piece of chalk in his hand and with something to write about. What can he write about? We have already recommended that homework assignments be written on the board by students,
not by you. In the same way, at the beginning of the hour, other students
are writing on the blackboard their assignments from the day before, getting them ready for class criticism and correction. After the assignment
for the day has been copied, a designated student should erase it. After
the assignments of the day before have been criticized, discussed, and corrected, another student is designated to erase. As far as possible keep your
hands free of the board eraser. Designate the area to be erased; designate
the student who is to erase it. You are thereby keeping students in contact
with board work. If a student successfully states a point that you intended
for a summary, acknowledge the achievement by having the student come
to the board and add to the summary points. In this fashion, ability to
summarize receives the accolade it deserves.

On other occasions, the blackboard is best avoided. Suppose you are
teaching a short poem. You have no copies in the text you are using. In
this case, do not write the poem, short though it is, on the blackboard.
Instead, mimeograph the copies you need and distribute them. The blackboard is a group experience, and sometimes you want the sense not of
group experience, but of an individualized one. A copy of one's own, like
a room of one's own, accentuates individualized values not shared with
anybody.

Generally, you'll have to cut your own stencils, but students, your own
or those on the staff of office aides, will run, collate, and staple them for
you. Use your mimeograph facilities liberally. When possible, have your
name and the name of the class typed in, and let students know that this
material is theirs to keep. The mimeograph, Rex-o-graph, and other duplicating devices, save you great amounts of time and energy, many more
times your original investment in cutting the stencil. They also help rapport.
Material cut by you, with your name and the class number on it, is more
personal than the same material studied out of flossy, glossy work books.
Students know you cut it for them. They will be pleased by these signs of
the effort you have taken. Don't stint on the amount of *meaningful* mimeograph material you prepare. Such material can be poems, drill materials in
spelling, usage, and grammar, reading comprehension materials, and anything else you encounter that can be useful in class. (The A. B. Dick Com-

pany has prepared suggestions as to the use of their machine in the classroom.[6])

The blackboard's strength is in recapitulation of material; the duplicating machine's strength is in the presentation of material. You can present duplicated material and from it work up your summaries on the blackboard, integrating the merits of duplication processes and the blackboard.

Evaluation in English

Objective tests or essay tests? Both have strengths and weaknesses. Nothing tests organizing ability like the essay; nothing tests knowledge of facts like the objective test. As an English teacher you will test organizing ability and facts and you will be the target of strongly outspoken proponents of one or another form of testing.

Efforts to assess organizing ability by the objective test and knowledge of facts by the essay test have led the College Entrance Examination Board, in its booklet "A Description of the College Board Achievement Tests" [7] to explain to high school seniors how its modified essay test gives greater objectivity:

> The English Composition Test provides an *indirect* measure of your ability to write English. It does not require you to write an essay, but it does require you to do a number of things, which, taken together, show reasonably well whether you have the power to do so.
>
> This indirect approach to the measurement of writing ability often puzzles people. They wonder why it would not be easier and better to have a student show his writing ability by giving him a pencil and telling him to write. In a national testing program, this method would be not easier but more difficult because of the enormous labor that would be required to read and mark some 100,000 essays. Furthermore, experience has shown that the writing of a one-hour essay provides a poorer basis for measuring a student's writing ability than does the indirect approach of the English Composition Test, which also takes an hour. There are several reasons for this, but the two that are probably most important follow. In the first place, a student's writing performance is apt to vary from day to day and from topic to topic. There is thus no way to tell whether a particular essay, taken all by itself, represents the student at his best, his worst, or his average. And in the second place, readers do not agree very well in their marking of essays. That is, the same essay may get a high mark from one reader and a low mark from another.

The booklet goes on to describe its ways of indirectly, and objectively, measuring writing ability, by "scrambled" paragraphs, scrambled poetry, and the appropriateness of figures of speech and style.

Efforts to retain the essay test and to give it greater objectivity are described by Highet[8] and by Thorndike and Hagen,[9] but these efforts are time consuming. The essay test is easy to prepare, but hard to correct; the objective test is hard to prepare and easy to correct. Both are hazardous for you because the objective test may tap the superficial and the trivial; the essay test is subject to the way you feel about the student, your reaction to his handwriting, and how much sleep you have had. Since neither method of testing is infallible, you must learn humility in your assessments of your students.

Your face-to-face assessments based on your personal reaction to students, their behavior, their apple-polishing, their aggressiveness, and their agreeableness will tend to reward the active participant rather than the quiet, thoughtful, withdrawn student, or the ebullient one. This is in part unfair, in part justifiable, because classroom manner and behavior are legitimately assessable by you, provided that you are not hopelessly subjective and do not have a preconceived pattern of the kind of student you want to have around you.

Learn the techniques of item analysis[10] so that your objective test will be truly objective and will truly test, because many an objective test that looks like one isn't. Item analysis is one way of testing a test, to see if the people who should do well are, and those who should do poorly are. Objective testing is part of a technology of testing, a complicated matter of reliability, validity, statistics, percentiles, and norms—matters which you should have studied in education courses—and, specifically in the field of English, you will find excellent objective test items. Study these materials for hints and suggestions as to how to develop your own.

Research, Resources, and Techniques

1. Two books that relate Information Theory to the work of the English teacher:

a. Norbert Wiener's *The Human Use of Human Beings* (Doubleday Anchor, 1954) shows how basic to modern science and to your questioning technique is the polarizing way of counting and of asking.

b. Joshua Whatmough's *Language: A Modern Synthesis* (Mentor, 1957) integrates the mathematics of electronic circuits with language, in an excellent introduction to new directions in linguistics.

2. These articles from *Scientific American* analyze group behavior and pathology; if you see them as a source of illumination for classroom behavior, you won't be wrong:

a. Ernest Gruenberg's "The Epidemiology of Mental Health" (March 1954, p. 38) points out that certain mental illnesses, like tarantism and other group disorders, are infectious. Are the ripples that sweep over your class and impede classroom management related to the illnesses discussed in this article?

b. Robert F. Bales' "How People Interact in Conferences" (March 1955) discusses how groups arrive at consensus. Lesson planning, class management, group discussion, committee work, and debate are aspects of your work clearly affected.

c. Edward T. Hall's "The Anthropology of Manners" (April 1955, p. 54) describes how students from different ethnic and socioeconomic backgrounds have different concepts of good manners, humor, courtesy, and acceptable behavior. Negro, Jew, Italian, Irish, and New England Protestant may not have the same ideas as to what constitutes socially desirable conduct.

d. Muzafer Sherif's "Experiments in Group Conflict" (Nov. 1956, p. 54) reports how strife and conflict in a summer camp were experimentally contrived and controlled. How would you *reverse* the procedures here discussed for satisfactory classroom outcomes?

e. Marvin K. Opler's "Schizophrenia and Culture" (Aug. 1957, p. 103) describes how ethnic and cultural patterns affect mental disease. Thus schizophrenia among the Irish is not the same as among the Italians. Are there ethnic, racial, and other group differences in the patterns of classroom misbehavior, or do all students misbehave the same way, irrespective of their background? How would your answer affect your management of your class?

3. Luella B. Cook's "The Search for Standards" (*E. J.*, May 1960, p. 321) discusses in general, nonspecific terms some concepts in evaluation.

English
CHAPTER 12 and Self-Understanding

Adjustment versus Nonconformity

Should students be administered Miltown or benzedrine at the beginning of each school day? Tranquilized or stimulated? Some occasions call for tranquillity; other for stimulation. If pills will do, why read literature? If vitamins, why eat food? Because we are not only chemical laboratories, but thinking and feeling creatures. Much of us is chemistry, but just as much is spirit.

The spirit wants to find out about itself and why it behaves as it does. English does this, as does psychological experimentation; coupling psychology and English will gain for you some of the most exciting class sessions you ever will have. Let your students watch themselves as they behave under experimental conditions.

Some risks are possible, but minimum precautions will avoid them. Pictures like those in the Thematic Apperception Test[1] or the Symonds' Adolescent Fantasy Test[2] can be found in magazines. Detach the captions and have students spin stories about the pictures. Such pictures are used in psychological testing; in the hands of a trained psychologist they reveal patterns of psychological and emotional disturbance. If you were to attempt to discuss these patterns, or to diagnose the emotional lives of your students on the basis of the stories, you would be trespassing into dangerous areas where you, with your training, have no business being. But you are safe in showing untitled pictures from *Life* or *Look,* inviting them to title the pictures, discuss them, and write brief paragraphs on them. Thereafter, compare the paragraphs and point out agreements and disagreements, but do not indicate in any way that these are diagnostic instruments. If, indeed, it would be presumptuous for a trained psychologist to interpret and diagnose in this group situation, in casual classroom circumstances, how can you? Nevertheless, self-understanding can proceed by your pointing out the way people project themselves onto unclear and amorphous structures and the way different people see things differently. You are illustrating differences in taste, not accounting for them. You are illustrating differences in temperament and outlook, not sorting them into higher and lower ranks.

The nonsense syllable (discussed on p. 128) is described fully in Woodworth,[3] where you will find other possibilities adaptable to your classroom. For example, match a list of nonsense syllables with spelling or vocabulary words. At the end of five minutes, test to see how many nonsense syllables are successfully matched with the key word. Get the average for the class. Readminister until you get the classical curve of learning that Ebbinghaus discovered. Show this to the class. Test the class the next day on the list. Note the results. Test again on subsequent days until you now develop Ebbinghaus' other classical curve, the curve of forgetting. You will have personalized psychology, as biology can be personalized by seeing a drop of one's own blood under the microscope.

Or you can try a variant that shows how learning and forgetting are related to height, weight, and mathematics. If you keep scores for each individual student in your class on the learning and forgetting of nonsense syllables, you will soon have enough data to draw a curve on the distribution of the learning and forgetting scores. Measuring the height and weight of the members of your class will give you another curve, in which most members of the class group around the middle and some exceptions are off at the ends of the distribution. Next have students report to class with ten pennies and have them do the probability experiment in coin-tossing that is described in most elementary statistics texts,[4] and you will have five curves dealing with learning, forgetting, height, weight, and coin-tossing.

The bell-shaped curve is sometimes called the Curve of Random Distribution. What's random about learning, forgetting, height, weight, and coin-tossing? What goes on in coin-tossing that is similar to the distribution of learning ability among human beings, or else the distribution of genes contributing to learning ability? What does this say about the heredity-environment controversy? What does it say about the underlying principles of democracy? What does it tell each student about his limitations and opportunities?

After you have explored these considerations deriving from one aspect of psychology, you can turn to another kind of curve, the kind encountered in social psychology, Floyd Allport's J-curve of Social Conformity.[5] Ask your students how often they have seen people smoking in a bus or driving through a red light. Your students will agree that these things don't happen very often and that most people behave the same way, under these conditions. The J-curve is so known because if this conforming behavior is graphed, the resulting curve looks like an inverted J, with most people grouped together, undifferentiated, with a few exceptions trailing off.

The bell-shaped curve tells us that people are different. The J-curve tells us that people are generally the same. Which best describes human behavior? If both do, in different circumstances, what are the circumstances? If a teacher declares that he marks on the curve, which curve is he talking about? In what circumstances is it defensible to mark on the J-curve? On the bell-shaped curve? To the extent that you set up standards, police them, and reduce the randomness of procedures, you are justified in marking on the J-curve, in which you will approach homogeneity of grades with a minimum of scatter. This is the kind of grading done in many professional institutions (for example, medical schools) where screening in original selection of the school population and rigidity of standards make it possible for the great majority of students to pass. Does this mean that medical education attempts to stamp out individuality? Hardly.

Is this beyond your work as an English teacher? You are dealing with the dimensions of homogeneity and heterogeneity of people, with the sense of individuality as contrasted with the need to belong, and with the way grades reflect an underlying philosophy of the differences or sameness in people. Poetry expresses it in Matthew Arnold's "Dover Beach," in which the individual is spiritually troubled because he feels his individuality being stripped from him or his individuality as a human being invaded. Arnold wanted to be marked on the J-curve. But Edna St. Vincent Millay, in "God's World"—"O world, I cannot hold thee close enough!"—sought to be part of the continuum of things and to find her pace in the grand design of the bell-shaped curve. Similarly, Frost's "Provide! Provide!" and Yeats' "To a Friend Whose Work Has Come to Nothing" deal with the J-curve's clumping of conforming behavior. Frost's satire and Yeats' loftiness are suitable for your brighter students in the junior and senior years. After you have compared the meaning of *hard* in both poems, discussed the reason for the comma after *Abishag* in the Frost poem, and compared *stock exchange* in Frost with *a place of stone* in Yeats, you will want your students to see how conformity—or its more recent formulation, consensus—can corrupt, because that is what both poems are about.

Self-Understanding Is Not Self-Improvement

Great teachers and great creative spirits are not always persons of exemplary conduct. Abelard, Byron, Shakespeare, Shelley, Wordsworth, and many others transgressed against socially desirable behavior. You do not gain self-improvement when you teach for self-understanding. Even the psychoanalyst, who goes so deeply into the psyche, wants his patients to understand themselves but does not assume that this understanding leads to better conduct; self-understanding may lead to unhappiness because many motives are better left unexplored. The bank-robbery film *Rififi*, showing that crime does not pay and inevitably requires a price, convinced certain people that safe-cracking can be safe; a rash of bank robberies followed and understanding did not lead to self-control. The fence-whitewashing episode in *Tom Sawyer* is a study in deception. Do you think your alert students have learned from the episode to avoid deception or to sharpen up their practices in it?

On the other hand, there can be no self-improvement without self-understanding. Your classes may have students assiduously studying English to become better spellbinders, just as some students in Socrates' day sought out sophists who taught them to be demagogues, and just as slick politicians have profited by speech training. In gaining insight into the mental processes of others, they have learned little about themselves; there has been self-enhancement without self-improvement. See Plato's *Symposium,* in which Alcibiades illustrates self-enhancement without self-improvement. Socrates illustrates self-improvement without self-enhancement. As an English teacher, you seek self-improvement in your students and you reject self-enhancement; to encourage self-improvement you must see that they achieve self-understanding; to differentiate self-improvement from self-enhancement, you must illuminate and deal with that other aspect of self, self-control. Our desiderata are self-understanding, self-improvement, and self-control.

The curriculum is a social instrument, paid for by the taxpayer, which attempts to have the student go as far in self-understanding as will have beneficial outcomes in citizenship and social responsibility; beyond that point the curriculum does not care to meddle and should not. Alcibiades, self-enhancing as he was, was never reached by the responsibilities of citizenship. He was an aware villain, sensitive, alert, cultured, and unprincipled. But others who had been exposed to the same curriculum could assess him better because they had been. The curriculum operates in the matrix of a class, a group, in which the best defense against an Alcibiades and the best knowledge of him is gained by an understanding of self. This was Socrates' defense too. Let us understand ourselves and we will do a better job of understanding tyrants, demagogues, and slick orators. This is what the curriculum requires of you and of your students, not psychoanalysis in depth.

Keep this *caveat* in mind as you read such otherwise helpful book as Elizabeth Berry's *Guiding Students in the English Class*.[6] You will find good suggestions in several of her case histories but remember the other side of the coin: the guidance program sometimes blueprinted for you, and the ability to express oneself, the understanding of self and others, and the appreciation of character in literature and of the beautiful poetic phrase and figure, can sometimes equip a man to be a better malefactor instead of a better citizen. Hence, in your program for self-understanding, do not aim at alteration of character but at awareness of it and its manifestations.

In such a program, you will waste time by plunging into suggestions that students write on, or consider, or discuss such topics as these:

> The kind of person I think I am.
> The kind of person I think others think I am.
> The kind of person I would like to be.
> Overcoming an inferiority complex.
> Getting boys to notice you.
> Should teen-agers go steady?
> They don't understand me.
> They brought me up wrong.

These suggestions are taken from English methods texts that will remain nameless. What's wrong with them? Nothing except the timing. These are extraordinarily difficult topics to write on (see the discussion on "How I Spent My Summer Vacation," p. 83), but they are appropriate if they emerge from reading or discussion. They should be the outcome of considerations encountered in discussing *The Good Earth,* or *Lost Horizon,* or *Elizabeth, the Queen.* They are perfectly acceptable topics, provided that they emerge from a task that the class has undertaken and, even more important, *after* you and the class know each other.

Indeed, your self-understanding program will fall on its face, no matter what your topics, your resources, and your timing, unless *you* have understanding. Glance back at pages 134-136, 137-139, and 190 to remind yourself of why self-understanding in you is a necessary preliminary to your self-understanding program. Let's assume you have it. Then everything contributes. You will impart self-understanding whether you teach punctuation, Shakespeare, or the business letter. Not a single aspect of the English curriculum but will offer an opportunity. You will not need any such special topics as those listed above to gain it, contribute though they may.

But suppose you don't have it? How can you avoid playing the hypocrite? How can you gain self-understanding before attempting to impart it to your classes? By remembering, and by setting aside time every day, ten, fifteen, or twenty minutes, when you recall yourself during adolescence, your friends, your ambitions, your home, your family, what you cherished, what you loathed, whom you envied, whom you scorned, what made school subjects easy, what made them hard. Be thorough, be minuscule, about your recollections.

The probabilities are that you were an obedient, docile pupil, the kind that would ultimately become a teacher, so that it is more difficult for you to remember the behavioral infractions in which most other people indulge during adolescence. You were, most likely, the "good" child, if not the goody-goody kind. Do you remember your teen-age reactions to your friends who weren't? Let these contribute to memory too.

In addition to this encouragement of recall, keep in mind what was said earlier about the observant eye and the accessible ear (p. 25): the temptation to give helpful advice comes out as yammering. Whenever possible, instead of making statements, ask questions. Inquire; do not state.

CASE STUDY 17 *   A per diem substitute dreaded the telephone calls that summoned her to work because her days were nightmares. Students knew she was there for a day and discipline meant nothing. She dutifully tried to follow any lesson plans left for her, but they were impossible as the students rampaged on this day off. She tried to develop emergency lesson plans of her own that would stimulate and interest students, but these fell before the onslaughts of students given this opportunity to frolic. They would walk in, see her, and "Whee! Teacher's absent! We got a substitute! Let's have a blast!" At the very sight of her, all the mischief and deviltry in them bounced to the surface; they were maniacs suddenly liberated from strait jackets, in slow, average, and superior classes alike. Scolding, threats, pleas, cajolery didn't work.

To prepare herself for regular appointment, she was taking a workshop in secondary school problems. She presented her experience and asked the class and instructor what possibilities remained to her. After the class had made some half-sympathetic, half-humorous recommendations, which ranged from tranquilizers for herself to bludgeons for the students, the instructor commented, "What's wrong is that you're trying to teach them."

"I'm supposed to," she answered.

"It doesn't work. They don't listen to you. I'm reminded of a diametrically opposite situation. You're at home and somebody rings your bell, or you're walking out of a supermarket and somebody stops you, or you're in the street and somebody asks you for a minute of your time. This person has a clipboard and papers and wants to question you for a survey. This person is a complete stranger, somebody you don't know from Adam, but you stop, most often, even if you're in a hurry, to answer questions that have nothing to do with you. Why should you care if somebody's taking a survey? But they want your opinion and you'll stop whatever you're doing or wherever you're going to give it. Suppose you try that in your classes? Suppose you hand them a questionnaire of some kind as soon as they enter and tell them you're doing a survey and you need their opinion for research? They come in and find you not a person who's teaching them anything, but someone asking them something. Naturally you must have your materials prepared beforehand, and they

* Adapted from a student report.

must be broad enough in scope to be generally appropriate to most classes. You can have them check off preferences on national brands, whether soups or soaps; political candidates; which current movies they've seen and whether it was advertising or word-of-mouth recommendations that sent them to see the movie, prefer the candidate, or buy the soups and soaps. Do we select soups, soaps, political candidates, and movies the same way? Do they spend the same average time, Mondays through Sundays, in radio listening or television watching? Or throw forms of the Kuder Preference Record [7] at them. In any case, you're not telling, not instructing, but asking."

A week later, at the next class meeting, the substitute teacher reported: "I've had three days of assignments since the last meeting, but I can only report on the last two because I didn't have the materials ready for the first, which was miserable as usual. But the second and third day were miraculous. As soon as the first students walked into the room I handed them each three pages of stapled, mimeographed questions, and designated a couple to distribute to other students when they walked into the room, so that something unexpected was in their hands when they saw the regular teacher not there. The first thing on the questionnaire was a line for their names and section number—there wasn't going to be anything anonymous about this one—and then the instructions: 'Answer all questions as fully as possible,' and then the questions you suggested last time, plus some I thought of myself on corn-flake preferences, a check list of countries on who's more to blame for international crises, and something on whether they preferred reading the book first or seeing the movie first. In the first class I met, I walked around the room as they worked, and I was terrified to find that they could finish it in twelve to fifteen minutes. What would I do with them the rest of the time? I determined I wouldn't say anything, I wouldn't instruct, I wouldn't teach, but I'd only ask questions. I did. I asked only three. The first was, 'Which of these questions is most closely related to your interests?' the second was, 'Which is most closely related to your school work?' The third was, 'Who disagrees?' They fought and quarreled with one another and they were still fighting as they walked out of the room, leaving me the questionnaires. The second class went the same way, and that's how it's been since. But I still feel guilty about not teaching them so I asked them today which question was most closely related to the last work they did for their regular teacher. That gave me a chance, after twenty minutes or so, to swing into the lesson plans the regular teacher had left for me. By that time they had got over the hysteria of seeing a substitute and we could begin to work. But it would be impossible unless I had had some mechanism for first asking them questions, and this is it."

If self-understanding in your class must be preceded by self-understanding in you, and if self-understanding in you reveals some unpalatable characteristics about you, your reasons for teaching English, and the status of the English teacher, should not this sorry catalogue never have been opened in the first place? As a teacher, you are subject to all kinds of slings and arrows, from students, parents, community, and public opinion. There is nothing spectacular about your salary or your status. Do you have friends who are successful in business? How do they regard you? How, indeed, do you regard yourself when they discuss their business experiences, successes, and even failures?

How did you select teaching for your career? Did you back into it, *faute de mieux,* because nothing better presented itself? Did you go forward to it because you wanted nothing else as much? Did you enter teaching because you are afraid to compete? And does your fear of competing with other adults engender a compensatory braveness and fearlessness when you face younger human beings? In other words, does teaching please you because you can bully the helpless and fawn upon your superiors as part of your job?

Are you as scholarly as you have to be and no more? Do you feel restless because you haven't the time to learn more about your profession, or doesn't it bother you a bit? Do you weigh out as much of yourself as required to keep your tracks covered and your job done, but not an ounce more because that's all the tight-fisted authorities deserve and that's all they'll get? Or do you find it impossible, once you're in the classroom and facing your students, to stint of yourself, your ideas, and your enthusiasm, because the presence of your boys and girls needles you into efforts that spill over and refuse to be doled out?

These questions must be answered by you before you have any right to teach students self-understanding, but remember that if they reveal a public and a private face in you, hypocrisy isn't automatic. Let's assume that you have answered such questions and that the image of yourself that emerges isn't what the books tell you a teacher ought to be. Accept it; you have a right to. Virtually everybody operates with two sets of faces, from politicians seeking high office, to newspaper editors, to businessmen, to lawyers and doctors, to school administrators, so why not you? We're all human. Having a public and a private face does not imply hypocrisy. But this is a partial answer.

Being with teen-agers so many hours a day has its risks. You may become a superannuated teen-ager, petulant, petty, and narrow, because students, community, and public policy conspire in reducing you.

Membership in a professional organization answers this conspiracy. It puts spine into you. As a teacher you are eligible to join the National Council of Teachers of English, the A.F.L.-C.I.O, or political parties. If you join out of conviction, rather than out of conformity, this affiliation will strengthen you.

Now answers are never final, even in science. The alternatives available, an elucidation of the problems that make your answers inconclusive or tentative, are good answers, and you should furnish them. You are thereby answering as well as anybody can. By revealing the complexities surrounding the soul, eternity, political affiliation, economic equity, or beauty, you have answered effectively. By showing a student how he gets in his own way, in letting emotional needs distort perception, you have answered him. You must always be able to answer, even if you do not have the answers. "I don't know," is an excellent answer.

Ask questions of yourself to gain confidence that you can answer your students' questions without stalling and without spurious answers; if, therefore, you can answer any question, how long will you remain a classroom teacher? Will anybody able to ask so and answer so be content with the routinized repetitiveness of the teacher's work? Only if he has great dedication because the world offers great rewards, far greater than teaching affords, to such a person. So you must determine your level of purposefulness. Why should you remain a teacher, when you—who can ask and answer on this high plane—could do so much better for yourself in another career, in advertising, radio, television, politics, publishing, or newspaper work? Are you afraid to try because you don't have the proper connections and because timidity keeps you where you are? Or because twice or three times a week lessons go so well that you capture the creative joy that only the artist and scientist ever experience and that no amount of money in the world can compensate for? And because teaching this way yields a contentment that is not the same as a routinized rut, but is rather the craftsmanlike satisfaction that very few people are ever privileged to get? Which?

Unless you have engaged in this kind of self-understanding program aimed at yourself, you have not the right to ask your students to write about themselves, their ambitions, their fears, what they think of school and their best friends, how they reacted to their summer vacations, or any matter dealing with the first person singular. However, if you have, all these subjects are legitimately open to you. Indeed, what isn't?

On Energy

Can you make stupid students bright? No. Can you make stupid students less stupid? Yes. A low I. Q. can function poorly or it can function well. It can work at low efficiency or at maximum efficiency.

The average teacher is appalled with the necessity of teaching a slow class, but greets the possibility of teaching a bright one. Less energy is expended in teaching a bright class, more in teaching a slow one; but less energy is returned to the teacher in successfully teaching a bright class than in successfully teaching a slow class. The more you work effectively with a slow class, the greater your bounce at the end of the day. If so, what makes teachers reluctant to work with slow classes?

Far more than with a bright class, the slow class requires you to question your approach, your values, and your stereotypes. Stupidity is an extraordinarily complex affair and you should treat it with respect and give it your deepest powers of analysis. Dealing with stupidity takes more thought and preparation than dealing with brightness. Thought and preparation require energy. Invest it. As with all good investments, you will get a handsome return at the end of the day which you will be able to reinvest in your hobbies, your family, and your social life. Meanwhile your stupid class will become less stupid and more efficient.

| CASE STUDY 18 * | The teacher was very experienced, especially at keeping several irons in the fire. The student teacher thought it unprofessional of him to spend free periods at the pay telephone in the

* Adapted from a student report.

corridor speaking to parents and rounding up business for his summer camp and making appointments to show films and slides of his camp facilities to prospects, and then running upstairs to the teachers' room to play a rubber of superlative contract bridge before the bell rang. He had even asked the student teacher if she wanted a summer job as a counselor.

In the classroom of slow students that she was observing, he was altogether unhurried, almost as if, she suspected, he recuperated in the classroom from the weight of his outside interests of summer camp and contract bridge. It was in this class, the day before, that the regular teacher had asked the class for the meaning of *fatigue* and one of the students had said, "Work clothes." The student teacher, sitting in back of the room, had with difficulty stifled a laugh, but the regular teacher had nodded gravely, had admitted that this was one meaning of the term, and then had said, "The first meaning was *tired*. How can the same word mean *work clothes* and *tired?*" At the end of the discussion, the student teacher admiringly admitted, the class understood the meaning and use of the word.

Spring vacation was a few weeks off, and one day the regular teacher had a student write on the board:

? ? ? ? ? ?

lily	bonnet
avenue	egg
parade	basket
fashion	color

"Naturally this is a spelling list," said the regular teacher, "but all these words have something in common. Can you guess what it is? While you're writing the spelling list in your notebooks, I want you to figure out what word goes in place of the question marks. It's the word they all have in common." Hands went up; the second student got it—*Easter Vacation*—and was given the privilege of going to the board, erasing the question marks, and spelling out the words. He did so without error. The cooperating teacher called on another student, gave him a slip of paper, and, while the student was writing the contents on the board, asked the class: "Tell me if you understand the points."

By that time the student had finished writing:

He has the message wrong.
He has the wrong message.

Make the transition gradual.
Make the transition gradually.

The teacher asked, "Does everybody know the words in the first pair?" Everybody did. "In the second pair?" *Transition* required explanation and was thereafter included in the word list in their notebooks. The regular teacher asked, "Why did I put these four sentences on the board? I'll give you a minute." He turned his back on them and looked out of the window. Hands were up and waiting for him when he turned around again.

One student said, "In the top sentence you're talking about the way. In the next one you're talking about the message. Right?"

He nodded and called on another raised hand: "It's How and What. I don't know how else to say it."

The co-operating teacher seemed incredulous that the correct answer had been gotten so soon. "Perfect! Which is which?"

"In the first sentence it's How and in the second it's What. Okay?"

"Go on! Go on! You're doing great!"

"In the third it's What and in the fourth it's How."

"Come up front and put a perfect mark for yourself in the Delany book." He told the class, "Copy the four sentences in your notebooks. In one place the word *wrong* describes a name. In the other the same word describes an action. Where does it describe a name? Where does it describe an action?" They knew. He went on. "Now substitute *incorrect,* a synonym, for *wrong,* and read the sentences." After some faltering they substituted *incorrectly* for *wrong* in the first sentence and saw that it couldn't be substituted in the second without dropping the *-ly* suffix. Parallel discussion followed with the third and fourth sentences and he then detached himself from the side window sill on which he had been relaxing and went to the blackboard, writing *Adverb* and *Adjective.* "In which sentences do we see an adverb, and in which an adjective?"

As soon as he had the answers—on the third try—he said, "Fine! Now we're going to have a discussion. It's no secret that some of you are slow readers. Here's something that puzzles me. Notice that even the slow reader *speaks* at a normal rate. I'm not speaking any more slowly than usual, but you understand me when I speak at this speed, so that you *listen,* as well as *speak,* at a normal rate of speed. A person who's a slow reader can be a normal speaker and a normal listener. Does anybody know why?" There were shoulder shrugs and head shakes, but nobody volunteered. The teacher nodded. "I don't know how to answer that either. If I knew, believe me, I'd make a lot of people happier, including some in this class, who'd like to read better but don't know how to go about it. But that's a puzzle, isn't it, that people who speak and listen at a regular, normal rate, don't read at a normal rate? Many of my students are slow readers so I had an idea for an experiment. I don't know how it would work out, but it depends on slow readers being just as fast as anybody else in talking and listening. Maybe we've made a mistake in remedial reading. We keep giving you new passages to read. What would happen if you read and reread the *same* passage until you read it at a normal rate *aloud*. Get the difference?" He looked around the room and now there were nods. "What *is* the difference?" he asked, calling on a student.

The student arose. "We'd be getting one thing perfect before we went on to another."

"That's right. But wouldn't it be more boring than the other way, when you go on to new passages all the time?"

This time hands went up. The consensus: "No, because you wouldn't be fighting new words and new passages all the time, but getting better and better with one passage. You wouldn't be always in the dark with new passage after new passage, but one passage would get clearer and clearer. It would be less discouraging."

The regular teacher slapped his hand down on the desk. "We'll try it. Not today, because we don't have time enough, but we'll try it and see what the results are. I'll get some magazines from the library, and I'll tell you what passages to work on. Meanwhile," and he turned to the board and wrote:

"A *pessimist,* seeing an eight ounce glass containing four ounces of water, says, 'It's half empty.' What does the *optimist* say?" He turned around, to find half the hands in class waving.

"That's easy," he laughed. "Write the underlined words in your notebook."

A student called out, "Does *optimist* have anything to do with *optician?*"

The teacher shook his head doubtfully. "It may. If you look at something through rose-colored glasses, you're an optimist, all right, and you've been to an optician maybe, but if there's a connection it's way back, thousands of years back, and there's no way of knowing any more. The unabridged dictionary would tell you. But here's something I want you to figure out—who has more pep, the optimist or the pessimist—and why?"

Up to this point the student teacher had been able to keep adequate notes on the questions, answers, and reactions, but now the discussion exploded, becoming so excited and participation so general that it was impossible, despite her assiduity, to keep notes on the various points the students were raising, except in the sketchiest way. After a while, the co-operating teacher broke in, "The more you speak, the more there's a connection with the experiment. It's not going to be successful with everybody, only with those who have pep, and most of you agree the optimist is the one who has. So everybody who has pep can join the experiment and everybody who doesn't have pep enough can stay out of it and do it the old way. Now, before the bell rings, how can those four sentences we studied at the beginning of the period help in better reading?"

"You've got to know the difference between How and What," one student volunteered.

"Which words hang around together," said another.

After a few more students summarized in their own lame way, but to the apparent satisfaction of the co-operating teacher, the bell rang. He collected his papers and the student teacher came up and said, "You had them on their toes all the way. Can I discuss it with you now?"

The co-operating teacher shook his head and brushed her off, "Not now. I've got to run downstairs and call my broker about an order, and then I've got to call one of my partners about the agent's bill on a real estate parcel we just bought, and then I want to confirm an appointment for tonight with the parents of a possible camper. I'll be on the telephone about a half hour. Get yourself a cup of coffee and see me in thirty minutes in the teacher's room." He moved rapidly down the hall, calling over his shoulder, "Have you finished correcting those compositions for the creative writing class? We'll need to return them tomorrow!"

The student teacher, bewildered, met with the regular teacher at the appointed time and place. Puffing a small but expensive cigar, he said contentedly, "Now what's on your mind?"

"How do you do it?" asked the student teacher. "How do you juggle all those balls at the same time?"

"During the lesson?" the regular teacher inquired.

"No. You had them working every minute, but, before we discuss my notes, aren't you tired at the end of the day?"

The regular teacher smiled. "Why? Teaching, like learning, liberates energy; it doesn't fritter it away. I'm a better teacher because I'm in the market, in real estate, and I've got business interests. It broadens me. It doesn't narrow me. I can put more on the ball. I can draw on more experiences. Do you know that kids sense it too? Did you see how they delivered for me? When I talked about pep, they listened because I'm an expert on the subject. I bring energy into a classroom because I get some of it from the outside, and I walk out with more than I brought in. Some people around this school don't like me because I make them feel dusty. Believe me, they're poor teachers. But forget me; let's talk about the lesson. That slow class moved fast, didn't it? They can't take too much of anything at one time, so you can't keep them at one thing too long. Nevertheless, it *was* the same thing all the way through, only I didn't let them know it. It was reading, reading, and more reading that I was interested in; the spelling was part of it, the vocabulary study was part of it, that experiment idea was part of it, and the optimist-pessimist bit was part of it. It all added up to reading. I wasn't going to preach that reading was complex, but I was giving them complexity without telling them that that's reading." He suddenly grew sheepish. "You liked it?"

The student teacher nodded. "It was exciting."

The regular teacher leaned forward. "Confidentially, and don't tell my dusty colleagues I told you, but I'm in teaching for kicks. That's the only reason for teaching. Those stupid kids were never given birth to properly. I'm helping them give birth to themselves. A friend of mine's a successful obstetrician. He says every time he delivers a baby it's the same miracle all over again; he can't ever get over the miracle of it, and he's delivered hundreds and hundreds. With me it's the same way, but I'm helping these kids give birth to themselves. Money? I make more on the outside, but every day in the classroom it's an *accouchement* and I can see those kids putting their hands into their brains and pulling out ideas and feelings nobody ever gave them credit for having. Several times a week they walk out of my class beside themselves for joy, stupid as they are, because they never knew they had it in them and there it is, red-faced, hollering, and clawing for food and air—an idea, a sentiment, an intimation, a feeling —their babies! With every idea, more pep and more self-confidence. It helps me too. Nobody has to tell me I'm a successful teacher, so I don't feel there's any unfinished business behind when I walk out at the end of a school day. I feel like a bird. I can meet with people and talk deals and take care of business. My mind's free."

"And active," the student teacher said admiringly.

The Guidance Function in English

Unquestionably, the apex of your work in English is guidance, but not before you have attempted, even if not attained, self-understanding. Console yourself that it will never be attained, but without the conscientious attempt you have no right to meddle with the plans, hopes, and dreams of others. Furthermore, nobody can substitute for the kind of job you, and only you, the English teacher, can do, whether school psychologist or school architect, even though these people have tried to do so.

Can student morale be improved by school architecture? The author recently discussed this with the principal of a beautifully designed vocational school, a veritable showplace of the best in modern architecture, spacious, airy, with a Mondrian exterior, wide corridors, and a handsome mural. I asked the principal if the décor had improved the behavior of the student body over behavior in the rundown building formerly occupied.

"Not with the lower classmen," the principal replied. "We have as much vandalism with them as we had before. But I believe that the building has improved the morale and behavior in the seniors, though it's hard to tell because we never had any trouble with our seniors, even in the old building. By the time our students are in their last year, they've settled down and they're pretty responsible. They're proud of being seniors. There's always less trouble with the eighteen-year-olds than with the thirteen- and fourteen-year-olds. The seniors had morale before, and the building just adds to it. The younger kids haven't grown up to it yet, and the building doesn't accelerate the growth process."

Architecture, no matter how beautiful, doesn't compensate for the job that only you can do. Every dollar that goes into a beautiful school structure and is diverted from more teachers is a less efficient dollar in gaining an educated citizenry. Architecture is not as basic to education or to guidance as teaching is. Education can go forward successfully in dark basements if you have the right teachers. School architecture without adequate staff represents frightful waste. We are wasting on structures and wanting in educators.

This waste affects your guidance program. Basic values will be pushed aside for whipped cream. Careers are important, but so is satisfaction in work. Getting along with people is fine, but not prostrating yourself before them is too. Pleasantness should not become obsequiousness, nor gregariousness prostituted to dependence on the opinions of others. Publishers like Science Research Associates[8] have excellent materials on guidance that will never replace Browning's portraits of people, Pope's descriptions of social relationships, or a *New Yorker* treatment of human interaction.

Your guidance program aims for effective social citizens who are not only polite to others but bold in stating their opinions and whose responsibility to society does not stop with unquestioning loyalty to any *status quo* they have been born into. The lives of Schweitzer, Einstein, Freud, Loyola, and Pasteur show that a man can deeply influence the world by living deeply inside himself and that social outcomes result from individual insights. Living in society sometimes requires tractability, sometimes inflexibility, depending on the face that society puts forward. When you teach usage (see p. 63) you teach judgment as to conformity and nonconformity, in turn relating usage to guidance, and in turn to social understanding.

A student teacher offers an example of guidance through utilization of individual experiences in paragraph writing:

> I was fortunate enough to observe our co-ordinator teach a lesson on the introductory paragraph, a technique the students could use in many assigned topics. . . . He distributed issues of *Reader's Digest* and *Coronet* to each student and said, "These magazines, even in this television age, have maintained great popularity. What's their secret?" He then instructed students to read *only* the first paragraphs of several pieces in the magazines and to raise their hands when they found an introduction so fascinating that they wished to continue. He then had students read their choices aloud, asking for a show of hands if the others found the item interesting. Four or five articles led the rest. He then asked what the paragraphs had in common. After consideration, the students replied that all began with anecdotes that hinted at the possible conclusion, thus engaging the reader's curiosity. He then discussed the values of this method: each person could achieve individuality because each would have different experiences to draw on even when writing on a topic assigned to almost forty students. The lesson was followed by an assignment, a composition which had to begin with a personal experience. Almost forty papers individually flavored by the writer's personality and experience and demonstrating more effort and care than the average set of compositions were turned in.

Another example from another student teacher, indicating that guidance is more an attitude than a plan:

> One boy in class obviously had many problems which affected his work. He seemed twisted in knots inside. It was easier to ignore him than get entangled in helping him. One day I was watching the class as they wrote papers on "Is Suicide Ever Justified?" in which they related their papers to *Romeo and Juliet*. Fifteen minutes passed and this boy had written nothing. I approached him.
>
> "Having trouble?" There was no answer. "Why haven't you written anything?"
>
> "Can't think of anything to write, Miss ————."
>
> "But you were supposed to prepare for this at home."
>
> "Yes, Miss ————."
>
> "Did you?"
>
> "No, Miss ————."
>
> He spoke in a low tone, politely and with eyes averted. I went back to the desk. Ten minutes passed and he still hadn't written anything but his heading. Finally I called him up. "Could anything make you commit suicide?" I asked.
>
> "No. Nothing."
>
> "Why nothing?"
>
> "Because while we live there's always the possibility of a second chance. When we're dead, there's nothing. Perhaps Romeo would have met another girl, just as he met Juliet after Rosaline."
>
> I was amazed. Here, from a difficult boy, I had not only an opinion, but one that was related to the text. "Why don't you write *that?*" I asked. And he did. He turned in a paper, short because of the limited time in which he wrote it, but the grammar, usage, style, and ideas were swell. Several days later he read his paper to the class.

Another student writes on world crises and how these affect personal guidance:

> I have become acutely conscious of the responsibilities of the English teacher. He is more truly a "Teacher of Life." He must run the gamut of all phases of experience, not only those in the four school walls. Subject matter in the English classroom varies from "It's what's up front that counts," to "Will our rockets be the first up front?" The English teacher must discuss both extremities (are they really so far apart?) and in doing so instill values and ethics. I observed a class discussion centered on a dot which had been chalked on the board. The teacher told the class to imagine that this was a button which if pushed would cause instant death. Then he asked, "If you were walking on the street, minding your own business, and a stranger came up to you and offered you

a million dollars to push such a button, would you? The person who would die would not be related to you and would mean nothing to you."

One boy said he would. Then the teacher asked if he would do it for $999,999.99. Again the boy said he would. This continued, diminishing each time, until the boy said he wouldn't, and the figures on the board were:

$990,999.99
$990,999.98

and at this point he asked the boy the difference between the two; the boy answered a penny. "Then," said the teacher, "you would commit this action for one cent." The boy gulped, the class laughed, and the teacher had begun to make his point: right and wrong are distinguishable even though the differences are sometimes unclear, and small transgressions lead up to great evils.

Another student teacher shows the basic source of infection that causes many guidance programs to turn sour:

I've heard much, read much, and been amused much by pupil boners, but what about teacher boners? One in particular is self-satisfied and thick to boot, and I'm afraid she's not as exceptional as she should be. In introducing two poems on Lincoln, she dogmatically told the class that his famous pose (top hat, and stooped over) was caused by his sad life. She insisted that he was pictured pen in hand in another portrait because he had written the Fourteenth Amendment.

And another shows how character analysis is directly related to guidance:

In teaching the closing chapters of *The Good Earth,* I wanted to show that money could not buy Wang Lung peace and contentment. How could I interest the class in this decision of a remote Chinese? So I told them a story I had seen on the Alfred Hitchcock show of a man who bet his little finger against a new Cadillac. Would they bet on losing a little finger to gain a new car? Some would; others wouldn't. I asked if they would sell an arm for $100,000. Only one boy would. But no one would sell his eyes for a million dollars, or any price. I wanted to know why not, and one girl answered that there are some things money can't buy. After that I was set. We went into Wang Lung's life, what money couldn't buy for him, and he was less the remote Chinese after that.

And another shows how the teacher can make or break the guidance situation and how self-understanding in the teacher is preliminary to any guidance program:

In some psychological plays and novels, a single event in the main character's life throws sudden light on all that has gone before. I experienced the same illuminating flash. My annoyance with disciplinary matters and inattention was a personal one, unknowingly, that any person should be behaving that way, and especially to *me*. An incident which involved me, the regular teacher, a student, and indirectly an entire home room class, made this clear.

During an extended home-room period, I was helping my co-operating teacher straighten out some clerical work on records of student lateness; excessive lateness results in a bad character report. One boy was being reported for this. He was indignant and arguing and shouting at the teacher. But the teacher continued talking quietly and easily. I was half-amused by the boy's self-righteousness ("I was only late four times; that's not excessive; you can't do that to me!") and half-angry at his shouting. I would have reported him for misconduct, as well as for lateness. The teacher, however, remained calm and easy-going. Not only did the student calm down, but the teacher saved face—because the student turned out to be right! What looks like disrespect is often some problem within the student's own character. The teacher knew the boy and his weaknesses. Rather than counter the student's shouting with his own, he calmed the student down. How unpleasant I would have made it!

The Kinds of Interest There Are

Half a block off New York's fashionable Park Avenue you will find one of the city's 600 schools. The 600 schools are the city's problem schools, to which are sent the worst behavioral problems in the other schools. When the school was set aside to house this group, the people in the neighborhood, understandably concerned, objected to the school authorities but no other site was apparently available in time to meet the outcries in the newspapers that something be done and quickly about the juvenile delinquents; therefore, there they were and Park Avenue half a block away.

Around the other corner is a subway station, and each morning you can see them charging or slouching up the subway steps, coming from frightful slums and headed toward the city's street of privilege, status, and luxury. Some of them loiter at the corner, making plans to cut school for the day. Others go toward the school; unobtrusively around are policemen. Sickness is on the loose.

This is what comes of absence of interest. Elsewhere we have compared interest to a financial return on a financial investment, and perhaps the original meaning of *influence* or *coming between,* in its absence, tells why people on their way to the subway avoid these youngsters. Nothing has ever attempted to influence them, neither parents, nor society, nor a financial investment in their energy possibilities. They are an illustration of what the absence of guidance can do in reducing humanity to animality. If guidance is an investment of energy on your part to secure a sense of direction and purpose in your students, is it too late to do anything for these youngsters, or, as newspapers call them, punks? Yes, if our investment continues at its present level; no, if we increase our investment to compensate for the investment in them that was never made. They can only be salvaged if an investment in them is made. If society withholds this investment, they will never be salvaged.[9]

Several miles north are two of the best high schools in the United States, housing picked students selected by examination. In both these schools the parents association is fantastically active, the students compete feverishly for admission to the better colleges, and interest in careers, grades, and status, keeps the guidance office in a never-ending hubbub.

The teachers in the 600 school are paid a special bonus for consenting to teach there; the teachers in the two high schools are paid no more than teachers in other high schools in the city. Is society recognizing that it must increase its investment in the underprivileged? Admiral Rickover would insist that bonuses be paid better teachers handling picked youngsters.

What should the values in guidance be at both extremes? In the first instance, guidance can do nothing until the groundwork has been laid by adequate investment—more teachers, after-school supervision, summer programs, part-time employment opportunities, recreational facilities, and psychological care. This, of course, is not guidance; it is rehabilitation. In the second instance, guidance can move in all the way. If rehabilitation is needed with an occasional student, the ever-present parents association pays for a part-time social worker.

As an English teacher, you cannot involve yourself with rehabilitation, but you will have some students who cannot be made accessible to guidance without prior rehabilitation. They will require more of your time than the others, and you must give it, not unstintingly because you have not that much to spare. But when you have both punk and normal youngster, give more time to the punk than to the others, despite Admiral Rickover, until that time when society opens its purse strings and invests in him more than it has. Before being constructive with your normal youngsters, head off destructiveness in your abnormal ones. Wherever possible, whenever time permits, give them individual attention, talk with them, and listen to them. You will not have time for much more, but this is the best guidance program you can develop for them—until that distant day when the money flows in their direction.

Research, Resources, and Techniques

1. Dr. Ralph Rabinovich gives a physician's opinion in "Our Adolescents and Their World" (*E. J.*, May 1955, p. 261): "Basically the adolescent hasn't changed very much through the years. . . . As ever, he likes to give the impression that he knows all, while deep down he feels uncertain." The article also discusses the need for clarity in the teen-ager as to family role, sex role, place in school, standards and controls, and guidance. Parents and teachers should maintain suitable controls because "the teen-ager is searching for answers to questions about the important social and political realities of our time." Would this be as true of the stupid teen-ager as the bright one?

2. Charlotte Devree's "High School Seniors' Agony" (*New York Times Magazine*, Dec. 15, 1957, p. 14) describes the tensions and worries of the college-bound and how guidance can help this group.

3. Here's a sampling from *English Journal* on the directions you can take in guidance and self-understanding:

a. Morris Finder's "Teaching English to Slum-Dwelling Pupils" (April 1955, p. 199) corroborates what we have been saying about upward mobility, loyalty to one's own people, and how to spare college graduates the feeling that there's no room in the world they aspire to nor in the underprivileged world from which they come. Mr. Finder says that the aspiring individual has a responsibility for upward mobility of his group too.

b. Marquis E. Shattuck and Thomas Cauley's "Using a Modern Textbook in Composition" (April 1955, p. 215) shows how the questions teen-agers ask themselves can be formalized and restated for fruitful classroom discussion, research, and writing.

c. John C. Gerber's "The Greater Struggle Necessary" (Feb. 1956, p. 59) sets a scope of activity for you, thus: "Student adjustment is certainly a desirable goal of education. . . . In English classes . . . it is not likely to be achieved when the teacher makes a fetish of it at the expense of intellectual discipline. . . . The English instructor can best aid his students become adjusted by insisting upon a rigorous study of language and literature. . . ." Gerber's article illustrates the toughness and aggressiveness you should have. It's a special kind that leads to standards and acceptance of your students, without confusing acceptance and compliance.

d. Grace Daly Maertens' "Organizing the Class to Care for Individual Needs" (Oct. 1958, p. 414) is intended for the new teacher, but some of the suggestions require at least a term's experience before you have self-assurance enough to put them into effect. A target to shoot for at the end of your first year's work—not to be undertaken prematurely.

4. You will get an excellent picture of the character and feeling of the adolescent, presented from the psychoanalytic point of view, in Irene M. Josselyn's *The Adolescent and His World* (Family Service Association of America, New York, 1952).

5. What about the tough, aggressive adolescent? Read these:

a. James L. Hymes, Jr., presents an excellent discussion in *Behavior and Misbehavior: A Teacher's Guide to Action* (Prentice-Hall, 1955). This book bears rereading and more—internalizing! You'll find realism and honesty here.

b. Gertrude Samuels' "One Answer to Delinquency—Work Camps" (*New York Times Magazine*, Sept. 8, 1957, p. 22) shows that if you make an investment in people you get a superb return. People are the safest investment there is.

c. Here is a pioneer work on working with tough youth: Paul L. Crawford, Daniel I. Malamud, and James R. Dumpson's *Working with Teen Age Gangs: A Report on the Central Harlem Street Clubs Project* (Welfare Council of New York City, 1950). Observe the publication date. With all the answers in, why has society been so recalcitrant about correcting this situation?

d. Walter Bernstein's "A Reporter at Large—The Cherubs Are Rumbling" (*New Yorker*, Sept. 21, 1957, p. 129) is hard-hitting journalism on juvenile gangs. A superb piece. Worth discussing with all your classes, even with the college-bound.

6. Should you adjust yourself to your students, or should your students adjust themselves to you? Of whom is greater flexibility—not flaccidity—required? Read these articles and judge:

a. John and Mary Collier's "An Experiment in Applied Anthropology" (*Scientific American*, Jan. 1957, p. 37) shows how judicious use of the social sciences enabled a poverty-stricken people in the Andes to improve their condition. The innovators from the outside world gained a change in these backward Indians by first changing themselves. Would this be also true in gaining classroom change?

b. A parallel experience is reported by Walsh McDermott, Kurt Deuschle, John Adair, Hugh Fulmer, and Bernice Loughlin in "Introducing Modern Medicine in a Navajo Community" (*Science*, Jan. 22, 1960 and Jan. 29, 1960), which indicates that the best intentions require most preparation. Your students will be persuaded that you are there to help them only after you adjust to them—not by expecting them to adjust to you. Does this mean compromising your values and your ideals?

7. Does human communication begin with negativism? If so, how does communication ultimately form affirmative assertions? René A. Spitz, in *No and Yes* (International Universities Press, 1957), states that the earliest gesture is negativistic. Nevertheless, the positive emerges from it. How can you, in the classroom, make the positive emerge from the negative?

8. This assemblage of articles from *Scientific American* should help in promoting your understanding of your classes and subsequently in the self-understanding that your classes show:

a. Solomon E. Asch shows in "Opinions and Social Pressure" (Nov. 1955, p. 31) that courage of one's own convictions is a rare quality. In the face of apparent group pressure, many people will disbelieve their own senses. Hence, how can a classroom group compel conformity to its patterns? How can minority opinion, or individual opinion, withstand prevailing classroom opinion?

b. A. M. Guke's "The Social Order of Chickens" (Feb. 1956, p. 42) presents parallels between the barnyard and the classroom. In both you have social ranking and social order. What can the teacher, and the farmer, do about it?

c. Robert A. Butler's "Curiosity in Monkeys" (Feb. 1954, p. 71) shows that curiosity is as powerful and as basic a drive as hunger and sex. Therefore, how can you stimulate curiosity in your classes? How can you pique the incurious student into becoming curious?

d. A highly important point is made by Curt Stern in "The Biology of the Negro" (Oct. 1954, p. 80) that individual differences cannot be obliterated by education, but ethnic differences can.

e. John Cohen's "Subjective Probability" (Nov. 1957, p. 128) relates gambling patterns to the reasons why people take chances, and to the Duncan Cass, Micawber, and Barry Lyndon personality types.

f. Carl Rogers gives a brief account of his well-known techniques in " 'Client-Centered' Therapy" (Nov. 1952, p. 66).

The English Teacher's Colleagues

CHAPTER 13

The Curriculum and English

High school teachers must reconcile future satisfactions and deferred career outcomes with the adolescent's present-mindedness and group needs. Present needs and future planning are not mutually exclusive. Education has current benefits and immediate relevance in addition to future advantages, but when the adolescent asks, "Why don't people understand me? Why do I have arguments with my parents and teachers?" (p. 10), every high school teacher can contribute an answer:

(a) English syllabus materials—Hamlet and Laertes, Brutus and Cassius, *Johnny Tremain,* Frost's "Mending Wall"—bear on this question of communication.

(b) In social studies, class structures, political parties, caste, and legislative lobbies in opposition illustrate dispute and difference in society and government, without breakdown of communication, even when communication is strained.

(c) In modern languages, translations are poor substitutes for the original, either denotatively or connotatively. Both denotation and connotation are needed for successful communication, and the adolescent

389

must determine whether his communication difficulties are denotative or connotative.

(d) Science requires language guaranteeing the same experimental result time after time, and hence communication as tight as possible, to avoid inaccuracy and misunderstanding. True, denotation is maximized and connotation minimized in scientific writing, but has this avoided scientific polemic?

(e) Mathematical concepts are communicable not only in this school or town, and here and now, but throughout the universe and backward and forward in eternity.

Hence, all high school subjects deal with the adolescent's cry that nobody understands him. Subjects overlap. Consider two. In one, mathematics, interrelationships with English are considered tenuous, and common programs between English and mathematics are not usual. In the second, social studies, interrelationships are more intimate and common programs (as in core) more frequent. These interdisciplinary relationships affect the adolescent and affect you:

Mathematics is pattern, elegance, design, *not* computation. Computation is drill. Mathematics deals little with rote drill except as a vision of pattern, elegance, and design emerges. Unless drill in mathematics forces this emergence, it is a waste of time.[1] Unfortunately, too many mathematics teachers waste time so.[2]

Pattern and design make things predictable. An adolescent can predict the results of heaving a brick or baseball through a glass pane, but though he knows the glass will shatter, he does not know the design of the shatter-pattern. However, if a diamond cutter cuts a valuable raw diamond into smaller stones, he can predict the pattern of shatter before one judicious tap of the mallet on his chisel produces the stones, in the shapes and sizes predicted, all ready for polishing. Why can the diamond cutter predict? Because diamonds have grain and structure. Glass has no such structure. We cannot, therefore, predict the pattern of shatter in glass, while predictions can be made about shatter-patterns in diamonds.

The pool player "calls his shots" on a similar analysis of patterns and vectors. Or the mathematics teacher will say that $(a^2 - b^2)$ always factors into $(a + b)$ $(a - b)$. Thus you say to your students, "Things are predictable to the extent that we can ascertain their structure. Do you want to predict? Then you must analyze your problems to determine their structure and the way the grain lies before using mallet and chisel. If you can see no structure, you can always try a glass cutter." This was Alexander's approach to the Gordian knot.

Still, the adolescent's prime concern is his problem ("Why don't people understand me? Why do I have arguments with my parents and teachers?") or any other question he may ask himself (p. 10), not the techniques of algebraic factoring or the special trade secrets of the diamond cutter or the glazier. Yet these throw light on his problem, because human beings are proper subjects for mathematical scrutiny. Mathematics assists in personal problem solving. Where life, literature, poetry, and language have design, the teacher of mathematics may be a valuable partner for you.

More usual a partner is the teacher of social studies, a specialist in the patterns—if any—of history and society. Your social studies colleague will tell you of two alternative philosophies of history: (1) "There is nothing new under the sun," meaning that history repeats itself and hence has pattern. (2) "What we learn from history is that we cannot learn from history," meaning that history does not repeat itself and hence has *no* pattern.

In either case, men choose to remember; so history emerges and experiences accumulate, whether the historian favors Alternative 1 or Alternative 2. History makes us experientially older than we are chronologically or physiologically. If we can learn from experience, we can learn from history, irrespective of our bias toward either alternative philosophy of history. We have not yet burst through many of the thought barriers of the past, and are still at the same conceptual boundaries, where television merely implements the Cassandra myth, jet propulsion implements the Daedalus (or flying carpet) myth, and subatomic physics implements Zeno. Hence the problem-beset adolescent can with profit look to the past because the past extends his experiences and extends him. If an adolescent girl has problems with Momma in dating, clothing needs, and spending money, the American Revolution, between mother-country and daughter-colonies, is reminiscent of these problems, nor do we degrade historical considerations by this analogue. Rather we mutually enrich both history and mother-daughter problems by the breakdown in communication and value systems that in 1775 changed the world. Edmund Burke and Charles Fox offered advice to mother-country and daughter-colony that is as applicable to the misunderstandings of mother and daughter as are advice-giving newspaper columns.[3]

Be attentive to your colleagues. Learn from the foreign language teacher that the far away has importance to the hereabouts, that studying German, Italian, Yiddish, and Spanish leads to richer living in New York, Chicago, San Francisco, Montreal, and in any nearby urban center. A foreign language will help you live more richly in America as well as in Europe and will help you learn about Americans.

The art teacher will help you answer the adolescent's questions, "What's 'sharp'? How can I be a sharp dresser? What makes a car looks snappy? How can I furnish my room so that it will be in good style?" The music teacher has material relevant to the rock-and-roll fever. The science teacher will contribute answers to questions dealing with the secrets of life and the ways of finding out secrets—which adults call scientific method.

Starving the Tool Subject That Feeds You

Schaar writes: "Introductory chemistry courses in high school and college actually kill the desire of most students to select chemistry as a career, instead of whetting their appetites for more." [4] Norbert Wiener, in explaining the demise of Latin, describes how each man kills the thing he loves to teach.[5]

Teachers of science and mathematics may therefore be murderers of interest in science and mathematics. Dissatisfaction with high school teaching in science and mathematics has led the Ford Foundation and the National Science Foundation to subsidize programs, workshops, and institutes to inform these teachers on recent research. The success of these endeavors, at the moment of writing, is questionable. In reporting on one workshop, Gruber commented, "Science teachers must do more than study what scientists know; they must understand how scientists think." [6]

To "understand how scientists think" may be an esthetic experience, rather than a scientific one. If the science curriculum wants such understanding, but is frustrated by some science and mathematics teachers, then perhaps the English teacher is better trained to teach the esthetics of scientific method than are these science and mathematics teachers. For example, consider the technology of getting the out-of-reach:

(1) A student sees a coin beneath a sidewalk grating. How does he get it? He finds a long-enough stick and to it affixes a wad of well-chewed gum.

(2) A scientist knows of a bed of sulphur a mile or so below the surface in Louisiana. How does he get it? Instead of a stick and gum, he sinks

concentric pipes, sends steam down one pipe, and brings the molten sulphur up in another, by what is known as the Frasch process.

(3) Technology, not technique, differentiates the coin-hunting student and the sulphur-hunting scientist. Both have used techniques to gain the out-of-reach, but the technology separating chewing gum and the Frasch process is vast. Knowledge of the adhesive properties of chewing gum is not the same as knowledge of the properties of steam and the solubility of sulphur ores, but scientific method has been used in bringing coin and sulphur within grasp.

Some superior students in English are mediocre in mathematics and science, though certainly as intelligent as the students who shine in mathematics and science. What accounts for the difference in one student —superior in English, social studies, and foreign language, but incompetent in physics, chemistry, or algebra—and another who has this competence? Are the constituents, the factors, the qualities of intelligence different in each student?

Perhaps the difference is not intellectual but emotional, the different patterns in catharsis of emotion, the ability to tolerate the passing of time while no solution unfolds itself, the ability to wait it out until the climax —the solution—appears. Perhaps the difference is explained by Trilling's analysis of the first Kinsey report, and the contrasting definitions of sexual potency, frequency versus control, expression versus management, rushing goals versus stalking them.[7]

The good mathematics student is not in a rush toward climax. He is able to sit out the solution because he has inner faith that solution will come if he sits long enough at the problem. He enjoys the preliminary love-making. But the poor mathematics student has no such inner faith in the possibilities of solution and therefore no patience. Would you make the intelligent student a better mathematician or scientist? Slow him down. He has brains enough but does not allow himself time enough. Mathematics is not harder than the close study and understanding of "Bishop Blougram's Apology" or Christina Rossetti's "The Convent Threshold"—not harder, just slower. A professor of mathematics recently wondered how to increase the reading rate of his mathematics students, who read material slowly, word by word, and carry over this slow reading to newspapers, magazines, and fiction, materials not warranting so slow a pace. Conversely, the student with rapid reading rate cannot read science and mathematics at the same pace as a short story.

The competent teacher of mathematics and science differentiates between memorization and mastery. Politicians don't. Consequently, politicians will legislate funds for one kind of science education while scientists clamor for another. Scientists understand that the politician's kind of science education will produce technicians but not creative scientists. Possibly no kind of education will produce the scientist we need most, the imaginative, creative scientist, and perhaps we can only pray for his occasional emergence. But we can supplement prayer with directed efforts.

Scientists—not politicians—want a heavy infusion of the humanities in science education. Heisenberg[8] and Wiener[9] know that poetry, music, and art furnish additional dimensions in which creative imagination can work. The creative scientist approaches his problems as one approaches a problem in aesthetics. Lawrence Kubie, the psychiatrist, has said that science is emotion.[10]

Turner has said that science is appropriate to liberal arts education, but let's reverse direction.[11] Can liberal arts programs redesign science education? Can the humanities redesign mathematics? In brief, can poetry make science and mathematics clearer to the ordinary student and enrich them for the better one? Can English raise the routine technician into the imaginative scientist?

Certainly not by teaching Millay's "Euclid alone has looked on Beauty bare," even though the later lines,

> Let . . .
>
> cease
> To ponder on themselves, the while they stare
> At nothing, intricately drawn nowhere
> In shapes of shifting lineage,

illuminate the organized fantasy of mathematical thinking. To stare this way is to immerse yourself in concept and symbol, as the mathematician does; however, understanding and feeling the lines will not persuade the student competent in English but slow in mathematics to work the problems in the back of that chapter of his algebra text.

Nor will Sandburg's fog coming in on little cat feet, or its first cousin, Ezra Pound's "Dawn enters with little feet/like a gilded Pavlova," elucidate infinitesimals.

Nor will the approach to poetry recommended earlier—teaching two poems simultaneously, mutually to elucidate each other—solve simultaneous equations, though two equations are juxtaposed, and a far-fetched relationship between this approach to teaching poetry and the solution of simultaneous equations may be seen by the indulgent reader.

Nor will Gamow and Stern's *Puzzle-Math*,[12] which beds down mathematical puzzles in a context of narrative; it tells a story in the guise of a mathematical problem to reduce the resistance of the student to mathematics and science.

Instead we mean this:

Dante Gabriel Rossetti's " 'Tis visible silence, still as the hour glass," from "The House of Life," is the poetized version of Thomas Young's proof of the wave theory of light, in which light, suitably out of phase, produces darkness. Shelley's

> Life, like a dome of many-colored glass,
> Stains the white radiance of Eternity,
> Until Death tramples it to fragments,

from "Adonais," is Newton's diffraction grating. The dialectical confrontation of opposites that we see in Pope's

> Damn with faint praise, assent with civil leer,
> And without sneering, teach the rest to sneer;
> Willing to wound, and yet afraid to strike,

from "Epistle to Dr. Arbuthnot," and in Samuel Johnson's

> Since hope but sooths to double my distress,
> And ev'ry moment leaves my little less,

from "London," like the Chinese philosophical opposition of Yang and Yin, or, dimly, the antimatter of Lee and Yang, are a remote first approximation to protons and electrons. Shakespeare's Sonnet 81 ("Or I shall live your epitaph to make") deals with the conservation of energy. Amy Lowell's

> In a pattern called a war.
> Christ! What are patterns for?

from "Patterns," seeks structure, as science does.

But, more important (even in this scant sampling of the thousands available), each selection must be read slowly. For fullest meaning each passage must be closely inspected, looked at and then away from. In such poetry, rewards do not come easily. The full message appears slowly, in its own time and not yours, like an unfolding flower. Dynamite cannot force understanding, but patience will persuade it to come.

The mathematics student must do the same, if he is to get an image of mathematics and not to memorize it. He invests his energy in waiting it out and inviting concepts to invade him. But this waiting is not passive; it is extraordinarily active. There are sallies, thrusts, encirclements, and retreats; he invades and is invaded, while sitting.

You, the English teacher, do the same when you challenge students to determine whether a name or an action is missing from a fragment sentence (p. 62), or when you challenge students to see how the entire plot structure of *Tale of Two Cities* hangs on Jerry Cruncher's fingernails, cantilevered thereon, or how, in Wordsworth's "Daffodils," the inward eye is the bliss of solitude.

Science and mathematics teachers are getting subsidies because they are vital to national defense. Those who make the country's laws do not care much about who makes its songs, by evidence of the money allotted to poetry, because poetry is supposed not important to national defense.

Yet poetry is the key to the differences among the routine technician, the merely competent engineer, and the creative scientist, to the difference between the student who memorizes mathematics and the one who has imagination to play with it. Sir Charles Snow says, "Anyone who has ever worked in any science knows how much esthetic joy he has obtained. . . . One can't help feeling an awareness of beauty. The subjective experience, the esthetic satisfaction, seems exactly the same as the satisfaction one gets from writing a poem or a novel, or composing a piece of music. I don't think anyone has succeeded in distinguishing between them." [13]

George Meredith's "Melampus" describes how we learn about nature. First, we must have no fear. Melampus, picking up "a brood of snakes" whose mother had been killed by others "through savage fear of them," suddenly, "with love exceeding a simple love of the things/ That glide in grasses and rubble of woody wreck" is licked by the snakes and understands the language of the creatures of the woods.

Fear? Love? What have they to do with the mastery of science and mathematics?

Let's return to our students, the one excellent in English and social studies and a complete washout in mathematics and science, and the other who shines in these latter. Can you deny that something like fear lurks in the first, an absence of confidence when a math or science problem comes over the horizon? Why are bright girls less effective in science and mathematics than bright boys? They are certainly as self-assured in

English and social studies, but this feeling departs when they face the science text. Always? No, not always, but more than men, women falter with the sciences when they have intellect enough to master them. Unlike Melampus, they avoid snakes, make what you will of Meredith's symbolism as a precursor to Freudian symbolism.

Mastery of science and mathematics is not only an intellectual matter. We also need an absence of trepidation, a feeling of self-assurance, a faith that there is a solution around somewhere—or that no solution is possible —and a sense of esthetic delight when the solution comes, everything slots into place, and things fit. Only so can the intellect work.

Mastery of science and mathematics requires work, but there will be no work forthcoming unless place is made for emotiveness and esthetics. Work takes time. Melampus "knew the hours: they were round him, laden with seed," and, through hours of work, "not unsolicited, sought by diligent feet," to find order in disorder, "making harmony breathe of life and disease," and pattern in the haphazard, so that "with music wrought of distraction his ear enlarged."

Where does the poet enter?

These days the physicist finds several dozen subatomic particles, of different characteristics, littering his way. Science always tries to get the most economical explanation for things, an endeavor known in biology as Morgan's Canon, in psychology as the Law of Parsimony, and in philosophy as Occam's Razor. But how economical can you be in explanation when you are dealing with several dozen particles untidily in your way? "Scientists know their kinds of beauty when they see them. They are suspicious, and scientific history shows they have always been right to have been so, when a subject is in an 'ugly' state. For example, most physicists feel in their bones that the present bizarre assembly of nuclear particles, as grotesque as a stamp collection, can't possibly be, in the long run, the last word." [14]

Let the physicist consult with the poet here. Dryden says

> From Harmony, from heav'nly Harmony
> This universal frame began;
> When Nature underneath a heap
> Of jarring Atomes lay,

and Melampus "drew the Master of harmonies, voiced or stilled," and none of this is experimental, but the untidy litter of several dozen subatomic particles will never be swept away without this sense of harmony and order. Perhaps (the poet may ask) these are not particles but positions? Perhaps you have several dozen positions rather than several dozen particles?

Only experiment can answer, and the poet can only suggest, but faith is nonexperimental and the scientist must have the faith of Melampus that "never in woods/ Runs white insanity fleeing itself; all sane/ The woods revolve," meaning simply that the universe is rationally ordered. The scientist has faith that he lives in a rationally ordered universe; he doesn't necessarily have faith that he will find out what this rational order is.

Of your two students, one needs the faith that the other has and can get it from poetry, grammar, and the study of plot structure.

Do Plus Do Makes Core

We have warned you against the soft beguilements of your social studies colleagues to meet with them behind the woodshed and set up a common program. Beware the troth unless you are admitted as an equal partner to the venture (remember what was said on p. 183) but, if you are, go all the way. This will not be far enough, to the great disappointment of your social studies colleague; what he wants from core, ultimately, is to tell you how to teach English; what you want from him are additional resources that whip up the interest and motivational level of your classes. Between these two divergent aims lies a great area where common work is possible.

Thus a core program on the Civil War would include: the poems of Whitman, Whittier, and Lowell; *The Red Badge of Courage, Andersonville, Freedom Road, Gone with the Wind;* suitable biographical material on Lincoln, Herndon, Grant, Lee, Judah Benjamin, Mrs. Suratt, Carl Schurz; the essays of Emerson, Thoreau, William Lloyd Garrison, and the newspaper editorials of Horace Greeley; the speeches of Wendell Phillips. But not Carl Sandburg as historian or any of the other buffs—leave these for your colleague. Civil War biography is suitable, but Civil War history is not. When your colleague asks artfully if you aren't setting up arbitrary and artificial boundaries, ask only if he will take over the teaching of "When Lilacs Last in the Dooryard Bloom'd."

You want to increase the interest level of your classes—and core can help do so. Use the social approach in core to give flesh-and-blood and everyday reality to something as far out in the ethereal blue yonder as lyric poetry. A remote lady lyricist like Emily Dickinson who didn't get around as much as another lady lyricist like Elizabeth Browning will reflect the difference in lyricism in the life she led; a third like Christina Rossetti will have a different story to tell. A fourth like Edna St. Vincent Millay, still another. Do these four reflect different societies, different social values, different concepts of citizenship? Of course, and to that extent involve you legitimately in core, with a comparison of Victorian nine-teenth-century England and Victorian pre-Raphaelite England, academic New England and sophisticated New York.

A major concern of your social studies colleague is the constellation called economics, politics, civics, and citizenship education. Assist him here, but not subserviently, by such things as the business novel—*Cash McCall, Jefferson Selleck, Executive Suite*; the political novel *Advise and Consent*; the political plays— *State of the Union* and *The Best Man*; and by concentration in your journalism unit on political columnists like James Reston and Walter Lippmann and on reading assignments in political maga-zines like *The Reporter* and *Time.*

Your social studies colleague will be teaching the economics of the stock market, but though you can fish in the same pond you have other fish to fry. You will want students to read the financial page and to recog-nize that certain stories are planted by corporate public-relations experts to attract prospective stock purchasers, that annual reports are written to maintain management in office, that financial-page reporting is more con-servative in tone than most economists are, and that dividends and earn-ings reports are generally honest and appear in press only after insiders have had an opportunity to react. An effective device is to discuss a divi-dend and earnings report and say, "Some people will make and others will lose thousands of dollars from this newspaper story. How will this money be made or lost?" If you are too poor an economist in the ways of the Wall Street bulls and bears, your social studies colleague will elucidate long and short selling to the fascination of your class. You can also enlarge their financial horizons by bringing in copies of *Wall Street Journal, Forbes,* and *Fortune,* showing how minutely business and corporate activities are chronicled and that, daily, fortunes are being made and lost. Does this make your teen-agers eager to get in or anxious to keep away?

Or come election and your social studies colleague is urging students to assist in getting out the vote. You can supplement these efforts by having your students analyze their own voting preferences.

Much has been written by marriage brokers who want to join English and social studies in a shotgun wedding. Much is good, but you should be selective; the dowry is not worth the loss of liberty. Inspect it thoroughly and afterward do your best with it in splendid isolation. You can still be friends.

Art, Music, and Foreign Language

Art and music in particular sharpen the senses; but unless your own senses have been sharpened by frequent exposure to them, you are not equipped to sharpen the senses of your students by these means. The best of modern painting educates vision to new ways of seeing things and the best of modern music to hearing things. If you have been indifferent to art and music, it may be risky for you to integrate them with English. If, however, you have often gained emotional and intellectual rewards from them and if you have been truly moved, they offer a rich supplement to the English curriculum.

Modern painting, for example, is as involved with the texture of things as with the likeness of things; ask your class to look closely at a square inch of desk top or brick wall and to consider the way to go about drawing it. Or you can have them lean back, eyes closed, and listen intently to street sounds, traffic sounds, corridor noises. How many sounds do they hear? How many sights and sounds are passing them by? Can they listen to more than one sound at a time? Can they listen to two at a time? Three? Can they make the drawing of a square inch of the desk top's wood grain as interesting as a human face or a landscape? What makes sounds and sights interesting to us?

Just as projective geometry and the chemistry of paints and pigments revolutionized Renaissance art, so the microscope and camera have influenced modern art. Similarly, technology has influenced music; noises exist today that never existed before and from these the composer has fashioned new, exciting, and stimulating kinds of music.

How closely, how minutely, can your class pay attention to the sights they see and the sounds they hear? Line up the two index fingers, one behind the other, at arm's length with the index fingers two or three inches apart; move your head from side to side; which finger appears to move and which to remain still? This example of what the physicist calls parallax, in which the nearer index finger appears to move and the further to remain still, is reminiscent of well-known optical illusions. Common sense tells us that both fingers are still, but the evidence of our eyes tells us otherwise. If so, how dependable is the evidence of our eyes? Art and music teach us how to pay close attention to the too-often unseen and unheard parade before our senses.

What prevents this concentrated attention? Consider with your class how, when nobody is looking, the boys enjoy making muscles in front of the bathroom mirror and the girls study their faces and figures and how we become embarrassed about this self-analysis and private boasting when others are around. Concentrated attention is weakened because of the presence of others. We deprive ourselves of the attention we can give ourselves and the sights and sounds that come up to us. The more concentrated the attention we can give to the square inch of desk top and the sounds coming into the classroom, the closer the attention we give ourselves simultaneously.

Or does too concentrated attention endanger our grip on ourselves? You may remember, and your class will be interested in, two Pavlovian experiments that deal with sight and sound and how these cause breakdown. In one, a dog was rewarded with food in the presence of an ellipse and punished in the presence of a circle; in the second the dog was rewarded in the presence of a 256 cycle-per-second tone and punished when a 512 cycle-per-second tone was sounded. Through progressive modifications, the circle and ellipse gradually approached each other, as did the 256 and 512 cycle-per-second tones, until the dogs could no longer discriminate and became neurotic. Ask your students if that may account for their greater willingness to listen to popular music than to a Beethoven symphony, to look at a Norman Rockwell magazine cover in preference to a Cézanne painting. Are their discriminations too greatly challenged for neurological safety? Or are their discriminations being sharpened? Do sharpened discriminations make it easier or more difficult to live with others? Are sensitive people easier or more difficult to get along with? Are understanding people easier or more difficult to get along with? What's the difference between sensitivity and understanding? How can close, concentrated attention to sights and sounds make us more sensitive and more understanding so that we can get along more comfortably rather than less so?

Perhaps, in fact, closer apprehension of sights and sounds would make us less apprehensive of others, and, as an example, you can suggest that students think of the last time they were excited and lost their tempers. Would it have helped if they had been more sensitive to the unseen and unheard parade before their senses? Or, on the other hand, it may be better to be more closely in touch with others than with ourselves, lest we open up a Pandora's box. We know that some people are not artistic, musical, or poetic, and never will be. You ought not harass or persecute students because they will not or dare not press too closely upon the perceptual thresholds that separate ellipse from circle. Better that they not be too sensitized. The organism may not be able to take it.

On the other hand, you must not allow smugness to grow within them. The student who will not go deep, deep, deep with Emily Dickinson, or Prokofieff, or Paul Klee must question the defenses that cause him to go on the offensive with "That's all a lot of junk," when, in truth, the junk around is within him. You don't want him gibbering between circle and ellipse, but you don't want him thinking that he can distinguish one from the other, because he can't; because he can't, he thinks there's no distinction. However, not all students are so insensitive, but they seem to be because other matters crowd in on them, like friends, social activities, and gaiety. In the presence of these fevers, how can you be brought more intimately into contact with sights, sounds, and yourself? It's very difficult. Even though people go to concerts and galleries together, the ultimate feat of appreciation remains a private one.

Research, Resources, and Techniques

1. One of the world's great authorities in child psychology, Jean Piaget, in "How Children Form Mathematical Concepts" (*Scientific American,* Nov. 1953, p. 74) and in "The Child and Modern Physics" (*Scientific American,* March 1957, p. 46), indicates that the growth process may damage basic insights as well as improve them. Growth may mean loss of valuable and original insights, as well as the gain of them. Does this remind you of Wordsworth's "Ode on Intimations of Immortality"? Wordsworth and Piaget seem to agree that education for mathematics and science must recapture some of the young child's original visions, blunted and diffused by developmental processes.

2. Lejaren A. Hiller, Jr., in "Computer Music" (*Scientific American,* Dec. 1959, p. 109), relates modern mathematics to musical composition. "It is possible, at least in theory, to construct tables of probability describing a musical style, such as Baroque, Classical, or Romantic, and perhaps even the style of an individual composer." If the mathematics

teacher and the music teacher have this in common, what common programs can you work up with your colleagues? And without diluting English content? Note that Beethoven (1770), Wordsworth (1770), and Napoleon (1769) were born within a year of each other. What does this tell you of the romantic movement in politics, music, and poetry? What of Lincoln (1809), Poe (1809), and Chopin (1810), all cut short before the full expression of their powers? Any units here with the Music Department or the Social Studies Department?

3. Did you know that mathematicians are studying English?

a. Anthony G. Oettinger's *Automatic Language Translation* (Harvard University Press, 1960) deals with denotation and connotation in language and how these make translation machines possible.

b. Also see *Automatic Teaching: The State of the Art,* edited by Eugene Galanter (Wiley, 1959), for the basic polarization process common to good questioning, to teaching machines, to language teaching, and to logic.

4. Discoveries in the structure of language have been closely associated with advances in mathematics.

a. Charlton Laird's *The Miracle of Language* (Premier, 1957) should be read by every English teacher. See especially the chapter "More Leaky Grammars."

b. Joshua Whatmough's "Natural Selection in Languages" (*Scientific American,* April 1952, p. 82) presents a mathematical formulation of language changes and shifts. The same author's *Language: A Modern Synthesis* (Mentor, 1957) illustrates the relationships of English to physics and neurological processes. An excellent, thoughtful, and creative book.

c. For a better picture of linguistics, the science that binds language and mathematics, see the Viking Fund Publication in Anthropology, No. 24, *Essays in Linguistics,* edited by Joseph Greenberg, for the Wenner-Gren Foundation for Anthropological Research (University of Chicago Press, 1957).

d. The bases of measurement of man and his languages are discussed in S. S. Stevens' "Measurement and Man" (*Science,* Feb. 21, 1958, p. 383).

5. General discussions of the relations between science and the humanities are becoming more numerous. Two exemplify the tone of these discussions:

a. Joseph Gallant's "Literature, Science, and the Manpower Crisis" (*Science,* April 26, 1957, p. 787) is an appraisal of the English teacher's role with respect to the teaching and recruitment of scientists.

b. Howard Mumford Jones' *One Great Society: Humane Learning in the United States* (Harcourt, Brace, 1959) points out that support for the humanities must be brought into line with support for the sciences.

6. For the responsibilities of journalism in wedding the humanities and science, see:

a. Eric Larrabee's "Science, Poetry and Politics" (*Science*, April 17, 1953, p. 395);

b. William Seifriz' "A New University" (*Science*, July 16, 1954, p. 87), which calls for a greater emotional appeal in scientific writing, and for scientific papers with a personal, *poetic* touch.

7. The concern that the greatest of modern scientists feel for an equivalent development in the humanities is represented by this material:

a. Norbert Wiener, one of the world's outstanding mathematicians, in *The Tempter* (Random House, 1959), becomes a novelist and in this book exposes the conniving that goes on in science. Compare it with Eleazar Lipsky's novel *The Scientists* and with the novels of C. P. Snow, another distinguished scientist who has turned to literature.

b. Norbert Wiener's *The Human Use of Human Beings* (Doubleday Anchor, 1954) may help you if you plan a core program. You may find stimulation in this important book, which touches on mathematics, science, economics, law, social studies, and language.

c. Two world-famous physicists also show their concern for the relationships between the humanities and science. Werner Heisenberg's "From Plato to Max Planck" (*Atlantic*, Nov. 1959, p. 109) and Erwin Schrödinger's *Science and Humanism: Physics in Our Time* (Cambridge University Press, 1952) reflect the feeling that scientific development is limited unless reinforced by development of the humanities.

8. One of the oldest ways of elucidating a mathematical problem is telling a story about it. Hence narrative and plot are related to mathematical teaching:

a. George Gamow and Marvin Stern's *Puzzle-Math* (Viking, 1958) offers thirty-two stories and anecdotes illustrating various mathematical points.

b. Would you like to see how one tells a story to illustrate Diophantine equations? Read the tale of the three shipwrecked sailors and the pile of coconuts in Paul S. Herwitz' "The Theory of Numbers" (*Scientific American*, July 1951, p. 52).

9. A standard work, very valuable, that will be useful in common programs with the Art Department is Viktor Lowenfeld's *Creative and Mental Growth: A Textbook on Art Education* (Macmillan, 1947).

10. Some disquieting discussions on the quality, or lack of it, in science education in high school:

a. Bernard E. Schaar, "Avenues of Service" (*Science*, June 12, 1953, p. 643).

b. Howard E. Gruber, "Science Teachers and the Scientific Attitude: An Appraisal of an Academic Year Institute" (*Science*, Aug. 19, 1960, p. 467).

b. Fletcher G. Watson, "A Crisis in Science Teaching" (*Scientific American,* Feb. 1954, p. 27).

c. British Association for the Advancement of Science, *Science in Schools,* edited by W. H. Perkins (Butterworth's, 1958).

11. Milton Millhauser's "Advice to My Son" (*E. J.,* Jan. 1959, p. 21) offers reasons for studying Latin, among which is *not* included any benefits accruing to the study of English. Notice the agreement with Norbert Wiener's regret that Latin has disappeared from the curriculum.

12. Some suggestions for core programs between English and social studies follow:

a. Henry W. Bragdon's "Teaching Writing Through History" (*Atlantic,* Nov. 1959, p. 118) pleads for social studies topics as effective springboards in meaningful writing. Discuss it with your social studies colleague.

b. Lorraine Lowry's "Windows on the World" (*E. J.,* Feb. 1960, p. 15) deals with teaching for world understanding. The article offers a good list of suggested readings.

c. Elwood C. Karwand's "Teaching Literature of the Orient" (*E. J.,* April 1960, p. 261) discusses a literature unit for world understanding.

d. Charles Stephen Lewis' "The Orient—Blind Spot in High School Literature" (*E. J.,* Jan. 1956, p. 26) considers joint work with your social studies colleague in a unit on world understanding. The article concentrates on literary resources in teaching and understanding of Asian peoples, but you can undertake a parallel program on Latin America or Africa.

13. Carrie Stegall's "Now They Are Real Buddies" (*E. J.,* Feb. 1959, p. 78) considers how different subject matter teachers can work together on the English program.

Lesson Planning

CHAPTER 14

The Kinds of Lessons You Will Teach

The developmental lesson that develops an idea or a concept is the most intellectually stimulating of the lessons you will plan. But other types of lessons are also important. What are they?

After your students enter your classroom, sit down, come to order, and copy the assignment, your lesson will be a drill, a review, a recitation, a lecture, or a development in which a problem is presented and a solution attempted.

The drill lesson generally comes straight out of a work book and deals with drill in fundamentals like usage (*Between you and I; beside* or *besides*), sentence fragments (*When he saw me. He laughed.*), run-ons, comma splices, capitalization (*are those flowers roses? are those flowers rose's?*), spelling (your list of demons), and similar corrective or remedial materials. These become developmental when taught in depth and in ways discussed throughout this book, yet the place for pure rote drill is secure and justifiable. Remember that drill is not teaching, just part of it.

In the recitation you fire questions at students and get factual answers. ("Do you think Cassius has pop-eyes or sunken eyes?" "Sunken eyes because the book says he has a lean and hungry look." "Why didn't you put an apostrophe in *theirs* to show possession?" "Because *theirs* is one of the exceptions.") Or else you get students to explain why the dangling modifier in the work book is so funny. (*Standing on tiptoe, the church emerged from the mist.*)

In the review lesson, where you sharpen up students for College Boards or for midterm examinations, you are less interested in strengths than in weaknesses. When review indicates that the class has achieved competence, let the class know that mastery has been reached. In review lessons, as in contract bridge, lead from strength to weakness and deploy from mastery toward areas of unsureness. Capitalize on strength to attack weakness.

In the lecture, unless you are talking for pure love of your own voice, use the blackboard to stress the points you wish the students to retain, plant questions that you will want opened for later discussion, and hold students responsible for the content you are presenting. Thus, if after completing *Arrowsmith,* you lecture on the literature of the Twenties, and you evaluate the place of Fitzgerald, Mencken, O'Neill, Masters, and Anderson (Sherwood or Maxwell), your students should be taking notes and preparing themselves for a subsequent discussion.

In other lessons, your students will sit quietly at their desks, writing a composition and reading silently while you bring your records up to date. Are they wasting time? No. The English period should also offer relaxation. At another time they may assemble in groups, doing some committee assignments, while you go from group to group to expedite or clarify discussions.

All such lessons require preparation and planning and the assembling of materials. From *English Journal, Scholastic,* and other sources, you should have filing folders filled with such materials. Do not depend on your school library's back issues. You should have your own subscription to these magazines. When you've finished reading the current issue, decide what you can use, tear it, and include it in your filing folder. Put markers on these folders for ready reference—*Macbeth, Dangling Modifiers, Return of the Native, Topic Sentences for Paragraph Development, Robert Frost,* and *Some Interesting Hobbies.*

Whatever the lesson, you must plan. But the developmental lesson requires most planning of all. Further, it requires canniness and conniving.

You Are a Vile Name

These days *manipulator* is a dirty, pejorative word. Those who control opinion and response, like people in advertising and public relations, are so designated; the manipulator is a kissing cousin to the brain-washer and suspected.

But, for better or worse, you are a manipulator too. You prepare lessons, you plan outcomes, you affect the minds of your students. Of course, your intentions are the best but nonetheless you manipulate the beliefs, values, and judgments of your students. Furthermore, you do so by the subtlest of means, by motivating them, by discussions, by questions of the right kind, by comparisons, by arranging illustrations—a veritable arsenal of techniques by which, if you teach successfully, no student will be the same for having known you. You cannot teach any other way, if you are worth your salt; how to manipulate successfully is your abiding concern. But let's move from nasty words and for *manipulation* substitute *lesson planning;* do you feel better now?

Recently, in a Westchester suburb, a teacher, asked by his supervisor to submit lesson plans, refused; the issue was joined; the newspapers heard of it and sympathized with the teacher, who claimed that he could not predict how class discussions would go on any day that he walked into the classroom. He planned on the basis of student interest and he could not preplan this interest. Nor would he strait-jacket his students or himself. For forty-eight hours he was a hero to the newspapers (and to a well-known admiral). Nevertheless, justice was with the supervisor and not the teacher.

To depend on spontaneity and inspiration in teaching is to invite catastrophe. Spontaneity and inspiration are desirable, but they develop best when you plan for them. Don't rely on their day-by-day availability. Next, supervisors cannot allow overlap, gaps, or patchwork in the student's orderly education as he leaves one teacher and goes on to another. For one prima donna to refuse to plan, or divulge his plans, is to throw school operations into anarchy; other teachers, as well as the supervisor, will not know what was accomplished.

So much goes on in the average lesson—horseplay, whispering, somebody coming in with a message, requests to leave the room, littered floors because students have aimed a wad of paper at the waste basket and have missed, the cry of "Two points!" if they have succeeded, tittering, twittering, traffic screeches, noisy gum chewers, girls inspecting and repairing make-up—and you are pulled in so many directions that your lessons become a mulligan stew of forgetting where you left off or what comes next, unless you have a fixed point, a lodestar, an unshakeable point of reference, which is what your lesson plan ought to be.

With a good lesson plan, you can without worrying let the interruptions flood in. You are in control. You know what you are about. The good lesson plan states, so that others can understand (hence it is not casually scratched notes on the back of an envelope), what you will teach, why you will teach it, how you will teach it, and to whom you will teach it. Restated, your lesson plan will clearly and communicably declare:

1. the topic;
2. the reasons for teaching that particular topic;
3. the relevance of the topic to your class of teen-agers;
4. problems, questions, and materials relating to the topic;
5. summary of important considerations emerging from the lesson;
6. applications of the lesson.

Let's now attack these points *seriatim.*

The Topic

Generally the topic is given by the course of study you are being paid to teach. It requires no thought from you. Like the tablets of the Law handed to Moses on Sinai, you ask no questions about the topic while you teach —although you can freely question the curriculum at teacher meetings and professional meetings, in writing, and in those other circumstances that a free democracy permits. In the classroom, you teach what you are told to teach, which is fully stated by your syllabus.

Your syllabus for English should be somewhere around your school, perhaps under dust. Study it to see what authority requires you to teach and how these requirements are modifiable.

You will find a galaxy of topics, from *Hamlet,* to the mass media, to the comma-splice, to speech, to poetry, to self-insight, to community undertakings and surveys. These topics are specified and classified and thus your thinking here in your lesson planning is minimal.

The Aim

You must ask yourself, "Why should this topic be taught? For what reasons? Why should it (whether *Hamlet,* the mass media, the comma-splice, speech, poetry, or community undertakings and surveys) be learned? Why did the wise elders include it in the syllabus?"

The possible reasons for teaching *Hamlet* can be good or bad, general or specific, vague or precise. To some extent they overlap with reasons for teaching *Macbeth* or *Julius Caesar,* but they should have their own independent *raison d'être.* Are these possible aims in teaching *Hamlet?*

1. To compare the need for revenge with love and forgiveness.
2. To learn how the dead can command the living.
3. To compare the understanding of humanity in Shakespeare with the humanity of understanding in *Hamlet.*
4. To determine how passion in *Hamlet* leads to compassion and understanding in the reader.

These, however, are inclusive of the play as a whole. Other aims would be more restricted to that day's portion, meaning that each time you set foot into the class you must have a specific aim (or intention) in mind. For example, still on *Hamlet:*

1. To determine whether men cause ghosts to appear, or ghosts cause men to see them. (I:1)
2. To study whether Hamlet is justified in his distress over his mother's marriage. (I:2) To compare I:2 with Deuteronomy 25:5-10, and to determine whether the incestuous aspect of the marriage is affected because Gertrude had a son.
3. To analyze why older people want to preach to younger people. (I:3)
4. To compare supernatural and natural horror, and to analyze why the assurances of an afterlife should frighten, rather than comfort, us. (I:4 and I:5)

A group of student teachers were asked, "Why teach 'Mending Wall'? For what reasons should high school students learn it? What should your intentions be in teaching it?" Here are some answers:

1. To show that "good fences" do not always make good neighbors.
2. To see that the wall represents all arbitrary barriers between men, like prejudice and misunderstanding.
3. To compare isolationism and co-operation.
4. To compare the revolt that challenges tradition with the conventions that uphold restraints.
5. To show that man cannot live without walls, limits, and self-limitations.
6. To relate fences and the "turf" of juvenile gangs.
7. To compare how imagination wars against things as they are and conservatism with things as they could be.
8. To show how obedience to tradition leads to stagnation.

Whatever *your* reason for teaching "Mending Wall," you must ask "Why, why, why should this be taught?" of everything in the syllabus. Your answer will begin with some infinitive: "To show . . ." "To compare . . ." "To analyze . . ." "To prove . . ." "To discuss . . ." followed by the outcome you intend.

Notice how you simultaneously accept and challenge the syllabus. You are being paid to teach it. Like an honest person you will. But you must satisfy yourself as to the sense it makes, else you will be an automaton. You must know why that topic has been included in the job you do. Do not accept the topic blindly, but insist on finding out for yourself what rationale put it in the course of study.

Conscientious analysis may leave you unconvinced of the importance of sentence diagraming or *Silas Marner.* You will teach them because you have contracted to do so, but not because you have any good reasons for wanting to teach them. Your teaching will in that event suffer. You will not be alone and you need not feel guilty. Resign yourself to sections of the syllabus that you do not enjoy teaching, teach them though you must. In fairness to the people who developed the syllabus, however, you should make a sincere effort to see what values persuaded them to include material that you would like to be rid of.

Note that reasons for teaching a topic can be complex, but that they should not be vague. (See our earlier discussion, p. 250, on the difference between simplicity and clarity in the teaching of poetry.) Don't be afraid of having a complex intention, or aim, in your lesson plan, but this complexity should have no vagueness about it. The examples that follow present aims that strive for clarity and do not shrink from complexity. The problems dealt with are significant. They are not watered down. The bright student can cope with them. The stupid student will respond to them after suitable rephrasing:

> "Richard Cory": to show how snobbery is partial suicide; to show that the snob cuts himself off from life.
>
> *Tale of Two Cities:* to show that hate has lower survival value than love; to show that self-sacrifice for a worthy end insures survival.
>
> *Julius Caesar:* to show that massive historical efforts require massive emotions; that people of little emotional capacity have little political energy; that without emotional directedness we have no political or social directedness; that politics is in part an emotive matter.
>
> *Paragraph structure:* to show that an idea has a beginning, a middle, and an end; to show how every idea can be related to another idea by suitable

transitions; to show that ideas grow by well-known growth patterns; to show the logic, the psycho-logic, the chrono-logic, and the patho-logic of ideas.

Sentence structure: to determine what a name is; to determine what an action is; to ascertain how names act.

Parts of speech: to ascertain description and the differences between name-description and action-description.

Macbeth: to show that unbridled ambition is as much self-murder as murder of others; to show that rule over others is justified only by rule over self.

Note that the aim is a statement of purposefulness and direction and that it insures against awkwardness and aimlessness. Your aim clearly and explicitly states what you will attempt in the lesson. No fuzziness should mar the aim, complex though it may be, when you succinctly state the fixed point of that lesson, your lodestar, from which you may depart but to which you must always return, despite the distractions in a period purposed or accidental, the interruptions, the petty climaxes, that can easily cause you to lose sight of the one main thread that leads you through the labyrinth of the class hour. Hence the importance of the aim.

Motivation

But having analyzed to a hair and concluded why a particular topic should be taught, where is the student? The student walks into the classroom carrying with him, invisibly, a life of his own, compounded of family, friends, needs, values, status, socioeconomic situation, and resistances. Material must be taught because it is unfamiliar. But it cannot be taught unless it is related to the familiar, the invisible compound of family, friends, needs, and so on. When the student walks into the classroom, the invisible compound is prepotent, not your Aim. In consequence, you must relate the lesson's Aim to the invisible compound, and you can do so only by knowing your customers and how they are being invisibly motivated. What will startle, puzzle, pique, tantalize, interest the invisible compound? Unless your Aim sets the invisible compound to resonating, no teaching can occur —telling, yes, but not teaching.

So you must consider your audience, its characteristics, needs, urges, aspiration—the *to-whomness* of your lesson—and how to introduce *Why* to *Who*. Favorite means are anecdotes, newspaper clippings, or audio-visual aids, but best of all is a question with this twofold relationship, combining teen-ager interest and involvement with the material, that gets the lesson moving (hence motivation) and off the ground at the opening of the lesson.

Thus, as prelude to "The Devil and Daniel Webster," a teacher asked: "How often did you sell your soul to the devil today?" and followed it with "Did you feel bad when you did so, or triumphant?"

In *Julius Caesar,* III:2, in a lesson comparing Brutus' and Antony's speeches, the teacher began with, "If you were a candidate for office, would you depend more on a debate with your opponent, a slogan, or a campaign song?"

In teaching T. S. Eliot's "Macavity: the Mystery Cat," the lesson opened with "Who is the more successful criminal, a man who is careful about life or a man who is careless about it?"

In teaching a unit on journalism, the teacher asked, "Is it preferable for a newspaper to rely only on its own reporters or on prepared releases?"

Eugene O'Neill's *Beyond the Horizon* was introduced with, "In order to make our dreams come true, which should be greater, ambition or ability?"

"Is true maturity acting older than you are, or acting your age?" introduced John Steinbeck's "Flight."

"Would a girl find it more adventurous to fall in love with a villain or with a criminal? For whom would she be more likely to sacrifice herself?" introduced "The Highwayman."

"If you could live forever, at which age would you prefer to be? Which age would your parents prefer you to be? Your friends? Your grandparents?" introduced Shelley's "The Cloud."

"Which is stronger, curiosity or carefulness?" introduced Tennyson's "Ulysses."

These questions simultaneously deal with the topic and with teen-ager interests. They do not merely entertain. The student teacher who went to the rear of the room, bent down, and drew a chalk line down the center of the floor, dividing the classroom into two, and then, after backing her way down to the front of the room, straightened herself out, somewhat red-faced from her posture, and asked the class, "What was I doing just now?" in an effort to motivate "Mending Wall," was confusing interest with motivation. Motivation is not a stunt or an entertainment gimmick, but arises from the material to be taught and its connections with the needs, experiences, and drives of the people to be taught. These connections must interest, challenge, pique, or excite the student. They should not be trivial.

Superficial aims and motivations won't work in a classroom. Meaningful ones are difficult to achieve, but if you want to teach successfully you can't settle for less. Nothing substitutes here for considerable portions of thought about the material you teach, the adolescents you teach it to, and the way to bring these together.

For example, the real danger of overmotivating a lesson is caused by the confusion between entertainment and teaching, arising when you can't quite come to grips with the materials you are to teach. You become over-concerned with what will appeal to your students. You, rather than the materials, are on display. You evade whatever issues reside in the materials; you do not think about them sufficiently or go deeply into them in order to lead your students deeply into them. You become carried away by slick-ness, showmanship, and trivia.

Keep your eye on the problem. Some classifications of Motivation into extrinsic and intrinsic and of Aim into immediate and general (or proximal and distal) are harmless and not particularly enlightening. They will not ease your burden when you break your brain analyzing why you should teach *Great Expectations,* or why students should learn Shakespeare, or what goes on in the minds of stupid children.

How can you tell when you have gone into your material with suitable depth? How can you tell when you are not deceiving yourself about the adequacy of your preparation and your planning?

Development

Your preparation is assured by the thought level and the sequential arrangement of your questions. We have already discussed questioning techniques (p. 345), but good questions of the pivotal, polarizing, or thought type, are one guarantee that you have prepared yourself adequately to teach. A second guarantee is an arrangement of questions that has a beginning and an end, proving that you know where you've come from and where you're going to.

A good lesson has this logic. It has a structure and an orderly sequence, almost like a play. Your questions should lead to discussion that should in turn lead into the next question. How do you know they will? You have plotted it so beforehand. If the plot sometimes gets out of hand and the lines you assigned never get spoken and others are substituted by your refractory actors, you may not have plotted poorly but more richly than you imagined. Remember this twist in development the next time you pass that way.

The more clash your questions engender the better. The adolescent, especially the male, enjoys conflict, but it should be controlled and have qualities of fun. You are not a comedian or an old sobersides, but ideas are always fun, even for stupid students, provided that your ideas present problems of significance and reflect development, growth, and sequence.

Almost like a one-act play, where issues are presented, played off one against another, and finally resolved, your lesson should proceed step by step to a series of clearly indicated peak points where it rests, regroups forces, breathes a while, and proceeds to the next point. In pulses, one aspect, then another, then another of the lesson is brought forward. Remember the concept of the one-act play, but also remember that the play, though not broken by intermissions, is broken into facets, subunits within a larger unit of plot. So is your lesson development.

Each aspect or facet is characterized by at least one thought question, by related illustrative materials, and by opportunities for discussion. Questions not only implicate the class in the material, but in sequence implicate themselves in their successors; they have linkages. How? By the quality of suspense, of unfinished business, so that even when a student's response merits a "Very good!" from you, it should be accompanied by a sense of incompletion, a sense that it is very good mainly because it pushes the unfinished business forward and not because it furnishes any final answers or completes anything at all.

Therefore your lesson has architecture. This architecture must be set down on paper. In class, you should have this paper handy in case you forget any of the matter, but you should have it as clearly as possible in mind and in memory. If you feel more comfortable with your paper in hand, keep it there. If you do not need the paper, leave it on the desk. In either case, commit your lesson plan to paper.

An additional assurance that your development and its architecture evidence sound and logical preparation derives from its readability for others. Should your supervisor want to know what you are doing, he can read your lesson plan. Reading it, he will know whether you have adequately presented the material. Good supervision will be able to react appropriately to the lesson plan. Commit your plan to paper so that good supervision can react constructively to it.

The Summary

Your lesson should not be vague. You should be able to tie it together. It should have punch, direction, climax, and it should add up to a sum, or summary. Halfway through the lesson you should be able to state briefly, so that the class will understand, what has gone on. At the end, you, or some student, should be able to recapitulate.

These recapitulations should also be down on paper because they state the goal you originally anticipated reaching when you stated your aim for the lesson. Hence your summaries, both medial and terminal, are related to your initial aim. Unlike the aim, which is stated as an infinitive phrase, the summary is a statement:

> Hamlet turns against Ophelia because he turns against love.
> The chief difference between Carton and Darnay is purposefulness.
> A preposition connects a noun to the sentence.
> We expand the topic sentence by comparisons, contrasts, and examples.
> Connect paragraphs by appropriate transitions.
> Sound it; see it; spell it.
> "Kubla Khan" shows us how we are the authors of our dreams and how they are written.
> Newspapers print news and withhold it.
> In "Luke Havergal," Robinson urges suicide when guilt is intolerable.
> Your own conclusions are best supported by reading both *Time* and *The Reporter.*
> Per Hansa was killed by Beret's superstitions, rather than by his hard life on the prairie.
> In "Provide, Provide," Frost uses the jingling rhyme scheme to drive home his satire.

By the summary, you prove that your lesson has something to say and something to leave with your students. Also, you prove that you have been in command of the development and that your lesson has gone the way you planned. The summary attests to your ability to manage—a better word than *manipulate*—the outcomes you want your students to reach.

Planning for the Long Haul

Long-term planning takes maturity and experience. Don't rush it. Day-by-day planning can be effectively blueprinted by the beginning teacher, but at least a semester's experience is advisable before you try juggling such things as student-teacher planning, core programs, and the other long-term units occasionally described in *English Journal* and some methods texts. Take it easy. First control your day-by-day planning and observe how it goes. At the same time, find out what you can about your school's policy toward such programs, what the experiences of your colleagues have been, and where performance has fallen short of or exceeded promise.

Such planning takes a capable hand at the wheel and you are too new to teaching to be successful with it. But prepare yourself, as experience grows, to move into such comprehensive planning, where you take a unit, perhaps The Civil War, Our State, The American Cowboy, Careers, or some other that you will read and hear about, and determine that you'd enjoy exploring it. The topic should be of real interest to you, and one of which you have some knowledge. Long-term planning will challenge your professional ability, and you should not undertake it prematurely. Indeed, the average teacher should not tamper with such programs at all, as supervisors, enthusiastically pushing them on their staffs, have found to their regret.

But, given the better teacher, such long-term planning represents learning at its peak. Students learn creatively, imaginatively, and enthusiastically. Poetry becomes integrated with fashion, art with home economics, fiction with history, accompanied throughout by great elation and great industry. You get to know your students, they get to know the material, and the material becomes an aspect of deeply personalized experience. Sounds fine, doesn't it? But beware until you achieve competence, because long-term planning, ineffectively handled, can become a disorganized, diffuse bore that wastes everybody's time. Indeed, some time-wasters among your colleagues love such programs because they sound so good, mean so little, and give them a chance to soldier on the job while seeming ever so advanced in their educational philosophy. Long-term planning is fine for snow jobs—but there are fakers and leeches in art, medicine, industry, and in religion, so don't be disillusioned when you encounter them in teaching.

Some time from now, when you feel professionally ready, you will ask yourself:

> What do students know?
> What have they experienced?
> What can they contribute?
> Can they search out resource material?

Such questions must be answered by you at each stage of long-term planning, and not only at the outset. Consider a relatively simple matter in long-term planning, the class newspaper (p. 117), which sounds like a viable, realistic opportunity for joint teacher-student planning, but which allows the disinclined to goof off, places a heavier than usual burden on those who can type and cut stencils, and requires continuing enthusiasm in you when problems of layout, proofreading, and other mechanics arise. Yet how special and affecting is the heart-warming sense of accomplishment in students when the class newspaper is collated, stapled, and distributed, with everybody getting a by-line! This little, unambitious thing means so much and is so treasured by the class!

You must be alert in seizing upon on-going activities, interests, and behavior, threading them into your long-term planning. A classroom is a vibrating entity. You have no dearth of springboards from which to dive into such long-term projects as joint teacher-student planning if you are the kind of teacher who plunges. At every step you will be helping students formulate, digest, refine, consider, and analyze. You will be hip-deep in activity, attentive both in leading and in following. Joint planning and long-term planning require even more alertness than day-by-day planning.

CASE STUDY 19

Three matters exploded that Club Day:

One group of students asked why students were forbidden to smoke when faculty could; if teachers could smoke in rest rooms, why couldn't some place be assigned to students too?

Another group asked why they were restricted to the school cafeteria throughout lunch period. Why did they have to hang around the smelly cafeteria when they were finished, like convicts in a prison movie, when they wanted to stroll outside?

A third group maintained that Student Court dispensed injustice rather than justice. The faculty member assigned to Student Court acted as if you were guilty until found innocent.

"What can be done?" asked the teacher.

"Nothing," the class said. Teachers stuck together and certain rules were blindly and stubbornly enforced.

"I'm more optimistic," the teacher said. "I don't give up so easily. I want you to find out who made the smoking rules, who made the cafeteria rules, and who wrote the by-laws for the Student Court."

"Nobody tells us anything," the class scoffed.

"I'll find out for you," the teacher said. That afternoon the teacher met with the principal and presented the plan that was taking shape in his mind. The principal thought that the inquiry into Student Court practices and the survey of student cafeteria behavior were worthwhile, but was uneasy about consequences on community and parents of the school smoking inquiry. The teacher assured the principal of responsible, tactful supervision, and the principal gave his blessings, which were mixed with doubts about the smoking inquiry.[1]

The next day the teacher met the Student Court faculty adviser for lunch, warned him to expect a deputation, and briefed him on what the students would ask. The faculty adviser was completely affable.

When the teacher informed the class of his meetings with the Student Court faculty adviser and the principal, they were suddenly eager to go ahead, now that an official imprimatur had been given. Though skepticism lurked in some, most were interested in setting up the three committees suggested by the teacher, a *Smoking Room Committee*, a *Student Court Committee*, and a *Student Cafeteria Committee*.

These were the committee assignments:

The Smoking Room Committee agreed that it had no concern with nonsmokers and that it was to avoid making smoking attractive to them. It would ask these questions of smokers only:

(1) How many cigarettes do you smoke a day?

(2) Do your parents know you smoke?

(3) Do you smoke week-ends or school days?

(4) If students had a smoking room in school, would there be more smoking or less?

Other questions submitted were tendentious. Such questions as "How would you like to have a smoking room in school?" were ruled out because the answers would be predictable. This wasn't a thinly disguised petition, but a questionnaire. Other committee members were sent to the city charter to track down the fire-department regulations. Others went to the encyclopedia for materials on the history of tobacco and smoking. (Since this took place before the recent turmoil on lung cancer, no responsibilities were assigned in this area.)

The Student Court Committee was to ask members of the Student Court these questions:

(1) How many cases do you handle a term?

(2) What is the per cent of cases innocent, per cent guilty, per cent suspended sentence?

(3) What percentage of cases are repeaters?

Suggested questions like "Why don't you take the word of witnesses for the defense?" were ruled out because they prejudged. The teacher cited the old chestnut of "Have you stopped beating your wife?" which proved the term's most successful witticism.

Assignments were given of the two trial scenes in *Tale of Two Cities* in order to compare trial by jury and trial by fury (the phrase was coined by a student); the chairman of the committee, who planned to practice law and was one of the best readers in the class, was sent to the encyclopedia for materials on evidence and practice and procedure; other assignments were on the trial of Silas Marner by his brethren, precedents set in the then-fresh Nuremberg Trials, Macaulay on the trial of Warren Hastings, and a recent book by Judge Bernard Botein.[2]

The Student Cafeteria Committee had to collect information on these points:

(1) altercations between students observed in the cafeteria;

(2) the times witnessed when students aimed waste at receptacles, "Two Points" versus a miss, and how often students picked themselves up to pick up the waste and place it in a receptacle;

(3) instances of sneaking ahead on the serving line;

(4) gang feeling and other instances of irresponsibility.

In addition the committee was to interview the cafeteria dietitian, the librarian, and the chairman of the physical education department and find out what manpower could be spared to supervise students in the library or in available play space in the event that it would be possible to excuse students from the cafeteria.

The three committees met different results. The faculty adviser of the Student Court, despite his earlier affability, claimed he had no information with which to answer the committee's questionnaire and abruptly—or so the committee reported to the teacher—despatched them to the principal's office if they wanted that material. He claimed he kept no duplicate copy of his reports. The experience of this committee did not lead to improved school citizenship.

The Smoking Room Committee provided a most interesting series of classroom discussions, which caused students to think quite deeply about their reasons for wanting to smoke. Though the statistics on student and parent interviews revealed an absence of public opinion favoring a smoking room, a subgroup of the committee reported on the introduction of tobacco to Europe, how nicotine got its name, and why it was called the "pipe of peace." This last matter, reported in an off-hand manner, immediately exploded into a rewarding discussion. The student described Indians pledging peace over a pipe, adding, with a grin, "Like we do in the boys' lavatory." When the teacher said that smoking was as much psychological as physiological, the class looked puzzled. The teacher explained that the physiological need set in after the habit was established, but originally the reason for smoking was psychological, to imitate grown-ups, to become more intimately one of the gang, to pledge peace—and suddenly the class recognized the social pressures to smoke, the need to respond to gregariousness and to feel more intimately part of the group, and how smoking was a psychological symbol. Smoking stated an absence of hostile intentions and thus served similar purposes with them and with the Indians. Their reports on the circumstances in which they first smoked reflected a prior need to be grown up or more closely identified with the group. Their original physiological distress in smoking verified that tobacco was an important psychological symbol.[3] "Social and cultural pressures to conform are probably important in initiating the smoking habit." [4]

But didn't this underscore the need for a smoking room? Others on the committee reported that smoking could be a physical hazard, if not watched. Society was particularly careful about fire hazards in public schools.[5] Could the city be sued if a student were injured? Yes. When they went on field trips, their parents signed release forms freeing the city from suit for damages. Would their parents sign similar release forms permitting them to smoke in school? Some students claimed their parents would. Others said that their parents wouldn't feel happy about possible additional hazards from student smoking, even if under official school auspices. Thus, in class discussion, the students quickly talked student smoking rooms into greater and greater remoteness. Public opinion, parental opinion, and conflicting opinion would make it difficult indeed for principals or any other educational administrators to set aside space for student smoking rooms.

The greatest rewards accrued to the Student Cafeteria Committee. They reported that the librarian had no objections to the fuller use of library facilities during lunch hours, provided that students could show passes from teachers assigned to the cafeteria, and provided that the number of students sent was not excessive. A library squad augmented by three additional students would enable him to handle the anticipated increase. The principal was told and undertook the matter on a trial basis. Within minutes a pass system was worked out by the librarian and the teacher in charge of the cafeteria. Posters went up that week announcing the change in cafeteria procedure, and the school newspaper hailed the change and the class for its constructive efforts.

The batting average was not bad. Of three projects one, the cafeteria, was successful. The second, the smoking room, provided a valuable forum for self-understanding, even if the original goal was not achieved and, indeed, was rejected by the class as unwise. The third encountered the roadblock already described—an unsympathetic, silly, and defensive teacher.

When long-term planning deals with the community, it should involve the principal and other administrators. When students seek favorable public opinion on school-bond issues, they have a right—not merely a privilege—to persuade other citizens and to affect changes in attitude and belief. But unless you secure the co-operation of your principal, you may find yourself in an unprotected position when some citizen of the opposite persuasion says, "What are these kids doing out of school, away from their books, stirring up the community in what's none of their business? Who's their teacher?" When your long-term planning involves community matters, you will be well advised to take counsel with your supervisors. Not all citizens favor school bonds, school buildings, or increases in teacher salaries.

But once administrative backing is secured, the scope for work becomes so vast, the opportunities so illimitable, that you must keep tight rein on yourself lest you wander too far afield. Tax rates and school-bond issues lead you to letter writing, speech, analysis of neighborhood characteristics, journalism, skits, but these experiences are no substitutes for symbolic and conceptual learning. These must be had from books and the written word.

The best hedge against a hodge-podge of poorly digested and ill-unified community experiences is an effective reading program. Getting students out to the community to learn its operations, its power structure, and how it endures is part of education, but it must not obscure the fact that learning comes more efficiently through books than through experience. Pure community experiences, without books, tend too often to become boon-doggles.

Finally, there is planning that goes beyond day-by-day planning, long-term planning, or joint teacher-student planning. Call it lifetime planning; it takes place in a teacher married to education—even if not to the class-room—forever. It is unplanned planning. This English teacher carefully notes in the Sunday newspaper the television programs for the following week that may be appropriate for class work. In a restaurant this teacher learns from the juke-box what the teen-ager is listening to. In a super-market this teacher discovers what the delivery boys are getting in an average tip. This teacher goes through an occasional copy of *Variety* to learn what the entrepreneurs of show business are beaming at youth. He reads *Business Week* to see how businessmen turn a profit in the youth market. In an art gallery he sees how painters see things and how a square inch of desk top can furnish the subject of a large canvas; at a concert he vows to listen more acutely to the sounds in corridors and classroom during change of period; sights and sounds should not be re-stricted to painters and composers. He remembers a joke told over a bridge table to bring to class. He keeps files of clippings for possible class discussion. He lives, indeed, not as a white-collar clerk whose time clock hermetically compartmentalizes work from play, but as a professional whose work and play interact.

Everything is English. Very little cannot in one way or another be brought into the orbit of the English syllabus. This is your master plan.

By it, every week-end, you will set aside several hours to contemplate what you will be teaching the following week. You will prepare yourself to face the week. You will organize yourself, your ideas, your materials, and you will put these down on paper as explicitly as you can. On your free week-end time? Yes, to make all your waking hours more truly yours. This investment of a fraction of your week-end will make the re-mainder of the week more richly exciting, and all yours. Plan it so.

Research, Resources, and Techniques

1. Franklin A. Miller, James H. Moyer, and Robert B. Patrick's *Planning Student Activities* (Prentice-Hall, 1956) is a thorough, well-organized book on cocurricular and extracurricular programs. See especially the section on school publications and school newspapers. The section on school dramatics, unfortunately, is somewhat brief.

2. Irvin C. Poley's *Speaking of Teaching* (Germantown Friends School, 1957) offers suggestions for teaching the bright student.

Notes

Notes to Chapter 1

1. Alfred C. Kinsey, Wardell P. Pomeroy, and Clyde E. Martin, *Sexual Behavior in the Human Male* (Saunders, 1948).

2. Sheldon and Eleanor Glueck, *Delinquents in the Making* (Harper, 1952).

3. *Seventeen,* "Research from *Seventeen*" (320 Park Avenue, New York); "Profiles" (Eugene Gilbert and the Gilbert Youth Survey), *New Yorker,* Nov. 22, 1958, p. 57, and Nov. 29, 1957, p. 57.

4. Weston La Barre, *The Human Animal* (University of Chicago Press, 1955), p. 226.

5. William W. Wattenberg, *The Adolescent Years* (Harcourt, Brace, 1955), p. 150: "Folk wisdom is rich with expressions showing that we expect young people to take on the characteristics of their parents. We predict conduct by saying 'Like father, like son; like mother, like daughter.' . . . We take it for granted that a boy or girl will accept his parents' religion, echo their prejudices, and even defend their politics. . . . In the process of personality development, parents exert a potent influence by being objects of identification for their children. Both admirable and troublesome characteristics are passed along in this way."

6. Lester D. and Alice Crow, *Adolescent Development and Adjustment* (McGraw-Hill, 1956), p. 156.

7. Marynia F. Farnham, *The Adolescent* (Harper, 1951), Chap. 6.

8. Arthur Bestor, *Educational Wastelands* (University of Illinois Press, 1953).

9. Jacques Barzun, *House of Intellect* (Harper, 1959).

10. Arthur Bestor, *The Restoration of Learning* (Knopf, 1955).

11. Harold Rugg and B. Marion Brooks, *The Teacher in School and Society* (World Book, 1950).

12. Carleton Washburne, *A Living Philosophy of Education* (John Day, 1940).

13. Reuel Denny, *The Astonished Muse* (University of Chicago Press, 1957).

14. Bestor, *The Restoration of Learning.*

15. Nelson L. Bossing, *Principles of Secondary Education* (Prentice-Hall, 1955), Chap. 7.

16. George A. Miller, *Language and Communication* (McGraw-Hill, 1951); Colin Cherry, *On Human Communication* (Technology Press and Wiley, 1957).

17. B. C. Brooks, "The Teaching of English to Scientists and Engineers," in *The Teaching of English,* ed. Randolph Quirk and A. H. Smith (London: Secker and Warburg, 1959).

18. Cherry, *op. cit.*

19. Paul Goodman, *Growing Up Absurd* (Random House, 1960).

20. Edgar Friedenberg, *The Vanishing Adolescent* (Beacon, 1960).

21. Bestor, *The Restoration of Learning.*

22. Harold Laski, *American Democracy* (Viking, 1948), p. 339.

23. David Riesman, "Secondary Education and 'Counter-Cyclical Policy,'" in *Constraint and Variety in American Education* (Doubleday Anchor, 1958), p. 126: "The high school teacher has in fact lost relative status in recent years as more and more parents are themselves high school graduates."

24. Aristophanes, *The Clouds*; Zachariah 8:5: "And the broad places of the city shall be full of boys and girls playing in the broad places thereof."

25. *Time,* Feb. 16, 1959, p. 23.

26. "Tonsure," *Encyclopaedia Britannica.*

27. Robert Neese, *Prison Exposures* (Chilton, 1959).

28. Division of Surveys and Field Services, *Free and Inexpensive Learning Materials* (Nashville: George Peabody College for Teachers, 1960).

29. Nelson L. Bossing, *Teaching in Secondary Schools* (Houghton Mifflin, 1952), Chap. 11.

30. Edwin H. Sauer, *English in the Secondary School* (Holt, Rinehart and Winston, 1961); J. N. Hook, *The Teaching of High School English* (Ronald, 1959); Robert C. Pooley, *Teaching English Grammar* (Appleton-Century-Crofts, 1957); The Commission on the English Curriculum of the National Council of Teachers of English, *The English Language Arts in the Secondary School* (Appleton-Century-Crofts, 1956); Dwight L. Burton, *Literature Study in the High Schools* (Holt, 1959).

31. Citizenship Education Project, *Hours on Freedom* (Teachers College, Columbia University, 1951).

32. Arthur Koestler, "The Anatomy of Snobbery," in *The Anchor Review,* No. 1 (Doubleday Anchor, 1955).

33. William H. Whyte, Jr., *The Organization Man* (Doubleday Anchor, 1957).

Notes to Chapter 2

1. Ernst Cassirer, *Language and Myth* (Dover, n.d.; originally published by Harper, 1946), p. 82.

2. Jean Piaget, *The Construction of Reality in the Child* (Basic Books, 1954).

3. Dorothea McCarthy, "Language Development in Children," in *Manual of Child Psychology,* ed. Leonard Carmichael (Wiley, 1954).

4. George Philip Krapp, *Modern English* (Scribner, 1909).

5. Sigmund Freud, *Dictionary of Psychoanalysis* (Wisdom Library, 1957).

6. Ernest Jones, *The Life and Work of Sigmund Freud,* Vol. 1 (Basic Books, 1953), p. 245.

7. Quoted in Robert S. Woodworth, *Experimental Psychology* (Holt, 1938), p. 341.

8. G. H. Kent and A. J. Rosanoff, *American Journal of Insanity,* 67 (1910), 37-96, 317-90; Ira Progoff, *Jung's Psychology and Its Social Meaning* (Evergreen Books, 1958); David P. Boder, "The Adjective-Verb Quotient: A Contribution to the Psychology of Language," *The Psychological Record,* 3 (1940), 309-44; Eva Ruth Balken and Jules H. Masserman, "The Language of Phantasy II," *Journal of Psychology,* 10 (1940), 75-86; C. M. Cofer and J. P. Foley, "Mediated Generalization and the Interpretation of Verbal Behavior," *Psychological Review,* 49 (1942), 513-40.

9. C. E. Osgood, G. J. Suci, P. H. Tannenbaum, *The Measurement of Meaning* (University of Illinois, 1957).

10. Cassirer, *op. cit.*

11. Edward Sapir, "Grading: A Study in Semantics," in *Selected Writings,* ed. David G. Mandelbaum (University of California Press, 1949), p. 122; Wendell Johnson, *People in Quandaries* (Harper, 1946), Chap. 6.

12. Modified from a song by Abe Burrows.

13. Robert C. Pooley, *Teaching English Grammar* (Appleton-Century-Crofts, 1957).

14. Ogden Nash, "Manuscript Found under a Serviette in a Lovely Home," *New Yorker,* Sept. 22, 1956, p. 49; Nancy Hale, "Department of Amplification," *New Yorker,* Oct. 13, 1956, p. 124; A. S. C. Ross, "U and Non-U," in *Noblesse Oblige,* ed. Nancy Mitford (Harper, 1956).

15. "Notes and Comments," *New Yorker,* June 21, 1958.

16. J. N. Hook, *The Teaching of High School English* (Ronald, 1959), p 372.

17. George W. Hartmann, *Gestalt Psychology* (Ronald, 1955).

18. John J. DeBoer, Walter V. Kaulfers, and Helen Rand Miller, *Teaching Secondary English* (McGraw-Hill, 1951), p. 58.

19. Pooley, *op. cit.*

20. DeBoer *et al., op. cit.*

21. George W. Hartmann, *Educational Psychology* (American Book, 1941), pp. 117-20.

22. George W. Hartmann, "The Relative Influence of Visual and Auditory Factors in Spelling Ability," *Journal of Educational Psychology,* 22 (1931), 691-99; D. H. Russell, *Characteristics of Good and Poor Spellers* (Teachers College, Columbia University, 1937).

23. Frieda Radke, *Word Resources* (Odyssey, 1955).

24. Harry Shefter, *Six Minutes a Day to Perfect Spelling* (Pocket Books, 1954).

25. Emma Bolenius, *Everyday English Composition* (American Book, 1917).

26. Radke, *op. cit.*, p. 193.

Notes to Chapter 3

1. Paul Klapper, *The Teaching of English* (Appleton, 1915), p. 2.

2. William Strunk, Jr., *The Elements of Style,* rev. E. B. White (Macmillan, 1959).

3. J. N. Hook, *The Teaching of High School English* (Ronald, 1959).

4. Harry Shefter, *Shefter's Guide to Better Compositions* (Washington Square Press, 1960).

5. Eric Johnson, *E. J.,* Feb. 1958, p. 76.

6. Paul B. Diederich, "The Rutgers Plan for Cutting Class Size in Two," *E. J.,* April 1960, p. 229.

7. Celia B. Stendler, *Field Projects and Problems in Educational Sociology and Social Foundations of Education* (Dryden, 1956).

8. Paul Mort and William S. Vincent, *Modern Educational Practice* (McGraw-Hill, 1950).

9. The Citizenship Education Project, *Hours on Freedom* (Teachers College, Columbia University, 1951).

Notes to Chapter 4

1. Albert J. Harris, *How to Increase Reading Ability* (Longmans, Green, 1956).

2. Oscar S. Causey (ed.), *The Reading Teacher's Reader* (Ronald, 1958).

3. United States, Works Progress Administration, New York City, Report on Official Project 661-97-3-55 W. P. 1, 1939; U.S., WPA, Technical Series, Education Circulars 1-9 (Washington, 1937); Will Scarlet, *Remedial Reading in the New York City High Schools* (National Council of Teachers of English, 1938).

4. Gertrude Hildreth, *Teaching Reading* (Holt, 1958).

5. Ernest R. Hilgard, "Methods and Procedures in the Study of Learning," p. 517, and Carl I. Hovland, "Human Learning and Retention," p. 613, in *Handbook of Experimental Psychology,* ed. S. S. Stevens (Wiley, 1951).

6. *Ibid.*

7. Woodburn Heron, "The Pathology of Boredom," *Scientific American,* Jan. 1957, p. 52.

8. Alfred Adler, *The Practice and Theory of Individual Psychology* (Harcourt, Brace, 1943).

9. William W. Wattenberg, *The Adolescent Years* (Harcourt, Brace, 1955); Lester D. and Alice Crow, *Adolescent Development and Adjustment* (McGraw-

Hill, 1956); Elizabeth B. Hurlock, *Adolescent Development* (McGraw-Hill, 1955).

10. L. M. Terman and M. Lima, *Children's Reading* (Appleton-Century-Crofts, 1927); E. M. Anderson, "A Study of the Leisure Time Reading of Pupils in Junior High School," *Elementary School Journal*, 48 (1948), 258-67.

11. M. M. Lewis, *How Children Learn to Speak* (Basic Books, 1959).

12. Frieda Radke, *Word Resources* (Odyssey, 1955).

Notes to Chapter 5

1. Arthur Jersild, "Emotional Development," in *Educational Psychology*, ed. Charles E. Skinner (Prentice-Hall, 1951).

2. Lee Cronbach, *Educational Psychology* (Harcourt, Brace, 1954).

3. *Time*, March 31, 1959.

4. *Ibid.*, March 17, 1958, p. 75.

5. Werner Heisenberg, "From Plato to Max Planck," *Atlantic*, Nov. 1959.

6. Jacques Barzun, *House of Intellect* (Harper, 1959), p. 81.

Notes to Chapter 6

1. Margaret Webster, *Shakespeare Without Tears* (Premier Books, 1957), p. 12.

2. Jack A. Wapen and Leroy S. Layton (eds.), *Julius Caesar* (Globe Book Company, 1952), p. v.

3. Gabriele D'Annunzio, *The Triumph of Life* (Modern Library, 1923), p. 101.

4. Eleanor Stoker Boll, "Should Parents or Cupid Arrange Marriages?" *New York Times Magazine*, Dec. 13, 1959.

5. Robert Graves, *Occupation: Writer* (Creative Age, 1950), p. 117.

6. "P and G Plans Multi-Million Dollar Push as Gleem Is Introduced in New York," *Advertising Age*, Feb. 8, 1954, p. 1.

7. Tyrone Guthrie, "Why and How They Play Hamlet," *New York Times Magazine*, Aug. 14, 1960.

Notes to Chapter 7

1. Dylan Thomas, "Ballad of the Long-Legged Bait," in *Collected Poems* (New Directions, 1953).

2. Herbert Read, "Obscurity in Poetry," in *The Nature of Literature* (Horizon Press, 1956), p. 89.

3. W. H. Auden and Norman Holmes Pearson, *Poets of the English Language*, Volume 5 (Viking, 1953), p. 395.

4. Thomas H. Johnson (ed.), *Poems of Emily Dickinson*, Volume 2 (Belknap Press, Harvard University, 1955), p. 752.

5. Robert Frost, *Complete Poems* (Holt, 1949), p. 61.

6. *Ibid.*, p. 318.

7. Carl Sandburg, *Complete Poems* (Harcourt, Brace, 1950), p. 3.

8. *Ibid.*, p. 183.

9. John Livingston Lowes, *The Road to Xanadu* (Houghton Mifflin, 1930).

10. William Dement, "The Effect of Dream Deprivation," *Science,* June 10, 1960.

11. Lowes, *op. cit.*

Notes to Chapter 8

1. Robert F. Scott, *Voyage of the* Discovery (Transatlantic, 1951); R. F. Scott, *Scott's Last Expedition* (Beacon, 1957).

2. Leslie Fiedler (ed.), *Art of the Essay* (Crowell, 1958).

3. Charles B. Shaw (ed.), *American Essays* (Mentor, 1960).

4. John Lincoln Stewart, *The Essay* (Prentice-Hall, 1952); John Ashby Lester, *Essays of Yesterday and Today* (Harcourt, Brace, 1943); Andrew Thomas Smithberger, *Essays British and American* (Houghton Mifflin, 1953); Margaret Bryant, *Essays Old and New* (Crofts, 1940).

5. Louis Kronenberger, *Company Manners* (Mentor, 1955).

6. George Orwell, *Collection of Essays* (Doubleday Anchor, 1954).

7. Gilbert Highet, *The Art of Teaching* (Vintage, 1954), p. 37.

8. Donald Cox, "Do Women Make the Best Biographers?" *Saturday Review,* July 9, 1960.

9. Joseph Wood Krutch, "No Essays—Please!" *Saturday Review Reader* (Bantam, 1951).

10. J. D. Salinger, *Catcher in the Rye* (Signet, 1953), p. 115.

Notes to Chapter 9

1. *Time,* Sept. 12, 1960, p. 79.

2. *Advertising Age,* Dec. 7, 1959, p. 1.

3. Martin Mayer, *Madison Avenue, U.S.A.* (Pocket Books, 1959).

4. T. S. Matthews, *The Sugar Pill* (Simon and Schuster, 1959).

5. Stanley Kelley, Jr., *Professional Public Relations and Political Power* (Johns Hopkins Press, 1956).

6. Frank Luther Mott, *American Journalism* (Macmillan, 1941), p. 598.

7. Joseph Turner, *Science,* Dec. 18, 1959.

8. William H. Whyte, Jr., *Is Anybody Listening?* (Simon and Schuster, 1952).

Notes to Chapter 10

1. Plutarch, *Lives* (Modern Library, 1932), p. 1025.

2. *Ibid.*, p. 1026.

3. *Ibid.,* p. 1028.

4. *Ibid.*

5. Joseph Albert Mosher, *The Essentials of Effective Gesture* (Macmillan, 1917); Albert M. Bacon, *A Manual of Gesture* (Silver, Burdett, 1872).

6. David Efron, *Gesture and Environment* (King's Crown Press, 1941).

7. Gordon W. Allport and Philip E. Vernon, *Studies in Expressive Movement* (Macmillan, 1933).

8. Sam Duker, "Goals of Teaching Listening Skills in the Elementary School," address at the National Council of Teachers of English, Chicago, 1960.

9. Helen Jennings, *Sociometry in Group Relations* (Washington: American Council on Education, 1959).

10. Robert Erman, "The Job Interview," *High Points,* Feb. 1959, p. 70.

11. *The New York Times,* June 5, 1960.

12. Ralph A. Micken, *Speaking for Results* (Houghton Mifflin, 1958); Lee Norvelle, Raymond G. Smith, and Orvin Larson, *Speaking Effectively* (Dryden, 1957).

Notes to Chapter 11

1. Francis Bello, "The Information Theory," *Fortune,* Dec. 1953, p. 136.

2. Colin Cherry, *On Human Communication* (Technology Press, Massachusetts Institute of Technology, 1957).

3. *Ibid.,* p. 26.

4. Gilbert Highet, *The Art of Teaching* (Vintage, 1954), p. 219.

5. J. N. Hook, *The Teaching of High School English* (Ronald, 1959), p. 20.

6. A. B. Dick Company, 485 Lexington Avenue, New York 17.

7. College Entrance Examination Board, "A Description of the College Board Achievement Tests" (Educational Testing Service, Box 592, Princeton, New Jersey).

8. Highet, *op. cit.,* p. 118.

9. Robert L. Thorndike and Elizabeth Hagen, *Measurement and Evaluation in Psychology and Education* (Wiley, 1955), pp. 35-49.

10. *Ibid.,* p. 74.

Notes to Chapter 12

1. Henry A. Murray, *Explorations in Personality* (Oxford University Press, 1938).

2. Percival M. Symonds, *Adolescent Fantasy* (Columbia University Press, 1949).

3. Robert S. Woodworth, *Experimental Psychology* (Holt, 1938), p. 13.

4. Quinn McNemar, *Psychological Statistics* (Wiley, 1949), p. 39.

5. Floyd H. Allport, "The J-Curve Hypothesis of Conforming Behavior," *Journal of Social Psychology,* May 1934, p. 141.

6. Elizabeth Berry, *Guiding Students in the English Class* (Appleton-Century-Crofts, 1957).

7. G. F. Kuder, *Kuder Preference Record* (Science Research Associates, 228 South Wabash Avenue, Chicago).

8. Science Research Associates, *Guidance* (228 South Wabash Avenue, Chicago).

9. Gertrude Samuels, "Visit to a 600 School," *New York Times Magazine,* March 2, 1958, p. 12.

Notes to Chapter 13

1. Max Beberman, *Emerging Program of Secondary School Mathematics* (Harvard University Press, 1958).

2. L. R. Genise, "Impact of the Maryland and Yale Programs," *Arithmetic Teacher,* Feb. 1960.

3. *Time,* Jan. 21, 1957, p. 70.

4. Bernard E. Schaar, "Avenues of Service," *Science,* June 12, 1953, p. 643.

5. Norbert Wiener, *The Human Use of Human Beings* (Doubleday Anchor, 1954): ". . . the people who *taught* Latin and the people who *used* Latin became ever more widely separated classes, until the teachers completely eschewed the problem of teaching their disciples anything but the most polished and unusable Ciceronian speech. In this vacuum they ultimately eliminated any function for themselves other than that of specialists; and as the specialty of Latinism thus came to be less and less in general demand, they abolished their own function. For this sin of pride, we now have to pay in the absence of an adequate international language far superior to the artificial ones such as Esperanto, and well suited for the demands of the present day" (p. 90).

6. Howard E. Gruber, "Science Teachers and the Scientific Attitude: An Appraisal of an Academic Year Institute," *Science,* Aug. 19, 1960, p. 457.

7. Lionel Trilling, "The Kinsey Report," in *The Liberal Imagination* (Doubleday Anchor, 1953), p. 216.

8. Werner Heisenberg, "From Plato to Max Planck," *Atlantic,* Nov. 1959, p. 109; also Erwin Schrödinger, *Science and Humanism: Physics in Our Time* (Cambridge University Press, 1952).

9. Wiener, *op. cit.*

10. Lawrence Kubie, "Some Unsolved Problems of the Scientific Career," *American Scientist,* Oct. 1953, p. 596; also Edwin G. Boring, "Psychological Factors in the Scientific Process," *American Scientist,* Oct. 1954, p. 639.

11. Joseph Turner, editorial, *Science,* Dec. 11, 1959.

12. George Gamow and Marvin Stern, *Puzzle-Math* (Viking, 1958).

13. Charles P. Snow, "The Moral Un-Neutrality of Science," *Science,* Jan. 27, 1961, p. 255.

14. *Ibid.*

Notes to Chapter 14

1. Bernhardt S. Gottlieb, *Understanding Your Adolescent* (Rinehart, 1957): "If you give the adolescent the satisfaction of smoking, by the time he is thirty he will generally stop entirely or modify the habit to such an extent that it no longer constitutes a danger in inducing lung cancer" (p. 59). Further: "Much has been said and written about how smoking stunts a youth's growth, diminishes his lung capacity, and makes him susceptible to tuberculosis or cancer of the lungs. These statements have no basis in fact, and they should not be used as arguments to keep an adolescent from smoking. The facts indicate that smoking is not harmful in early youth but may be harmful in late life. The nicotine in tobacco tends to constrict the arteries. In youth the circulatory system is flexible and collateral circulation is readily established. Theoretically, after the age of thirty, with progressive loss of flexibility and the thickening and hardening of the arteries, the effects of nicotine cannot so easily be mollified" (p. 58). And: "The time tables, as it were, for drinking and smoking are in direct reverse. Smoking, our mores to the contrary, has few detrimental effects in youth, but constricts circulation in adulthood. Alcohol, inasmuch as it warps judgment and is difficult to use in moderation should—in theory—be avoided in youth, or kept at a minimum, but can be beneficial in adulthood" (p. 106).

2. Bernard Botein, *Trial Judge* (Simon and Schuster, 1952).

3. J. K. Finnegan, B. S. Larson, H. B. Hoag, "The Role of Nicotine in the Cigarette Habit," *Science,* July 27, 1945, p. 94.

4. From Eric D. Wittkower and Kerr L. White, "Psychophysiologic Aspects of Respiratory Disorders," *American Handbook of Psychiatry,* ed. Silvano Arieti (Basic Books, 1959), Vol. 1, Chap. 35, p. 700.

5. See *The New York Times* for Dec. 2, 1958, on the fire at Our Lady of Angels School, Chicago, in which 87 children and three nuns died. Authorities in all responsible communities constantly check for school fire hazards.

Bibliography

Adler, Alfred, *The Practice and Theory of Individual Psychology.* New York: Harcourt, Brace, 1943.

Adler, John C., "The Metatextbook Factor in Writing." *English Journal,* XLVIII (December 1959).

Allison, Luther, "A Functional Unit on Occupations." *English Journal,* XLVIII (February 1959).

Allport, Floyd H., "The J-Curve Hypothesis of Conforming Behavior," *Journal of Social Psychology,* May 1934.

Allport, Gordon W., and Vernon, Philip E., *Studies in Expressive Movement.* New York: Macmillan, 1933.

Alwin, Virginia, "Developing a Unit." *English Journal,* XLVIII (September 1959).

Anati, Emmanuel, "Prehistoric Art in the Alps." *Scientific American,* January 1960.

Anderson, E. M., "A Study of the Leisure Time Reading of Pupils in Junior High School." *Elementary School Journal,* 48 (1948).

Anderson, William S., *An Investigation of Reading Achievement as an Affective Determinant in the Perception of Verbal and Non-Verbal Symbols.* Doctoral Dissertation. Ithaca: Cornell University, 1955.

Arieti, Silvano (ed.), *The American Handbook of Psychiatry.* New York: Basic Books, 1959.

Asch, Solomon E., "Opinions and Social Pressure," *Scientific American,* November 1955.

Auden, W. H., and Pearson, Norman Holmes, *Poets of the English Language,* Volume 5. New York: Viking, 1953.

Bacon, Albert M., *A Manual of Gesture.* Morristown, N.J.: Silver, Burdett, 1872.

Bahn, Harold E., *Toward an Improved Teaching of Shakespeare in the Secondary School: Proposals Based on Experiences with Graduates in New Jersey High Schools at the New Jersey State Teachers College, Montclair, 1944-51.* Doctoral Dissertation. New York: Columbia University, 1955.

Bales, Robert F., "How People Interact In Conferences." *Scientific American,* March 1955.

Balken, Eva Ruth, and Masserman, Jules H., "The Language of Phantasy II," *Journal of Psychology,* 10 (1940).

Barlow, Elizabeth R., *Improving Sentence Patterns in Written Compositions in Grade Nine.* Doctoral Dissertation, Boston, Boston University, 1955.

434

Barzun, Jacques, *The House of Intellect*. New York: Harper, 1959.

Beberman, Max, *Emerging Program of Secondary School Mathematics*. Cambridge: Harvard University Press, 1958.

Bello, Francis, "The Information Theory." *Fortune*, Dec. 1953.

Bens, John H., "Teaching Literature in the World of Mickey Spillane." *English Journal*, XLV (February 1956).

Bernstein, Walter, "A Reporter at Large—The Cherubs are Rumbling." *New Yorker*, September 21, 1957, pp. 129-159.

Berry, Elizabeth, *Guiding Students in the English Class*. New York: Appleton-Century-Crofts, 1957.

Bestor, Arthur, *Educational Wastelands*. Urbana: University of Illinois Press, 1953.

———— *The Restoration of Learning*. New York: Knopf, 1955.

———— and Kilpatrick, T. H., "Progressive Education—a Debate," *New York Times Magazine*, September 8, 1957.

Blake, Howard E., *Class Size*. Doctoral Dissertation, New York: Columbia University, 1955.

Bluefarb, Sam, "The Sea—Mirror and Maker of Character in Fiction and Drama." *English Journal*, XLVIII (December 1959).

Bluestone, George, *Novels into Film*. Baltimore: Johns Hopkins Press, 1957.

Bode, Carl, "The Buxom Biographies." *English Journal*, XLIV (February 1955).

Boder, David P., "The Adjective-Verb Quotient: A Contribution to the Psychology of Language." *The Psychological Record*, 3 (1940).

Bolenius, Emma, *Everyday English Composition*. New York: American Book, 1917.

Boll, Eleanor Stoker, "Should Parents or Cupid Arrange Marriages?" *New York Times Magazine*, December 13, 1959.

Boring, Edwin G., "Psychological Factors in the Scientific Process." *American Scientist*, October 1953.

Bossing, Nelson L., *Principles of Secondary Education*. Englewood Cliffs, N.J.: Prentice-Hall, 1955.

———— *Teaching in Secondary Schools*. Boston: Houghton Mifflin, 1952.

Botein, Bernard, *Trial Judge*. New York: Simon and Schuster, 1952.

Braddock, Richard, "Films for Teaching Mass Communication." *English Journal*, XLIV (March 1955).

Bragdon, Henry W., "Teaching Writing Through History." *Atlantic*, November 1959.

Breault, C. W., "Three Steps to Short Stories." *English Journal*, XLV (March 1956).

Britton, Jane, "Let Them Talk—The Community Will Listen." *English Journal*, XLIV (March 1955).

Broening, Angela M., Falk, Ethel Mabie, Hatfield, W. Wilbur, McEntyre, Doris E., and Southwick, Margaret, *Conducting Experiences in English*.

The National Council of Teachers of English. New York: Appleton-Century-Crofts, 1939.

Brooks, B. C., "The Teaching of English to Scientists and Engineers," in *The Teaching of English,* ed. Randolph Quirk and A. H. Smith, London: Secker and Warburg, 1959.

Brown, Dana Worrall, Brown, Wallace C., Bailey, Dudley, *Form in Modern English.* New York: Oxford University Press, 1958.

Brown, Donald P., *Auding as the Primary Language Ability.* Doctoral Dissertation, Stanford, 1955.

Brunstein, James J., "Ten Uses for Commercial Television in the English Classroom." *English Journal,* XLVII (December 1958).

Bryant, Margaret, *Essays Old and New.* New York: Crofts, 1940.

———— and Aiken, Janet Rankin, *Psychology in English.* New York: Columbia University Press, 1940.

Bullock, Harrison, *Helping the 'Non-reading Pupil' in the Secondary School.* Doctoral Dissertation, New York: Columbia University, 1955.

Bulman, Learned T., "Biographies for Teen-Agers." *English Journal,* XLVII (November 1958).

Bureau of Secondary Curriculum Development, *Using Mass Media in Teaching English.* Albany: New York State Education Department, 1960.

Burton, Dwight L., *Literature Study in the High Schools.* New York: Holt, 1959.

———— "Teaching Literature to Our Youths Today." *English Journal,* XLIV (May 1955).

Butler, Robert A., "Curiosity in Monkeys." *Scientific American,* February 1954.

Calitri, Charles, "Macbeth and the Reluctant Reader." *English Journal,* XLVIII (May 1959).

Carlsen, G. Robert, "English and the Liberal Arts Tradition in the High School." *English Journal,* XLIV (September 1955).

Carroll, Jane Z., "A Plan for Meeting Individual Differences in Composition and Reading." *English Journal,* XLVIII (November 1959).

Casimir, H. B. G., "Broken English." *Scientific American,* March 1956.

Cassirer, Ernst, *Language and Myth.* New York: Dover, n.d.

Causey, Oscar S., (ed), *The Reading Teacher's Reader.* New York: Ronald, 1958.

Chamberlain, Essie, *Essays Old and New.* New York: Harcourt, Brace, 1934.

Chauncey, Henry, "The Plight of the English Teacher." *Atlantic,* November 1959.

Cherry, Colin, *On Human Communication.* New York: Wiley, 1957. Published jointly by the M.I.T. Technology Press and John Wiley and Sons.

Christopher, Georgia, "Literature and the Beginning Teacher." *English Journal,* XLVIII (September 1959).

Citizenship Education Project, *Hours on Freedom.* New York: Teachers College, Columbia University, 1951.

Coan, Otis W. and Lillard, Richard G., *America in Fiction: an Annotated List of Novels That Interpret Aspects of Life in the United States*. Stanford: Stanford University Press, 1956.

Cofer, C. M., and Foley, J. P., "Mediated Generalization and the Interpretation of Verbal Behavior," *Psychological Review*, 49 (1942).

Coggin, Philip A., *The Uses of Drama*. New York: Braziller, 1956.

Cohen, John, "Subjective Probability." *Scientific American*, November 1957.

Collier, John, and Collier, Mary, "An Experiment in Applied Anthropology," *Scientific American*, January 1957.

Comerford, Joseph F., *Perceptual Abilities in Spelling*. Doctoral Dissertation. Boston, Boston University, 1955.

Cook, Luella B., "The Search for Standards," *English Journal*, XLIX (May 1960).

Cook, Stanley S., *A Comparative Study of Aims Held by Parents, Students, and Teachers for an English Program in a Suburban High School*. Doctoral Dissertation, Detroit, Wayne University, 1955.

Coombs, Robert W., *The Appraisal of Personal Problems of High-school Seniors*. Doctoral Dissertation, Los Angeles, University of Southern California, 1955.

Corbin, Richard, "Grammar and Usage." *English Journal*, XLIX (November 1960).

Cox, Donald, "Do Women Make the Best Biographers?" *Saturday Review*, July 9, 1960.

Crawford, Paul L., Malamud, Daniel I., Dumpson, James R., *Working with Teen Age Gangs: a Report on the Central Harlem Street Clubs Project*, Welfare Council of New York City, 1950.

Creed, Howard, "The Rime of the Ancient Mariner." *English Journal*, XLIX (April 1960).

Cronbach, Lee, *Educational Psychology*. New York: Harcourt, Brace, 1954.

Cross, E. A., and Carney, Elizabeth, *Teaching English in High Schools*. New York: Macmillan, 1950.

Crow, Lester D., and Crow, Alice, *Adolescent Development and Adjustment*. New York: McGraw-Hill, 1956.

Cutts, Norma E., and Moseley, Nicholas, *Teaching the Disorderly Pupil in Elementary and Secondary School*. New York: Longmans, Green, 1957.

Dakin, Dorothy, *How To Teach High School English*. Boston: D. C. Heath, 1947.

D'Annunzio, Gabriele, *The Triumph of Life*. New York: Modern Library, 1923.

De Boer, John J., Kaulfers, Walter V., and Miller, Helen Rand, *Teaching Secondary English*. New York: McGraw-Hill, 1951.

Deighton, Lee C., "Developing Vocabulary: Another Look at the Problem." *English Journal*, XLIX (February 1960).

Dement, William, "The Effect of Dream Deprivation," *Science*, June 10, 1960.

Denney, Reuel, *The Astonished Muse*. Chicago: University of Chicago Press, 1957.

Devree, Charlotte, "High School Seniors' Agony." *New York Times Magazine,* December 15, 1957.

Dewey, John, *Democracy and Education.* New York: Macmillan, 1939.

———— *Experience and Education.* New York: Macmillan, 1956.

Diederich, Paul B., "The Rutgers Plan for Cutting Class Size in Two," *English Journal,* XLIX (April 1960).

Division of Surveys and Field Services, *Free and Inexpensive Learning Materials.* Nashville: George Peabody College for Teachers, 1960.

Duker, Sam, "Goals of Teaching Listening Skills in the Elementary School," address at the National Council of Teachers of English, Chicago, 1960.

Eastman, Max, *Enjoyment of Poetry.* New York: Scribner, 1951.

Educational Film Guide. New York: H. W. Wilson.

Efron, David, *Gesture and Environment.* New York: King's Crown Press, 1941.

Emig, Janet, "We Are Trying Conferences." *English Journal,* XLIX (April 1960).

Erman, Robert, "The Job Interview." *High Points,* Feb. 1959.

Evans, Bertrand, "Writing and Composing." *English Journal,* XLVIII (January 1959).

Farnham, Marynia F. *The Adolescent.* New York: Harper, 1951.

Felice, Sister Mary, "An Approach to Teaching *A Tale of Two Cities.*" *English Journal,* January 1959.

Fidone, William, "An Above-Average Class Studies *Hamlet.*" *English Journal,* XLV (November 1956).

Fiedler, Leslie (ed.), *Art of the Essay.* New York: Crowell, 1958.

Filbin, Robert L. "Teaching Reading." *Atlantic,* November 1959.

Finder, Morris, "Teaching English to Slum-Dwelling Pupils." *English Journal,* XLIV (April 1955).

Finnegan, J. K., Larson, B. S., and Hoag, H. B. "The Role of Nicotine in the Cigarette Habit." *Science,* July 27, 1945.

Forsdale, Louis (ed.), "Adapting Literary Materials to Television." Part II, *English Journal,* XLV (January 1956).

Freeman, Bernice, "Teaching Short Stories." *English Journal,* XLIV (May 1955).

French, Ruth E., "The Potential of Speech in the English Program." *English Journal,* XLIX (November 1960).

———— "Planning Speech Training for All Youth." *English Journal,* XLV (September 1956).

Freud, Sigmund, *Dictionary of Psychoanalysis.* New York: Philosophical Library, 1957.

Fridone, William G., "The Theme's the Thing." *English Journal,* XLVIII, (December 1959).

Friedenberg, Edgar, *The Vanishing Adolescent.* Boston: Beacon, 1960.

Friedman, William, and Friedman, Elizabeth S., *The Shakespearean Ciphers Examined.* New York: Cambridge University Press, 1957.

Frost, Robert, *Complete Poems.* New York: Holt, 1949.

Gainsburg, Joseph C., and Spector, Samuel I., *Better Reading*. New York: Globe Book Company.

Galanter, Eugene (ed.), *Automatic Teaching: the State of the Art*. New York: Wiley, 1959.

Gallant, Joseph, "Literature, Science, and the Manpower Crisis," *Science*, April 26, 1957.

Gamow, George, and Stern, Marvin, *Puzzle-Math*. New York: Viking, 1958.

Genise, L. R., "Impact of the Maryland and Yale Programs." *Arithmetic Teacher*, Feb. 1960.

Gerger, John C., "The Greater Struggle Necessary," *English Journal*, XLV (February 1956).

Glueck, Sheldon, and Glueck, Eleanor, *Delinquents in the Making*. New York: Harper, 1952.

Goldstein, Miriam, "Humanities Through Television." *English Journal*, XLIX April 1960).

Goodman, Paul, *Growing Up Absurd*. New York: Random House, 1960.

Goodman, Roger B., and Lewin, David, *New Ways to Greater Word Power*. New York: Dell, n.d.

Gordon, Edward J., "Levels of Teaching and Testing." *English Journal*, XLIV (September 1955).

Gottlieb, Bernhardt S., *Understanding Your Adolescent*. New York: Rinehart, 1957.

Gottschalk, Hans, "English Augmented—Diversity or Depth?" *New York State Education*, December 1959.

Gowers, Sir Ernest, *The Complete Plain Words*. London: Her Majesty's Stationery Office, 1954.

Grambs, Jean D., Iverson, William J., Patterson, Franklin K., *Modern Methods in Secondary Education*. New York: Dryden, 1956.

Graves, Robert, *Occupation: Writer*. New York: Grosset (Universal Library) 1950.

Greenberg, Joseph (ed.), Viking Fund Publications in Anthropology #24, *Essays in Linguistics*, Wenner-Gren Foundation for Anthropological Research. Chicago: University of Chicago Press, 1957.

Greene, Jay E., *Essays for Modern Youth*. New York: Globe, 1960.

Gregory, Emily Betts, "Managing Student Writing." *English Journal*, XLIV (January 1955).

Grim, Paul R., and Michaelis, John U., *The Student Teacher in the Secondary School*. Englewood Cliffs, N.J.: Prentice-Hall, 1953.

Grissom, Loren V., "Student Leadership in Evaluating Compositions." *English Journal*, XLVIII (September 1959).

Gruber, Howard E., "Science Teachers and the Scientific Attitude: An Appraisal of an Academic Year Institute." *Science*, August 19, 1960.

Gruenberg, Ernest, "The Epidemiology of Mental Health." *Scientific American*, March 1954.

Guke, A. M., "The Social Order of Chickens." *Scientific American,* February 1956.

Guthrie, Tyrone, "Why and How They Play Hamlet." *New York Times Magazine,* August 14, 1960.

Hahn, Hans, "Is There an Infinity?" *Scientific American,* November 1952.

Hale, Nancy, "Department of Amplification," *New Yorker,* Oct. 13, 1956.

Hall, Edward T., "The Anthropology of Manners." *Scientific American,* April 1955.

Hamalian, Leo, and Volpe, Edmond L., *Essays of Our Time.* New York: McGraw-Hill, 1960.

Hand, Harry E., "Sex in The Modern Novel—A Teaching Problem." *English Journal,* XLVIII (November 1959).

Harris, Albert J., *How to Increase Reading Ability.* New York: Longmans, Green, 1956.

Hartley, Helene W., "English in a Community of Conflicting Interests." *English Journal,* XLIX (March 1960).

Hartmann, George W., *Educational Psychology.* New York: American Book, 1941.

——— *Gestalt Psychology.* New York: Ronald, 1955.

——— "The Relative Influence of Visual and Auditory Factors in Spelling Ability," *Journal of Educational Psychology,* 22 (1931).

Hartung, Charles V., "Doctrines of English Usage." *English Journal,* XLV (December 1956).

Hatfield, W. Wilbur, "Will Structural Grammar Help?" *English Journal,* XLVII (December 1958).

Hazard, Patrick D., "Behind the Tinsel Curtain." *English Journal,* XLV (March 1956).

——— and Hazard, Mary, "Juilliard, Jazz, and the Golden Gate Bridge," *English Journal,* XLVIII (September 1959).

Heilbroner, Robert, *The Wordly Philosophers.* New York: Simon and Schuster, 1953.

Heilman, Robert B., "Literature and Growing Up." *English Journal,* XLV (September 1956).

Heisel, Dorelle Markley, "Let's Remove the Perennial Hardy." *English Journal,* XLV (January 1956).

Heisenberg, Werner, "From Plato to Max Planck," *Atlantic.* November 1959.

Heller, Lejaren A., Jr., "Computer Music," *Scientific American,* December 1959.

Heron, Ina Honaker, "Changing Images of the Small Town." *English Journal,* XLVII (December 1958).

Heron, Woodburn, "The Pathology of Boredom." *Scientific American,* January 1957.

Herwitz, Paul S., "The Theory of Numbers." *Scientific American,* July 1951.

Hess, Eckhard H., and Polt, James M., "Pupil Size as Related to Interest Value of Visual Stimuli." *Science,* August 5, 1960.

Hewes, Gordon W., "The Anthropology of Posture." *Scientific American,* February 1957.

Higgins, Frank and Higgins, Audrey, "Teaching Guide for *Richard III." English Journal,* XLV (March 1956).

Higgins, V. Louise, "Approaching Usage in the Classroom." *English Journal,* XLIX (March 1960).

Highet, Gilbert, *The Art of Teaching.* New York: Knopf, 1950. (reissued, Vintage, 1955).

Hildreth, Gertrude, *Teaching Reading.* New York: Holt, 1958.

Hilgard, Ernest R., "Methods and Procedures in the Study of Learning," in *Handbook of Experimental Psychology,* ed. S. S. Stevens. New York: Wiley, 1951.

Hook, J. N., "The National Council Looks Ahead," *English Journal,* XLIV (January 1955).

——— *The Teaching of High School English.* New York: Ronald, 1959.

Hovland, Carl I., "Human Learning and Retention." in *Handbook of Experimental Psychology,* ed. S. S. Stevens. New York: Wiley, 1951.

Hurlock, Elizabeth B., *Adolescent Development.* New York: McGraw-Hill, second ed. 1955.

Hyman, H. H., and Sheatsley, P. B., "Attitudes on Desegregation." *Scientific American,* December 1956.

Hymes, James L., Jr., *Behavior and Misbehavior: a Teacher's Guide to Action.* Englewood Cliffs, N.J.: Prentice-Hall, 1955.

Incorporated Association of Assistant Masters in Secondary Schools, *The Teaching of English.* Cambridge: Cambridge University Press, 1957.

Ives, Sumner, "Linguistics in the Classroom." *College English,* XVII (December 1955).

Jacobson, Frank B., "Two Ring Circus in the Mass Media." *English Journal,* XLIV (May 1955).

Jarrell, Randall, *Poetry and the Age.* New York: Knopf, 1953. (reissued, Vintage, 1955).

Jennings, Helen, *Sociometry in Group Relations.* Washington: American Council on Education, 1959.

Jersild, Arthur, "Emotional Development," in *Educational Psychology,* Charles E. Skinner (ed.), Englewood Cliffs, N.J.: Prentice-Hall, 1951.

Jespersen, Otto, *Growth and Structure of the English Language.* New York: Doubleday Anchor, 1955.

Jewett, Arno, "Creative Activities for Observing the Lincoln Sesquicentennial." *English Journal,* XLVIII, (January 1959).

Johnson, Eric W., "Stimulating Reading in the Junior High School." *English Journal,* XLVIII (February 1959).

Johnson, Falk S., "New Rules for 'IE-EI' Spelling." *English Journal,* XLIX (May 1960).

Johnson, Jotham, "The Changing American Language." *Scientific American,* August 1955.

———— "The Language of Homer's Heroes." *Scientific American*, May 1954.

Johnson, Thomas H. (ed.), *Poems of Emily Dickinson, Volume 2.* Cambridge, Mass.: Belknap Press, Harvard University, 1955.

Johnson, Wendell, *People in Quandaries.* New York: Harper, 1946.

Jones, Ernest, *The Life and Work of Sigmund Freud,* Volume I. New York: Basic Books, 1953.

Jones, Howard Mumford, *One Great Society: Humane Learning in the United States.* New York: Harcourt, Brace, 1959.

Jones, W. Powell, *Practical Word Study.* New York: Oxford University Press, n.d.

Josselyn, Irene M., *The Adolescent and His World.* New York: Family Service Association of America, 1952.

Kaplan, Milton A., "Television Drama: a Discussion." *English Journal,* XLVII (December 1958).

Karwand, Elwood C., "Teaching Literature of the Orient." *English Journal,* XLIX (April 1960).

Keene, Katherine, "Students Like Corrections." *English Journal,* XLV (April 1956).

Kegler, Stanley B., "Techniques for Teaching: Listening for Main Ideas," *English Journal,* XLV (January 1956).

———— and Simmons, John S., "Images of the Hero—Two Teaching Units." *English Journal,* XLIX (September 1960).

Kelley, Stanley, Jr., *Professional Public Relations and Political Power.* Baltimore: Johns Hopkins Press, 1956.

Kent, G. H., and Rosanoff, A. J., *American Journal of Insanity,* 67 (1910).

Kiley, Frederick S., "Served on a Black Platter." *English Journal,* XLV (November 1956).

Kinsey, Alfred C., Pomeroy, Wardell P., and Martin, Clyde E. *Sexual Behavior in the Human Male.* Philadelphia: Saunders, 1948.

Klapper, Paul, *The Teaching of English.* New York: Appleton, 1915.

Klausmeier, Herbert J., *Teaching in the Secondary School.* New York: Harper and Brothers, 1958.

Kline, Morris, "Projective Geometry." *Scientific American,* January 1955.

Koestler, Arthur, "The Anatomy of Snobbery," in *The Anchor Review, No. 1.* New York: Doubleday Anchor, 1955.

Krapp, George Philip, *Modern English.* New York: Scribner, 1909.

Kronenberger, Louis, *Company Manners.* Indianapolis: Bobbs, Merrill: (reissued, Mentor Books, 1955).

Krutch, Joseph Wood, "No Essays—Please!" *Saturday Review Reader.* New York: Bantam, 1951.

Kubie, Lawrence, "Some Unsolved Problems of the Scientific Career." *American Scientist,* Oct. 1953.

Kuder, G. F., *Kuder Preference Record.* Chicago: Science Research Associates, n.d.

Kurath, Hans, "The American Languages." *Scientific American*, January 1950.

La Barre, Weston, *The Human Animal*. Chicago: University of Chicago Press, 1955.

La Brant, Lou, "As Of Now" *English Journal*, XLVIII (September 1959).

———— "Inducing Students to Write." *English Journal*, XLIV (February 1955).

Laird, Charlton, *The Miracle of Language*. Cleveland: World Publishing Co., 1953.

Lambert, Robert, and Mack, Dorothy, "Anecdotal Autobiographies." *English Journal*, XLVIII, 9 (December 1959).

Lamberts, J. J., "Basic Concepts for Teaching from Structural Linguistics." *English Journal*, XLIX (March 1960).

Lang, Daniel, "Man In Space—Reporter at Large." *New Yorker*, November 15, 1958.

Larrabee, Eric, "Science, Poetry, and Politics," *Science*, April 17, 1953.

Laski, Harold, *American Democracy*. New York: Viking, 1948.

Lazarus, Arnold Leslie, "Guards for Our Future Security." *English Journal*, XLIV (September 1955).

Leichty, V. E., "How Slowly Do They Read?" *English Journal*, XLV (May 1956).

Lester, John Ashby, *Essays of Yesterday and Today*. New York: Harcourt, Brace, 1943.

Levine, Seymour, "Stimulation in Infancy." *Scientific American*, May 1960.

Lewis, Charles Stephen, "The Orient—Blind Spot in High School Literature." *English Journal*, XLV (January 1956).

Lewis, M. M., *How Children Learn to Speak*. New York: Basic Books, 1959.

Lowe, Helen R., "Solomon or Salami." *Atlantic*, November 1959.

Lowenfeld, Viktor, *Creative and Mental Growth: A Textbook on Art Education*. New York: Macmillan, 1947.

Lowes, John Livingston, *The Road to Xanadu*. Boston: Houghton Mifflin, 1930. (reissued, Vintage, 1959.)

Lowry, Lorraine, "Windows on the World." *English Journal*, XLIX (February 1960).

Lynn, Kenneth S., "Authors in Search of the Businessman." *Harvard Business Review*, October 1956.

Maertens, Grace Daly, "Organizing the Class to Care for Individual Needs." *English Journal*, XLVII (October 1958).

Maloney, Henry P., "Stepsisters of Print: The Public Arts in the High School English Class." *English Journal*, XLIX (November 1960).

Marquardt, John L., *English Language Instruction in the American High School as Viewed within the Framework of the Adolescent Needs Concept*. Doctoral Dissertation. New York: Columbia, 1955.

Marshall, Marion, "Helping Seventh Graders to Spot Plots." *English Journal*, XLVII (January 1958).

Mathews, M. M., *Words: How To Know Them*. New York: Henry Holt and Company, 1956.

Matthews, T. S., *The Sugar Pill*. New York: Simon and Schuster, 1959.

Mauk, Grant, "Speak Up," *English Journal*, XLIV (May 1955).

Mausner, Bernard, and Mausner, Judith, "The Anti-Scientific Attitude." *Scientific American*, February 1955.

Mayer, Martin, *Madison Avenue, U.S.A.* New York: Harper, 1958. (reissued, Pocket Books, 1959.)

McCall, Roy C., "Taking Literature out of Cold Storage." *English Journal*, XLIV (January 1955).

McCarthy, Dorothea, "Language Development in Children," in *Manual of Child Psychology*, ed. Leonard Carmichael. New York: Wiley, 1954.

McClennen, Joshua, *Masters and Masterpieces of the Short Story*. New York: Holt, 1957.

McDermott, Walsh, Deuschle, Kurt, Adair, John, Fulmer, Hugh, Loughlin, Bernice, "Introducing Modern Medicine in a Navajo Community." *Science*, January 22, 1960 and January 29, 1960.

McNemar, Quinn, *Psychological Statistics*. New York: Wiley, 1949.

Mersand, Joseph, "English Meets the Challenge," *English Journal*, XLIX (February 1960).

Micken, Ralph A., *Speaking for Results*. Boston: Houghton Mifflin, 1958.

Miller, George A., "Information and Memory." *Scientific American*, August 1956.

——— *Language and Communication*. New York: McGraw-Hill, 1951.

Miller, Franklin A., Moyer, James H., and Patrick, Robert B., *Planning Student Activities*. Englewood Cliffs, N.J.: Prentice-Hall, 1956.

Millhauser, Milton, "Advice to My Son," *English Journal*, XLVIII (January 1959).

Montaigne, Michel de, *Selected Essays*. New York: Modern Library, 1949.

Mort, Paul, and Vincent, William S., *Modern Educational Practice*. New York: McGraw-Hill, 1950.

Mosher, Joseph Albert, *The Essentials of Effective Gesture*. New York: Macmillan, 1917.

Mott, Frank Luther, *American Journalism*. New York: Macmillan, 1941.

Muize, Ray Charles, "Two Methods of Teaching English to College Freshmen." *Journal of Educational Psychology* (January 1954).

Murray, Henry A., *Explorations in Personality*. New York: Oxford University Press, 1938.

Mylonas, George E., "Mycenae, City of Agamemnon." *Scientific American*, December 1954.

Nash, Ogden, "Manuscript Found under a Serviette in a Lovely Home," *New Yorker*, Sept. 22, 1956.

Neese, Robert, *Prison Exposures*. Philadelphia: Chilton, 1959.

Norvelle, Lee, Smith, Raymond G., and Larson, Orvin, *Speaking Effectively*. New York: Dryden, 1957.

"Notes and Comments," *New Yorker,* June 21, 1958.

Oettinger, Anthony G., *Automatic Language Translation.* Cambridge: Harvard University Press, 1960.

Ogden, C. K., and Richards, I. A., *The Meaning of Meaning.* New York: Harcourt, Brace, revised edition, 1953.

Opler, Marvin K., "Schizophrenia and Culture." *Scientific American,* August 1957.

Orwell, George, *Collection of Essays.* New York: Doubleday Anchor, 1954.

Osgood, Charles E., *Method and Theory in Experimental Psychology.* New York: Oxford University Press, 1953.

―――― Suci, G. J., and Tannenbaum, P. H., *The Measurement of Meaning.* Urbana: University of Illinois, 1957.

Page, Ellis Batten, "Teacher Comments and Student Performance." *Journal of Educational Psychology,* August 1958.

Penfield, Wilder, and Roberts, Lamar, *Speech and Brain-mechanisms.* Princeton: Princeton University Press, 1959.

Perdew, Philip W., *The American Secondary School in Action.* Boston: Allyn and Bacon, 1959.

Perkins, W. H. (ed.), *Science in Schools.* London: Butterworth's, 1958.

Perrin, Noel, "Wake Me Up for the Hoedown." *New Yorker,* November 28, 1959.

Piaget, Jean, "The Child and Modern Physics," *Scientific American,* March 1957.

―――― *The Construction of Reality in the Child.* New York: Basic Books, 1954.

―――― "How Children Form Mathematical Concepts," *Scientific American,* November 1953.

Pierstorff, Marion B., "Promoting Critical Thought in the Study of Character Conduct in Literature." *English Journal,* XLVII (October 1958).

Plato, *The Republic.* Translated by W. H. D. Rouse. New York: Mentor, 1956.

Plutarch, *Lives.* New York: Modern Library, 1932.

Poley, Irvin C., "Drama In the Classroom" *English Journal,* XLIV (March 1955).

―――― *Speaking of Teaching.* Philadelphia, Germantown Friends School, 1957.

Pooley, Robert C., "Dare Schools Set a Standard in English Usage?" *English Journal,* XLIX (March 1960).

―――― "The English Teacher's Preparation in Speech," *English Journal,* XLV, (April 1956).

―――― "The Professional Status of the English Teacher." *English Journal,* XLVIII (September 1959).

―――― *Teaching English Grammar.* New York: Appleton-Century-Crofts, 1957.

Progoff, Ira, *Jung's Psychology and Its Social Meaning.* New York: Grove Press Evergreen Books, 1958.

Rabinovich, Ralph, "Our Adolescents and Their World." *English Journal,* XLIV (May 1955).

Radke, Frieda, *Word Resources.* New York: Odyssey, 1955.

Raeff, Marc, "We Do Not Teach Them How To Think." *New York Times Magazine,* January 26, 1958.

Ragle, John W., "Something Old, Something New, Something Borrowed—." *English Journal,* XLV (April 1956).

Read, Herbert, "Obscurity in Poetry," in *The Nature of Literature.* New York: Horizon Press, 1956.

Riesman, David, "Secondary Education and 'Counter Cyclical Policy,' " in *Constraint and Variety in American Education.* New York: Doubleday Anchor, 1958.

———— "Thoughts on Teachers and Schools." *Anchor Review #1.* New York: Doubleday Anchor, 1955.

Robb, Inez, "Price of Nonconformity." *New York World-Telegram,* June 20, 1960.

Rogers, Carl R., " 'Client-Centered' Therapy." *Scientific American,* November 1952.

Rosenson, Julius S., "The Oral Approach to Sentence Sense." *English Journal,* XLVII (October 1958).

Rosenzweig, Mark R., and Postman, Leo, "Frequency of Usage and the Perception of Words," *Science,* February 7, 1958.

Ross, A. S. C., "U and Non-U," in *Noblesse Oblige,* ed. Nancy Mitford. New York: Harper, 1956.

Rugg, Harold, and Brooks, B. Marion, *The Teacher in School and Society.* New York: Harcourt, Brace, and World, 1950.

Russell, D. H., *Characteristics of Good and Poor Spellers.* New York: Teachers College, Columbia University, 1937.

———— "A Second Study of Characteristics of Good and Poor Spellers." *Journal of Educational Psychology* (March 1955).

———— "Some Research on the Impact of Reading," *English Journal,* XLVII (October 1958).

Salinger, J. D., *Catcher in the Rye.* New York: Little, Brown, 1951 (reissued in paper, new American Library, 1954.)

Sallback, Robert P., "Teaching Students to Organize." *English Journal,* XLVII (November 1958).

Samuels, Gertrude, "One Answer to Delinquency—Work Camps." *New York Times Magazine,* September 8, 1957.

———— "Visit to a 600 School." *New York Times Magazine,* March 2, 1958.

———— "Why They Rock 'n' Roll." *New York Times Magazine,* January 12, 1958.

Sandburg, Carl, *Complete Poems.* New York: Harcourt, Brace, 1950.

Sanders, John, "Begin a Theme with Proust." *English Journal,* XLV (November 1956).

Sapir, Edward, "Grading: A Study in Semantics," in *Selected Writings*, ed. David G. Mandelbaum. Berkeley: University of California Press, 1949.

Sauer, Edwin H., *English in the Secondary School*. New York: Holt, Rinehart and Winston, 1961.

Scarlet, Will, *Remedial Reading in the New York City High Schools*. National Council of Teachers of English, 1938.

Schaar, Bernard E., "Avenues of Service." *Science*. June 12, 1953.

Schierbeek, A., *Measuring the Invisible World*. New York: Abelard-Schumann, 1959.

Schrodinger, Erwin, *Science and Humanism: Physics in Our Time*. New York: Cambridge University Press, 1952.

Scott, Robert F., *Scott's Last Expedition*. Boston: Beacon, 1957.

——— *Voyage of the* Discovery. Hollywood-by-the-Sea, Fla.: Transatlantic, 1951.

Seidman, Jerome M. (ed.), *The Adolescent: a Book of Readings*. New York: Dryden, 1953.

Seifriz, William, "A New University," *Science*, July 16, 1954.

Seligman, Daniel, "The 'Business Novel' Fad." *Fortune*, August 1959.

Shannon, J. P., "The Case of Shannon vs. Novels." *Clearing House,* October 1954.

Shattuck, Marquis E., and Cauley, Thomas, "Using a Modern Textbook in Composition." *English Journal*, XLIV (April 1955).

Shaw, Charles B. (ed.), *American Essays*. New York: Mentor, 1960.

Shefter, Harry, *Shefter's Guide to Better Compositions*. New York: Washington Square, 1960.

——— *Six Minutes a Day to Perfect Spelling*. New York: Pocket Books, 1954.

Sherif, Muzafer, "Experiments in Group Conflict." *Scientific American*, November 1956.

Shostak, Robert, "Meet Me at the Fair." *English Journal,* XLVIII (February 1959).

Skinner, B. F., *Verbal Behavior*. New York: Appleton-Century, 1957.

Sledd, James, "Grammar or Gramarye?" *English Journal*, XLIX (May 1960).

Smith, Dora V., "Teaching Language as Communication," *English Journal*, XLIX (March 1960).

Smith, Everett C., "Industry Views the Teaching of English." *English Journal*, XLV (March 1956).

Smith, Glenn E., *Counseling in the Secondary School*. New York: Macmillan, 1955.

Smith, Hugh L., Jr., "Jazz in the American Novel." *English Journal*, XLVII (November 1958).

Smithberger, Andrew Thomas, *Essays British and American*. Boston: Houghton Mifflin, 1953.

Snow, Charles P., "The Moral Un-Neutrality of Science." *Science*, January 27, 1961.

Spencer, Herbert, *On Education*. New York: Cambridge University Press, 1960.

Spiegler, Charles G., "Report on a 'Tough' School." *New York Times Magazine*, November 24, 1957.

Spitz, René A., *No and Yes: On the Genesis of Human Communication*. New York: International Universities Press, 1957.

Squire, James R., "Individualizing the Teaching of Literature." *English Journal*, XLV (September 1956).

———— "Literacy and Literature." *English Journal*, XLIX (March 1960).

Staats, Mabel M., "Continued Next Week." *English Journal*, XLIX (February 1960).

Stageberg, Norman C., *Some Structural Ambiguities. English Journal*, XLVII (November 1958).

Stegall, Carrie, "Now They Are Real Buddies." *English Journal*, XLVIII (February 1959).

Steinberg, C. S., *The Mass Communicators*. New York: Harper, 1958.

Stendler, Celia B., *Field Projects and Problems in Educational Sociology and Social Foundations of Education*. New York: Dryden, 1956.

Stern, Curt, "The Biology of the Negro." *Scientific American*, October 1954.

Stevens, S. S., "Measurement and Man." *Science*, February 21, 1958.

Stewart, John Lincoln, *The Essay*. Englewood Cliffs, N.J.: Prentice-Hall, 1952.

Stockwell, La Tourette, "Best Sellers and the Critics." *English Journal*, XLIV (January 1955).

Strom, Ingrid M., "Does Knowledge of Grammar Improve Reading." *English Journal*, XLV (March 1956).

———— *A Study of the Relationship between the Ability to Read Materials of an Informational or Literary Nature and the Ability to Analyze the Grammar and Syntax of the Materials Read*. Doctoral Dissertation, Minneapolis, University of Minnesota, 1955.

Strunk, William, Jr., *The Elements of Style*, rev. by E. B. White. New York: Macmillan, 1959.

Symonds, Percival M., *Adolescent Fantasy*. New York: Columbia University Press, 1949.

Terman, L. M., and Lima, M., *Children's Reading*. New York: Appleton-Century-Crofts, 1927.

Thieme, Paul, "The Indo-European Language." *Scientific American*, October 1958.

Thomas, Cleveland A., "Semantic Concepts for Secondary School English." *English Journal*, XLIX (March 1960).

Thorndike, Robert L., and Hagen, Elizabeth, *Measurement and Evaluation in Psychology and Education*. New York: Wiley, 1955.

Thornton, Helen, "English for Technical Students." *English Journal*, XLIV (September 1955).

Trilling, Lionel, *The Liberal Imagination*. New York: Doubleday Anchor, 1953.

Trow, William Clark, Zander, Alvin C., Maru, William C., and Jenkins, David H., *Journal of Educational Psychology* 41 (1950).

Turner, Joseph, editorial, *Science*, December 11, 1959.

Vallins, G. H., *The Pattern of English.* New York: Oxford University Press, 1956.

Van Schaick, Sally, "The Composition-Reading Machine." *English Journal,* XLIX (April 1960).

Waggoner, Hyatt Howe, *The Heel of Elohim: Science and Values in Modern American Poetry.* Norman: University of Oklahoma Press, 1950.

Wannberger, Carl G., "Writing—A Way of Life." *English Journal,* XLVIII (February 1959).

———— "They All Can Learn to Write." *English Journal,* XLV (November 1956).

Wapen, Jack A., and Layton, Leroy S. (eds.), *Julius Caesar.* New York: Globe, 1952.

Warner, John F., "Anthologies in the High School Classroom?—Never!" *English Journal,* XLVIII (October 1959).

Washburne, Carleton, *A Living Philosophy of Education.* New York: John Day, 1940.

Watkins, Ralph K., *Techniques of Secondary School Teaching.* New York: Ronald, 1958.

Watson, Fletcher G., "A Crisis in Science Teaching." *Scientific American.* February 1954.

Wattenberg, William W., *The Adolescent Years.* New York: Harcourt, Brace, 1955.

Webster, Margaret, *Shakespeare Without Tears.* Cleveland: World, rev. ed. 1955. (reissued, Premier paperback, Fawcett World Library).

West, William W., "How To Avoid Work." *English Journal,* XLV (December 1956).

Whatmough, Joshua, *Language.* New York: St. Martin's, 1956.

———— "Natural Selection in Languages." *Scientific American,* April 1952.

Whitney, Algard P., *Improvement of Reading through Supervision.* Doctoral Dissertation. New York: Columbia University, 1955.

Whorf, Benjamin Lee, *Language, Thought, and Reality,* ed. John B. Carroll. New York: Technology Press of M.I.T. and John Wiley, 1956.

———— "Science and Linguistics," *Technology Review,* April 1940.

Whyte, William H., Jr., *Is Anybody Listening?* New York: Simon and Schuster, 1952.

———— *The Organization Man.* New York: Simon and Schuster, 1956 (reprinted, Doubleday Anchor Books, 1957).

Wiener, Norbert, *The Tempter.* New York: Random House, 1959.

———— *The Human Use of Human Beings.* New York: Doubleday Anchor, 1954.

Williams, Elizabeth, "Teaching Judgment of Prose Fiction." *English Journal,* XLVII (November 1958).

Williams, Greer, *Virus Hunters*. New York: Knopf, 1959.

Williams, Robert D., "Linguistics and Grammar." *English Journal*, XLVIII (October 1959).

Wilson, Edmund, *A Piece of My Mind*. New York: Farrar, Straus and Cudahy, 1956.

Wilson, John S., "What Makes 'Pop' Music Popular." *New York Times Magazine*, December 8, 1957.

Wittich, Walter A., and Halsted, Gertie Hanson, *Educators' Guide to Free Tapes, Scripts, and Transcriptions*. Randolph, Wisconsin: Educators' Progress Service.

Wittkower, Eric D., and White, Kerr L., "Psychophysiologic Aspects of Respiratory Disorders," *American Handbook of Psychiatry*, ed. Silvano Arieti. New York: Basic, 1959.

Wolfe, Don M., "Fruitful Long Paper: The Autobiography." *English Journal*, XLV (January 1956).

Woodworth, Robert S., *Experimental Psychology*. New York: Holt, 1938.

Yatron, Michael, "Carl Sandburg: the Poet as Nonconformist." *English Journal*, XLVIII (December 1959).

Zahner, Louis, "Composition at the Barricades." *Atlantic*, November 1959.

Zamchick, David, "Paperback Buying Patterns." *English Journal*, XLIX (May 1960).

——— "Problems in Paperback Publishing." *English Journal*, XLVII (December 1958).

Zink, Priscilla M., "*Hamlet*—Caviare to the Generals." *English Journal*, XLIV (January 1955).

Zollinger, Marion, and Dawson, Mildred A., "Evaluation of Oral Communication." *English Journal*, XLVII (November 1958).

Index